THE POWER OF SATIRE:
MAGIC, RITUAL, ART

THE POWER OF
SATIRE:
MAGIC, RITUAL,
ART

BY ROBERT C. ELLIOTT

PRINCETON, NEW JERSEY

PRINCETON UNIVERSITY PRESS

Copyright © 1960 by Princeton University Press
L.C. Card: 60-5746
ISBN 0-691-01276-8

Publication of this book
has been aided by a grant from the Ohio State University
Development Fund and also by the Ford Foundation program
to support publication, through university presses, of works
in the humanities and social sciences

First PRINCETON PAPERBACK Edition, 1966
Second Printing, 1970
Third Printing, 1972

Printed in the United States of America
by Princeton University Press, Princeton, New Jersey

FOR
LUCY WOODBRIDGE BIRKENHAUER
AND
MARY CURTIN ELLIOTT

PREFACE

THIS BOOK deals with what John Dryden called the underwood of satire and the timber trees: that is, with the origins of satire in primitive magic and incantation and also with some of satire's towering achievements. My aim is both theoretical and historical: to elucidate an early connection of satire with magical power and to show how that original connection survives, in underground and distorted ways, in satire written today.

The materials of the first chapter or two are, I am afraid, relatively intractable. For a study of this kind the literature of medieval Ireland, for example, is remarkably rich. But the literature reflects a culture so remote from our own, its manners, its values, its modes of expression so foreign to us today, that a good deal of guidebook exposition will be necessary. I am aware of the problem; but because my whole enterprise is based on the "primitive" material, we will have to make our way through some moderately heavy growth before we can survey the timber trees. The critical analyses in Chapter IV of Shakespeare's *Timon of Athens*, Molière's *Misanthrope*, and Swift's *Gulliver's Travels* have validity, I hope, apart from the historical and theoretical considerations of the preceding chapters. But I have tried to do more than give adequate readings of the works in question. These works embody, I believe, highly sophisticated treatment of primitive themes and concepts. They are unquestionably great works of art in their own right, but they are also exemplary manifestations of the development of certain forms of satire and as such are generically bound to (although not, of course, defined by) the magical imprecations of Old Irish bards and ancient Greek soothsayers. They may even derive some of their literary power from that relationship.

These considerations have enforced the plan of the book. Chapter I presents some of the historical evidence for the early relations of satire with magic. Chapter II attempts to account theoretically for the magical efficacy attributed to satire and to show how literary satire develops out of its magical background:

how the timber trees grow from out the underwood and come to loom over it. Chapter III treats briefly the establishment of formal verse satire in Rome and the tenuous relations of that form with the primitive past. Chapter IV consists of analyses of *Timon*, the *Misanthrope*, *Gulliver* in terms of a theme important in Old Irish and other early satire. Chapter V deals with the work of two twentieth-century satirists, Wyndham Lewis and Roy Campbell, from the point of view of the major interests of the book. Chapters VI and VII treat of various continuities between primitive satire and sophisticated literary satire. An appendix considers briefly the curse and its relation to early satire.

My primary interests in this book are literary; but in trying to understand some of the curious forms early satire takes—and the beliefs out of which the forms arise—I have gained what help I could from non-literary disciplines, chiefly anthropology and psychology. It is hardly necessary to say that neither of these disciplines has achieved the status of exact science. Rules of evidence are not established nor are criteria of verification agreed upon. Within the fields themselves there is bitter controversy over theory, techniques, even ends. As a layman in these matters I have been forced to choose my authorities as best I could: to choose between competing schools on the basis of what seemed to me theoretical consistency and the adequacy of the theories to deal with the material given. Any such choice is obviously open to basic criticism, but the choice has to be made. And even if the choice is wrong, the loss need not be total; for, though some of the theories may be provisional, there is no question that, as E. R. Dodds says, they have cast light into dark places; and an uncertain light is better than none.

Let this single apology stand for many: I am not a linguist, not a classicist, not an anthropologist, and so on. I am uncomfortably aware of the risks I take in venturing into foreign fields. But I have had the help of learned friends, and I comfort myself with the knowledge that "fields" are artificial constructs: in any work aspiring to synthesis one must face up to the risks entailed. I believe the risks worth taking.

One word on definition. *Satire* is notoriously a slippery term, designating, as it does, a form of art and a spirit, a purpose and a tone—to say nothing of specific works of art whose resemblances may be highly remote. My use of *satire* throughout will be pragmatic rather than normative; that is, it will comprehend responsible uses of the term as I encounter them. I shall depend upon context and qualifying terms to convey the relevant sense of *satire* intended at any given time.

ACKNOWLEDGMENTS

I am glad to be able to thank publicly The Ohio State University, which granted me time to write and money to help support the publication of this book; librarians at Ohio State, Yale, and Harvard Universities, who were consistently helpful; my graduate students, on whom I tried out ideas and materials and who provided ideas and materials of their own. I have had the advantage of expert editorial assistance from Elizabeth Brown Wenzel and expert typing from Virginia Kohls.

My debt to scholars in the field of satire, particularly F. N. Robinson, G. L. Hendrickson, and Mary Claire Randolph, is even greater than the frequent references to them in the notes would indicate. I met Professors Robinson and Hendrickson after they had retired from teaching; they were both most generous with counsel.

A number of friends and colleagues read parts of the manuscript of this book at one stage or another of its evolution and made helpful criticisms; others contributed expert knowledge when I was out of my depth. I think most immediately of Morton W. Bloomfield, Sigurd Burckhardt, Marvin Fox, Thalia Phillies Howe, Martin Price, the late Paul Radin, Robert G. Shedd, Francis L. Utley, Jay Vogelbaum, Morris Weitz, Kurt H. Wolff. Professor George Sherburn made valuable suggestions on my *Gulliver* chapter. The Chairman of my Department, Robert Mark Estrich, has, in his official capacity and as a friend, encouraged my work from the beginning; I owe him many thanks in both categories. Roy Harvey Pearce has been my most interested, most critical, most helpful reader. To him and to all the others I am grateful indeed.

Acknowledgment is made to the following for permission to quote from copyrighted material:

Anne Wyndham Lewis, for Wyndham Lewis, *Men Without*

Art, 1934; Robert M. McBride Co., for Wyndham Lewis, *Apes of God*, Copyright 1932; Hutchinson and Co., for Wyndham Lewis, *Rude Assignment*, 1950; The Macmillan Co., for William Butler Yeats, *Collected Poems*, Copyright 1956; and for Yeats, *Collected Plays*, Copyright 1952; Henry Regnery Co., for Roy Campbell, *Selected Poems*, 1955; Faber and Faber, Ltd., for Roy Campbell, *Talking Bronco*, 1946; Mrs. Mary Campbell, for Roy Campbell, *Flowering Rifle*, 1939; David Orr, for Hugh MacDiarmid, *The Battle Continues*, 1957; Oxford University Press, for R. S. Rattray, *Ashanti*, 1923, and for Rattray, *Ashanti Law and Constitution*, 1929.

The editors of *ELH* have kindly given me permission to use material from two articles of mine that originally appeared in that journal.

CONTENTS

THE POWER OF SATIRE:
MAGIC, RITUAL, ART

CHAPTER I

SATIRE AND MAGIC: HISTORY

You'll accidentally find
    in barrows of books,
wrought-iron lines of long-buried poems;
handle them
    with the care that respects
ancient
    but terrible weapons.
    —VLADIMIR MAYAKOVSKY, "AT THE TOP OF MY VOICE"

1. GREECE

AT THE END of his play *Poetaster*, Ben Jonson justifies his satire and threatens his enemies. The climax of the threat comes in these lines:

> I could doe worse,
> Arm'd with ARCHILOCHVS fury, write *Iambicks*,
> Should make the desperate lashers hang themselues.
> Rime 'hem to death, as they doe *Irish* rats
> In drumming tunes.

Behind Jonson's boast lie themes and traditions and beliefs which point both ways in time: backward into the dimmest recesses of history, forward to the latest poetic flyting to come from the press. The first two chapters of this book are in effect a gloss on Jonson's threat. They set forth the history of the concepts implied and a theoretical framework by which we can try to understand the concepts themselves and the extraordinary power they have exerted through the whole course of satirical literature.

Archilochus, whose power Jonson claims, was a Greek satirist of the seventh century B.C. According to tradition, he was the first who "dipt a bitter Muse in snake-venom and stained gentle

3

Helicon with blood"; travelers are warned to pass softly by his tomb, lest the wasps that settle there be aroused.[1] Even today, of course, we speak of satire as "venomous," "cutting," and "stinging," although as we use these terms we may be a little self-conscious about the extravagance of what are, for us, mere metaphors. It was not always so. Our language preserves the memory of a once-powerful belief: Archilochus' verses had demonic power; his satire killed. Indeed, all satire "kills," symbolically at any rate, and Archilochus is the archetypal figure in the tradition.

The curious legend which attributed deadly power to Archilochus' verse was widespread in antiquity, carried great authority. We shall examine it closely, but the best approach is indirect: like so many others, by way of Aristotle. In the *Poetics* Aristotle says that poetry broke into two kinds, the graver sort of poets producing hymns and panegyrics, the meaner sort "invectives" (variously translated: satires, lampoons), which were written in the iambic meter: "hence our present term 'iambic,' because it was the metre of their 'iambs' or invectives against one another." Homer's *Margites* is the first poem of this kind we know, says Aristotle; by presenting "a dramatic picture of the Ridiculous," it outlines the general forms comedy will take. In fact, the *Margites* "stands in the same relation to our comedies as the *Iliad* and *Odyssey* to our tragedies." As soon as comedy appeared in the field, says Aristotle, "those naturally drawn to the one line of poetry became writers of comedies instead of iambs," because the new mode was grander and more highly esteemed than the old.

Comedy originated, according to Aristotle, in improvisations—the improvisations of the authors or leaders of the Phallic Songs, "which still survive as institutions in many of our cities."[2] Thus far we have Aristotle's authority that comedy developed out of

[1] Gaetulicus in *The Greek Anthology*, Bk. VII, No. 71; cited in *Elegy and Iambus*, ed. and trans. J. M. Edmonds (London, 1931), II, 97.

[2] *Aristotle on the Art of Poetry*, 4.1448ᵇ-1449ᵃ, trans. Ingram Bywater (Oxford, 1909), pp. 11-13. The Greeks (for that matter, the Romans) had no single word equivalent to our *satire*. In dealing with early satire I shall not attempt to distinguish among *lampoon, invective, abuse, ridicule*, etc.; and so long as some element of formalization has gone into the utterance, I shall use these terms, together with the Greek *iambi* (iambics), as generally equivalent to *satire*. For further discussion of the term, see the Preface and Chap. III below.

4

invective or satire, and we want now to follow the lead provided by the reference to the Phallic Songs. These songs, we know, were a feature of the fertility rituals common to many peoples over Europe and Asia Minor. The exact form of the songs has not been preserved, although a brief scene in Aristophanes' *Acharnians* (ll. 237 ff.) seems to incorporate the principal elements of the rite. Working with this scene and much analogous material, F. M. Cornford has been able to reconstruct hypothetically the form required by the ceremonial purpose. The Phallic Song, in his view, was divided antiphonally between a chorus and a leader or succession of leaders; it consisted of invocation of the god: "Hymen, O Hymenaee" or "O Phales, Phales!" (the image of the god would have been in evidence, erect on a pole) and an iambic element, improvised by the leaders and directed at individuals—presumably stingy persons who had refused to contribute food or money—who were attacked by name.[3] The great purpose of these rituals was to spread the benign influence of fruitfulness throughout the land, among crops, herds, and among the people. Traditionally we associate feelings of gaiety and abandon—even orgiastic abandon—with such ceremonies, as in the Maypole dance, whose kinship with the ancient phallic rites we know. But the iambic component of the Phallic Songs breaks sharply into the mood of solemn joy. How are we to account for it?

The entire rite is magical. Its purpose was to stimulate fertility, the sacred energy of life. Its method was to coerce by magical means the responsible spirits or powers. The ceremonial had two aspects, as it were: the invocation of good influences through the magic potency of the phallus, the expulsion of evil influences through the magical potency of abuse. "The phallus itself is no less a negative charm against evil spirits than a positive agent of fertilisation," writes Cornford. "But the simplest of all methods of expelling . . . malign influences of any kind is to abuse them with the most violent language."[4] Similarly, D. S. Margoliouth

[3] Francis M. Cornford, *The Origin of Attic Comedy* (London, 1914), pp. 35-52.

[4] Cornford, p. 49. Regular choral matches in abuse were apparently connected with certain of the ceremonies; see pp. 110-111. An analogue to these practices may be found in ancient India. Professor A. Berriedale Keith, discussing the elements out of which the Sanskrit drama migh.

in his commentary on the *Poetics* notes that violent abuse forms the most effective spell against demons; he cites Apollonius of Tyana, who got rid of a vampire by insulting her.[5] The scurrilous Fescennine verses sung at Roman wedding processions, and by soldiers at triumphs, had somewhat the same apotropaic function. So, when the joyful invocation of the god Phalles was interrupted by invectives, the purpose was magical, and the iambic verses themselves were thought to have magic properties. Cornford is explicit in his summary: "There can be no doubt that the element of invective and personal satire which distinguishes the Old Comedy is directly descended from the magical abuse of the phallic procession, just as its obscenity is due to the sexual magic; and it is likely that this ritual justification was well known to an audience familiar with the phallic ceremony itself."[6] Aristotle's remarks have thus led us to our first evidence that in their early manifestations satire, invective, and ridicule may be closely associated with magic.

A discussion of Archilochus arises naturally out of this back-

---

have developed, describes a primitive dramatic ritual marked by the following ceremony: "A Brahman student and a hetaera are introduced as engaged in coarse abuse of each other, and in the older form of the ritual we actually find that sexual union as a fertility rite is permitted. . . . The ritual purpose of this abuse is undeniable; it is aimed at producing fertility. . . ." *The Sanskrit Drama* (Oxford, 1924), pp. 24-25. Cf. the rites cited by Mircea Eliade, "Agriculture and Fertility Cults," *Patterns in Comparative Religion,* trans. Rosemary Sheed (London, 1958), pp. 331-66, esp. p. 358.

[5] *The Poetics of Aristotle,* trans. with commentary by D. S. Margoliouth (London, 1911), p. 143.

[6] Cornford, p. 50. Perhaps there is a recollection of the kind of ritual just discussed in the Elizabethan Lord of Misrule ceremony. The Puritan Phillip Stubbes has a characteristically brilliant description of the wild goings-on, then adds: "They haue also certain papers, wherin is painted some babblerie or other of Imagery woork, & these they call 'my Lord of mis-rules badges:' these they giue to euery one that wil giue money for them to maintaine them in their hethenrie, diuelrie, whordome, drunkennes, pride, and what not. And who will not be buxom to them, are mocked & flouted at not a little." *Anatomy of Abuses* (1583), Part I, ed. F. J. Furnivall (London, The New Shakespeare Society, 1877-79), p. 148. This may be compared also with Cornford's account (p. 39) of the ancient Greek children's songs in various festal processions: a choral verse was sung by the whole company before every house door; when householders refused to give liberally to the group, iambic verses of ridicule and abuse were improvised against them.

ground. Despite the anticipations just discussed, ancient tradition is fairly strong that Archilochus was the first individual satirist of record. He was generally credited with having "invented" iambic verse, the measure in which "ruthless warfare ought to be waged," Ovid was to say.[7] More important, however, was the story of Archilochus himself, with its mystery and melodrama, its widely-flung influence. Briefly, it is this: Archilochus was born on the island of Paros; he came, on his father's side, from a family of hereditary priests of Demeter. His father was Telesicles, founder of Thasos, his mother a slave. Archilochus was betrothed to Neobule, daughter of the Parian noble Lycambes. For some reason (perhaps because Archilochus made public the matter of his irregular birth), Lycambes "broke the great oath made by salt and table," as Archilochus put it, and refused to sanction the marriage.[8] In the terrible violence of his rage Archilochus composed iambics against the father and his household and recited (or sang) them at the festival of Demeter. Lycambes and his daughter (according to some versions, daughters) hanged themselves.[9] Archilochus went on to further triumphs, and further miseries, in the islands of the Aegean. He established a towering reputation as a poet. Hundreds of years after his death writers compared him to Sophocles, to Pindar, even to Homer, some indeed placing him next to Homer over all other poets. There is evidence that when he was killed in battle, Archilochus became the center of a heroic cult on his native island of Paros; and, according to Dio Chrysostom and others, the man who killed him was banished from the temple by Apollo for having slain a servitor of the Muses.[10] By piecing together

[7] See, for example, Clement of Alexandria, *Miscellanies*; Horace, *Ars Poetica*, l. 79; Plutarch, *Music*, 28—all cited in *Elegy and Iambus*, ii, 85-89; and Ovid, *Ibis*, ll. 53-54, 307. The derivation of the word *iambi* is obscure. Archilochus used it of his own poetry, and, writes J. M. Edmonds, "it is certain that when the word came to be used to describe a form of literature, it came to connote ridicule and invective, and the idea of ridicule seems to have joined in it with that of improvisation." "An Account of Greek Lyric Poetry," *Lyra Graeca*, ed. and trans. J. M. Edmonds (London, 1927), iii, 604.

[8] Fragment 96, *Elegy and Iambus*, ii, 149.

[9] For an attempt to account for the varying forms of the story, see François Lasserre, *Les Epodes d'Archiloque* (Paris, 1950), pp. 47 ff.

[10] *Elegy and Iambus*, ii, 93.

scraps of commentary with the Fragments of Archilochus that have survived, we can embellish the story further; but central to it, and crucial, is the account of the poet's terrible triumph over Lycambes and Neobule.

Until recently, modern scholars have been inclined to treat the tale as a late invention (antedating Horace, it is true, who knew it and presumably expected his audience to know it well) — an invention based upon a false interpretation of a Fragment of Archilochus. The improbability of such a theory, however, has been made clear by Professor G. L. Hendrickson: that a story of such wide currency as that of Archilochus and Lycambes could have been spun out of a grammatical interpretation perhaps hundreds of years after Archilochus' death is simply not credible. Instead, Hendrickson shows, the legend, if it be such, grew inevitably out of belief: "the wide-spread popular belief in the destructive, supernatural power of words of ill-omened invective or imprecation, uttered by one who believes himself wronged."[11]

The invectives of Archilochus have much in common with the curses of tragic mythology: that of Thyestes, for example, which doomed the house of Atreus; or that of Oedipus on his sons. For a Greek audience these curses were not a matter of dramatic convention or of supernatural machinery; they were part of reality. When in the *Electra* the chorus, hearing the death agony of Clytemnestra, cries out, "The curses are fulfilled!" the moment must have been charged with a meaning but dimly available to us today. Similarly, there can be no question about the wide-spread belief in the efficacy of the personal curse: witness the curse tablets, *defixiones* (metal tablets engraved with a more or less elaborate imprecation against a personal enemy and then buried), which have been recovered in great numbers over the past fifty years. So common was belief in curse and incantation that Plato proposed extremely harsh penalties for these and other magical practices.[12] (Plato also forbade iambic poets to hold any

[11] "Archilochus and the Victims of His Iambics," *AJP*, xlvi (1925), p. 103.

[12] See the discussion by E. R. Dodds, *The Greeks and the Irrational* (Berkeley, Cal., 1951), pp. 194-95, who says that few of the *defixiones* seem to date from earlier than the fourth century B.C. Hendrickson, p. 106, believes, however, that "they merely carry on in written form (perhaps under oriental influence) the same habit of oral imprecation which

citizen up to laughter [935]; but the motivation here seems to
have nothing directly to do with fear of magic.) These matters
will be discussed more fully later, but the point is this: Archilochus had sources of power similar to those drawn on by the
curser.[13] Just as the curse was believed to be fatal, so, as Hendrickson says, "the popular fancy demanded and assumed, as a matter of course, destruction for the objects of the imprecations of
the more famous iambists. That their ill-omened vows and invectives should be effective was a part of their preeminence, and
that their victims should escape with less than death would have
been a derogation of their fame." Whether the iambics of Archilochus were believed to have magic potency because of his own
personal command over the Word, which was magical in and of
itself, or whether his power derived from his ability to bring
about divine intervention, it is difficult to say. But Hendrickson's
thesis is convincing: Lycambes and his daughter were driven—or
were believed to have been driven—to suicide by the preternatural
power of Archilochus' poetry.[14]

The whole tradition is adequately summed up in a sepulchral
epigram on Archilochus: "Cerberus, whose bark strikes terror
into the dead, there comes a terrible shade before whom even
thou must tremble. Archilochus is dead. Beware the acrid iambic
wrath engendered by his bitter mouth. Thou knowest the might
of his words ever since one boat brought thee the two daughters
of Lycambes."[15]

The attribution of magic power need not surprise us. In the

---

is implied in the multitudinous curses of early mythology." For Plato,
see *The Laws*, Bk. xi, 933, trans. A. E. Taylor (London, 1934), pp. 327-
38.

[13] See the Appendix for discussion of the curse and its relation to archaic satire.

[14] J. Vendryes observes that we treat the Archilochus story as legend,
"flattering on the whole for the talent of Archilochus, if not for his character. But it is not correct to interpret it as a legend; it is probably necessary to take the story in a literal sense. Archilochus really condemned
Lycambes and Neobule to death; he hurled a magical incantation against
them, from which they could not escape. He had the secret of avenging
himself on his enemies." *Revue Celtique* (referred to hereafter as *RC*),
xxxiv (1913), pp. 94-96.

[15] *The Greek Anthology*, Bk. vii, 69, trans. W. R. Paton (London,
1917), ii, 43.

early stages of cultural development, poetry is almost always associated with magic, whether white or black, or both. The poet's function has not yet been differentiated; in addition to being celebrant and perhaps mocker or maker of invectives, he is likely to be prophet, historian, genealogist, even healer.[16] All "antique poetry," according to Johan Huizinga, "is at one and the same time ritual, entertainment, artistry, riddle-making, doctrine, persuasion, sorcery, soothsaying, prophecy, and competition."[17] In this cultural situation the poet can hardly be said to *compose* verses; rather, as the more or less passive instrument of divinity, he transmits them. He is inspired, "breathed into," by the god. I do not mean to claim that Archilochus was a shaman or a primitive medicine-man. But it is well to remember that he was a priest of Demeter. Given his status in a relatively "primitive" culture, and given his extraordinary power of utterance, it is not difficult to understand why magical power was attributed to his verse.

The poetry of Archilochus survives in dishearteningly inadequate bits and pieces; at least one Fragment, however, is long enough to give us a sense of the power his satires must have developed. This, the Strassburg Fragment (97A), is a fierce imprecation against a former friend who is embarking on a journey by sea. The poet prays—demands—that the vessel be wrecked, that the traveler be "tossed by the waves and naked [where] the savage Thracians may receive him with their *kindly* hospitality; and there may he have his fill of suffering and eat the bread of slavery. Shivering with cold, covered with filth washed up by the sea, with chattering teeth like a dog, may he lie helplessly on his face at the edge of the strand amidst the breakers—this 'tis my

---

[16] Aelian writes (*Various History*, 1250): "If ever the Spartans required the aid of the Muses on occasion of general sickness of body or mind or any like public affliction, their custom was to send for foreigners at the bidding of the Delphic oracle, to act as healers and purifiers. For instance they summoned Terpander . . . Tyrtaeus . . . and Alcman." J. M. Edmonds comments: "Here in 7th Century Greece is the poet as medicine-man . . . doubtless his original rôle." Both quotations are from Edmonds, "An Account of Greek Lyric Poetry," *Lyra Graeca*, III, 610.

[17] *Homo Ludens*, trans. R. F. C. Hull (London, 1949), p. 120. Cf. N. Kershaw Chadwick, *Poetry and Prophecy* (Cambridge, 1942), p. 14; Dodds, *The Greeks and the Irrational*, pp. 80-82; F. M. Cornford, "Was the Ionian Philosophy Scientific?" *JHS*, LXII (1942), pp. 5-7.

wish to see him suffer, who has trodden his oaths under foot, him who was once my friend."[18] The total conviction of hate carries down undiminished through twenty-five centuries: we sense the force of the implacable will behind the words. Even these few lines make a famous characterization of Archilochus more meaningful: "And he drank the bitter wrath of the dog and the sharp sting of the wasp; from both of these comes the poison of his mouth."[19]

Ancient writers most often characterize Archilochus' satire in terms like these; the emphasis is on the bitterness, the hatred, the abuse. One other element, however, should be noticed. In the Fragment just quoted Archilochus speaks from a sense of outraged justice; the former friend had trampled on his oaths, as had Lycambes. A tone of righteous indignation informs a number of the Fragments: "he shall not escape for this despite done to me" (92); "Lord Apollo, reveal Thou the guilty and destroy them . . ."(27). It is this quality which prompts Bruno Snell to view the Strassburg poem as something more than a curse, something more even than the invectives of the Homeric heroes, who used abuse as a weapon of battle. Here invective is attached to a feeling of moral mission; the satirist (if we may call him so) is at this early date concerned with punishing vice.[20]

[18] Trans. Hendrickson, "Archilochus and the Victims of His Iambics," p. 115. For an excellent poetic translation of this and other poems of Archilochus, see Richard Lattimore, trans., *Greek Lyrics* (Chicago, 1955). A sizable Fragment of Archilochus probably bearing on the Lycambes story (but not an imprecation) has recently been recovered; see François Lasserre, "Un nouveau poème d'Archiloque," *Museum Helveticum*, XIII (1956), pp. 226-35.

[19] The characterization is by Callimachus; see Frag. 37a in *Callimachus and Lycophron*, trans. A. W. Mair (London, 1921), p. 239. Cf. Pindar: "But I must refrain from the violent bite of slanderous calumny; for, though far removed in time, I have seen the bitter-tongued Archilochus full often in distress, because he battened on bitter abuse of his foes." "Pythian Odes," II, 53-56, in *The Odes of Pindar*, trans. Sir John Sandys (London, 1946), p. 177; and Horace's well-known "Archilochum proprio rabies armavit iambo," *Ars Poetica*, l. 79.

[20] *The Discovery of the Mind*, trans. T. G. Rosenmeyer (Oxford, 1953), pp. 54-55. Werner Jaeger emphasizes that the poem is "dictated by a hatred which is *justified*, or which Archilochus believes to be justified," and comes to similar conclusions about the early sense of moral mission. *Paideia: The Ideals of Greek Culture*, trans. Gilbert Highet (Oxford, 1946), I, 121-24.

One wonders, of course, whether the punishment of Lycambes and Neobule, through the agency of iambic verse, *actually* brought about their deaths; whether we ought to take the story *au pied de la lettre*, as Vendryes thinks we should take it. It is impossible to say. The tradition is strong and it is the tradition, which is founded in and grows out of belief, that is significant. Lycambes and Neobule may in fact have hanged themselves as a result of the satirical onslaught, just as a man of the Murngin tribe in Australia lies down and dies when he feels that his soul has been stolen from him by black magic.[21] On the other hand, they may have survived the imprecations, as Pliny established that, despite the tradition, the sculptor Bupalus survived the iambics of Hipponax a century after Archilochus' death. Historical fact or legend, it hardly matters. For a very long time the story of Archilochus' word-slaying of Lycambes commanded belief. The satirist had access to uncanny powers because the story said he did. In light of the belief, we may read with new insight the simple vaunt of Archilochus: "One great thing I know, how to recompense with evil reproaches him that doeth me evil."[22]

All satirists, of course, have made this boast, although not all have been specific about the nature of their powers. Ben Jonson is blunt enough, as we have seen: armed with Archilochus' fury, he will write iambics which will "make the desperate lashers hang themselues." In the twentieth century Roy Campbell asserts similar claims: just as a lion breaks the spine of a giraffe, so his verse will drive hated rival poets to their doom.[23] The farther we are removed in time from Archilochus and the beliefs of his age, the more incongruous such threats are likely to appear. Dekker refused to be cowed by Jonson, and retaliated with *Satiromastix*. Auden, Spender, MacNeice, Day Lewis were publicly

---

[21] W. Lloyd Warner, "The Social Configuration of Magical Behavior," in *Essays in Anthropology Presented to A. L. Kroeber* (Berkeley, Cal., 1936), pp. 405 ff.

[22] Fragment 65. Cf. the similar boast in the recently recovered Fragment. Lasserre translates: "Je sais aimer qui m'aime, haïr mon ennemi, le poursuivre d'injures: la fourmi mord!" In Lasserre's interpretation, these are lines Archilochus claims to have addressed to Neobule, his betrothed. See "Un nouveau poème d'Archiloque," p. 227.

[23] See the last lines of the title poem in Campbell's *Talking Bronco* (London, 1946).

unaffected by Campbell's blast, however "wounded" they may have been privately. Neither Jonson nor Campbell, we may assume, would really have expected otherwise. But although the satirist no longer wields overt magical power, the old tradition remains vital, still exerting a strenuous attraction on our imaginations.

Greek satirists who followed Archilochus were believed to have powers similar to his. Best known of them was Hipponax, the sixth-century poet who wrote the first choliambics and to whom the ancients attributed (mistakenly) the invention of parody.[24] Hipponax, it is said, was a small, misshapen man, sensitive about his appearance. Two sculptors, the brothers Bupalus and Athenis, made a statue of him, exaggerating his deformity and exposing it to public ridicule. Against the distortion of the image Hipponax opposed the power of the word, but with uncertain results. A Renaissance translation of Pliny's account of the affair is colorful: Hipponax "so coursed them with bitter rimes & biting libels, that as some do thinke and verily beleeve, being weary of their lives, they knit their necks in halters, and so hanged themselves. But sure this canot be true . . . ," for, says Pliny, the sculptors survived the verses and went on to create images of the gods on Delos and elsewhere.[25] Pliny's rationalistic denial could not of course stem the progress of the legend which had long been fixed in tradition and was carried by epigrams like this: "Avoid, O stranger, this terrible tomb of Hipponax, which hails forth verses, Hipponax whose very ashes cry in iambics his hatred of Bupalus, lest thou wake the sleeping wasp, who not even in Hades has lulled his spite to rest, but in a halting measure launcheth straight shafts of song."[26]

Theocritus introduces the theme of justice which often appears in accounts of magical power: "Here lies the bard Hipponax. If you are a rascal, go not nigh his tomb; but if you are a

[24] For translations of the surviving Fragments of Hipponax, see *Herodes, Cercidas, and the Greek Choliambic Poets*, trans. A. D. Knox (London, 1929), pp. 15 ff.

[25] *The Historie of the World: commonly called the Natural Historie . . .*, trans. Philemon Holland (London, 1634), Bk. xxxvi, Chap. v.

[26] *Greek Anthology*, Bk. vii, 405, Paton ed., ii, 219. The "halting measure" refers to the fact that Hipponax wrote iambics ending in a spondee.

true man of good stock, sit you down and welcome, and if you choose to drop off to sleep you shall."[27]

The common element in these tales of the satirists is obvious. Out of hate and desire for revenge the poet writes iambics against his enemy. We may conjecture that the verses expressed the hatred and the will that the enemy die, directly, and that, perhaps concomitantly, they employed mockery and ridicule, which, under certain circumstances to be discussed later, can themselves be fatal.[28] In the Strassburg Fragment of Archilochus the hatred and the willed death are strikingly clear. As to the ridicule, an ingenious reconstruction by Hendrickson enables us to get some sense of the tone of Archilochus' opening attack on Lycambes. The reconstruction is hypothetical, but seems most reasonable: "What is this that you say, father Lycambes? Who has robbed you of the reason on which before you leaned so securely? But now in truth are you become a laughing-stock to your fellow-townsmen. What god pray, or in anger at what, has kindled you to stir up a creature garrulous like me, looking for nothing better than themes for his iambics? You have seized in fact a cicada by the wing, which shrills by nature and without occasion, and when touched shrills the louder. What do you mean? Do you desire to become notorious at any cost? You shall pay for your rashness with a penalty that shall endure for long."[29]

It would be a mistake to build too much on this, but one cannot help being struck by the mocking, supremely self-confident tone and by the explicit reference to ridicule as one of the means of attack. Later we shall examine these matters more analytically, but for the moment this much should be clear: the iambic verses of a major poet, expressive of his hate, his will to destroy, his mockery, were believed to exert some kind of malefic power. The power seems to have resided, not in secret, esoteric spells or in

[27] Number xix of the Inscriptions in *The Greek Bucolic Poets*, trans. J. M. Edmonds (London, 1923), p. 377. Other Greek satirists to whom are ascribed comparable powers are Semonides of Amorgos and Callimachus. See Hendrickson, "Archilochus and the Victims of His Iambics," pp. 103, 111.

[28] See Chap. II, 2, below.

[29] The reconstruction is based upon three Fragments of Archilochus (94, 95, 143), a paraphrase of Archilochus by Lucian in "The Mistaken Critic," and an epigram of Catullus (40). See "Archilochus and Catullus," *CP*, xx (1925), pp. 155-57.

the mechanics of sympathetic magic, but in the character of the poet himself—in his command over the word.[30] The word could kill; and in popular belief it *did* kill. This is the essence of Archilochus' story. It is crucial for an understanding of the image of the satirist as it develops over the centuries, as it exists in our own day.

2. ARABIA

Other literatures offer similar evidence of the relation of satire to magic: Irish, in particular, but also Arabic. The basic divisions of Arabic poetry are encomium and satire, and both were thought originally to be magical. The pre-Islamic Arabs believed that the poet possessed supernatural wisdom by reason of his alliance with spirits. He was the oracle of his tribe; he was prophet, teacher, encomiast; but above all he was a warrior and his weapon was satire. The poet's chief function was to compose satire (*hijá*) against the tribal enemy. The satire was like a curse; it was thought always to be fatal, and it was as important an element of waging war as the actual fighting itself.[1] Arab tribesmen thought of the *hijá* concretely, as a weapon which rival poets hurled at each other as they would hurl spears; and indeed a man at whom the *hijá* was directed might dodge, just as he would try to dodge a spear, by ducking and twisting and dancing aside. The poet-satirist led his warriors into battle, uttering his wild imprecations, shod with one sandal, his hair anointed on one side only, his mantle hanging loose.[2] The outcome of battle was

---

[30] A distinction should be made here between what I call magical satire and the more familiar magical spells known the world over. The magical spell has a set, invariable form; its efficacy depends on getting the spell "right," that is, uttering it exactly according to the established formula. Magical satire, on the other hand, is usually extemporaneous and each satirical utterance unique. Satire may have to conform to canons of its own, as we shall see; but it has not the closed, invariable structure of the spell.

---

[1] See Ignaz Goldziher, "Ueber die Vorgeschichte der Hiġâ-Poesie," *Abhandlungen zur Arabischen Philologie* (Leiden, 1896), pp. 1-105, esp. p. 26; and Reynold A. Nicholson, *A Literary History of the Arabs* (London, 1907), pp. 72-74.

[2] In the strange rites she engages in before her death, Dido (*Aeneid*, IV, 509 ff.) wears her hair unbound, her garment uncinctured, and one sandal only. These practices probably have something to do with the belief that knots and constrictions may hinder magical action—though why

thought to depend directly on the efficacy of his imprecation. Through degeneration of the magical content in this practice seems to have come the custom of bragging, insulting, defying the enemy (a regular preliminary to combat throughout the entire ancient Near East), as Goliath insults David in the Old Testament. What was once black magic became mere boasting.[3]

Edouard Farès distinguishes formally between certain verses of the Arabic poets which professed overtly to command supernatural agencies—they were in fact stereotyped spells—and the *hijá* proper, which was extemporized verse, employed humor, ridicule, and sometimes obscenity, and was designed to attack the enemy's honor.[4] The supreme obligation of life in pre-Islamic Arabia was to preserve one's honor unsullied; in attacking honor, therefore, ridicule attacked life itself—hence the extraordinary effects attributed to the mocking verses. Even in much later times people sometimes preferred death to being satirized. Thus, although a formal distinction may be made between magical verse and ridiculing verse, no such distinction can be made functionally. Both were "magically" potent. After a great battle, Muhammed said, according to Farès: "the satires of the three poets caused more damage . . . than whole flights of arrows" (p. 200).

In early times the Arabian tribesmen periodically held formal contests of honor in which individuals, or sometimes entire tribes, competed in boasting and ridiculing and abusing each other. These were ritual occasions, and again the satires of the poets were probably thought to exert magical influence. In any event, the slanging matches often ended in murder and sometimes in tribal war.[5]

---

one sandal is retained is not clear. See the articles on shoes and sandals and on knots in Hastings' *Encyclopaedia of Religion and Ethics* (New York, 1912); James G. Frazer, *The Golden Bough*, 3rd ed. (London, 1914), Vol. III: *Taboo and the Perils of the Soul*, pp. 309 ff.

[3] See Theodor Gaster, *Thespis: Ritual, Myth and Drama in the Ancient Near East* (New York, 1950), pp. 135-36. An interesting modern literary treatment of this theme may be found in Jean Giraudoux, *Tiger at the Gates*, trans. Christopher Fry (New York, 1955), Act II, pp. 40-42. I owe the reference to Miss Georgianna Wuletich.

[4] *L'honneur chez les Arabes avant l'Islam* (Paris, 1932), pp. 214-18; see also pp. 198 ff.

[5] Huizinga, *Homo Ludens*, pp. 66-68. Huizinga's discussion of contests in courtesy and in vilification is most interesting, but it ignores the magical background.

While satire among the Arabs was preeminently a weapon of war—a public weapon—it also had its private manifestations. Jarwal ibn Aus, surnamed the Dwarf, a poet of the seventh century A.D., wandered from tribe to tribe reciting panegyrics for which he was rewarded, and exploiting the universal fear of satire. Like Aretino, the Scourge of Princes, he extorted money from those in high station but at the same time stirred up great anger against himself. Caliph 'Umar found it necessary to imprison the poet in the interest of public safety and the general peace.[6]

Arabic women, too, exerted power through their mastery of satiric verse, which they employed both as propaganda and as invective. They are said to have been feared by even the greatest rulers: Muhammed, who usually avoided bloodshed whenever possible, is reported twice to have ordered the execution of female satirists. According to S. D. Goitein, the odd poetic power wielded by these women explains "why King Saul was so upset when the 'dancing women' in their songs of triumph ascribed, or, as the Bible says, 'gave' to David the slaying of ten thousands and to him only thousands, or why Barak refused to wage war against Sisera unless Deborah would accompany him. The biting satires of the woman judge, some of which were later included in the so-called Song of Deborah (Judges 5) were a most effective means of activating the languid tribes." There is still a strong and popular tradition among the Jewish women of Yemen, says Goitein, of commenting in satiric verse on public events.[7]

Over the centuries, the deadly mockery and invective of the *hijá* gave way to the lampoon by which the poet reviled his enemies, whether personal or public. Nicholson (p. 200) translates a fragment of a satire from the seventh century A.D. which may still have been thought to have magic power. (No examples of the earliest Arabian poetry survive.)

> Negroes are better, when they name their sires,
> Than Qahtán's sons, the uncircumcised cowards;
> A folk whom thou mayst see, at war's outflame,

[6] Clément Huart, A *History of Arabic Literature*, trans. Lady Mary Loyd (New York, 1903), p. 45.
[7] *Jews and Arabs* (New York, 1955), pp. 30, 202-03.

More abject than a shoe to tread in baseness;
Their women free to every lecher's lust,
Their clients spoil for cavaliers and footmen.

The most famous of early Arabian satirists was Jarír, an eighth-century poet as well known for encomium ("Let us be praised like this or in silence!" cried the Caliph after hearing one of Jarír's eulogies) as for satire. One of Jarír's greatest triumphs was gained at the expense of a rival poet, Rá'i, and his tribe, the Banú Numayr. Rá'i and his son Jandal insulted Jarír grossly. Jarír turned on them and exclaimed in verse:

O Jandal! what will say Numayr of you
When my dishonouring shaft has pierced thy sire?

With that he hurried to his home, where he spent the night with a jug of date-wine and a lamp, crawling about naked on his bed. At daybreak he rushed from his house, shouting triumphantly "Allah Akbar!" and rode off to find Rá'i and his companions of the Numayr. Without greeting them he burst into a satire of eighty verses. Rá'i and his fellows sat with bowed heads in silent mortification. When Jarír came to the final verses: "Cast down thine eyes for shame! for thou art of Numayr. . . ." Rá'i rose: "Saddle! Saddle!" he cried to his comrades: "You can not stay here longer, Jarír has disgraced you all." Rá'i's tribe bitterly reproached him for the ignominy he had brought upon Numayr; and, says the story, "hundreds of years afterwards his name was still a byword among his people."[8]

The degeneration from the original potency of satire is clearly evident here. The "dishonouring shaft" is a metaphor, recalling the more dreaded "shafts" which satirists had launched in times gone by. Rá'i does not drop dead, as might once have been expected; he and his tribe suffer no physical harm, but their honor is affected and they are shamed. Social sanctions have replaced the deadly powers once commanded by the poet, but the shadow of these powers is still discernible.

3. IRELAND

Ireland is the great and fertile source of material on the early relation of satire to magic. History, myth, saga, folktale—these

---

[8] Nicholson, pp. 244-46.

intertwined in such a way that no separation of categories is possible—are shot through with accounts of the power of the poets and of the dramatic role played by satirists in the days of the Christianizing of Ireland and in the dim times before that. Just one example at this point from saga:

" 'And thou, O Carpre, son of Etain,' saith [King] Lugh to his poet, 'what power can *you* wield in battle?'

" 'Not hard to say,' quoth Carpre. 'I will make a *glám dicind* on them. And I will satirize them and shame them, so that through the spell of my art they will not resist warriors.' "[1]

The poet's confidence in his power is illimitable; the source of his power may well be similar to that tapped by Archilochus and the Arabian poets.

Pre-Christian Ireland has no history, at least in one sense, for it had no writing; but the heroic sagas, surviving in texts dating from the eighth century A.D. and later, are based on oral traditions which unquestionably go back hundreds of years before the time of the texts themselves. Until recently the saga material was generally accepted by Irish historians as representing historical fact, or at least the substratum of historical fact. They believed that the history of Ireland was known, if not in precise detail, then in general outline, as far back as about 2,000 years B.C. Some Irish annalists claim, for example, that Amergin White Knee composed the first poem in Ireland in 1700 B.C.[2] Historians thought that the great Irish heroes Cú Chulainn, Fergus, Finn, etc., were actual personages, around whom, it was conceded, a good deal of legend had accumulated. In the last generation or so this euhemerism has been subjected to heavy criticism.[3] Much

---

[1] The *glám dicind* has been variously translated as a "metrical malediction," "extempore satire," and, most recently, as an "endless, biting attack." It will be discussed later. The quotation is from *The Second Battle of Moytura*, trans. Whitley Stokes, *RC*, XII (1891), pp. 91-92; the saga is reproduced in part in *Ancient Irish Tales*, ed. Tom Peete Cross and Clark Harris Slover (New York, 1936), pp. 28-48; referred to hereafter as Cross and Slover. Throughout this section I have regularized the spelling of certain proper names.

[2] Douglas Hyde, "Bards (Irish)," Hastings' *Encyclopaedia of Religion and Ethics*.

[3] The most magisterial work is Thomas F. O'Rahilly, *Early Irish History and Mythology* (Dublin, 1946); see especially Chap. XIV, "History or Fable?" pp. 260 ff. Irish euhemerism reached a wonderful kind of ab-

of what was once taken to be the history of pre-Christian Ireland (this includes the genealogies, some of which go back to Adam) has been shown to be myth or inspired fabrication. Most of the great heroes of saga were mythic, says O'Rahilly; they were gods, not men, and were euhemerized probably very early in the Christian era. On the other hand, much legendary material has been imported into the stories of actual persons like St. Columba. This is not to say, of course, that the medieval texts are worthless for the uses of history, even factual history. Quite the contrary. They preserve, at least in part, a strong and conservative oral tradition which has its roots far back in pre-Christian times. More important, they preserve data about, say, ancient religious beliefs and social practices which may be accepted as factual if the proper material from other cultures and other sources is available for cross-checking, as it often is.[4]

By and large, however, it is impossible to separate history and myth in the Irish material. The natural and supernatural "penetrate and continue each other," says Marie-Louise Sjoestedt, "and constant communication between them ensures their organic unity." Fortunately, for our purposes, to distinguish between historical fact and legend is not of major consequence. We are dealing with belief (itself a kind of fact) and only indirectly with the particular deed: whether the satirist actually killed his foe by the power of his verse-making (or, indeed, whether or not the satirist even existed in history) is less important than whether his culture, or his tradition, allotted him that kind of power. In Irish story from the beginning to the twentieth century, evidence of belief in the close relation of satire and magic is overwhelming. The problem for the historian, indeed, is *not* to be overwhelmed by it.

---

surdity when one scholar wrote of the famous power of Finn to acquire occult knowledge by chewing his thumb: Finn, he said, "when in deep thought, seems to have been in the habit of biting his nails." Cited by O'Rahilly, p. 262.

[4] See Marie-Louise Sjoestedt, *God and Heroes of the Celts*, trans. Myles Dillon (London, 1949), pp. xviii-xix. Elsewhere, Professor Dillon, using social, linguistic, and literary evidence from Ireland and from India, argues that "Ireland, on the margin of the Indo-European area, has preserved Indo-European characteristics that have been lost in most other regions of the west." "The Archaism of Irish Tradition," *Proceedings of the British Academy*, xxxiii (1947), p. 246.

From ancient saga, then, from the law tracts, some of which antedate the sagas, and from archeological evidence, it has been possible for scholars to reconstruct, however tentatively, the culture of pre-Christian Ireland and its major institutions. It was a culture in which the role of the poets (*filid*) was of the highest importance. The poets were not yet mere men of letters (nor were they to be until the devastation of Ireland in the seventeenth century); the command over the word gave access to many forms of the higher knowledge, and, as we might expect, the *filid* were prophets, medicine-men, historians, genealogists, lawgivers, encomiasts, "hard-attackers," and much else besides. One of the earliest references to Celtic poets is that of Diodorus Siculus in the first century B.C.; Diodorus, to be sure, is writing of the Celts of Gaul, but we may assume that there was a fairly close relation between the practices and beliefs he describes and those of the Celts of Ireland. The Gauls are "terrifying in aspect," says Diodorus; they are "boasters and threateners" and yet they have sharp wits:

"Among them are also to be found lyric poets whom they call Bards. These men sing to the accompaniment of instruments which are like lyres, and their songs may be either of praise or of obloquy. . . . [The Gauls] obey, before all others, [the Druids] and their chanting poets, and such obedience is observed not only by their friends but also by their enemies; many times, for instance, when two armies approach each other in battle with swords drawn and spears thrust forward, these men step forth between them and cause them to cease, as though having cast a spell over certain kinds of wild beasts."

Diodorus' comment is much to our point: "In this way, even among the wildest barbarians . . . Ares stands in awe of the Muses."[5]

This early coupling of druids and poets anticipates a similar association frequently found in Irish saga. The words for *druid* and *poet* were often used interchangeably, even within the same text, and apparently no sharp differentiation was made between the powers appropriate to each.[6] Druids, of course, were prophets:

[5] *Diodorus of Sicily*, Bk. v, 31, trans. C. H. Oldfather (London, 1939), III, 177-81.

[6] Carolus Plummer, *Vitae Sanctorum Hiberniae* (Oxford, 1910), I,

they foretold the coming of the saints, the outcome of battles, the span of a man's life, the sorrows that were to cluster about unhappy Deirdre. But poets, too, though less consistently, had this power. Ferchertne in *The Colloquy of the Two Sages* is called a "great poet and a prophet," and Marbán, the swineherd who was brother to a king, was "a saint, a prophet, and a poet."[7] Clearly the poet has access to powers over and above the natural course of things. "Pour tout dire," says Vendryes, "c'est quelqu'un qui connait la vertu des mots."

The major function of the *filid* was the familiar one of *laus et vituperatio*, praise and blame. It may be that the duality of the office is indicated symbolically in a story from *Cormac's Glossary* (a compilation of the ninth or tenth century) about the bard Senchán Torpeist, chief poet of Ireland. The tale goes that Senchán and his retinue of fifty poets, all dressed with extraordinary magnificence, were setting out on a pleasure cruise to Mann. (The numbers and richness of costume testify to the prestige of the poet.) A "foul-faced gillie" insisted that he be taken along. His aspect was unbelievably hideous: ". . . when any one would put his finger on his forehead, a gush of putrid matter would come through his ears on his poll. . . . Rounder than a blackbird's egg were his two eyes; blacker than death his face; swifter than a fox his glance; yellower than gold the points of his teeth; greener than holly their base; two shins bare, slender; two heels spiky, black-speckled under him. . . . He shouted mightily to Senchán . . . : 'I should be more profitable to thee than the proud and wanton crew that is around thee.' "

After the foul gillie outdoes Senchán in completing the mysterious quatrains of a female poet, he is suddenly metamorphosed into a "young hero with golden-yellow hair curlier than crosstrees of small harps: royal raiment he wore, and his form was the

---

clxi. Material illustrative of a number of themes to be discussed below can be found indexed in Tom Peete Cross, *Motif-Index of Early Irish Literature* (Indiana University Publications, Folklore Series No. 7, 1952).

[7] *The Colloquy of the Two Sages*, trans. Whitley Stokes, *RC*, xxvi (1905), p. 50; *The Proceedings of the Great Bardic Institution*, trans. Owen Connellan, in *Transactions of the Ossianic Society*, v (1860), p. 89. For a good example of a poet to whom "was revealed all that would be thereafter," see *The Adventures of the Sons of Eochaid Muigmedón*, trans. Whitley Stokes, *RC*, xxiv (1903), pp. 191-93.

noblest that hath been seen on a human being. . . . It is not . . . doubtful that he was the Spirit of Poetry."[8] Though the transformation of the monster is a common theme in Irish folklore, the hideous aspect of this spirit may symbolize the well-authenticated concern of the satirist with destruction and rancor and death, while the golden aspect may represent his function as encomiast. In any event, the double role was well recognized: Cormac has an etymology, false but no less significant for that, proposing that *file*, poet, is derived from "poison (*fi*) in satire and splendour (*li*) in praise."[9]

The *filid* were organized into a tightly-knit, exclusive, nearly autonomous body. The training in the esoteric knowledge of their profession was rigorous and required years of study of the obscure and secret language of their art. In the early days, according to saga, they roamed Ireland in bands, exacting hospitality wherever they went, making exorbitant demands on whomever they pleased. They could be refused nothing, partly because of the great prestige accorded their art, but chiefly because of the universal terror inspired by their satire. Kings, saints, warriors, monks, peasants—all lived in fear of the cutting verses of the ruthless poets. Hundreds of years later Edmund Spenser testified that "none dare displease" the bards "for feare to run into reproch . . . and to bee made infamous in the mouthes of all men."[10]

[8] Trans. Whitley Stokes in *Transactions of the Philological Society* (1891-94), pp. 181-85. For a variation of the story, see *Proceedings of the Great Bardic Institution*, trans. Connellan, in *Transactions of the Ossianic Society*, v (1860), pp. 115 ff.

[9] Fred N. Robinson, "Satirists and Enchanters in Early Irish Literature," in *Studies in the History of Religions Presented to Crawford H. Toy*, ed. D. G. Lyon and G. F. Moore (New York, 1912), p. 110. It is curious to find a similar false etymology of the Greek *iambus*. A. W. Mair, in a note to Callimachus, Fragment 37a, says that the Ambrosian grammarian derives *iambus* from *iós* = poison (*Callimachus and Lycophron*), p. 239. One of the Irish words for satirist is *cainte*; Cormac derives it from *canis*, "a dog, for the satirist has a dog's head in barking." Compare Callimachus' characterization of Archilochus: "And he drank the bitter wrath of the dog and the sharp sting of the wasp: from both of these comes the poison of his mouth."

[10] James F. Kenney, *The Sources for the Early History of Ireland* (New York, 1929), I, 3; Spenser, *A View of the Present State of Ireland*, ed. W. L. Renwick (London, 1934), p. 94.

At various times the poets aroused such hostility that the kings resolved to banish them. Geoffrey Keating, the seventeenth-century Irish historian, records four such occasions, on one of which Cú Chulainn came to the rescue of the *filid* and retained them (they are said to have numbered 1,000) for seven years. The best-known intercession on behalf of the poets, however, was that of Colum Cille (St. Columba). At the famous assemblage of Druim Ceat in the year 575 A.D., King Aed was determined to banish the whole host of the *filid* who had become intolerable in numbers and, according to some accounts, in their exactions. But St. Columba managed to appease the king, though his appeasement was stiffened by warnings of danger:

> This is what I have read in the circle of science:
> blessed is he who is praised, woe is him who
>   is satirised, O Aed.
>
> Fair the sap that is sucked from noble sayings:
> woe to the inconspicuous [?] land that is
>   satirised![11]

The poets were allowed to remain in Ireland, their numbers considerably reduced, after they and the kings entered into a solemn pact, which was ratified by the saints.[12]

The various legal compilations of ancient Ireland are among our most fruitful—and often among the most puzzling—sources of information about the early culture. The laws pay a remarkable amount of attention to satirists, both male and female; the injurious effects of their verse constituted a serious social problem.[13] In ways often not clear to us, the laws attempt to restrain the uncontrolled exercise of satire and to afford restitution for the damage inflicted by the poets' baleful activities. Satire is sometimes linked with such purely physical crimes as bodily

[11] Keating, *The History of Ireland*, trans. Rev. Patrick S. Dinneen and others (Irish Texts Society, 1908), III, 79-95; *The Eulogy of Saint Columba*, trans. Whitley Stokes, *RC*, xx (1899), p. 45.

[12] For a full discussion, and exemplification of the result of the pact, see *Proceedings of the Great Bardic Institution*, trans. Connellan, *Transactions of the Ossianic Society*, v, 21 ff.

[13] I follow closely Robinson, "Satirists and Enchanters," in *Studies in the History of Religions*, pp. 104-108. Most of my material on Irish satire comes directly or indirectly from Robinson's magnificent article.

assault, sexual attack on a man's wife, or theft of his cattle.[14] Damages awarded depend on the rank of the person injured; to satirize a king's son is a more serious offense than to satirize a minor chief (II, 157).

Women satirists are treated with particular harshness in the laws; sometimes they are equated with common scolds (although in saga, as we shall see, they had most uncommon powers); at other times they are classified with liars, thieves, and road-side trollops. A woman who is the victim of a satire, however, is entitled to full restitution; if the satire is made by her husband "until she is laughed at" and made game of in public, then she may leave him even though she is bound by son and security; and she may take her dowry with her.[15]

Most references to satire in the laws treat it as though it were what we would call a misdemeanor or a crime; but that is by no means always the case. Some satire is lawful and the satirists are highly rewarded for their services—among them for collecting taxes in areas where, apparently, "points of satire" were feared more than were "points of weapons" (V, 13). From other sources we learn that treaties invoked the satirist's power, sometimes with that of the druids, as a threat to those who might think of violation.[16] Satire had its public value even as it threatened personal welfare.

The language itself, as Robinson shows, reflects the way the early Irish thought about satire; it does not distinguish between the magically efficacious verses we are to consider and the "real" satire of a later, more sophisticated period. Many Irish words frequently associated with satire are perfectly familiar to us: words for "laughter," "ridicule," "disgrace," "reviling," and the like. But another class of words used in the same connection appears strange: words for "blemishing," "cutting," "piercing," and "reddening," for example. *Rinntaid* is the name for "a man of satire, who wounds or cuts each face." The poet Néde, when asked what art he practiced, answered: "reddening a countenance,

[14] *Ancient Laws of Ireland* (hereafter *ALI*), ed. Eugene O'Curry and others (Dublin, 1865-1901), II, 157; V, 512-13.

[15] *ALI*, V, 295. See Mary Claire Randolph, "Female Satirists of Ancient Ireland," *Southern Folklore Quarterly*, VI (1942), pp. 75-87.

[16] Plummer, *Vitae Sanctorum Hiberniae*, I, cii, note 8.

piercing flesh," and a glossator comments: "the edge of his satire like a point in flesh."[17]

The curious emphasis here on reddening, cutting, and blemishing flesh is seen to have particular point when we look at some of the stories. A famous one concerns the abovementioned Néde who had been adopted by his uncle Caier, king of Connaught. Caier's wife seduced Néde by promising him half of the kingdom if he would sleep with her. She persuaded him to make a satire against Caier. Néde pronounced a *glám dícind* upon his uncle:

> Evil, death, short life to Caier!
> Let spears of battle wound him, Caier!
> Caier . . .! Caier . . .! Caier under earth,
> Under ramparts, under stones be Caier!

Three colored blisters, namely, Stain, Blemish, and Defect, broke out on Caier's face. He fled to hide his disgrace. A year later the repentant Néde found Caier hiding under a flagstone behind a fort. Caier died of shame at the sight of Néde. A rock flew up and pierced Néde's head.[18] From our point of view, Néde's quatrain is a spell, rather than a satire;[19] but, as the linguistic evi-

---

[17] From *The Colloquy of the Two Sages* as trans. by Howard Meroney, "Studies in Early Irish Satire," II, *Journal of Celtic Studies*, I, No. 2 (Nov. 1950), p. 217. The idea that satire raised blisters on a victim's face was originally an importation from juridical folklore, Meroney says; he believes that much of what looks like magic in the old tales may be explained by "the vagaries of school-men notorious for distortions of word and fact" (pp. 218 ff.).

[18] In *Three Irish Glossaries*, trans. Whitley Stokes (London, 1862), pp. xxxvi ff.; Robinson's briefer version follows Stokes: "Satirists and Enchanters,"pp. 112-114.

[19] Meroney believes that the quatrain represents a conflation of two themes: one of magic interment, the other of stigmatization. "Studies in Early Irish Satire," II, pp. 212-215. In the Book of Ballymote there is an elaborate prescription for making a *glám dícind* against a king who has refused to pay for a poem. The ritual involved first a council of thirty laymen, thirty bishops, and thirty poets to decide whether the satire should be made; "and it was a crime for them to prevent the satire after the reward (for the poem) was refused." Then seven poets, representing the seven degrees of the *filid*, ascended a hill at sunrise when the wind was blowing from the north, and stood with their backs to a hawthorn tree. Each sang a stave of a lampoon into a slingstone and a thorn of the hawthorn, which they left at the butt of the tree. If the satire was unjustified the earth would swallow the poets. "But if it were the king

dence just cited shows, and as we shall see in more detail later, the Irish, like the Arabs, made no distinction between this kind of word magic and the mocking verses of poets designed to hold their victims up to ridicule and shame. Somehow, we notice, shame results from Néde's verse, just as it results (or *should* result, all satirists have claimed) from the verse of Horace, Pope, or of, say, Auden.

A poignant tale has to do with Luaine, who had replaced the unhappy Derdriu (Deirdre) in King Conchobar's affections. Luaine and the king were to be married; but it happened that Aithirne the Importunate, a great satirist, and his two sons, also poets, were overcome by the beauty of the girl. They were filled with desire for her, so that "they preferred not to be alive unless they should forgather with her." The poets threatened to make a *glám dícind* against Luaine unless she accepted their solicitations. "The damsel refused to lie with them. So then they made three satires on her, which left three blotches on her cheeks, to wit, Shame and Blemish and Disgrace, black and red and white. Thereafter the damsel died of shame and bashfulness."[20]

When King Aed determined to banish the poets from Ireland, his reason, as given in the earliest version of the *Eulogy of St. Columba*, was simply that they were too numerous. A later version, however, introduces the theme of oppressiveness: ". . . Ireland's men were not able to find out what to do with them [the *filid*]; for the person who was satirised there, if he did not immediately die, there used to grow poisonous ulcers upon him . . . ; but upon the poet himself grew the ulcers, and he used to die immediately, if it was without fault that he satirised."[21] The in-

---

that was in the wrong, the earth would swallow up him and his wife and his son and his horse and his arms and his dress and his hound." Trans. Whitley Stokes, *RC*, XII (1891), pp. 119-121. Both Robinson (p. 109) and Meroney (p. 218) are suspicious of the authenticity of this account; and it is true that most references to the *glám dícind* involve no such elaborate carryings-on.

[20] *The Wooing of Luaine and the Death of Aithirne Here*, trans. Whitley Stokes, *RC*, XXIV (1903), pp. 273-85.

[21] Meroney, "Studies in Early Irish Satire," II, p. 222. For a version expanded still further and including reference to the *glám dícind* and the three blisters Shame and Blemish and Defect, see Appendix B to the Bodleian *Eulogy of St. Columba*, trans. Whitley Stokes, *RC*, XX (1899), pp. 421-22. Meroney characterizes this tract as "worthless," because it

troduction of the blisters and the retribution theme may be the invention or importation of a poet or it may be that he was following a well-established tradition. A great deal of hostility toward the *filid* is expressed in the early literature; such traditions help account for it.

All this seems wildly remote from the twentieth century and from our conception of satire and its effects. Yet the tradition is by no means dead: Hugh MacDiarmid, for example, today regards himself "as a purely Celtic poet, carrying on (newly applied in vastly changed circumstances) the ancient bardic traditions of a very intricate and scholarly poetry, and with all the bardic powers of savage satire and invective. . . ." Part of his job is "to keep up perpetually a sort of Berserker rage . . . in the way of the old heroes," to be a real bard who " 'sang' things till they 'became.' "[22] MacDiarmid is one of the most complex poets of our time, self-consciously of the avant-garde; yet he has written poetry that is a direct throwback to the magical ethos we have been considering. His verse, he threatens an enemy poet, is designed

> To remove the haemorrhoids you call your poems
> With a white-hot poker for cautery,
> Shoved right up through to your tonsils![23]

The language might be that of Aithirne the Importunate—or of a *defixio* of the fourth century B.C.

Again, is it not curious that today we too speak of satire as "blistering"? that we too "die of shame," as did the victims of Irish satire? We speak figuratively, of course; but behind our use of the terms lies a sense of physical damage: not magical damage, to be sure, but the possibility of "real" damage, even real blisters. The Celts, comments Sir John Rhŷs, are a thin-skinned race, and he quotes a Welsh saying: "The cheek hides not the heart's affliction."[24] Today medical researchers interested in the

---

represents a conflation of several different, Meroney would say unrelated, themes.

[22] *Lucky Poet: a Self-Study in Literature and Political Ideas* (London, 1943), pp. 166, 79, 81.

[23] *The Battle Continues* (Edinburgh, 1957), p. 1.

[24] *Celtic Folklore* (Oxford, 1901), II, 634. Rhŷs discusses the possible psychosomatic implications of the Irish satirist's ability to blemish the face of his victim.

correlation between emotional disturbance and skin eruptions echo the language of proverb: "The skin is . . . a canvas," write Doctors Wittkower and Russell, "on which the psyche reveals itself."[25] It will not do to dismiss the Irish tales out of hand. We are all thin-skinned in the face of Shame, Blemish, and Disgrace.

From time to time Irish satirists encountered a class of men whose magic was greater even than their own: that is, the saints. On one occasion certain poets demanded a gift of St. Columba. He had nothing with him, asked them to come to his home, where he would grant their boon. They refused and threatened to satirize him. "When Columb cille heard the poets threatening to satirize him . . . he was seized with great shame, and so grievous was that shame that those present saw smoke arise from his head." He put his hand to his forehead to wipe away the sweat, and the sweat was turned into gold. He gave it to the poets. "And so it was that God saved the shame of Columb cille."[26]

The most celebrated, the most feared and hated and admired, satirist of Irish saga was Aithirne the Importunate, the poet of Ulster, who has been mentioned above as responsible for the death of Luaine.[27] Like Archilochus, Aithirne was destined for great deeds from the beginning. According to one tale, his mother, pregnant with Aithirne, requested a drink of ale from the brewer. She was refused. Aithirne, importunate even before birth, intoned a spell from his mother's womb; the ale casks burst, the ale ran ankle-deep through the house, and his mother helped herself to three draughts.[28] This is one of the few instances in which any kind of levity is attached to Aithirne's

[25] Eric Wittkower and Brian Russell, *Emotional Factors in Skin Disease* (New York, 1953), see pp. 4, 24, 88-92. The ability of a hypnotist to raise blisters on a patient under controlled conditions is well known; see Flanders Dunbar, *Emotions and Bodily Changes*, 3rd ed. (New York, 1946), pp. 372-409, esp. p. 379.

[26] O'Donnell's *Life of Columb Cille*, trans. Richard Henebry, *Zeitschrift für Celtische Philologie* (hereafter ZCP), IV (1903), pp. 297-99. Plummer points out that in some cases the saints' hospitality was "dictated less by Christian charity, than by dread of the tongue of satire." *Vitae Sanctorum Hiberniae*, I, ciii, cxiii.

[27] Robinson says that for the Irish, Aithirne is *the* representative satirist: "in the metaphorical language of poetry *sciath aithirni*, 'the shield of aithirne,' became a 'kenning' for satire." "Satirists and Enchanters," p. 116.

[28] *Aithirne's Mother*, trans. E. J. Gwynn, ZCP, XVII (1928), pp. 154-55.

name; his associations are overwhelmingly with terror and destruction and death. Aithirne made a bardic circuit of Ireland,
going lefthandwise from kingdom to kingdom, making fantastic
exactions, exploiting the fear of his satire wherever he went. The
one-eyed King Eochaid of Connaught offered Aithirne as appeasement whatever his people had of jewels and treasures.
" 'There is, forsooth,' saith Aithirne, 'the single eye there in thy
head, to be given to me into my fist.' 'There shall be no refusal,'
saith Eochaid. . . . So then the king put his finger under his
eye, and tore it out of his head, and gave it into Aithirne's fist."[29]

The poet proceeded to Leinster, where he demanded on threat
of satire to sleep with the queen. The king's honor was at stake
here (as, we may suppose, was the honor of Lycambes when he
was faced by public ridicule from Archilochus; and as was the
honor of Arabian chieftains threatened with mockery by the
poets); but the terms of the issue may seem grotesque to us. The
king's solicitude for his honor, which would be destroyed by the
poet's satire, requires that he submit to Aithirne's demand:
"Thou shalt have the woman for my honour's sake. Nevertheless
there is not in Ulster a man who could take her unless I gave
her to thee for my honour's sake." We need not read our own
sexual morality into medieval Ireland to see the reality of the
conflict.[30] It is painful for the king to prostitute his wife, although whether loss of honor was entailed is not clear. But it
would be death for him to refuse the poet. These tales are unquestionably products of a "shame" culture—a culture in which
man literally lives by his good name.[31] If his name is enhanced,
he flourishes; if it is defiled, he dies. In such a culture the poets
are truly creative. By their encomium they create honor; they
make good names. But they are also truly destructive, for their

[29] *The Siege of Howth*, trans. Whitley Stokes, RC, VIII (1887), p. 49.
The following material is from the same tale. Cf. the activities of Jarwal
ibn Aus, the Arabian satirist, mentioned in Section 2 above.

[30] In a similar episode in the same tale the issues at stake are horribly
increased, as though to make the conflict more extreme and the power
of satire more fearsome. In Munster, Aithirne demands to sleep with the
queen. "And that night on which the woman was brought to bed [i.e.,
was to give birth], this is the night that she slept with Aithirne, for sake
of her husband's honour, that his honour might not be taken away" (p.
49).

[31] For discussion of the concept, see Chap. II, 2, below.

satire eats away honor, which is to say, it destroys life itself. Aithirne's magic was great.

When Aithirne and his sons, overcome by lust, made their fatal satires against Luaine, the beloved of King Conchobar, the Ulstermen finally rebelled. Conchobar cried for vengeance; the leading men of Ulster recalled that "many a time Ulster has found reproach of battle" from Aithirne; Luaine's mother cited the saying of a wizard: "Women-troops grieve at the destruction of men by Aithirne's words. . . ." But Cathbad, the great druid, gave warning: "Beasts of prey will be sent against you by Aithirne, namely, Satire and Disgrace and Shame, Curse and Fire and Bitter word." Nevertheless, the Ulstermen followed Aithirne the Importunate to his fortress, and there they walled the satirist up, together with his two sons, his two daughters, and his whole household, and they burned the place upon them.[32]

The tale, oddly enough, does not end there; the last lines record the outrage of the poets of Ulster at the slaying of Aithirne. Amargen, the chief poet, said: "Great grief, great pity, the destruction of Aithirne the greatly famous. . . . Woe (to him) that wrought the man's destruction, woe to him that caused his slaughter! . . . He had a spear which would slay a king. . . ."

Apparently the poets' allegiance to their order overrides questions of morality, justice, and responsibility, although from other testimony we find that poets were normally enjoined to follow a fairly rigid code of behavior. One of the old laws holds that as every king is bound to truth and every bishop is bound to purity, so every poet is bound to fairness in all his compositions.[33] To complicate the story of Aithirne further, there is an ancient tract on the privileges and responsibilities of the poets in which Aithirne is taken as the representative of the entire order of *filid*. He is still the fierce satirist: "no man of sense ventures his fist in hot coals round which spring up flames," he warns; but the "testament" he offers calls for a lofty standard of personal conduct as well as a high standard of art.[34] (We think of the standard implied in Juvenal's *inprobior saturam scribente cinaedo*:

[32] *The Wooing of Luaine and the Death of Aithirne Here*, trans. Whitley Stokes, *RC*, xxiv (1903), pp. 279-85.

[33] *ALI*, v, 459.

[34] E. J. Gwynn edits the tract; see *Eriu*, xiii (1942), pp. 3-4.

"more shameless than a pederast writing satire.") It seems impossible to reconcile this testament with the best-known stories of Aithirne, but clearly the poets of Ulster, at least in the story of Luaine, were not distressed by a moral dilemma. Their allegiance was to poetry and the poet.

Not all satirists attained to the individual notoriety of Aithirne, but the stories of their powers and of the fears they inspired lace the tales of early Ireland. When they are not chief actors, they provide motivation for the heroes or rationalization for the heroes' actions. Their roles are eerie and menacing; they seem like evil spirits rather than poets who could also praise. For example, one of the most famous fights in all the voluminous literature of fighting in Irish saga—that between Cú Chulainn and Fer Diad in the great story of *The Cattle-Raid of Cooley* (*Táin Bó Cúalnge*)—is brought about directly by the intervention of the satirists. Fer Diad, the champion of Connaught, refused to accompany the messengers of Queen Medb summoning him to battle with Cú Chulainn, who was his friend and foster-brother.

"Then did Medb despatch to Fer Diad the druids and the poets of the camp, and lampooners and hard-attackers to the end that they might make the three satires to stay him and the three scoffing speeches against him, to mock at him and revile and disgrace him, that they might raise three blisters on his face,—Blame, Blemish, and Disgrace, that he might not find a place in the world to lay his head. . . .

"Fer Diad came with them for the sake of his own honor and for fear of their bringing shame on him, since he deemed it better to fall by the shafts of valor and bravery and skill than to fall by the shafts of satire, abuse, and reproach."[35]

On the day of his death, Cú Chulainn was hounded by satirists as though by furies. He had, of course, had encounters with them earlier in his career. Richis, a woman satirist, was particularly unscrupulous. She sought revenge on Cú Chulainn for the death of her son and demanded that Crimthann aid her. Approaching Cú Chulainn, she took off her clothes, exploiting her knowledge of a *geis* (a kind of taboo) on Cú Chulainn which

[35] *The Ancient Irish Epic Tale Táin Bó Cúalnge*, trans. Joseph Dunn (London, 1914), pp. 218-19; I reprint the version in Cross and Slover, p. 288.

forbade that he look on a naked woman. He hid his face down-wards and was defenseless. "Attack him now, O Crimthann," said Richis. Cú Chulainn's followers warned of the danger, but he could not look up. He was saved when one of his men hurled a stone at Richis and broke her back.[36] But on his last day no human intervention could save Cú Chulainn. Evil powers closed implacably upon him: portents of doom were everywhere and the meaning of cryptic prophecies became manifest. Three times on the bloody plain of Muirthemne satirists demanded his spear from him, threatening that they would revile him or his people or his race. Cú Chulainn's fear of being satirized ("I have never yet been reviled because of my niggardliness or my churlish-ness") and his preeminent role as protector of his people's honor caused him each time to "give" his spear to the satirist: each time he flung it, killing the satirist and nine men beside, but disarming himself; and each time the spear was hurled back at Cú Chulainn. The last cast wounded him mortally.[37] Cú Chu-lainn's death was brought about by magic of many kinds, but the most deadly, the final fatal agency, was the word of the poet which threatened the hero's honor.

In addition to their command over the skins, the lives, and the honor of men, some of the great Celtic satirists were able to blight the land itself—a curious reversal here of the function of satire in the rituals of Greece, where it promoted fertility. For a whole year, it is said, Laidcenn, chief poet of Niall of the Nine Hostages, "kept satirising and lampooning the men of Leinster and cursing them, so that neither grass nor corn grew with them, nor a leaf, to the end of a year."[38] It is as though Lear's earth-

---

[36] *The Intoxication of the Ulstermen*, trans. William M. Hennessy; reprinted in Cross and Slover, p. 237. Richis' daughter Gris, also a satirist, employed a more conventional satirist's weapon to more formidable pur-pose, but she came to no better end. Gris made a demand on the girl Maistiu which was refused; thereupon Gris so belabored Maistiu "with blemishing lampoons that she died thereof before her." Maistiu's lover broke the female satirist's head apart with a rock. *The Prose Tales in the Rennes Dindsenchas*, trans. Whitley Stokes, RC, xv (1894), p. 335.

[37] *Cuchulainn's Death*, trans. Whitley Stokes, RC, iii (1876-78), pp. 178 ff.; Cross and Slover, pp. 335 ff. See Sjoestedt, *Gods and Heroes of the Celts*, pp. 78-79.

[38] *The Death of Niall of the Nine Hostages*, trans. Kuno Meyer, *Otia Merseiana* (University College, Liverpool, 1899-1904), ii, 84 ff.; Cross

rending curses had actually been effective. The poet Forgoll (who had some of Aithirne's characteristics) merely had to threaten King Mongán: "The poet said he would satirise him with his lampoons, and he would satirise his father and his mother and his grandfather, and he would sing (spells) upon their waters, so that fish should not be caught in their river-mouths. He would sing upon their woods, so that they should not give fruit, upon their plains, so that they should be barren for ever of any produce."[39]

Mongán promised all in his possession, including his wife, to appease the poet. One of the few times that Aithirne the Importunate met his match was when he satirized the river Modarn which flooded in anger so that he had to pronounce a eulogy to bring it back within its banks: "that is the praise that washes out satire."[40]

Beliefs as firmly planted as these having to do with the magic powers of satire, particularly the power over life, die hard. In Chaucer's time the Welsh poet Dafydd ap Gwilym wrote a satire on a rival poet, Rhys Meigen, who heard it recited and, it is said, promptly fell dead.[41] Early in the fifteenth century a harsh and unpopular Lord Lieutenant of Ireland, an Englishman named John Stanley, incurred the bitter hatred of Hugh O'Higgins and his son Niall. They satirized Stanley, who died within five weeks "of the virulence of the lampoons."[42] Many years later, we find the same malefic power attributed to the poet. The Reverend Patrick S. Dinneen writes of Egan O'Rahilly, who flourished in the late seventeenth and early eighteenth centuries:

---

and Slover, pp. 514 ff. Robinson, "Satirists and Enchanters," pp. 118-19, cites this and other examples of the satirist's ability to blast the land.

[39] *The Voyage of Bran*, trans. Kuno Meyer (London, 1895), I, 49; Cross and Slover, pp. 548-49. On the other hand, Amergin White Knee (whose wife was a satirist, as he doubtless was in his negative function) "sang . . . to increase fish in the creeks." *The Book of Conquests of Ireland*, ed. R. A. Stewart Macalister and John MacNeill (Dublin, n.d.), Part I, cap. 186; Cross and Slover, pp. 21-22.

[40] Part of this is conjectural; see E. J. Gwynn in *Eriu*, XIII (1942), pp. 3, 57-58.

[41] H. Idris Bell and David Bell, eds., *Dafydd ap Gwilym: Fifty Poems* (London, 1942), p. 40.

[42] *Annals of the Kingdom of Ireland, by the Four Masters*, trans. John O'Donovan (Dublin, 1856), IV, 819.

"It is said that, like Archilochus of old, he killed a man by the venom of his satire, and that a fierce attempt was made to satirize himself; that he laboured the livelong night to neutralize its effects; and that when morning came he asked his daughter to look out. . . . The daughter brought word that some of his cattle had perished during the night. The poet . . . said: 'Thank God! the victory was gained over them and not over me.' "[43]

English writers of the sixteenth century and later were well acquainted with this Irish tradition: Sidney ends *An Apologie for Poetrie* with a curse on him who "cannot heare the Planet-like Musicke of *Poetrie.*" Not a fatal curse, however: "I will not wish unto you . . . to be driven by a *Poets* verses (as *Bubonax* was) to hang himselfe, nor to be rimed to death, as is said to be done in *Ireland.*"[44] The belief that Irish satirists could rhyme rats and mice to death was widely current. One of the best-known stories is of the poet Senchán, from whom mice stole an egg, the only food he would eat. In his fury he satirized the mice to such effect that ten fell dead at his feet.[45] For centuries Irish poets were credited with this useful control over rodents, and in the popular mind rat-killing and man-killing were inevitably linked. References to these powers are scattered throughout English literature.[46] Ben Jonson, as we have already seen, connects ancient Greece with Ireland through the lethal power of verse. Rosalinde (*As You Like It* [III, ii]), who, as Dr. Johnson observed, is a learned lady, makes a mild joke about Irish rat-rhyming, while an author in the Martin Marprelate controversy sounds serious:

[43] Dinneen's Introduction to his translation of *The Poems of Egan O'Rahilly* (Irish Texts Society, 1900), p. xxxi. The quoted passage is dropped, interestingly enough, in the second edition.

[44] Sidney has combined the names of Hipponax, the satirist, and Bupalus, the victim (see Section 1 above); but he clearly equates the power of the Greek iambist with that of the Irish poet.

[45] *Proceedings of the Great Bardic Institution*, trans. Connellan, *Transactions of the Ossianic Society*, v (1860), pp. 75 ff. On the following, see Robinson, "Satirists and Enchanters," pp. 95-97, and the Rev. J. H. Todd's remarks on rhyming rats to death in *Proceedings of the Royal Irish Academy*, v (1850-53), pp. 355 ff.

[46] For a fine, swinging English rat-curse of the fourteenth century, see Kenneth Sisam, ed., *Fourteenth Century Verse and Prose* (Oxford, 1923), p. 170.

I am a rimer of the Irish race,
And have already rimde thee staring mad;
But if thou cease not thy bold jests to spread
I'll never leave till I have rimde thee dead.[47]

Still later Sir William Temple asserts that tales of rhyming rats
to death come from the same root as accounts of the *"Gothick
Runers"* who turned their rhymes "to Incantations and Charms,
pretending by them to raise Storms . . . to cause Terror in their
Enemies . . . ," and so on.[48] Swift (or whoever wrote the "Letter
of Advice to a Young Poet") knew of the tradition and so did
Pope, who adapted lines of Donne's *Second Satire* thus:

> Songs no longer move,
> No Rat is rhym'd to death, nor Maid to love.

Remnants of the old beliefs persisted among the folk well into
the nineteenth century—and doubtless still persist. It is said that
the rural Irish of the 1820's dreaded nothing so much as "the
satirical severity of their bards. Many a man, who would kindle
into rage at the sight of an armed foe, will be found to tremble
at the thought of offending a rhymer."[49] Whether rats were so
affected is not clear, although the scholar Eugene O'Curry tells
of contemporary efforts—some successful—to banish rats (rather
than to kill them) by satire. Indeed O'Curry himself, who admitted to being something of a poet, tried his hand at rat-
rhyming, but without success. The rats, he surmises, were unable
to understand his hard words.[50] Robert Browning knew the tradition (as his "Pied Piper" might indicate): he wrote to his
publisher Edward Moxon, threatening to rhyme a hostile critic
to death "like an Irish Rat!"[51] In the 1880's David Fitzgerald
claimed to possess modern specimens of rat-rhyming poems him-

---

[47] As cited by J. H. Todd, *op.cit.*, p. 356. For other references in the
period, see Ben Jonson, *Staple of News*, 4th Intermean, ll. 54-55; Thomas
Randolph, *Jealous Lovers*, v, ii.

[48] "Of Poetry," in *Sir William Temple's Essays on Ancient and Modern Learning and on Poetry*, ed. J. E. Spingarn (Oxford, 1909), pp. 66-67.

[49] Quoted from J. H. Hardiman's *Irish Minstrelsy* by Owen Connellan,
Trans. Ossianic Society, v (1860), p. xxx.

[50] J. H. Todd, *op.cit.*, pp. 362-66.

[51] *New Letters of Robert Browning*, ed. W. C. DeVane and K. L.
Knickerbocker (New Haven, 1950), pp. 37-38.

self.[52] Finally, to round up this hasty summary, Yeats exploits magnificently the mythic associations of the belief in these bitter lines from "Parnell's Funeral" (1934):

> Come, fix upon me that accusing eye.
> I thirst for accusation. All that was sung,
> All that was said in Ireland is a lie
> Bred out of the contagion of the throng,
> Saving the rhyme rats hear before they die.

But this has led us away from the point at hand. Thus far in the discussion of Irish satire emphasis has been on what the ancient satirists were said—and, one assumes, believed—to be able to effect through their verse. Few examples of the satires themselves have been given. Few exist, and these, as we shall see, nearly incomprehensible; for the closer the primitive satires are to magic, the less "meaning," in the discursive sense, are they likely to have. Writing about the meaning of magic, the contemporary anthropologist Bronislaw Malinowski says that magic is not built up in the narrative style: "it does not serve to communicate ideas from one person to another; it does not purport to contain a consecutive consistent meaning. It is an instrument serving special purposes, intended for the exercise of man's specific power over things, and *its meaning*, giving this word a wider sense, can be understood only in correlation to this aim. It will not be therefore a meaning of logically or topically concatenated ideas, but of expressions fitting into one another and into the whole, according to what could be called a magical order of thinking, or perhaps more correctly, a magical order of expressing, of launching words towards their aim."[53]

Malinowski, to be sure, is discussing magical spells which are strictly formularized and thought never to change, while the magical satire of Ireland is said to be extemporaneous. Still, early Irish satires are unquestionably the product of a "magical order of thinking" and are therefore but minimally available to logical (or literary) analysis.

[52] "Early Celtic History and Mythology," *RC*, vi (1883-85), p. 195. Fitzgerald notes that an Icelandic rhymer, Hallgrim Peterson, "sang a fox to death."

[53] *Argonauts of the Western Pacific* (London, 1932), p. 432. Cf. Malinowski's longer discussion in *Coral Gardens and their Magic* (London, 1935), ii, 213-50.

Magical satire existed in written form in Ireland as early as the ninth century; how far back it may have gone in oral tradition before that, it is impossible to say. A tale incorporating what is said to be the first satire ever made in Ireland begins with these words:

Who first was satirized in Ireland?
That is not hard to answer: Bres Mac Eladain.
Who satirized him?
That is not hard to answer: The poet Cairpre Mac Edaine of the Tuatha Dé Danaan.
What was the cause of this satire?
That is not hard to answer. The poet came seeking hospitality to Bres.

Bres, it develops, was king of the Fomorians (a mythical people of Ireland), unpopular because of his stinginess: "Never did either man or woman go from him drunk or happy." When Cairpre came seeking hospitality he was taken to a small, dark, narrow, house where there was no fire nor bath nor bed. The king sent him three small dry cakes on a little dish. On the next day Cairpre arose and he was not pleased. As he left the guest-house, he uttered a satire:

"Without food speedily on a platter,
Without a cow's milk whereon a calf thrives,
Without a man's habitation after the staying of darkness,
Be that the luck of Bres Mac Eladain."

"Not exists now Bres's wealth," he said. This came to be true, says the story, for Bres lost his wealth, his kingdom, and then his life.[54]

This "first" Irish satire is clearly an incantation, a spell enwrapped in the mysterious linkages of end and entrance rhyme, strong alliteration, assonance, and other metrical devices universally favored by magicians.[55] Néde's satire against his uncle

[54] *Cairpre MacEdaine's Satire upon Bres MacEladain*, trans. Vernam Hull, ZCP, xviii (1930), pp. 63-69. Cairpre, incidentally, is identical with the "Carpre" of *The Second Battle of Moytura*, he whose satire would render the enemy incapable of resisting warriors. See note 1 above.

[55] See James Travis, "A Druidic Prophecy, the First Irish Satire, and a Poem to Raise Blisters," PMLA, lvii, Pt. 2 (1942), pp. 912 ff.

Caier is similar; the poet wills in a heavily stylized quatrain the death and interment of Caier:

> Evil, death, short life to Caier!
> Let spears of battle wound him, Caier!
> Caier . . . ! Caier . . . ! Caier under earth,
> Under ramparts, under stones be Caier!

The stylization is more magical than literary, consisting chiefly in the accentuated repetition of the victim's name. Magicians everywhere employ the technique, for the name is the man, and when it is entrapped in the mysterious bonds of magical verse, the man himself is entrapped.[56]

To call these verses "satires" is, it would seem, to stretch the term almost beyond recognition. Our first impulse is to decide that the translation is imprecise, that the identification of magical spells with satire cannot be justified. Yet, as we have seen, the Irish language insists on the identification. The Irish do not differentiate between Cairpre's quatrain and what we think of as the "real" satire of a later time. As Robinson points out, the men who produce the magical verses, whether in history or in saga, are not mere enchanters; they are poets, and they compose magical verses as well as ridiculing verses as part of their proper function as poets—the function that requires them to blame as well as to praise. Furthermore, it should be observed that the magical satires are often occasioned by, and treat of, the same vices and follies which preoccupy Horace and Wyndham Lewis, Rabelais and Pope: stinginess, inhospitality, pride, the inflexibility of those in power. Finally, the magician satirists often propose to ridicule their victims and to shame them—this, most significantly, the precise aim of satirists in any age.

After advancing these justifications of the Irish use of the term *satire*, Robinson suggests that "the retention of one term

---

[56] The name was of great importance in early Ireland. For example, Cú Chulainn was forbidden by a *geis* (taboo) to "name himself to a single warrior"; his son Conla inherited the *geis*; and because neither would identify himself when they met each other, they fought and Cú Chulainn killed his son. See *The Death of Conla*, trans. Kuno Meyer, *Eriu*, I (1904), pp. 115 ff.; Cross and Slover, pp. 172 ff. For a discussion of the name-*geis*, see John R. Reinhard, *The Survival of Geis in Medieval Romance* (Halle, 1933), pp. 126 ff.

for all these products . . . is certainly defensible, and may be positively instructive in emphasizing the continuity of literary development."[57] This book, in effect, is an attempt to work out some of the implications of that instruction.

Not all early Irish satire has a magical ethos. A woman who was satirized "until she is laughed at" in public unquestionably sustained injury, for which she was entitled by law to restitution; but she was not "magically" injured. Again, ancient rhetorical treatises list as among the principal kinds of satire a category known as "incantation" (of which ten separate types are named and obscurely illustrated), but they also list other categories which seem to comprehend surprisingly familiar themes and methods.[58] In the literature itself are many examples of what Robinson calls "well-developed," that is, relatively sophisticated, satire. For instance, *The Instructions of King Cormac Mac-Airt*, a collection of proverbial morality thought to date from the first half of the ninth century, contains a long (122-line) diatribe against women which fits perfectly into a satiric tradition extending from the ancient Greek Semonides of Amorgos, through Juvenal, and into the Middle Ages and Renaissance, where anti-feminist attacks proliferate in startling abundance.[59] A sample of this gnomic instruction should make the point:

"O grandson of Conn, O Cormac," said Carbre,
"how do you distinguish women?"
    "Not hard to tell," said Cormac, "I distinguish them,
but I make no difference among them.
    They are crabbed as constant companions,
    haughty when visited,
    lewd when neglected,

    .   .   .   .   .   .

    [are] stubborn in a quarrel,

[57] "Satirists and Enchanters," pp. 98-99.
[58] For Meroney's translation of a bafflingly obscure rhetorical treatise on satire, see "Studies in Early Irish Satire," 1, *JCS*, 1, No. 2 (Nov. 1950), pp. 204-06. Cf. the discussion in the legal tracts (*ALI*, v, 229) of the seven kinds of satire and the regulations governing the "honor-price" to be paid to the victim of each kind.
[59] See Francis L. Utley's Introduction to *The Crooked Rib* (Columbus, Ohio, 1944).

not to be trusted with a secret,

.   .   .   .   .   .

boisterous in their jealousy.

.   .   .   .   .   .

lustful in bed .   .   .   .
better to whip them than to humour them,
better to scourge them than to gladden them

.   .   .   .

They are waves that drown you,
they are fire that burns you

.   .   .   .

they are moths for sticking to one,
they are serpents for cunning. . . .[60]

The themes are conventional; and the tone, the attitude, even the images are matched by dozens of predecessors and hundreds of followers from many lands. Misogynists have a strong and abiding brotherhood—one of the great cross-cultural institutions of history—but it is amusing to see how the nature of their enterprise, in its extreme specialization, limits the range of their utterance.

Between this easily recognizable satiric mode and the magical incantations considered earlier lies a kind of satire that seems to incorporate elements from both modes. We must be cautious in these matters. Translations are tentative and meanings often obscure; and the temptation to read one's own preconceptions into invitingly murky categories is great. Still, that mockery and ridicule were employed in early magical satires seems almost unquestionable.

The best examples of this kind of satire appear in the fascinating tale known variously as *Proceedings of the Great Bardic Institution* (a burdensome title given it by its translator, Owen Connellan) and as *The Great Visitation to Guaire*. I shall refer to it in this discussion as *The Great Visitation*.[61] At the opening

---

[60] *The Instructions of King Cormac MacAirt*, trans. Kuno Meyer, *Royal Irish Academy*, Todd Lecture Series, xv (1909), pp. 29-35.

[61] Analysis of these satires is complicated by the fact that much of *The Great Visitation* is sheer burlesque, which means that one is rarely sure in what sense to take any given passage. The first satire to be discussed, however, appears early in the tale, before comic distortions super-

of the tale the great poet Dallán Forgaill visits King Hugh (also known as Aed: the same king who had entered into a pact with the poets). Dallán has been bribed to request of King Hugh his magic shield, which made any enemy who looked on it as feeble as an old woman. Knowing that the request is improper, Dallán still asks for the shield and recites a poem praising King Hugh (the poem is given in the text). " 'That is a good poem,' says the king, 'whoever could understand it.' " Dallán allows the truth of the remark and translates the verses into ordinary language. He then recites two poems to the shield. The king offers to pay for the poems in gold, silver, and cattle. Dallán will take only the shield. " 'I will not give you the shield,' said Hugh. 'I will satirize you,' said Dallán."

" 'The powers and miracles of the king of Heaven and earth be on my side to save and protect me against thee! And dost thou remember, O Dallán,' said Hugh, 'that when the saints of Erin made peace between us (the kings) and you the bards of Erin, it was agreed that whosoever of you should compose a satire on us unjustly, three blotches of reproach should grow upon him; and if we should deserve it and that you should compose it justly, the same number should grow upon us.' "[62] Not all the power of all the saints who were present at the assembly can save you from being satirized, said Dallán; and he uttered his satire:

"O Hugh, son of Duach the Dark,
    Thou pool not permanent;

---

vene. It serves a thematic purpose, motivating and justifying the ridicule of the poets that follows. Thus it seems reasonable to treat the poem as a true example of magical satire. Professor Robinson has told me that he thinks this interpretation justified. See also Myles Dillon, *The Cycles of the Kings* (London, 1946), p. 92, n. 3. James Carney, *Studies in Irish Literature and History* (Dublin, 1955), thinks *The Great Visitation* may have taken substantially its present form in the tenth century or earlier (p. 170); other authorities tend to place it later. For summaries and discussion, see Carney, pp. 165-88; Dillon, *Cycles of the Kings*, pp. 79-98; Rudolf Thurneysen, *Die irische Helden-und Königsage* (Halle, 1921), pp. 254-67. Except where specified, I use Connellan's translation, *Trans. Ossianic Soc.*, v (1860), pp. 15 ff.

[62] Reference is to the assembly of Druim Ceat, at which St. Columba interceded with King Aed in favor of the poets. See Connellan's note, pp. 22-23.

Thou pet of the mild cuckoos;
Thou quick chafferer of a blackbird;

Thou sour green berry;
Swarms (of bees) will suck the herbs;
Thou green crop like fine clothes;
A candlestick without light;

Thou cold wooden boat;
Thou bark that will give dissatisfaction;
Thou disgusting black chafer;
Thou art more disgusting, O Hugh." (pp. 25-27)

Because King Hugh understands this poem no more than he had the first, Dallán undertakes an *explication de texte*: " 'O Hugh, son of Duach the Dark, thou pool not permanent;' that is equivalent to a summer pool when it experiences a great drought and that persons trample in it; its water entirely evaporates, and it is not replenished till the flood comes again; you are similarly circumstanced, for no matter how highly you may be praised, the same hospitality shall not possess you again in consequence of these satires."

Dallán discusses each phrase of the first quatrain and the first half of the second, explaining and expanding the enigmatic references and applying them specifically to Hugh. He is interrupted by the king and dismissed from court. The poet gathers his retinue and leaves exulting: "It is a wonder to me . . . what the publishers of stories have related, for they assert that whosoever composes satires wrongfully it will be worse for himself; and I believe that never have been made satires more unjustly or wrongfully than the satires I myself have composed, and yet I am now the better for uttering them, for I was without an eye on my coming to the place, and I have two good eyes now" (p. 31). Dallán, who has been blind, now sees. The omen is bad, however, for St. Columba had foretold that Dallán would have a remarkable warning before his death. The poet is taken to his house and three days later is dead.

As Connellan, the translator, confesses, it is impossible to know precisely what Dallán's satire means, and the translation can be no more than tentative. But this much is clear: the satire consists of a series of cryptic epithets identifying Hugh with unpleasant, ridiculous, or (it may be) demonic beings or things. Dallán's discursive expansion of "thou pool not permanent" indicates that the image is one of simple denigration based upon an elaborate series of implied analogies. Whether more than denigration is intended, we cannot know. The poet explains the cuckoo epithet of line two as follows: " 'Thou captive of a tamed cuckoo;' that is equivalent to a pet of a cuckoo, for there cannot be in a house a worse pet than this. It ceases to sing except a little, and he will as soon do so in winter as at any other time. And some assert that another bird nurses for it; its name is Cobcan, and he puts away his own bird and feeds the cuckoo's bird till it is able to provide for itself, when the cuckoo takes it away with her, and she has no more regard for that Cobcan than she has for any other bird. Similar to that is your case and of the learned professors of Erin, for they will not remember any good thou hast done after these satires" (p. 29). The explanation is notably undramatic and hardly clear; still one can detect the aim of denigration (perhaps to be achieved through ridicule), the satirist's familiar attention to ingratitude and lack of generosity, and the obsessive Irish concern with reputation. The image may have a magical significance as well; as Connellan points out, the song of the cuckoo, a sacred bird in pagan times, has ominous association among the Irish folk.[63]

Later in *The Great Visitation* two more satires are recorded, these uttered by Senchán Torpeist, chief bard of Ireland after Dallán's death. The first is Senchán's famous satire against the mice who had stolen his food; the second against Hirusan, chief of the cats, the tribe that should have suppressed the mice. The humor of the latter part of the tale complicates things: are Senchán's verses to be taken as proper examples of magical satire?

[63] Similarly, the black chafer of the last two lines of the satire is said to have a specifically demonic significance in Irish folklore. The chafer is possessed by the spirit of an emissary of Satan; it is the insect that betrayed to the Jews the way that Christ went when they were searching for Him. He who kills the chafer according to the proper ritual will have seven sins remitted from his soul. Connellan believes that the association of this insect with evil and black magic may go back to pre-Christian times. When Dallán calls King Hugh more disgusting than even this disgusting creature, something beyond simple invective may be involved, although again one cannot be sure.

or are they jokes? I do not know. Still, even if they are jokes, they will necessarily have a close formal relation to what they burlesque: that is, to the kind of magical satire uttered by Dallán. Senchán is furious with the mice who have nibbled at his egg: " 'I will satirize them,' said Senchán:"

> The mice though sharp are their beaks,
> Are not powerful in the battles of warriors;
> Venomous death I'll deal out to the tribe,
> In avengement of Bridget's leavings [i.e., the egg].

In an answering quatrain a mouse begs Senchán to spare them, to accept compensation instead: "Don't satirize us all, O learned bard." But the poet is unrelenting:

> Clear ye out of your spacious abodes,
> As we are prepared to convict you,
> Come ye all out of the hole (or burrow)
> And lie down (here) O ye mice! (pp. 75-77)

Ten mice, it is said, fell dead at his feet. Here are no allusive epithets such as Dallán employed, rather the relatively straight-forward expression in verse of the poet's will, somewhat as in Cairpre's satire on Bres (above, p. 38). The mockery or ridicule apparent is in what looks like a mock-heroic conception of the mice; but that may be an unjustified reading-in.

Senchán was much less successful in his attack on Hirusan, lord of the cats. This is the satire:

> "Hirusan pleading of nails,
> remnant of a badger,
> tail of a cow in heat,
> charioteer against charioteer,
> pleading against Hirusan."

Like Dallán, Senchán explains his satire: " 'Hirusan pleading of nails,' said he, that is, when the mouse is in the wall he [Hirusan] can only scratch the wall with his nails; 'remnant of a badger,' for the ancestor of the cats was once asleep at a lake-side and a badger came to him and struck the top of his two ears from him, and ever since every cat has scraggy, jagged ears;

'tail of a cow in heat,' for the tail of a cow in heat is no quicker than *his* tail when the mouse goes away from him. . . ."[64]

Hirusan felt the influence of the verses, even at a considerable distance, and he swore vengeance. He appeared before the poet: "Blunt-snouted, rapacious, panting, determined, jagged-eared, broad-breasted, prominent-jointed, sharp and smooth clawed, split-nosed, sharp and rough-toothed, thick-snouted, nimble, powerful, deep-flanked, terror-striking, angry, extremely vindictive, quick, purring, glare-eyed. . . ." Hirusan seized Senchán and carried him off on his back. The poet would have been devoured except that as the cat dragged Senchán past St. Kieran's (Ciarán's) cell, the saint picked up a flaming iron bar, hurled it at Hirusan, killing him, and thus the poet was saved.[65]

Senchán's satire is formally very similar to that of Dallán. The obscure epithets of which it is composed are shown by the poet to have some significant association with the object of the satire. In this case the ridicule is unmistakable: the cat's monstrous claws scratching vainly at the mouse hole, the mocking comparison of tails—the images of the quatrain work together to make Hirusan the butt of laughter. He is "injured" and appears before the poet in all his wrath, with the results we have seen.

Of the three satires in *The Great Visitation*, only the one against the mice is successful. The other two fail lamentably in their purpose. That is not to say, however, that the verses lacked magical power or that the poets were inferior practitioners. Dallán's satire against King Hugh carried with it all the magical efficacy usually associated with this kind of word-killing, but his magic encountered a superior magic: that which inhered in the pact between the poets and the kings, a pact given transcendent

---

[64] I use Carney's translation of the satire and its explanation, p. 175.

[65] A curious theme is introduced here. Senchán is furious with the saint for having saved him. If the cat had eaten him, as Senchán wished, then the poet's host, King Guaire, could be considered to have violated the laws of hospitality (his protection of a guest had failed) and Guaire would be subject to the satire of the whole Bardic Association. Senchán would prefer that Guaire "be satirized than that I should live and he not satirized." Cf. Aithirne's hope (*Siege of Howth*, p. 49) that his satires will incite the Leinstermen to kill him; then Ulster would be obliged to avenge him forever. For comparable themes in other cultures, cf. Frazer, *Golden Bough*, Vol. IV: *The Dying God*, p. 141.

authority by the participation of the saints. The lethal satire, in collision with the greater power, turned back upon its author and Dallán died. Similarly, Hirusan was magically affected by Senchán's mocking satire; but the cat's magic was mightier than that of the poet, and only the mightiest magic of all—that of a saint—saved Senchán from death.

We began this chapter with lines from Ben Jonson's *Poetaster*; it would be well to read them again:

> They know, I dare
> To spurne, or bafful 'hem; or squirt their eyes
> With inke, or vrine: or I could doe worse,
> Arm'd with ARCHILOCHVS fury, write *Iambicks*,
> Should make the desperate lashers hang themselues.
> Rime 'hem to death, as they doe *Irish* rats
> In drumming tunes.[66]

Jonson's threat has two roots, as we have seen, one extending back over two thousand years to Archilochus and the beginnings of Western civilization, the other stretching back in cultural (as opposed to chronological) time a distance beyond calculation. Both roots draw upon "primitive" beliefs which have had remarkable vitality throughout the entire history of satirical literature. The principal belief, of course, is that satire kills (or at least causes death), that magical power inheres in the denunciatory and derisive words of a poet whose function is to blame as well as to praise. In obscure ways these beliefs exert influence even today, as we shall see in later chapters. But our task now is to ask certain theoretical and historical questions about the material we have just examined: how can we account for the curious association of magic with satire in cultures as dissimilar as those of Greece, Arabia, and Ireland? Can the function of ridicule in preliterate and civilized societies today throw light on this and allied problems? Is it possible to demonstrate how and when archaic satire is divested of its magical trappings: is there a discernible point, that is, at which the satirist breaks with the magical background and begins producing the literary

[66] See "To the Reader," appended to *Poetaster* in *Ben Jonson*, ed. C. H. Herford and Percy Simpson (Oxford, 1927), IV, 322.

art we know? These are the questions we shall ask and try to
answer in the next chapter. After that we will be able to turn
to the great timber trees of our subject—trees which grow, we
must remember, out of the underwood which has thus far
claimed our attention.

CHAPTER II

SATIRE AND MAGIC: THEORY

"The original of ancient customs," said Imlac, "is commonly unknown, for the practice often continues when the cause has ceased; and concerning superstitious ceremonies it is vain to conjecture, for what reason did not dictate reason cannot explain."—SAMUEL JOHNSON, *Rasselas*

1. MAGIC, RITUAL, MYTH

ON THE BASIS of the material presented thus far, we can make some generalizations about the function of satire in its primordial form. In what follows I adapt certain ideas of Freud and of Jane Harrison, principally, in an effort to account theoretically for the origin of magical satire and its complex development. Much of the material is hypothetical, as it must be. In speculative studies like this, proof is impossible; the best one can hope to approximate is the kind of ambiguous truth, or, better, *adequacy*, with which scientists are content as they construct models of atomic and sub-atomic behavior. The models do not describe reality; they are not even capable of being "true," for they are necessarily incommensurate with what they purport to describe. They are mere tools of thought. But the models may be adequate in that they have a heuristic and so a valuable function. The formulations that follow may be looked at in the same way. Freud's speculations in *Totem and Taboo* are notoriously unhistorical, but even so historically-minded an anthropologist as A. L. Kroeber recognizes their potential for deepening our understanding of the nature of culture.[1] Freud's ideas (and those of Jane Harrison, F. M. Cornford, and others) applied to the origin and development of satire, will not eventuate in a formu-

[1] "Totem and Taboo in Retrospect," *American Journal of Sociology*, XLV (July 1939 to May 1940), pp. 446-51.

lation that can be tested historically; there is no history for much of this material. But they may help to form a model which will be adequate, one which will help us to understand the role of satire in culture.

As we have seen, in Greece, in Arabia, in Ireland, satire was originally magical—or, more accurately, the satirist was often thought to possess preternatural powers. It is most difficult, perhaps impossible, to be precise about the nature of those powers. Some satirists achieve their malefic ends merely by uttering their invectives (or mockery or riddling verses—whatever form their satire takes); the power seems to reside in the words themselves, often in a special concatenation of words, rhymes, and rhythms. Others call upon gods to blast their enemies, and still others practice certain magical rites as accompaniment to the deadly words. Different sources of power, or at least different methods of harnessing the power, are implied in the different practices. To resolve such distinctions falls in the province of the anthropologists; they, however, have been unable to agree upon categories or terminology adequate to deal with the staggeringly complex problems associated with belief in, and attempts to control, supernatural power. That such beliefs are ubiquitous, everyone grants. But what the relation of religion is to magic, for example; whether religion developed out of magic or magic out of religion; whether religion is antithetical to magic or perhaps complementary to it; or what the relations of witchcraft and sorcery and other demonic beliefs are to religion and magic and to each other—on these matters there is great confusion. Radcliffe-Brown, after discussing the failure of Frazer, Durkheim, and Malinowski to distinguish adequately between magic and religion, throws up his hands: "The only sound procedure, at any rate in the present state of anthropological knowledge, is to avoid as far as possible the use of the terms in question until there is some general agreement about them."[2]

No such agreement has been forthcoming, and as it is impossible in an enterprise such as this to avoid using the terms, one makes one's choice. I follow, in general, Ruth Benedict's treatment of the categories. "Magic," says Mrs. Benedict, "is

[2] A. R. Radcliffe-Brown, *Taboo* (Cambridge, 1939), p. 16. Cf. Joachim Wach, *Sociology of Religion* (Chicago, 1944), pp. 350-56.

technological and mechanistic, a compulsion of a passive universe to one's own ends; religion is animistic behavior and employs toward a personalized universe all the kinds of behavior that hold good in human relations." Elsewhere, shifting her terms slightly, she writes: "Just as the theory of the supernatural swings between two poles, one of which is magic power as an impersonal attribute of objects and acts [objects and acts, that is, have *mana*] and the other the will power of a personalized universe, so also religious techniques cover a gamut one extreme of which is mechanistic manipulation of impersonal magic power, and the other personal relations with the supernatural."[3] Functionally, the two categories, magic and religion, cannot be considered apart: "they are always alternative techniques for inducing power . . . by means other than those of the natural cause and effect sequences. . . . Both the animistic and magical techniques . . . have in common the fact that they rely upon wish fulfilments rather than upon mundane labor in order to attain their ends." Freud's distinction in *Totem and Taboo* between sorcery (*Zauberei*) and magic (*Magie*) is not unlike that made by Ruth Benedict. According to Freud: "Sorcery . . . is essentially the art of influencing spirits by treating them in the same way as one would treat men in like circumstances: appeasing them, making amends to them, propitiating them, intimidating them, robbing them of their power, subduing them to one's will—by the same methods that have proved effective with living men. Magic, on the other hand, is something different: fundamentally, it disregards spirits and makes use of special procedures and not of everyday psychological methods."[4] Richard Chase states the difference between magic and religion from a psychological point of view thus: "Magic is the envelopment and coercion of the objective world by the ego; it is a dynamic subjectivism. Religion is the coercion of the ego by gods and spirits who are objectively conceived beings in control of nature and man."[5] "If magic says, '*Let there be* such and such,' religion

---

[3] "Magic," *Encyclopedia of the Social Sciences* (1933); "Religion," in *General Anthropology*, ed. Franz Boas (New York, 1938), p. 637.

[4] Sigmund Freud, "Animism, Magic and the Omnipotence of Thoughts," *Totem and Taboo*, trans. James Strachey (New York, 1950), p. 78.

[5] *Quest for Myth* (Baton Rouge, Louisiana, 1949), pp. 84-85.

says, 'Please do such and such,'" writes Kenneth Burke. "The decree of magic, the petition of prayer"[6]—and within the two categories the ramifications of practice are endless: from the saint in communion with his God to the medicine-man threatening and cheating the spirits; from the elaborate magic ceremonials of the Trobriand Islanders to the simple "bewitching with the mouth" of the BaKxatla of South Africa.

Magic beliefs provide primitive man with a way of knowing his world and of coping with it. The motives behind the practice of magic are simple, Freud believed: they are human wishes, and magic is no more, fundamentally, than the projection of the human will. "All magic," says Paul Radin, "consists in the coercion of an object so that it will comply with the wishes and desires of the performer."[7] But before the object can be coerced there must be unconditional belief in the power of the coercer's will to achieve its end. This belief is part of what Freud has called the "omnipotence of thoughts" principle characteristic of preliterate mentality. The primitive mind tends generally, we would say, to overvalue mental processes, in the sense that "Things become less important than ideas of things: whatever is done to the latter will inevitably also occur to the former. Relations which hold between the ideas of things are assumed to hold equally between the things themselves. Since distance is of no importance in thinking—since what lies furthest apart both in time and space can without difficulty be comprehended in a simple act of consciousness—so, too, the world of magic has a telepathic disregard for spatial distance and treats past situations as though they were present."[8]

Behind the practice of magic, then, lies the will—a will assumed to be omnipotent, operating independently of space and time in a cause-and-effect relation which is not rationalized but which is *known* to be effective. Freud hypothesizes a kind of evolutionary development of the magical act. The primitive man's wishes are accompanied by a motor impulse, the will; the act of will itself prefigures, in a sense, the satisfaction to be

[6] *The Philosophy of Literary Form* (Baton Rouge, Louisiana, 1941), p. 4.
[7] *Primitive Religion: Its Nature and Origin* (New York, 1937), p. 25.
[8] *Totem and Taboo*, p. 85.

gained from the accomplishment of the desired end. In the act of willing there is a representation (Freud speaks of it as a "motor hallucination") of that which is desired; the representation brings its own satisfaction.[9] "No actual killing of the enemy," writes Mrs. Benedict, "could be so satisfactory in details of vindictiveness as the pre-enactment that is staged in the interests of magic by the Algonquian medicine man."[10]

As time goes on, says Freud, "the psychological accent shifts from the *motives* for the magical act on to the *measures* by which it is carried out—that is, on to the act itself. . . . It thus comes to appear as though it is the magical act itself which, owing to its similarity with the desired result, alone determines the occurrence of that result."[11] Hence, one would assume, the overwhelming concentration on method in most imitative magic: the insistence that the spell must be letter-perfect and must not change, that the rite must be impeccably performed. All this has relevance, I believe, for the development of magical satire; but for the moment I want to approach the matter from a somewhat different direction.

In her remarkable study *Ancient Art and Ritual* (which was written independently of Freud) Jane Harrison shows how primitive art develops more or less directly out of ritual. She considers, as part of her demonstration, various widely practiced tribal dances—those reenacting memorable events, for example.[12] When the hunters of a tribe return from a successful foray, they often reenact their exploits in dance. Doubtless the motives behind the dancing are complex, but prominent among them is the element of *mimesis*, of imitating and commemorating the exploit. But if the dance is repeated again and again, it becomes detached from the particular hunting expedition which may have prompted it, and is generalized. The dance comes to cele-

[9] For Freud's theory that a child "hallucinates the fulfilments of its inner needs" and thus experiences satisfaction, see "Formulations Regarding the Two Principles in Mental Functioning," *Collected Papers,* trans. under the supervision of Joan Riviere (London, 1925), IV, 13-21.
[10] "Magic," *Encyclopedia of the Social Sciences.*
[11] *Totem and Taboo,* p. 84.
[12] Jane Ellen Harrison, *Ancient Art and Ritual* (London, 1913), pp. 40-44. Freud's "Animismus, Magie, und Allmacht der Gedanken," a translation of which I have been using, appeared originally in 1913.

brate, not a particular hunt, but hunting. Then, once the dance has achieved this hypothetical abstraction, it is available for a different, this time a magical, use; for primitive man dances not only after an exploit but in anticipation of some major event. The dance which may have originated as a *re*-presentation, then becomes a *pre*-presentation, an action mimetic of something anticipated, rather than of something realized.[13] The men about to set out on a hunt or go into battle will dance their desires. The dance is a magical representation of what is intensely wanted, an objectification of what is willed.[14] We might say that it is a working out in anticipatory mimetic action of the fantasy that Freud speaks of. The magical pre-enactment of the dance is a coercion of the event to come; it is the will given monstrous efficacy, and if the magic is good, the end will already, in a sense, have been accomplished.[15]

Thus primitive magic is before all else practical. The emphasis is on the end to be achieved, on the coercion of the thing for utilitarian purposes. Like science, magic aims to control the world, to shape it, to bring it under man's sway for his immediate practical purposes. The cry of both magic and science, says Jane Harrison, is: "I'll do, and I'll do, and I'll do."[16] To the degree that this is true, so far removed is magic from art. For while art may grow out of practical needs and be used for practical ends, while it does have a social dimension, its primary

[13] "A 'presentation' is . . . only a delayed, intensified desire—a desire of which the active satisfaction is blocked, and which runs over into a 'presentation.' An image conceived 'presented,' what we call an *idea* is, as it were, an act prefigured." Harrison, *Ancient Art and Ritual*, p. 53.

[14] Before going on a war party a Winnebago "previsions his enemy. He destroys his courage, deprives him of his power of running, paralyzes his actions, and blunts his weapons." Paul Radin, *Primitive Man as Philosopher* (New York, 1927), p. 24.

[15] A simple pre-enactment, says Miss Benedict, gives a maximum possibility of emotional release. "The medicine man hollows out a shallow grave before him and lays in it a rotten log to represent his enemy. He chants over it the torments of the dying. He applies red-hot tongs to the points that are symbolically his enemy's eyes, heart, and groins. He seizes a spear and runs the 'body' through from side to side with violent thrusts." The emotional satisfaction derived from this magical pre-enactment is very great and it may be obtained in words as well as in acts. See Miss Benedict's example, "Religion," in *General Anthropology*, pp. 638-39.

[16] *Themis* (Cambridge, 1912), pp. 82-84; *Ancient Art and Ritual*, p. 221.

mode of being is apart from the exigencies of the world of affairs. Art, in this sense, is autonomous; it is analogous to contemplation and pure theory, is detached from the practicalities of life, while magic, like science (except in its very highest reaches), is firmly rooted in man's immediate concrete needs and demands.[17]

Magic is founded on belief. The ritual dance that we have been considering—or any comparable rite—will have its peculiar potency, it is clear, only so long as belief is unquestioned; once skepticism and doubt enter, the rite may continue to be practiced but its function will be far removed from what it was originally. In the beginning the dancers were "making" magic: they were "making" the death of the animal or of their foes; but when belief in the magical efficacy has gone, the makers, like the dance, become something else. They may become performers and the dance, detached from its immediate practical purpose and from the practically directed emotion which impelled it, a thing to be witnessed.[18] The dance, in fact, may become art.[19]

[17] Another view of these matters deserves consideration. Suzanne K. Langer, *Philosophy in a New Key* (Cambridge, Mass., 1942) holds that the direct motivation of magic "is the desire to symbolize great conceptions. . . . Its origin is probably not practical at all, but ritualistic; its central aim is to symbolize a Presence, to aid in the formulation of a religious universe" (pp. 48-49). However Mrs. Langer also writes: ". . . the driving force in human minds is fear, which begets an imperious demand for security in the world's confusion: a demand for a world-picture that fills all experience and gives each individual a definite *orientation* amid the terrifying forces of nature and society" (p. 158). But it is precisely out of this demand, it seems to me, that magic arises; it is man's *will*, as Freud says, given preternatural efficacy, and in this respect magic and other forms of "symbolization" are intensely practical. This truncated account hardly does justice to Mrs. Langer's views, which are part of a larger pattern and derive their power from it.

[18] "If an expression, which at first was automatic, is repeated for the sheer joy of expression, at that point it becomes aesthetic. . . . Anger enjoyed in being acted consciously is not mere instinctive anger, but dramatic . . . anger, a very different thing." L. A. Reid, "Beauty and Significance," *Proceedings of the Aristotelian Society*, N. S. xxix (1929), p. 144; cited by Langer, *Philosophy in a New Key*, p. 152.

[19] The wheel seems to come full circle when we speak, quite properly, says Freud (*Totem and Taboo*, p. 90) of "the magic of art" and compare artists with magicians. Cf. Richard Chase who writes (mistakenly, I think): ". . . besides being a compulsive technique magic is in and of itself an aesthetic activity." *Quest for Myth*, pp. 80-81.

Primitive man's wishes to control his hostile environment, his impulses of fear, hatred, longing, etc., must often have been translated directly into action, so far as that was possible. Freud quotes Goethe's Faust: "In the beginning was the deed." But inevitably the original impulse would have been accompanied by inhibitions, frustrations of one kind or another. Hatred of an enemy led directly to the desire to kill him. Between the impulse and the realization, however, would have intervened the sanctions of society which prevented the direct attack, fear of failure, of retaliation, inaccessibility of the object of hate, etc. The overpowering fear of hunger arising from crop failure, blight, or natural calamities may well have led to attempts to coerce directly, physically, the forces thought to be responsible for such matters. (Perhaps a reflection of this direct translation of impulse into physical action may be seen in the practice of the Selknam who, when a long spell of rain threatens their normal activities, take glowing logs and wave them around furiously in the air, "fighting" the rain. As they fight, they shout angrily: "When will you finally go away, bad rain?—Do, at last, go away, wicked rain!—Go to another place, impudent rain!"[20]) Inhibitions of a different order would eventually be set up here. At any rate, between the original impulse and the frustrated reaction arises Miss Harrison's "presentation," Freud's "hallucination"; and in accordance with the principle of the over-valuation of mental processes, the presentation is endowed with magical efficacy.

It would be folly to try to systematize rigidly the development of this presentation, but we may conjecture that out of it evolved many manifestations of magical activity, formally very different but all grounded in the same psychological phenomenon. Today, for example, as is well known, the forms which "black magic" takes among preliterate people are diverse beyond calculation. In some societies it is believed that disease and death can be transmitted to an enemy by thought alone. An Azande witch "performs no rite, utters no spell and possesses no

[20] Cited by Hans Kelsen, *Society and Nature* (Chicago, 1943), p. 38, from Martin Gusinde, *Die Feuerland-Indianer*, Vol. I: *Die Selknam* (Vienna, 1931), pp. 683 ff.

medicines. An act of witchcraft is a psychic act."[21] The Herero believe that merely by dissembling one's anger and thinking evil of one's enemy, one can bring harm to him—consume his power.[22] In order to "bewitch with the mouth" among the BaK-xatla of South Africa a man need have "only a bitter heart against his enemy." He uses no medicines or rites or spells, and observes no taboos; he simply says: *ke tla xo hutsa,* "I shall curse you," and the cursed one is doomed to grievous misfortune.[23] In other societies' words in the form of spells are the agents of power, although more often words and rites are combined. Malinowski describes Trobriand magic as "a specific power, essentially human, autonomous and independent in its action. This power is an inherent property of certain words, uttered with the performance of certain actions by the man entitled to do it through his social traditions and through certain observances which he has to keep. The words and acts have this power in their own right, and their action is direct and not mediated by any other agency. Their power is not derived from the authority of spirits or demons or supernatural beings. It is not conceived as having been wrested from nature. The belief in the power of words and rites as a fundamental and irreducible force is the ultimate, basic dogma of their magical creed."[24]

Still other groups manipulate evil powers through supplication or coercion of their gods. A sorcerer of the Kuraver of southern India makes an image of his enemy, recites a spell, then instructs the god as to what manner of ruin he is to bring on the enemy. The sorcerer threatens the god: "If you do not descend I shall come and put a thorn through your nose, and you will find it difficult to breathe. If you do not help me in my desperate plight I shall cut you in pieces, hang your limbs on the branches of a tree. . . . Come at noon precisely, catch my enemy, and bring him to the grave. . . . If not, I will cut your shoulder

[21] Edward E. Evans-Pritchard, *Witchcraft, Oracles and Magic among the Azande* (Oxford, 1937), p. 21.

[22] Lucien Lévy-Bruhl, *Primitives and the Supernatural,* trans. Lilian A. Clare (London, 1936), pp. 172-73.

[23] I. Schapera, "Oral Sorcery among the Natives of Bechuanaland," in *Essays Presented to C. G. Seligman,* ed. E. E. Evans-Pritchard and others (London, 1934), pp. 296 ff.

[24] *Argonauts of the Western Pacific,* p. 427.

on the right and on the left, and I will grip you by the throat till you are dead, dead, dead."[25] Thoughts, looks, words, objects, acts, gods, men, beasts—all these and more in multifarious combination go to make up the means by which magical (or magico-religious) ends are achieved. But in all their complexity these rites spring from one primordial demand—a demand that out of the fears and confusions engendered by a hostile world man shall be able to impose some kind of order. The magical forms which are the agent of this demand will vary in response to the pressures of many cultural imponderables: the structure of the society concerned, the system of beliefs by which it operates, the influence of powerful individual magic-makers, and so on. Just so, we may surmise, the forms of the "presentation," a matrix of ritual from which magical satire (and much else) may have developed, will differ according to the same cultural variables.

It seems to me that what we have been calling magical satire was in its remotest origins ritual. Satire was believed to be magically efficacious because the original ritualistic formula was efficacious; the belief remained attached to the satiric content of the formula long after the rite had been forgotten. A relatively early stage of this process may be seen in the Greek Phallic Songs, where the connection with ritual is unmistakable. In the Songs, we recall, the joyous invocation of fertility is interrupted by the violent invectives of the leaders.[26] Clearly, the motivation behind the whole ceremony is a wish of great intensity, a *demand* that life shall burgeon throughout nature. The ceremony is a bipartite enactment of that demand, a magical representa-

---

[25] W. J. Hatch, *The Land Pirates of India* (London, 1928), pp. 49-50.

[26] See Chap. 1, 1, above. An analogue to this rite occurs today among the Zuñi. During various fertility rituals *katcina* priests impersonate supernatural beings who are bringers of rain and bestowers of fecundity. Among these beings are the Koyemci, who are the sacred clowns "privileged to mock at anything, and to indulge in any obscenity." Grotesque and uncouth, they are "the most feared and the most beloved of all Zuñi impersonations. They are possessed of black magic. . . . One who begrudges them anything will meet swift and terrible retribution." As part of the ritual, the Koyemci stand before various householders' doors, "calling the inmates by name in song, and twitting them for stinginess, laziness, . . . [and] fondness for American ways." Ruth L. Bunzel, "Introduction to Zuñi Ceremonialism" and "Zuñi Katcinas," in *Annual Report of the U. S. Bureau of American Ethnology*, XLVII (1929-30), pp. 521, 952.

tion of it: the sacred words and the sacred emblem invoke life-giving influences; the sacred mockery and invective expel blight and dearth and evil.[27] No doubt the individuals who were satirized by name in the ceremony somehow represented what was to be driven out. How they were affected by the verbal assaults, we do not know, but the association of satirical attack with magical efficacy is very strong. It would be strong even outside a ritual context. It would be overwhelming at a sacred occasion which was dominated by the personality and the charismatic power of utterance of a poet like Archilochus. In those circumstances personal satire might well drive a victim to death.

Archilochus' verses against Lycambes were, in fact, part of a fertility rite. We know that Archilochus came from a family of hereditary priests of the great Earth-Mother Demeter. As late as the fifth century B.C. Demeter still had strong associations with the chthonic deities, particularly as she was worshipped on Paros, the island where Archilochus was born.[28] Archilochus recited (or sang) his fatal iambics against Lycambes at a festival on Paros in honor of the goddess. Whether his iambic song-poem was part of a competition or whether it had some other ritualistic function, is not known. But the association with the fertility cult is clear; it goes far toward explaining the attribution of magic to Archilochus' iambics.

Mythographers working in the wildly rich—and relatively un-

---

[27] Magical ceremonies for the expulsion of evil are very widespread and take many forms. While in the Phallic Songs words alone seem to be the magical agent, in other ceremonies objects and even human beings, representing death, disease, evil of all kinds, are expelled and sometimes put to death. At the Greek festival of the Thargelia, for example, two *pharmakoi*, i.e., human scapegoats, were draped with strings of black and white figs and led out of Athens. Cheese and barley cakes and figs were placed in their hands and they were ceremonially beaten on the genitals with leeks, branches of wild figs, and other plants. The climax of the terrible ceremony (which is said to have been practiced as late as the fifth century B.C.) came with the burning of the *pharmakoi* and the scattering of their ashes to the winds. From a fragment of the satiric poet Hipponax it seems likely that imprecation and invective accompanied the rite. Jane E. Harrison, *Prolegomena to the Study of Greek Religion* (Cambridge, 1922), pp. 95 ff. For a huge collection of scapegoat ceremonies, see Frazer, *Golden Bough*, Vol. IX: *The Scapegoat*.

[28] See Lewis R. Farnell, *The Cults of the Greek States* (Oxford, 1907), III, 29 ff., esp. 64-65.

touched—field of early Irish culture have discovered relations between Irish myth and the great seminal myth of the Mediterranean and Near-Eastern area: the myth of the dying god. R. A. Stewart Macalister writes of the Parthalon story: "There seems to be very little room for doubt that the story is essentially a 'ritual-pattern' narrative, analogous to those which recent research has identified in the ancient legends of Egyptian, Babylonian, Minoan, and other oriental centres, and which there is good reason to believe were universal." The story is, among other things, "the narrative of a fertility—ritual drama"; and Macalister carefully traces the parallels between the Parthalon story of Ireland and the Osirus-Horus story of Egypt. A similar ritual-pattern, he says, may be found in other Celtic literature, as, for example, in the accounts of the inaugural rites of the King of Tara. Macalister concludes: "It is not too much to say that from Ireland and from Egypt we appear to be listening to far-away echoes of one and the same primitive story, of sunrise and sunset, and of the death and rebirth of a god of vegetation."[29]

This approach to Irish myth had been anticipated in the work of Mr. Alfred Nutt, who in the 1890's was tracing parallels between Greek and Irish agricultural ritual, a root from which he thought sprang the myths of Dionysus and the myths of the Tuatha Dé Danann in Ireland. The Tuatha Dé, in general, are the ancestors of the heroes of Ulster: Cú Chulainn, Conchobar, Fergus, Aithirne (themselves originally gods, as we have seen); they are, in part, at least, says Nutt, "gods of growth and fertility." If we may judge by analogy with the Greek, the literature surrounding them consisted originally of "chants forming part of the ritual, and of legends accounting for and interpreting ritual acts. Out of such materials there would gradually arise a mythology," growing ever more complex and plastic the further it became removed from its original magico-religious function.[30]

Mr. Nutt's researches in myth and ritual show him to be closely allied to Sir James G. Frazer, Jane Harrison, Gilbert

[29] Introduction to Section IV of *Lebor Gabála Erenn: The Book of the Taking of Ireland*, trans. and ed. Macalister, Part II (Irish Texts Society, 1939), pp. 263-66; and Macalister's *Tara* (New York, 1931), pp. 94, 106 ff.

[30] "The Celtic Doctrine of Re-birth" in *The Voyage of Bran*, trans. Kuno Meyer, II, 194.

Murray, F. M. Cornford, and their followers—those of the Cambridge school—whose work has demonstrated, satisfactorily, I should think, that ritual is the great fertile core from which come many myths and many forms of art besides. In this context the primary act is the act of ritual—Jane Harrison's "representation"—a re-enactment or a pre-enactment in the interests of magical or religious control of a situation charged with emotional tension. Out of this ritual develops the myth, which is the spoken correlative of that which is enacted; it is the imaging, the story of the rite.[31]

The formulation has proved powerful and generative when applied to the materials of Ancient Greece, the Middle East, and elsewhere; whether it is equally applicable to early Irish culture, I do not know. I should suppose that it is. From this point of view, the many tales of the Irish satirists may be looked at as reflections in language of early ritual acts, acts probably having to do with fertility rites. Some connection between satirists and problems of fecundity and dearth, we have already seen: Laidcenn satirized the men of Leinster "so that neither grass nor corn grew with them, nor a leaf, to the end of a year." The poet Forgoll threatened to satirize King Mongán and his family and to "sing upon their waters, so that fish should not be caught in their river-mouths . . . upon their woods, so that they should not give fruit, upon their plains, so that they should be barren for ever of any produce." Amergin White Knee "sang . . . to increase fish in the creeks." When he blamed the rivers, they

---

[31] The more extreme members of the school hold that *all* myths develop from ritual. For important discussions, see J. E. Harrison, *Themis*, pp. 327-28; S. H. Hooke, "The Myth and Ritual Pattern of the Ancient Near East," in *Myth and Ritual*, ed. Hooke (Oxford, 1933), pp. 1-4; Lord Raglan, *The Hero* (London, 1936), pp. 121-32. A brief summary of the Cambridge school's theory of ritual origins is given by E. M. Butler, *The Myth of the Magus* (Cambridge, 1948), pp. 1-4. The position is controversial; for lively—if biased—accounts of the issues and lists of significant works, see Stanley E. Hyman, "Myth, Ritual, and Nonsense," *Kenyon Review*, xi (1949), pp. 455-75 and "The Ritual View of Myth and the Mythic," *JAF*, lxviii (1955), pp. 462-72. Probably the most powerful attack on the Harrison-Murray-Cornford school on their own grounds is that of A. W. Pickard-Cambridge (the E. E. Stoll of classical anthropology) in *Dithyramb, Tragedy, and Comedy* (Oxford, 1927). Gaster's recent *Thespis* offers impressive confirmation of the ritual-origin theory.

fell. Even Aithirne the Importunate, in his encounter with the river Modarn, is involved, though obscurely, in this kind of activity.[32]

Irish satire is most often concerned with problems of social fecundity—with the offering of poor or inadequate food or ungracious hospitality. Consider the legendary first satire of Ireland, composed by Cairpre Mac Edaine, poet of the Tuatha Dé Danaan, against King Bres, whose offer of hospitality consisted of a wretched hovel and three dry cakes. Cairpre was angry and said:

> "Without food speedily on a platter,
> Without a cow's milk whereon a calf thrives,
> Without a man's habitation after the staying of darkness,
> Be that the luck of Bres Mac Eladain."

This is unquestionably magic; it seems reasonable to think of it as part of the negative aspect of a fertility rite—part of the same kind of occasion which prompted ritual invective against stingy persons in ancient Greece.[33]

Many tales of the Irish poets have to do with their implication in riddle-solving or verse-capping contests, an implication they share with Norse gods, Greek heroes, Brahmin kings, and many others in literature and legend all over the world. The contests are far more than mere tests of skill; they are originally sacred activity, concerned with the magical power which inheres in secret knowledge. The competitive propounding and solution of enigmatic problems (particularly those dealing with mysterious origins), the search for the secret name, the capping of obscure verses according to the proper formula—these all have to do with unlocking and controlling powers which lie mysteriously at the heart of things. "Competitions in esoteric knowledge," writes Huizinga, "are deeply rooted in ritual and form an

[32] See Chapter I, 3, above, and Robinson, "Satirists and Enchanters," p. 119.

[33] Cornford, *Origin of Attic Comedy*, pp. 39-40; Frazer, *The Golden Bough*, Vol. VII: *Spirits of the Corn and of the Wild*, I, 108-09; and compare Phillip Stubbes' account of the Elizabethan Lord of Misrule ceremony (see Chapter I, 1, note 6, above, for a brief quotation). The refusal of hospitality prompts curses in many cultures: see "Curses and Blessings," Hastings' *Encyclopaedia of Religion and Ethics*, p. 370b.

essential part of it. The questions which the hierophants put to one another in turn or by way of challenge are riddles in the fullest sense of the word, exactly resembling the riddles in a parlour-game but for their sacred import."[34] Irish satirists are frequently obliged to cap verses or to solve riddles. On one occasion Aithirne the Importunate, who was so niggardly that he never ate his meal where he could be seen, took a cooked pig and a pot of meal to a secluded spot and prepared to eat his fill. A man came toward him.

"Thou wouldst do it all alone," said the stranger, whilst he took the pig and the pot away from him.

"What is thy name?" said Aithirne.

"Nothing very grand," said he:

"Sethor, ethor, othor, sele, dele, dreng, gerce,

Son of Gerluscc, sharp, sharp, right, right, that is my name."

Aithirne was unable to cap the verse (it is called a satire), or perhaps unable to work the name into the magic bonds of a line of his own. The stranger walked off with the pig, and it is evident, says the story, that he was from God. Aithirne was not stingy from that day forth.[35] Here name-magic, verse-capping, and satire are entwined in a humorous context.

Much more serious is the great question and answer contest between old Ferchertne and the young Néde for the position of chief-poet of Erin and the vari-colored cape of feathers that went with it. The questions, antiphonally put, are majestically simple: "Whence hast thou come?" "What is thy name?" "What art dost thou practise?" "Hast thou tidings?" But each response is lengthy, hieratic, extremely obscure; and the agonistic structure is unmistakable.[36] In another tale a "foul gillie" shames the overbearing Senchán by completing the riddling verses of a

[34] *Homo Ludens*, pp. 105 ff. Cf. the excellent article on the Riddle in Hastings' *Encyclopaedia*.

[35] Sir John Rhŷs, *Lectures on the Origin and Growth of Religion as Illustrated by Celtic Heathendom*: The Hibbert Lectures, 1886 (London, 1888), p. 332; Robinson, "Satirists and Enchanters," pp. 116-17.

[36] In his powerful and gloomy prophecy of the terrible things to come to Ireland, Ferchertne lists this: "Everyone will buy a lampooner to lampoon on his behalf." Such a calamity, the context indicates, will be but one manifestation of the collapse of the old social order. *The Colloquy of the Two Sages*, trans. Stokes, RC, xxvi (1905), p. 41.

female poet (above, p. 22). Marbán, the saintly swineherd, over-comes the whole Bardic Association by virtue of his miraculous insight into the mysteries. He is forced to answer such questions as these from a leading poet of Leinster: " 'Do thou tell me,' said Dael Duileadh, 'what goodness did man find on the earth which God did not find? Which are the two trees whose green tops do not fade till they become withered? . . . And what is the animal which lives in the fire, and whose burning it would be if taken out of it, and whose life would be preserved by put-ting him into it?' "[37] Marbán answers infallibly; and one by one the poets are put down.

The riddle motif is seen in these tales in remarkably pure form; there is every reason to believe that in Ireland, as else-where, it develops from a ritual occasion. The fact that Irish satirists are frequently involved in these mysterious matters helps to confirm the theory that magical satire originates in ritual practice.

The hypothesis of ritual origin may throw some light on a puzzling passage in *The Siege of Howth*, the central tale dealing with Aithirne's depredations. After a year's circuit of Leinster, the land of his enemies, Aithirne departed, taking with him thrice fifty wives whom he had extorted from princes and nobles by threatening to satirize them. The Leinstermen pursued the satirist and the Ulstermen (Aithirne's compatriots) hurried to protect him. In a great battle the Ulstermen were routed; they fled to the fortress of Howth, where they were besieged: "Nine watches were they in Howth without drink, without food, un-less they drank the brine of the sea, or unless they devoured the clay." Then the episode in question: "Seven hundred kine, in sooth, had Aithirne in the middle of the fort; and there was not a boy or man of Ulster who tasted their milk, but the milking was cast down the cliff, so that of the Ulstermen none might find out Aithirne's food to taste it. And the wounded men were brought to him, and he would not let a drop go into their mouths, so that they used to bleed to death alone [unaided]. And the chiefs of Ulster used to come to him entreating a drink

---

[37] *The Great Visitation*, pp. 89-103. Cf. these questions with those cited by Huizinga (pp. 105-18) from the Rig-Veda and elsewhere.

for Conor [King Conchobar], and nought they got for him."[38] In ordinary terms the passage is incomprehensible. Why should Aithirne, niggardly though he is, throw the milk of seven hundred cattle over the cliffs rather than let his comrades, dying and living, drink?[39] Why would they let him? And why should he refuse his king? Is his power that great? Miss Eleanor Hull puts it all down to the "fierce barbarism of the period"; but that is merely to beg all questions.[40]

The passage is comprehensible, I believe, only in magical terms —only, that is, if we regard it as a reflection, obscure and doubtless much distorted, of a very ancient fertility rite. The connection of the satirist with growth and decay, fecundity and famine, we have seen. Here his role seems totally negative and blighting; he is the evil that causes famine, and the Ulstermen are saved only by the intervention of the supernatural hero, Cú Chulainn. The situation is thus the reverse of that in the Greek fertility rites: there the function of satire is to expel evil so that the earth may be fruitful; here the satirist (in this case, at least) destroys the milk which gives life. Precisely what ritualistic ends this act may have served, and what its implications were, we do not know; but we may be fairly confident that the act was magical and that Aithirne is associated with it by virtue of his role as satirist.

If the general hypothesis about ritual origin is correct, it would help to explain why magical potency was attributed to satire long after the satire had been effectively part of ritual. The form remained powerful after the rite had been forgotten.

[38] *The Siege of Howth*, trans. Stokes, *RC*, VIII (1887), pp. 53-55.

[39] In some sources Aithirne is the personification of inhospitality and stinginess. A tale from the *Book of Leinster* begins: "Aithirne the Importunate, son of Ferchertne, he is the most inhospitable man that dwelt in Erinn. He went to Mider of Bri Leith and took the cranes of denial and churlishness away from him surreptitiously; that is, with a view to refusal and churlishness, that no man of the men of Erinn should visit his house for hospitality. . . . 'Do not come, not come,' says the first crane. 'Get away,' says her mate. '[Go] past the house, past the house,' says the third crane." Trans. Sir John Rhŷs, *Lectures on the Origin and Growth of Religion*, p. 331.

[40] Introduction to her edition of *The Cuchullin Saga in Irish Literature* (London, 1898), pp. xlii-xliii.

2. THE USES OF RIDICULE

We have assumed that the tales of magical satire transmitted in legend and saga reflect what people actually believed, perhaps even reflect fact. That is, Lycambes and Neobule may really have hanged themselves; victims of Irish satirists may really have died of shame. Of course, we cannot know. But we can know whether ridicule and satire ever function in life in roughly the manner described by the ancient literature.[1] The best way to get at this will be to examine the cultural function of ridicule in societies in varying stages of development today. The materials we have dealt with—the underwood of our subject—have been largely sub-literary, but they have been ancient. The materials of this section will also be sub-literary, but modern. The break in continuity is thus more chronological than cultural, more apparent than real.

I risk introducing this material in order to approach the question of satire's malign efficacy from a new direction. After all, although the Irish believed that their poets exerted magical power, we no longer believe in magic; and pre-Christian Ireland is, in many senses, very far away. But if we discover that satire and ridicule today have functions somehow comparable to those described in saga, and if we can find hypotheses to account for those functions in terms appropriate to the twentieth century, we will be in a better position to understand the material discussed above and to understand the power exerted by satire and ridicule in our own culture.

One word more in defense of my method. When I cite a practice of the Eskimo or the Ashanti in the following pages, I often mean to suggest a comparison with ancient Greece or Ireland, or even with the United States. This does not mean that I think the societies equivalent or that the comparisons can ever be exact or that I am trying to ignore cultural differences, which are immense. Beneath the differences, however, are ineradicable human samenesses, some of which find expression in "primitive" modes of thought and behavior as easily identifiable in twentieth-century North America as in twentieth-century Ashan-

---

[1] Although we have used the term *satire* in a sense broad enough to include the idea of ridicule, I shall shift the emphasis in this section to *ridicule* because it has fewer purely literary associations.

ti or seventh-century Ireland. We are all primitive, whatever the level of our sophistication, in our deepest selves.[2]

Some anthropologists have found it useful to distinguish between cultures which rely heavily on feelings of guilt, and those which rely on fear of shame, as sanctions for behavior—as means, that is, for enforcing conformity to an accepted standard of behavior. In a guilt culture, an individual will obey internalized standards of morality without reference to outside forces. A Catholic alone on an island, for example—to cite an illustration suggested by Margaret Mead—would not eat meat on Friday. He would be responding to internal sanctions, would be following his conscience. Violation of such sanctions will produce a kind of torment, which, however, can be relieved by confession and atonement. Shame cultures, on the other hand, rely on external sanctions to govern behavior: what other people will think or say, whether they will praise or blame—these are the over-riding considerations. Probably no culture exists in which both internal and external sanctions are not operative, but societies vary greatly in point of emphasis.[3]

In a guilt culture if a man makes public his sin within the church or an appropriate public institution, the torment of his conscience will be allayed. In a shame culture if his wrongdoing becomes known, he will be criticized, shamed, rejected. One of the most powerful of all forms of public disapproval is ridicule. Probably as a result of childhood conditioning, few horrors are more to be dreaded by members of a shame culture than to be

[2] Cf. Dodds, *The Greeks and the Irrational*, pp. viii-ix.

[3] The guilt-shame classification of cultures is controversial. I employ it largely for descriptive reasons and intend no implications about values, the Protestant ethic, personality types, etc. For an account of the theory, see Ruth Benedict, *The Chrysanthemum and the Sword: Patterns of Japanese Culture* (Cambridge, Mass., 1946), pp. 222-24; various works of Margaret Mead, esp. her "Interpretive Statement" in her ed. of *Co-operation and Competition among Primitive Peoples* (New York, 1937), pp. 493-95; "Some Anthropological Considerations concerning Guilt," *Feelings and Emotions: The Mooseheart Symposium*, ed. Martin L. Reymert (New York, 1950), pp. 366 ff.; Geoffrey Gorer, "Pride, Shame, and Guilt," *Encounter* (April 1959), pp. 28-34. For careful analysis and criticism of the theory, see Gerhart Piers and Milton B. Singer, *Shame and Guilt: a Psychoanalytic and a Cultural Study* (Springfield, Ill., 1953).

publicly laughed at; suicide may be considered an appropriate response to public derision, and even the fantasy of ridicule holds terrors sufficient to stimulate the most violent reactions. Margaret Mead writes of an Indian alone in the middle of a lake who could be so shamed by his paddle breaking, and so fearful of ridicule to follow, that he would kill himself.[4] "Le ridicule," said La Rochefoucauld, "déshonore plus que le déshonneur."

In the training of Japanese children, according to Ruth Benedict, one of the most important character-moulding practices is the reiterated threat by the elders: "If you do this, if you do that, the world will laugh." The Japanese have a most highly developed sense of shame, to the degree that it seems equivalent to the Western idea of having a clear conscience, of avoiding sin. They live in acute consciousness of the eyes of others upon them. In World War II Japanese seamen were warned that, in the event their ship were torpedoed, they were to obey the strictest decorum in taking to the lifeboats; otherwise, "the world will laugh at you. The Americans will take movies of you and show them in New York."[5] If the world laughs, then one has been rejected by the world; and for a Japanese "ostracism is more dreaded than violence. He is allergic to threats of ridicule and rejection, even when he merely conjures them up in his own mind" (p. 288).

A generation ago a Japanese who wished to borrow money took a kind of oath: "I agree to be publicly laughed at if I fail to repay this sum." Actually, the debtor who could not meet his obligations was not made a laughing-stock; instead, at the New Year, when all debts were due to be paid, the insolvent debtor might commit suicide to "clear his name" (p. 151). And we remember that a major motive behind the honored custom of *harakiri* is the avoidance of public humiliation and shame.

[4] "Collective Guilt," *Proceedings*, International Congress on Mental Health (London, 1948), III, 58. Among the Jews, to shame one's neighbor in public is said to be like shedding his blood. Only three kinds of sinners, according to Rabbi Hanina, will never reascend from Gehenna: "He who commits adultery with a married woman, publicly shames his neighbor, or fastens an evil epithet [nickname] upon his neighbor." Baba Mezi'a, 58b, trans. H. Freedman, *The Babylonian Talmud*, ed. Rabbi Dr. I. Epstein (London, 1938), pp. 348-49.
[5] *Chrysanthemum and the Sword*, pp. 261-73, 29.

The sensitivity of the Japanese to ridicule may seem extravagant to us today; while we all recognize the great unpleasantness of public derision, still we are likely to think their reactions exaggerated: they are "thin-skinned." But the susceptibility of the Japanese is by no means unique. Ridicule is, as far as one can tell, ubiquitous, used by every people as a means of influencing behavior. Anthropologists say that one of the lowest cultures known to modern man was that of the aboriginal Tasmanians. They used ridicule for purposes of social control; a form of punishment was to make an offender clamber out on the low branch of a tree, while the tribe gathered round to point and jeer and mock at him—we think inevitably of the pillory of New England.[6] In contrast to Tasmania, one might cite Pope's boast:

> Yes, I am proud; I must be proud to see
> Men not afraid of God, afraid of me;
> Safe from the Bar, the Pulpit, and the Throne,
> Yet touch'd and shamed by Ridicule alone.

Or Mme de Staël's testimony: "Le ridicule a acquis tant de force en France, qu'il y est devenu l'arme la plus terrible qu'on y puisse employer."[7] In *The Red and the Black* Stendhal refers repeatedly to the overwhelming power of ridicule in post-Revolutionary France. Julien Sorel admires Comte Norbert's physical courage but recognizes simultaneously how the fear of appearing ridiculous terrifies the Comte and inhibits his actions; Mathilde de la Mole despises the young men of the court for their pusillanimity before the threat of ridicule.

In any society in which high value is placed upon the opinions of others, ridicule will clearly be a potent deterrent to deviant behavior; the more a person dreads shame, the more he will avoid situations which might bring upon him the bad name conveyed by public mockery. These sanctions are institutionalized over the world in an extraordinary variety of ways. The ambiguous power of fools and clowns in many societies may be derived in part from this kind of social complex. For example, among the Pueblo Indians the sacred clowns are said to have

[6] Henry Ling Roth, *The Aboriginies of Tasmania*, 2nd ed. (Halifax, Eng., 1899), p. 59.
[7] Cited in Larousse, *Grand Dictionnaire Universel du XIXe Siècle*, "Ridicule."

"a punitive and policing function in ceremonial matters and through their license in speech and song a somewhat similar function in domestic matters, ridicule being a strong weapon among the Pueblos. Probably most Pueblos would rather be ducked than mocked."[8] In other societies, as we shall see, people would rather be hanged than mocked; but the power is there among the Pueblos, its peculiar efficacy shaped and qualified by innumerable factors in the pattern of the culture concerned.

One of the most remarkable of all uses of ridicule for social control occurs among the Greenland Eskimos. When two men quarrel, a preferred way of resolving the difference is (or was) through an institutionalized contest in ridicule, invective, and satirical abuse known as the drum match or song duel. The two enemies face each other before the assembled tribe, who look on the affair as a festive occasion and are delighted with the lampoons, the obscene scurrilities, the mockery and jibing and flouting which the two contestants hurl at each other, each accompanying himself on a drum. Along with the duel in song may go complicated physical gyrations, such as snorting in an opponent's face, butting him, and tying him to the tent pole— indignities which the performers try to bear with surface impassivity. The match may continue at intervals over a long time, even years, and the opponents' ingenuity in abuse is likely to be stretched, even though they may recite well-known drum songs (or parts of them) that have been handed down by oral tradition. But finally the tribe makes a decision in the matter at issue (it often concerns a woman) in favor of one of the contestants. Then the two may become reconciled, or the match may end in blows or, rarely, even death. Loss of the decision is an extremely painful affair; for the loser not only has had publicly to bear the devastating mockery of his enemy, but at the end finds himself alone, against all the others, a laughing-stock. Occasionally, he may go into voluntary exile.[9]

[8] Elsie Clews Parsons and Ralph L. Beals, "The Sacred Clowns of the Pueblo and Mayo-Yaqui Indians," *American Anthropologist*, N.S. XXXVI (1934), p. 499. It is amusing that even Pueblo witches are subject to ridicule: after a witch has behaved outrageously, the god says, "You are bad, and this shall be your punishment; you shall be ridiculed by people." Elsie Clews Parsons, *Pueblo Indian Religion* (Chicago, 1939), I, 54 note.

[9] For the best account of the drum matches, see William Thalbitzer

Some flavor of the Eskimo songs may be preserved in translation, although one suspects that some of the English versions printed here tend to smooth out roughnesses and to force obscurities into patterns that would be familiar to Western readers. William Thalbitzer (whose translations, cited in the notes, are probably the most authentic) has commented on how primitive the drum songs are, on how little "art" goes into the language as compared to the delivery; and many authors speak of great obscurity.[10] Here, for one example, is a portion of Marratse's attack on Equerqo, who had stolen his wife:

> Words let me split,
> Small words, sharp words,
> Like the splinters
> Which, with my axe, I cut up.
> . . . .
> She [my wife] who was snatched from me
> By a prattler, a liar . . .
> That lover of human flesh,
> Cannibal, miscreant,
> Spewed up from starvation days.

Equerqo answers:

> Only amazement I feel
> At your preposterous words.
> Only anger they cause
> And the urge to laugh,
> You with your mocking song . . . .
> Did you think you could frighten me,
> I who many a time challenged death? . . .
> Yet never in combats of song

in his edition of *The Ammassalik Eskimo*, Meddelelser om Grønland (Copenhagen, 1923), XL, 166 ff.; also Knud Rasmussen, *The Netsilik Eskimos*, Report of the Fifth Thule Expedition, 1921-24, trans. W. E. Calvert (Copenhagen, 1931), VIII, Nos. 1-2, 323-24; Edward M. Weyer, *The Eskimos* (New Haven, 1932), pp. 226-28; Kaj Birket-Smith, *The Eskimos*, trans. W. E. Calvert, rev. C. Darrel Forde (London, 1936), pp. 54-55, 151; Huizinga, *Homo Ludens*, pp. 85 ff.

[10] *A Phonetical Study of the Eskimo Language*, trans. Sophia Bertelsen (Copenhagen, 1904), p. 62.

Did you challenge your foes for her.
Ah, but now she is mine.[11]

In a second example recorded by Rasmussen, Piuvkaq derides
Qaqortingneq:

Eager to breathe out,
I have made ready
This little bit of a song
Down along the wide road of song . . .
Mocking in exclamation,
Shapely of form,
Cutting in meaning,
Out westwards, out westwards.

. . . .

. . . here I have now come
To punish you with mockery.
It is I who plait together
Bits of song to answer you.
Loudly must the voice resound
To deafen noise and clamour!

I would rather fight a fist-fight,
All too oft words fade away,
Words melt away
Like hills in fog.[12]

A final example, less bland—one of dozens of songs and fragments of song preserved by Thalbitzer: "This one (him)/ I
envy him immensely/ his song/ as often as I begin to hear it/
this one/ *aja*/ I/ I can not (sing)/ believe me!/ the art of
making poems/ the art of upsetting/ I/ I cannot/." Thalbitzer
explains that the poem consists of ironical remarks: the opponent may be a skilled singer, but he cannot even paddle a kayak
without upsetting.[13]

These contests in ridicule fulfill several important social func-

[11] The poem was recorded by Knud Rasmussen, translated into German
by F. Sieburg, thence into English by Paul Radin; see Radin's "The Literature of Primitive Peoples," *Diogenes*, No. 12 (Winter 1955), pp. 26-27.
[12] Rasmussen, *The Netsilik Eskimos*, pp. 511-13.
[13] *Phonetical Study of the Eskimo Language*, p. 305.

tions. For one thing they provide first-rate entertainment extending over months for a people whose festal occasions are appallingly few. (Sometimes drum matches are held as pure entertainment; insults fly, the audience cheers, but emotions are feigned and it is all "in fun.") They also have a judicial function; quarrels that in other societies might have led to fighting and killing here are settled by action of the tribe, usually with no bloodshed and often with no apparent hard feelings remaining between the principals. Notice, however, that the decision is made without reference to the merits of the case initiating the contest. Justice is not an issue; victory goes to the greater master of the art of ridicule. Apparently the essential aim behind the institution is the restoration of peace within the community. The drum matches provide a means for the controlled release of hostile emotions.[14]

Interesting similarities exist between the Eskimo drum matches and other patterned forms of interactive insult and ridicule: flyting, for instance, or a practice known as the Dozens, engaged in by American Negroes in many sections of the country.[15] While rules for the Dozens change from place to place and from class to class, the basic pattern seems to be this: a boy or girl, man or woman may challenge another to "play the Dozens," or may threaten to "put him in" the Dozens. If the challenge is accepted, a crowd gathers expectantly and eggs on the rivals as they exchange insults and invective. The insults may be in verse or prose; they may be standardized or extemporaneous. In the "dirty" Dozens, obscene references will be made to the sexual behavior of the opponent's mother or sister, to incest or homosexuality—"Speckled Red" (Rufus Perryman) sings:

> Now you're a dirty mistreater,
> a robber and a cheater,

[14] See Birket-Smith, *The Eskimos*, p. 151. Further examples of institutionalized ridicule as psychological release will be considered below. Sometimes the song contests are followed by a kind of slugging match in which no defense is attempted, the point being to see who best can "take it." This suggests an interesting correspondence between the ability to bear psychical and physical pain. See Rasmussen, *Netsilik Eskimos*, p. 324.

[15] See John Dollard, "The Dozens: Dialectic of Insult," *The American Imago*, I (1939), pp. 3-25; William Elton, " 'Playing the Dozens,' " *American Speech*, xxv (1950), pp. 230-33, and references therein.

I slip you in the dozen,
        your Pappy is your cousin,
Your mama do the Lordy-Lord.

In the "clean" Dozens, normal taboos are respected. The on-lookers cheer and jeer and in general stimulate the participants to verbal attacks of increasing violence. Very often the Dozens leads to fistfighting between the principals, sometimes to knifings or shootings; but in some circumstances and locales the point of the duel seems to be that the principals should maintain surface equanimity, should not give way to anger, no matter how penetrating the ridicule and abuse. The one whose fury stultifies his verbal agility loses the contest, and a sure sign of being bested is to hit one's opponent.

Southern Italians play a game known as "la legge," The Law, which is close to the drum match—Dozens pattern. Roger Vailland's recent novel *The Law* is based on the game, describes its principles and rules in detail.[16] Players of The Law select a chief by lot; he dictates the law to the others: that is, he has the right "to praise and to blame, to insult, to insinuate, to revile, to slander, and to cast a slur on people's honor; the losers, who have to bow to the law, are bound to submit without sound or movement. Such is the fundamental rule of the game of The Law." Spectators witness this game, applauding the most effective performers, those, that is, whose taunts cut most deeply, who are artistic in the management of insult. In the novel the character Tonio, a loser at the game, is shown suffering under the ridicule of the chief; in his mind Tonio prepares "to make his tormentors swallow their own poison, sharpening the words he would hurl at them." Tonio bears the mocking insults impassively; but at the end, when the game is over, he vomits.

Close as the Dozens and The Law are to the drum matches, their function is more limited. They have entertainment value (socialized ridicule seems always to provide popular entertainment), and they act, as Dollard says of the Dozens, as a safety valve for aggression. But these particular forms of institutionalized ridicule do not have the juridical office of the drum match, where ridicule as a form of relatively gentle social control is seen at its clearest.

[16] Trans. Peter Wiles (New York, 1958), pp. 43 ff.

The Plains Indians of North America employed ridicule as a threat to hold their own warriors to tasks requiring exceptional bravery; it might be a man's glorious but dangerous office, for example, to plant a lance in the forefront of battle and not leave it until the battle was over or he was dead. Positions like these were not always in great demand. If a candidate refused to become lance-bearer in the Oglala Crow Owners' Society, members of the tribe attempted to persuade him to his duty by lectures and offers of gifts; if he persisted in his refusal he was subjected to the persuasive force of mockery and ridicule and impromptu songs of derision.[17] His situation was not unlike that of Fer Diad in Irish saga. Queen Medb forced him to fight the great champion Cú Chulainn by threatening him with satire: Fer Diad "deemed it better to fall by the shafts of valor and bravery and skill than to fall by the shafts of satire, abuse, and reproach."[18]

The same Indians make use of ridicule in less spectacular ways. When a man has persistently violated custom or propriety, his actions are likely to be made the subject of a prolonged discussion by the tribe, to the tune of organized jeering and hooting and laughter. Such treatment is usually adequate to bring the offender back into line; the Indians think of it as a severe but by no means intolerable form of social control.

Ridicule may be a very harsh control. In Southeastern Alaska the Tlingit Indians distinguish between the criminal act and the shameful act, the latter being punished by public ridicule. Mocking stories and songs, which may be composed by professional songmakers, are circulated against the offender, and grotesque wooden likenesses may even be set up in public places. The Tlingit are so sensitive to ridicule that the victims often die as a result of this punishment.[19]

[17] John H. Provinse, "The Underlying Sanctions of Plains Indian Culture," in *Social Anthropology of North American Tribes*, ed. Fred Eggan, enlarged ed. (Chicago, 1955), pp. 352, 356. Various articles in this volume discuss the use of ridicule by those in joking relation to one another.

[18] See Chap. 1, 3, above. Similarly, the fatal combat between Gunnlaug and Hrafn in the saga of Gunnlaug Serpent-tongue is finally provoked by ridicule. See *Three Icelandic Sagas*, trans. M. H. Scargill and Margaret Schlauch (Princeton, 1950), p. 41.

[19] Kalervo Oberg, "Crime and Punishment in Tlingit Society," *American Anthropologist*, N.S. XXXVI (1934), pp. 152-53.

"The fear of ridicule," writes Paul Radin, "is . . . a great positive factor in the lives of primitive peoples. It is the preserver of the established order of things and more potent and tyrannous than the most restrictive and coercive of positive injunctions possibly could be."[20] I know of no better evidence supporting Radin's statement than that provided by various practices of the Ashanti of West Africa, whose complex culture has been studied with meticulous and loving care by Captain R. S. Rattray. "The Ashanti," he writes, "was (and is), to our way of thinking, extremely sensitive to personal invective of every kind. To have 'a good name' was well nigh essential to his existence; to have 'a bad name' rendered life, in the narrow community in which he passed his days, unbearable. He was incapable of withstanding an atmosphere of adverse public opinion; public ridicule readily drove him to suicide."[21] And further:

"If I were asked to name the strongest of the sanctions operating in Ashanti to enforce the observance of the 'traditional rule of the community,' I think I would place the power of ridicule at the head of these forces of law and order. Indeed . . . the power of the sharp-edged weapon of derision seemed often the only sanction behind the law . . . it is doubtful if even the worst of humanly inflicted punishments was more dreaded than this subtle weapon which came in laughing guise to rob a man of his own self-respect and the respect of his associates. In the social world in which the Ashanti lived, there was not any escape for one who had incurred this penalty. What among ourselves, therefore, would be, at most, an unpleasant state of affairs, from which we might be glad to escape elsewhere for a time, became a punishment to an Ashanti from which there was not any escape, and one he could not face."[22]

Suicide among the Ashanti was considered a sin except in a few extreme circumstances; it was justified to avoid capture in war and to avoid the ridicule of one's companions. Rattray gives examples: on one occasion in his experience an old man, a member of a delegation come to honor a visiting dignitary, inadvertently broke wind as he made his obeisance. As soon as the cere-

---

[20] *Primitive Man as Philosopher*, p. 51.
[21] *Ashanti Law and Constitution* (Oxford, 1929), p. 326.
[22] *Ibid.*, p. 372.

mony was over, he hanged himself; for it is considered a disgraceful act in Ashanti to break wind in public, and ridicule was sure to follow. The universal opinion among his countrymen, says Rattray, was that he had followed the only possible course. He could never have "lived down" the withering sanction that would have ensued (pp. 372-73).

Again, if a group of Ashanti were eating together and one broke wind—Rattray quotes his informant: "the bowl of food would be placed upon that person's head that he might be used as a table." But, adds the informant: "if the man were among friends and was well liked, the rest of the party might cover their mouths with their hands and go outside that he might not see their laughter, because they might fear that the man who had offended would go away and hang himself, should he notice that the others were laughing at him." (p. 373, note.)

In the enormously complex relation of primitive man to his society, ridicule functions primarily as a social weapon, as an omnipresent threat against violation of social order and custom. Its power is frightful, for it can sever the delicate lifelines which bind man to the social body, outside of which he can conceive of no life for himself. Under the rejection of ridicule he dies; and while his death may be by his own hand, the mechanism is actually one of public execution. Thus it seems likely to me that the magic attributed to various archaic satirists may inhere in part in the power of ridicule to effect psychic damage. Ancient Greeks were not Ashanti; but we recall the tone of Archilochus' verses against Lycambes: "What is this that you say, father Lycambes? Who has robbed you of the reason on which before you leaned so securely? But now in truth are you become a laughing-stock to your fellow-townsmen. What god pray . . . has kindled you to stir up a creature garrulous like me, looking for nothing better than themes for his iambics? . . . Do you desire to become notorious at any cost?"[23] The threat is essentially this: I will laugh at you, and because I laugh, society will laugh. To be a laughing-stock in archaic Greece was presumably intolerable; Lycambes, says the story, hanged himself.

In New York on February 17, 1959, a young man shot two receptionists in the office where he had worked because, the po-

[23] See Chap. I, 1, above.

lice believe, the girls had ridiculed his surrealist paintings.[24] This juxtaposition is much too neat, of course, and the United States is not a shame culture; but the episode reminds us sharply of what everyone knows: that in some circumstances ridicule can still be intolerable.

It is astonishing to find that the same people for whom ridicule's destructive power holds such terrors institutionalize it for therapeutic purposes; they turn its primary function inside out, as it were, and ridicule, properly conducted, becomes a thing to be enjoyed for the health of society. Two hundred and fifty years ago, William Bosman, a Dutch factor who had lived fourteen years on the Guinea coast, wrote of the Ashanti:

"The Devil is Annually banished all their Towns with abundance of Ceremony. . . . This Procession is preceded by a Feast of eight Days, accompanied with all manner of Singing, Skipping, Dancing, Mirth and Jollity: In which time a perfect lampooning Liberty is allowed, and Scandal so highly exalted, that they may freely sing of all the Faults, Villanies and Frauds of their Superiours as well as Inferiours, without Punishment, or so much as the least interruption; and the only way to stop their Mouths is to ply them lustily with Drink, which alters their Tone immediately, and turns their Satyrical Ballads into Commendatory Songs. . . ."[25]

This was the *Apo* ceremony. In 1922 Captain Rattray witnessed precisely the same festival that Bosman had described; and with a fine sense of the continuities in these affairs he paid particular attention to the "lampooning Liberty" which had impressed his predecessor. *Apo*, the name of the ceremony, is a word that seems to be linguistically related to terms meaning "to speak roughly or harshly to," "to abuse, to insult," but also "to wash, to cleanse." In this happy period, this time ritually set apart from the rest of the year, ridicule and abuse are lucky and cleansing and enjoyable for all who participate. "Wait until

[24] Columbus *Citizen* (Feb. 18, 1959), p. 30.
[25] William Bosman, *A New and Accurate Description of the Coast of Guinea* . . . , Letter x (London, 1705), p. 158; cited in R. S. Rattray, *Ashanti* (Oxford, 1923), p. 151.

Friday," said the chief, "when the people really begin to abuse me, and if you will come and do so too it will please me."[26]

Here are three or four of the songs that are sung by women as they dance up and down the dusty road through the village:

> The god, Ta Kese, says if we have anything to speak,
>   let us speak it,
> For by so doing we are removing misfortune from the
>   nation.

> Do you people know the child who is head of this town?
> The child who is head of this town is called "the help-
>   ful one."
> When he buys palm wine he helps himself to the pot
>   as well.

> Your head is very large,
> And we are taking the victory from out your hands.
> O King, you are a fool.
> We are taking the victory from out your hands
> O King, you are impotent.
> We are taking the victory from out your hands.

> All is well to-day.
> We know that a Brong man eats rats,
> But we never knew that one of the royal blood eats rats.
> But to-day we have seen our master, Ansah, eating rats.
> To-day all is well and we may say so, say so, say so.
> At other times we may not say so, say so, say so.

All this is clearly ritual activity and so might well be thought of in connection with the magical satire discussed earlier. Perhaps even the killing ridicule can, from a certain point of view, be thought of as magical. But I am less concerned with that kind of differentiation than with another approach to the phenomenon—an approach made explicit by the Ashanti themselves. When Rattray asked questions about the licensed ridicule he had witnessed, he was given a careful explanation by the high-priest of the god Ta Kese as follows: "Your soul may be sick or

<hr/>

[26] This and the following material is from Rattray's detailed account of the ceremony in *Ashanti*, pp. 151 ff.

you 'may have hatred in your head against another, because of something that person has done to you. . . . Our forbears knew this . . . and so they ordained a time, once every year, when every man and woman, free man and slave, should have freedom to speak out just what was in their head, to tell their neighbors just what they thought of them . . . [and] also the king or chief. When a man has spoken freely thus, he will feel his *sunsum* [soul] cool and quieted. . . .' " Furthermore, the king will be better off; he will not be sickened by bad thoughts people have of him. Rattray suggests that the same logic may have been behind the Saturnalia of the ancients. Surely he is right: behind the Saturnalia, behind the annual Feast of Fools or Mass of Fools of medieval France, and behind many otherwise inexplicable activities.[27]

Consider a story that the French *philosophe* Pierre Bayle tells of the sixteenth-century Pope Hadrian VI: the Pope was "highly offended at some satirical verses written upon him, and fastened to Pasquin's statue [a famous repository of lampoons and squibs in Rome]; but he afterwards bore this with great calmness, when he came to know that this licentiousness of defaming was to be tolerated in obscure and invidious men, that they might comfort themselves in their hard fortune, by the pleasure and revenge they took in being suffered to defame eminent men."[28]

[27] Frazer records a Saturnalia among the Hos of northeastern India who at harvest time felt they had so much deviltry boiling within them that they had to "let off steam" in the interests of safety. The result was an orgiastic period during which "Sons and daughters revile their parents in gross language," servants treat their masters with the utmost freedom, etc. For this and many comparable festivals see *The Golden Bough*, IX: *The Scapegoat*, Part VI, 136-37 and 306-411. As for the Feast of Fools at which holy ritual was mocked and ridiculed, the sacraments profaned, and a wild kind of license held sway, a Doctor of Auxerre explained: "wine barrels break if their bung-holes are not occasionally opened to let in the air, and the clergy being 'nothing but old wine-casks badly put together would certainly burst if the wine of wisdom were allowed to boil by continued devotion to the Divine Service.' " Cited in Enid Welsford, *The Fool: His Social and Literary History* (New York, n.d.), p. 202.

[28] *The Dictionary Historical and Critical of Mr. Peter Bayle*, trans. Pierre des Maizeaux, 2nd ed. (London, 1734-38), V, 759. When Pope Hadrian wanted to throw Pasquin's statue in the river, he was warned that it would not be silent, but would croak like the frogs: i.e., would inspire a regular chorus of satirical verses.

The Pope's reasoning is similar to that of the Ashanti, although it is here less delicately expressed.

The high priest of Ta Kese was talking, in his own fashion, about the psychological dangers of repression, about the therapeutic value to be found in the patterned release of aggressive impulses. The Ashanti exploit this insight in several ways. For example, story-telling is an important activity among them, an activity engaged in, however, only under certain formal conditions. They tell stories only at night, and they precede each story by a public disclaimer that what is to follow is the truth; the teller will say: "We don't really mean to say so; we don't really mean to say so." Under these special conditions subjects ordinarily taboo can be talked about, laughed at, ridiculed. In former times a man who had a grievance against his superior—even a chief or the king—might make up a story about him, holding him up to thinly disguised mockery. The tale-teller would use no names and would be careful to insist that the story was all make-believe, but his audience would get the point. Such occasions, said Rattray's informant, were "good" for all concerned. And one further practice: if a man has been offended by a chief and wants to retaliate, yet is afraid, he may employ a technique of the most devious indirection. He and a friend will stage a violent quarrel in front of the chief; the aggrieved man will assail his friend with vituperation and ridicule and abuse. The real target—the chief—will have heard, the friend will not be hurt, and the offended man will feel much better.[29]

Negro cultures throughout West Africa and the New World characteristically have socially approved forms for the release in ridicule of pent-up feelings of aggression. Recognizing the dangers of repression (even though they may speak of the dangers as supernatural), the peoples of these cultures institutionalize ridicule for the health of their communities.[30]

[29] Rattray, *Akan-Ashanti Folk-Tales* (Oxford, 1930), pp. x-xii.

[30] See the examples and discussion in Melville J. Herskovits, "Freudian Mechanisms in Primitive Negro Psychology," in *Essays Presented to Seligman*, ed. Evans-Pritchard, pp. 77-78. Tales and myths which ridicule religious belief and the social order probably have a similar function. See, e.g., Paul Radin's remarks on the trickster myth as providing "an outlet for voicing a protest against the many, often onerous, obligations con-

One wonders if comparable practices in the United States today, conducted presumably for comparable motives, are equally sanative. Probably the best-known occasion for licensed ridicule of high public figures is the annual banquet of the Gridiron Club, an organization composed of fifty Washington, D.C., newspaper correspondents. In recent years as many as five hundred guests, from well-placed government officials up to the President of the United States, all dressed in white tie and tails, are entertained by the journalists. The feature of the evening is a series of skits, including songs (usually to traditional tunes) and dances (composed and performed by the newspapermen)—all designed to ridicule and caricature those in power. Some of the satire is said to be sharp, although examples available in the press are not notably severe. However, a modified censorship operates—it is a convention that "reporters are never present"— and it may be that published songs and jokes are not entirely representative. I reproduce a sample of the ridicule from the Spring 1957 celebration. A man impersonating Leonard W. Hall, former Republican National Chairman, sang of Vice President Richard Nixon's hopes of the Presidency in 1960:

> On a perch in the Senate, a Dicky bird sat,
> Singing Dicky, O'Dicky, O'Dicky!
> Every thought in his head was entirely on that:
> Just on Dicky, on Dicky, on Dicky![31]

(Neither Vice President Nixon nor President Eisenhower was present; President Roosevelt used to attend regularly and is said to have roared with laughter at satire against himself, but his successors have not shared his taste; they frequently have sent proxies.) In one important respect the Gridiron Banquet differs, at least officially, from other ceremonies we have glanced at: at every dinner it is announced: "Ladies are always present," an indirect way of saying that obscene jokes and sexual references, which might be expected on such occasions, are taboo.

Other organizations have their own more or less similar ver-

---

nected with the Winnebago social order and their religion and ritual." Primitive people, he says, have wisely devised many such outlets. *The Trickster: a Study in American Indian Mythology* (London, 1956), p. 152.
[31] *New York Times* (March 3, 1957), p. 70.

sions of the Saturnalia. At the annual lampooning banquet of the New York Financial Writers' Association in 1956, an attractive girl slithered up to the microphone and sang:

> I am Miss General Motors,
> What's good for me is good for the voters.

The newspaper account continues:

"Also lampooned was the all-out drive by industry to recruit new executive talent. Depicted was the problem of finding the proper niche for a none too bright prospect.

"His drinking habits suggest a sales post. The fact that he is a liar naturally indicates a post in market research. His lack of honesty makes him a natural in accounting. When it is finally brought out that he is illegitimate, it is decided to make him public relations vice president."[32]

Heresies like these can be uttered only at a time and at a place set apart, only under the special privilege of a ritual occasion. We are not far in this respect from the Ashanti tribesman, or, for that matter, from the Greeks. One of the principal charges made against Lucian in his dialogue "The Dead Come to Life" is that he ridiculed sacred Philosophy "without the sanction of a holiday."[33]

Most writers on the Gridiron banquet have described it as a uniquely American phenomenon, an affair, as Mr. Erwin D. Canham puts it, "which could not be imagined anywhere else in the world." In assessing the significance of the banquet, Mr. Canham says: "This, then, is freedom of speech in the American democracy. And many a diner comes away with the abiding conviction that as long as Gridiron shows are produced to the face of the nation's President, and its other great men, the republic is still safe!"[34] An Ashanti would probably not confuse the license of the *Apo* with freedom of speech, but he might agree that as long as the ritual is properly performed the nation

---

[32] Columbus *Citizen* (Nov. 14, 1956), p. 7.

[33] *Lucian*, trans. Harmon, III, 43. Europe today has lampooning festivals that conform to the saturnalia pattern. Erich Kahler has described to me, for example, the annual *Schnitzelbank* in Basle, Switzerland, at which extraordinary freedom of satirical utterance is permitted.

[34] "In the Glow of the Gridiron," *The Christian Science Monitor Weekly Magazine Section* (Apr. 6, 1940), pp. 4, 15.

will be safe. From our point of view it might be more reasonable to think of these occasions as providing sanctioned emotional release. Newspaper writers are notoriously a repressed lot.

Ridicule has many less esoteric functions in the Western world; like peoples on every level of cultural development, we use it as a means of enforcing conformity.[35] When a person is taken into a new group—a fraternity, the army, a new job—he may be forced to undergo a kind of initiation by ridicule, designed to see whether or not he can "take it" and to teach him his place in the new setting. Ordinarily, the hazing, while it may have unpleasant aspects, is not unduly painful; both group and individual regard it as a mark of inclusion, of acceptance.[36]

A much harsher ridicule, on the other hand, is directed at the true outsider, the one who deviates from accepted norms of behavior, appearance, etc. This form of discipline, which serves to integrate the laughers and either to bring the aberrant person into line or to thrust him irrevocably into outer darkness, occurs at all social levels, from the hipster's underground mockery of the square, to the undercutting wit of the socially established at the expense of the parvenu. Hugh Dalziel Duncan discusses ridicule used this way as a form of magic:

"We see ridicule used as magic art in the treatment of groups struggling for status. Each newly arrived immigrant group in

---

[35] We also use it as a device of rhetoric. It has always been considered a high point of wisdom, as Swift puts it, to "get the laughers on our side," and ridicule is effective in this respect. But theorists of rhetoric have always been ambivalent on the matter; if the powers of ridicule are great, so are its dangers. Plato would ban ridicule from his ideal state; Aristotle distinguishes carefully between the liberal and the illiberal jest, disapproving of the latter because of the pain it gives and the evil motives prompting it (*Ethica Nicomachea*, iv, 8, 1128a); Cicero (in *De Oratore*, ii, 217-290) discusses fully the function of ridicule in oratory and the ethical problems attendant on its use: what kinds of persons and what subjects may and may not appropriately be ridiculed, what language and what tone are proper to ridicule, etc. For discussion see Mary A. Grant, *The Ancient Rhetorical Theories of the Laughable*, University of Wisconsin Studies in Language and Literature, No. 21 (Madison, Wisc., 1924). The extensive controversy in eighteenth-century England over ridicule as a mode of rhetoric is studied by A. O. Aldridge, "Shaftesbury and the Test of Truth," *PMLA*, lx (1945), pp. 129-56, and by John M. Bullitt, *Jonathan Swift and the Anatomy of Satire* (Cambridge, Mass., 1953), pp. 75-82.

[36] See Joseph S. Roucek and associates, *Social Control* (New York, 1947), pp. 320-21.

America became a butt of ridicule for older groups who had risen to power and who therefore were able to set standards of Americanization. The immigrant is always a challenge, even a threat, to established customs. He makes us realize that two (or more) evaluations of action are possible. Laughter helps to resolve this. As we ridicule the newcomer, we overcome confusion through the euphoria arising within us as we laugh. Such ridicule is also used for control of minority groups. We ascribe ignoble and ludicrous characteristics to them, so that we can legitimize the 'need' for control. In magic art we do not hate and then ridicule, we ridicule so that we can hate. If such laughter is not checked by reason operating through imagination, as in great art, the butt of ridicule soon becomes the scapegoat, whom we torture and kill for our edification."[37]

Ridicule, says Duncan, is a way of reducing the burden of consciousness of the ridiculer through arousing hate; it is also a way of neutralizing the power of the victim. In the terms of Kenneth Burke, ridicule is a kind of rhetoric; it prepares the way for action. Before the Jew could be made a scapegoat in Germany, he had first to be made ridiculous. Before Christ was crucified, he was mocked.[38]

According to the shame-guilt formulation of the anthropologists with which we began this section, the effect of ridicule will vary from society to society, depending in part upon the valuation the society places on the opinions of others. Ridicule always hurts, but the hurt will increase in direct proportion as the culture tends to externalize sanctions of behavior. We may find it extremely painful, but our sensitivity is a far cry from that of the true shame culture, where to lose one's good name is virtually to lose one's title to existence, and where ridicule may be fatal. The daughters of Lycambes died, according to an epigram

[37] *Language and Literature in Society* (Chicago, 1953), pp. 24-25.
[38] Ridicule of this kind is of course always bitterly cruel; it destroys honor and self-respect. Duncan says that it is "never reflexive (like laughter arising out of great art). I may turn a joke, but not ridicule upon myself" (p. 23). When it *is* turned upon the self, the result is likely to be horrible, as was John Barrymore's public self-ridicule at the end of his career. Thomas Mann exploits the situation in his story "Little Lizzie"; Herr Jacoby's dance, in which he ridicules his own obesity and his impotence, brings on his death.

of Dioscorides, because of the "evil name" they had received from the "flood of horrible reproach and evil report" let loose upon their family by Archilochus. In Old Ireland, Luaine, like many other victims of the satirists, died of shame.[39]

The people who experience the malign effects of ridicule and satire are likely to account for them by recourse to magic. Even we, who do not believe in magic, may yet believe that belief itself can have a "magical" effect; yet we feel obliged to put such matters into terms more appropriate to our own time. In trying to explain the historical fact that under certain circumstances men kill themselves as a result of having been ridiculed (or in fear of being ridiculed), we would want to inquire closely into many features of a given instance. We would want to know of the negative value placed on shame by the culture concerned, for example. We would want to consider, following Durkheim, the degree to which the particular society was well or badly integrated.[40] We would want to inquire into the psychoanalytic implications of shame itself. The psychoanalyst Gerhard Piers writes: "Behind the feeling of shame stands not the fear of hatred, but the fear of *contempt* which, on an even deeper level of the unconscious, spells fear of abandonment, the death by emotional starvation."[41] I have no doubt that by examining these and other cultural and personal constituents of the general phenomenon, scientists would be able to account for the fact of death-by-ridicule in their own terms, that is, in terms of our day, just as they have been able to account (at least partially) for death by black magic.[42] But the materials we have

[39] *Greek Anthology*, Bk. VII, No. 351, trans. Paton, II, 189; and see above Chap. I, 3.

[40] Emile Durkheim, *Suicide*, trans. J. A. Spaulding and G. Simpson (Glencoe, Ill., 1951), pp. 152-216, esp. p. 208.

[41] *Shame and Guilt*, p. 16.

[42] W. Lloyd Warner writes of the Murngin of north Australia: "When the supposed theft of a man's soul becomes general knowledge, the sustaining social fabric pulls away from the victim. . . . The group . . . acts with all the ramifications of its organization and with the countless stimuli positively to suggest death to a suggestible individual. . . . [The victim] not only makes no effort to live . . . but actually . . . coöperates in his withdrawal. . . . He becomes what his society's attitudes make him, committing a kind of *suicide*." (He does not do violence to himself; he simply dies.) "The Social Configuration of Magical Behavior," in *Essays Pre-*

been considering belong to our day in a chronological sense only, not in a cultural sense. Most of the people we have dealt with live in an ambiance of magic. We want to inquire now at what point satire breaks out of that ambiance to become literature.

3. FROM MAGIC TO ART

One is astonished to learn that portrait caricature, in the strict sense—that is, the deliberate distortion of a particular individual's features for purposes of laughter or mockery—came into being as an art form no earlier than the end of the sixteenth century. To be sure, grotesque and comic art and the art of aggression have a long history indeed, but true caricature, which transforms features and exaggerates the eccentric in order to ridicule, seems to have been unknown before the work of the brothers Carracci in Italy.[1] How are we to account for this late development? Ernst Kris and E. H. Gombrich have a partial explanation: image magic, they point out, is one of the most powerful and abiding forms of magic known. Nearly all peoples at one time or another have believed in the magical identity of the image and its object, and the portrait, of course, is particularly amenable to this kind of association. Though belief in image magic is rarely held consciously in civilized countries, it is by no means dead, even among the sophisticated: "The lover who

---

sented to Kroeber, pp. 412-14. Using anthropological data of this kind, Dr. Walter B. Cannon of the Harvard Medical School has studied the matter from a physiological point of view. Extreme terror, with no outlet in action, he concludes, may bring about "persistent excessive activity of the sympathico-adrenal system" which in turn brings on a disastrous fall in blood pressure. This condition, combined with failure to take food and drink, may well produce quick death. Dr. Cannon compares victims of bone-pointing to victims of "shell shock." " 'Voodoo' Death," *American Anthropologist*, N.S., XLIV (1942), pp. 169-81.

---

[1] H. Brauer and R. Wittkower, *Die Zeichnungen des Gianlorenzo Bernini* (Berlin, 1931); cited by Ernst Kris and E. H. Gombrich, "The Principles of Caricature," in Kris, *Psychoanalytic Explorations in Art* (New York, 1952), pp. 189 ff. Annibale Carracci seems to have invented the word *caricature*, as used in its modern sense, as well as the thing itself. Bernini introduced the term into France in 1665, and Sir Thomas Browne used *caricatura* in the 1680's. See Denis Mahon, *Studies in Seicento Art and Theory*, Studies of the Warburg Institute, XVI (London, 1947), p. 259, n. 43; pp. 260-63, n. 45.

tears up the photograph of his faithless love, the revolutionary who pulls down the statue of the ruler, the angry crowd burning a straw dummy of a hostile leader—all testify to the fact that this belief in the magic power of the image can always regain its power whenever our ego loses some part of its controlling function." Caricature as an art form developed late because caricature "is a play with the magic power of the image, and for such a play to be licit or institutionalized the belief in the real efficacy of the spell must be firmly under control. Wherever it is not considered a joke but rather a dangerous practice to distort a man's features, even on paper, caricature *as an art* cannot develop."[2]

The ancestral development of caricature can be traced without difficulty: the first stage is that at which the crude image, with "likeness" no consideration, *is* the victim: to mutilate it is to mutilate him. Another stage may be represented by defamatory painting or hanging in effigy, where literal identification is not implied and the target is a man's honor or reputation rather than his person. (The effigies of football coaches which in the Midwest dangle freely in fall are probably to be thought of in these terms.) In a final stage, that of caricature proper, the victim's likeness is transformed—and so in a sense is he—but the transformation occurs within an aesthetic rather than a magical sphere. The form has been freed from its magical bonds and may now be developed as art.

If this interpretation is correct, caricature recapitulates in part, and at a very late date, the history of other art forms as well. Both tragedy and comedy, it has been shown, developed originally out of ritual drama. Professors Murray and Cornford, among others, have been notably successful in demonstrating

---

[2] *Psychoanalytic Explorations in Art*, p. 201 (the italics are mine); see also pp. 76-77, 180 ff. That image magic is still alive on a more primitive level hardly needs proof. I quote an Associated Press dispatch from the *New York Times* (March 20, 1955), p. 3: Olga Monzon, sister of an official of a recent Guatemalan government, was charged with practicing witchcraft against President Armas: "The rare charge said that she had placed a small rag doll in a jar containing a thick liquid, pieces of garlic, onion, tomato and some buckshot, had stuck some pins in the doll's head, then sent her maid to the cemetery to bury the jar. . . . Witchcraft experts here say the doll practice is intended to cause the death of the person represented by the doll."

how ancient ritual forms survive in the structure of the great classical genres.[3] For example, Murray shows that Aeschylus' *Supplices* (*The Suppliant Women*), possibly the earliest, certainly the most primitive, of extant Greek plays, is close indeed to the original choric dance from which tragedy evolved. The play is based upon a situation in which the fleeing Danaids implore refuge from their pursuers; they seek sanctuary, and in fact the subject of the play is the rite of sanctuary, the ritual in which "helpless and desperate people seek and find refuge at an altar." Only a step seems to divide the *Supplices* from the enactment of the ritual itself; but that step, like the shudder in the loins of the swan of Yeats's poem, is implicit with consequences beyond calculation. The *Supplices* is not a rite enacted at an altar; it is a play, performed at the theatre of Dionysus in Athens. "The performance," says Murray, "has been cut loose from its roots as a ritual act, and has started on its free career as a work of art. The leaven of drama is already working; and by the time Aeschylus reaches the second play of this trilogy we find him making one of the Danaids emerge as an individual character and stand out against her sisters."[4] The tragic drama as we know it is being born. But the birth had to wait upon the great emancipatory leap from the bonds of magic to the relative freedom of literature, from ritual, that is, to art.

To speak of a "leap" or a "step" in this connection is, of course, to oversimplify, for developments like these take place gradually and indeterminately; they undoubtedly result from the creative acts of gifted men, but hardly from a single conscious act. The movement from ritual to art is slow and inconclusive: who can say where one ends and the other begins? At an early stage, it seems probable, the Homeric myths, which formed the subject-matter of Greek drama, were accepted by the Greeks as reality. Even when the myths were "acted out," the chorus

[3] See Gilbert Murray's "Excursus on the Ritual Forms Preserved in Greek Tragedy," in Harrison, *Themis*, pp. 341 ff., and Cornford, *The Origin of Attic Comedy*.

[4] Gilbert Murray's Introduction to his translation of Aeschylus, *The Suppliant Women* (New York, 1930), pp. 9-10. The early dating of the *Supplices* is open to question; see T. B. L. Webster, "Greek Tragedy," in *Fifty Years of Classical Scholarship*, ed. Maurice Platnauer (Oxford, 1954), p. 74.

and those whom the chorus represented were thought of as one. The myth and its enactment formed a kind of undifferentiated present experience. Bruno Snell, who writes brilliantly of this matter, refers to a paean by Bacchylides (early fifth century B.C.) composed for his fellow-citizens the Ceans on the subject of the return of Theseus to Delos. In the ode, Theseus has leaped from his ship into the sea; he is borne by dolphins to the palace of Poseidon and then miraculously returned to the ship, bearing gifts from the gods. The paean ends: "The maidens [in the company of Theseus on shipboard] shouted with joy [at his appearance] . . . and the young men nearby sang the paean with graceful voice. Delian Apollo, cheer your heart with the choral songs of the Ceans and grant them a god-sent increase of good things." Snell comments: "The youths and maidens with Theseus merge with the chorus of the Ceans for whom Bacchylides wrote the ode; at the end of the poem the chorus is in the same situation as the mythical beings with whom the song concerns itself. The song of the mythical chorus becomes the song of the performing chorus. Here is the germ of drama, the source of impersonation: the transformation of myth into present reality. It leads us into the darkest recesses of the remote past."[5]

Tragedy developed, we know, out of a choral dance in honor of Dionysus; the dancers, disguised as animals, were probably in the beginning thought of as divine: the performers, that is, merged with the myth, the myth with the performers, just as today in the ceremonial dances of the Zuñi, when the priest dons the sacred katcina mask, he *becomes* the god whose representation he bears.[6] Some remnant of a conception like this must have survived among the Greeks at least until Lucian's time, for Lucian uses it as a valid subject for ridicule. In *Zeus Rants*, the orator Damis, attacking the Stoic Timocles, says: "Why, Timocles, you doughtiest of philosophers, if the playwrights have convinced you [of the existence of the gods by representing the gods themselves on the stage] you must needs

[5] *The Discovery of Mind*, pp. 90-91. For Bacchylides' ode, see *Lyra Graeca*, ed. Edmonds, iii, 99 ff.

[6] Ruth L. Bunzel, "Zuñi Katcinas: an Analytical Study," *Annual Report of the U.S. Bureau of American Ethnology*, xlvii, 847-48. The Zuñi phrase for this process of transformation is "to make him [the god] into a living person."

believe either that Polus and Aristodemus and Satyrus are gods for the nonce, or that the very masks representing the gods . . . are divine; and that is thoroughly ridiculous."[7] But the belief cannot have been strong that late, for as the drama develops, the very conditions of performance tend to militate against such magico-religious identifications. The chorus *enacts* a role, it *impersonates* the gods and heroes of myth; and gradually, as Snell shows, the meaning of the ritual is lost. Tragedy begins to take over many myths having nothing whatever to do with Dionysus, so that by the time of Aeschylus the original religious connection has disappeared. As the drama grows further and further from the ceremonial occasion which gave it birth (and from the magico-religious structure imposed by that occasion), it develops laws of its own. Freed from ritual, as Snell says, the drama turns into "play."[8]

Several times we have spoken of a particular art's having been cut free from the bonds of ritual (or magic or mythic belief). The point is this: ritual is a rigidly patterned activity; its efficacy depends on a precise and invariable repetition of a basic formula, deviation from which is destructive of the ceremony. Livy describes how on one occasion an extremely elaborate and costly ceremonial had to be repeated from the beginning because a minor officiant reciting a prayer omitted the full name of the Roman people and thus destroyed the efficacy of the rite.[9] "A rite regularly performed," writes Mrs. Langer, "is the constant reiteration of sentiments toward 'first and last things'; it is not a free expression of emotions, but a disciplined rehearsal of 'right attitudes.' "[10] Precisely: and until the ritual has become secularized and the discipline of the rehearsal relaxed, that which is

[7] *Lucian*, trans. Harmon, II, 153.

[8] *Discovery of Mind*, pp. 92-93. See also Harrison, *Ancient Art and Ritual*, especially p. 222. An aspect of this process may be illustrated from our own time. Edmond Doutté, *Magie et Religion dans l'Afrique du Norde* (Alger, 1909), p. 534, writes: "The poignant drama of the sacrifice of a god, if faith has disappeared, is only a ridiculous ceremony. . . . And in the carnivals we have the most typical example of what happens to a religious ceremony, emptied of its belief: it deteriorates into burlesque . . . and it becomes a game. . . . From that point on it can take on an indefinite number of complications, like any aesthetic phenomenon."

[9] See H. J. Rose, *Primitive Culture in Italy* (London, 1926), pp. 68-69.

[10] *Philosophy in a New Key*, p. 153.

potentially art remains entrapped in the formulaic repetitiveness of the act. The act of ritual, it has been said, is one of participation rather than of creation; when the compulsive character of the act has disappeared, then the materials of the rite become available for new uses, new meanings, new significance.[11] Art, says Wyndham Lewis, "is a civilized substitute for magic." I am arguing that it is a sublimation of magic. Not until concern shifts from ritualistic efficacy to aesthetic value does art become free and the individual artist a maker.[12]

By the classical age in Greece the drama has been freed sufficiently from ritual to make possible the astonishing literary achievement we know. But, as has been indicated, strong traces of ritual origins remained imbedded in the new forms. F. M. Cornford has been able to account for the curious structure of Aristophanic comedy by showing how certain stereotyped features of the ancient phallic rites form the basis of its plot-formula. A crucial element of the Phallic Songs, as we have seen, was the invective, the personal satire, improvised by the leaders of the ceremony. The extraordinary proliferation of invective against individuals and even against the audience in Aristophanes' plays needs no demonstration (one thinks, for a single example, of the contest in abuse between the Paphlagonian and the Sausage-seller in *The Knights*),[13] and we have already (above, p. 6) noted Cornford's comment: "There can be no doubt that the element of invective and personal satire which distinguishes the Old Comedy is directly descended from the magical abuse of the phallic procession, just as its obscenity is due to the sexual magic. . . ." In Aristophanes, of course, the invective has lost

[11] E. Kris and Abraham Kaplan, "Aesthetic Ambiguity," in Kris, *Psychoanalytic Explorations in Art*, p. 253. In the present work, see Section 1 of this chapter above, and Chap. VI below.

[12] One finds evidence of this development in many fields. For example, in a review of Morton W. Bloomfield's *The Seven Deadly Sins*, Margery M. Morgan writes: "Interestingly enough, the serious significance of the [Seven Deadly] Sins appears to have faded as their personification and dramatic projection in literature and art became more complete and vital." (*RES*, N.S. VI [1955], p. 77.) Perhaps the emphasis should be reversed: not *until* the serious, i.e., magico-religious, significance of the Sins fades do they become fully available for artistic elaboration.

[13] For ritual matches in abuse associated with the fertility cults, see Chap. I, 1 and 2, above.

its magical function, though what lingering sense of preternatural significance may have remained, it is difficult to say. The audience was probably aware of the ritual origin of the invective, for the Phallic Songs were still in use, as we learn from Aristotle, in Aristophanes' day. But in Old Comedy invective serves a new and more literary purpose: belief in the baleful efficacy of abuse has declined or died, and materials once dedicated to the practical ends of magic become the agent of comedy and satire— this last in a sense easily recognizable today.[14]

The same kind of development is evident in Aristophanes' use of the curse for comic purposes. For example, all meetings of the Assembly and the Senate in Athens were opened by a ritualistic imprecation against enemies of the state.[15] Aristophanes uses the solemn form of this public curse in *The Thesmophoriazusae*, but alters its matter wildly:

> Whoso is disaffected, ill-disposed
> Towards this commonwealth of womankind,
> Or with Euripides, or with the Medes
> Deals to the common hurt of womankind,
>
> . . . .
>
> or dares betray a wife
> For palming off a baby as her own;
>
> . . . .

[14] The terms are slippery. Not *all* invective or abuse, surely, was thought to have magical power. G. L. Hendrickson writes: "It should be obvious that at a time when superstitions of the magical influence of look or word were universally entertained, it is unreasonable to expect a nice distinction . . . between words believed to possess harmful magical power and words of mere angry petulance and abuse. Magic was not originally a separate compartment of human potentiality. Every man carried it with him and used it as occasion or emotion dictated. He cursed earnestly, that is with serious purpose to harm, and he cursed lightly, as a mere outlet to spleen. The one had magical power, the other had not. . . . To draw a nice line between the supernatural curse of magic and the abuse of mere billingsgate is to attempt the impossible. *Maledicere* for example may be a formal curse meant to inflict disaster, but it ranges all the way from this meaning to the abuse of wrangling slaves or the petulant jealousies of rival playwrites." "Verbal Injury, Magic, or Erotic Comus?" *CP*, xx (1925), p. 293. On the other hand, in some cultures even an angry thought has power to harm, and wrangling and abuse are feared as signs of an evil influence abroad.

[15] See Appendix on the curse.

> or, being a rich old woman,
> Hires for herself a lover with her wealth;
> Or, being a girl, takes gifts and cheats the giver;
> Or, being a trading man or trading woman,
> Gives us short measure in our drinking cups;—
> Perish that man, himself and all his house. . . .[16]

A form once pregnant with magical significance becomes the vehicle of sharp and amusing satire.

The personal curse is burlesqued even more extravagantly in *Lysistrata* when the Chorus of Old Men hurls imprecations at Myrrhina for her hilarious betrayal of Cinesias:

> [She is] Vile, vile, I repeat.
> Zeus, send me a storm and a whirlwind, I pray,
> To whisk her away, like a bundle of hay,
> Up, up, to the infinite spaces,
> And toss her and swirl her, and
> twist her, and twirl her,
> Till, tattered and torn, to the earth she is borne,
> To be crushed—in my ardent embraces.[17]

The solemn form is suddenly shattered by the bawdiness of the last line (only faintly indicated by Rogers' charming paraphrase), and what was once feared as deadly magic is now the instrument of Aristophanes' most characteristic humor. The magical form has become available for art.

A close examination of Aristophanes' plays would yield much more material to the same purpose; and as we read the drama of ancient Greece, looking for evidence of primitive origins, we are almost overwhelmed by the sense of how close these great plays—tragic and comic—are to their roots in magic and ritual. But the miraculous achievement of the Greeks was that they transcended those origins, that they broke through the bonds of magical invariability. Instead of the rite we have the *Oresteia* and the *Oedipus*; and instead of the hieratic abuse of the phallic procession we have *The Frogs* and *Lysistrata* and the rest.

Nothing approaching the quality of that achievement can be

---

[16] Lines 331-51, in *Aristophanes*, trans. Rogers, III, 161-63.
[17] Lines 972-79, *Aristophanes*, III, 95.

found, of course, in Ireland, where the magical substratum is much more apparent; but if we look carefully at some of the early tales we will find achievement of a similar *kind*, in which the breakthrough from magic to art is clearly discernible. Rather than multiply unfamiliar instances, I propose to choose as an example *The Great Visitation to Guaire*, in which the old magical satire (which we have already examined) is remarkably confronted with a new literary satire.[18] Despite the "barbarity" of the *Great Visitation*, it is in some respects astonishingly modern: in it satire becomes its own subject, thus prefiguring one of the most characteristic themes in modern literature.

We dealt in Chapter 1 with the opening section of the tale wherein Dallán Forgaill, trying to obtain a magic shield, uttered his unjust satire against King Hugh. The poet died, we recall, because the magic of his satire redounded onto his own head. After the death of Dallán, the Bardic Association selects Senchán to be the new chief poet. Abruptly, the tone of the story, which has been straightforward and objective, now shifts into burlesque. The poets determine to visit King Guaire, a promising host, as Senchán points out, because he has never been satirized for stinginess. In order not to place undue strain on Guaire's hospitality, Senchán decides to take on the visitation *only* "thrice fifty of the professors; thrice fifty students . . . ; thrice fifty hounds; thrice fifty male attendants; thrice fifty female relatives; and thrice nine of each class of artificers" (p. 39). (The numerousness of the poets is a steady complaint throughout early Irish literature.) King Guaire, who was warned of their coming, built an eight-sided mansion to receive the visitors; he foresightedly arranged that beside each first-class bed should be a truckle bed so that if disputes arose during the night among the notoriously quarrelsome poets, a small bed would be ready to receive the worsted one. The king welcomes the company effusively and promises that every one of their desires shall be satisfied.

From then on every man in Ireland is kept busy attending to the whims of the visitors. Some of the wishes are most extraordinary: Muireann, for example, widow of Dallán, utters a great

---

[18] For an equally good, and rather more sophisticated, example, see *Aislinge Meic Conglinne: The Vision of MacConglinne*, trans. Kuno Meyer, Intro. Wilhelm Wollner (London, 1892); reprinted Cross and Slover, pp. 551-87.

groan and declares that she will die unless her desire is satisfied. She wishes for "a bowl of the ale of sweet milk, with the marrow of the anklebone of a wild hog; a pet cuckoo on an ivy tree in my presence between the two Christmases . . . and her full load on her back, with a girdle of yellow lard of an exceeding white boar about her; and to be mounted on a steed with a brown mane, and its four legs exceedingly white; a garment of the spider's web around her, and she humming a tune as she proceeded to Durlus" (pp. 41-43). Even Senchán is startled and confesses that to satisfy that wish will be difficult. King Guaire kneels and prays for death; for if he cannot satisfy the desire he will be satirized, and he would rather die than hear himself satirized by the poets. Guaire's brother Marbán, however, is a saint (as well as a swineherd); through his intervention Muireann's wish, and several more equally fantastic, is fulfilled.

Despite this extraordinary pampering, Senchán becomes petulant and goes on a hunger strike; for three days and three nights he fasts, while Guaire sends his comeliest youths and maidens to tempt him with specially prepared food.[19] Senchán refuses one youth, he says, because "I knew your grandfather and he was chip-nailed, and since he was so, I shall not take food out of thy hands." The poet finally, however, agrees to eat an egg; but the mice nibble at it and Senchán satirizes them, with the results we have seen.

All this has been, of course, to put the poets in a very bad, and a very ridiculous, light. Marbán, the saint, finding their petulance and their pride intolerable, finally undertakes to humble them. He gains entrance to the poets' mansion by claiming a connection with the arts: "viz. through the grandmother of my servant's wife, who was descended from poets." One by one he challenges the chief poets to a contest in the poet's own specialty, and one by one they are humiliated. Oircne Aitheamuin, for example, who claims to be "skilful and highly learned," is particularly vulnerable: Marbán points out that he is the most ignorant man in the whole bardic order: his wife is unfaithful to him; she has given the poet's ring and his sword to her two lovers; and Oircne knows nothing of it. Marbán subdues most of

---

[19] Senchán's hunger strike is used, in a remarkable shift of context, as the central episode in Yeats's play *The King's Threshold* (1904).

the poets in competition requiring knowledge of the origin of things: whence originated the science of playing the harp? for example; or in riddle contests: what goodness did man find on the earth that God did not find? Each of the bards is overcome by his superior knowledge; and with the humiliation of Senchán, Marbán's triumph is complete. He imposes certain tasks upon the poets, puts a *geis* on them, and sends them on a long search, his final scolding directed to "you indolent, ignorant, bardic clan."[20]

A fascinating tale from many points of view, *The Great Visitation* is of crucial interest to us in its juxtaposition of primitive and more or less sophisticated satire. The author of the tale, as we have seen, presents the introductory episode of Dallán and King Hugh straightforwardly. Dallán is the type of the satirist-magician; like Aithirne the Importunate, he wields his magic ruthlessly; his motives are evil and his satire a mere form of power. When this power encounters a superior power—that implicit in the idea of justice as it is objectified in the pact between the poets and the kings—Dallán succumbs. We observe that Dallán's fellow-poets (like the colleagues of Aithirne) see nothing whatever wrong in Dallán's action, which he himself has admitted to be unjust. Senchán's eulogy of Dallán (p. 35) is unqualified. But the *story* (as opposed to the poets) insists clearly, if indirectly, that Dallán was wrong, that his punishment was deserved. The episode justifies the mockery of the poets that follows.

Senchán, Dallán's successor, is a trivial imitator of other chief bards. His exercise of the once mighty power of the satirist is successful only against mice; a cat (an extraordinary cat, to be sure) makes him beg for mercy in the most humiliating fashion, and he has to be saved by a saint. Clearly the bulk of the tale is devoted to puncturing the myth of the inviolability of the poets. While the threat of magical satire is still present—Guaire is motivated by it throughout—it is far in the background as the poets are shown to be intolerably petty, vain, and frivolous per-

[20] This summary has slighted some of the historical interest of the tale, particularly the description of the poets' search for the story of *The Cattle-Raid of Cooley* and the legendary account of its transmission. For a full discussion, see Carney, *Studies in Irish Literature*, pp. 165-88.

sons. Between their pretensions and their essential impotence, between what is implied in their status and their foolish actuality, stretches a gap which is defined by ridicule. Burlesque is employed as the agent of indirect criticism. In short, the satirists are satirized.

To understand the significance of this development, we can return to the statement of Kris and Gombrich quoted at the beginning of this section. Caricature, they say, "is a play with the magic power of the image, and for such a play to be licit or institutionalized the belief in the real efficacy of the spell must be firmly under control. Wherever it is not considered a joke but rather a dangerous practice to distort a man's features, even on paper, caricature as an art cannot develop." Similarly, satire *as an art* cannot develop so long as belief in its magical efficacy retains its hold over men's minds. While it is thought of as curse or spell, its primary mode of existence will be governed by the non-rational and non-literary formal relations of magic. But, when belief in its magical power has been brought under control of the ego (does the belief ever really die?), then, through the creative act of a poet, satire may break out of the forms which have restrained it and be free to develop in the ways appropriate to art. The early stages of the breakthrough are exemplified in *The Great Visitation to Guaire*, where magical satire becomes the occasion of literary satire. Just as Aristophanes was free to "play" with the curse, so the anonymous maker of *The Great Visitation* was free to mock at the old magic. He was free, that is, to help transform satire from magic into art.

The major purpose of this chapter has been to account for the widespread association of satire and ridicule with magic and to show at what point and under what conditions satire breaks out of magic into literature. In examining *The Great Visitation to Guaire* as an exemplary work in this process, we encountered the theme of the satirist satirized—a theme that appears (in various guises) with remarkable regularity throughout the history of satirical writing. We shall follow some of the later manifestations of the theme, but first it would be well to establish a kind of base camp on more solid ground. We have been dealing with highly esoteric aspects of satire. In the next chapter I propose to discuss briefly the very center of the literary tradition of satire: that is, the formal verse satire as it was established in Rome. We shall be concerned with the sources of the formal satire, with its structure, and primarily with its function as that is defined by the great practitioners: Horace, Persius, Juvenal.

CHAPTER III

ROMAN VERSE SATIRE

indignatio facit versum
—JUVENAL, SATIRE I

As WE MOVE from the realm of magic, blisters, and incantatory death into the reassuringly familiar field of "real satire," we face the problem posed by the quotation marks around our central term. Is it sheer nonsense to use the word "satirist" to refer to Archilochus, Dallán Forgaill, Horace, and Swift? Have the verses of Hipponax against Bupalus, Aristophanes' *The Knights*, Juvenal's Sixth Satire, *The Great Visitation to Guaire*, *Le Misanthrope*, Orwell's *1984*—have these *really* enough in common to justify our calling them satires? Has the word *really* any meaning in this context?

The juxtaposition of three comments from major classical writers nicely dramatizes the puzzle. Aristotle, we know, traces the origin of comedy to the invectives, the iambics, the (we would say) satirical utterances of the leaders of the Phallic Songs. Second, Horace, writing of Lucilius, the "first" Roman satirist, says this:

hinc [the writers of Old Comedy] omnis pendet Lucilius,
    hosce secutus
mutatis tantum pedibus numerisque

("It is on these that Lucilius wholly hangs; these he has followed, changing only metre and rhythm.")[1] And, third, we have the well-known statement of Quintilian as he compares Greek and Roman literary achievement: "Satura . . . tota nostra est ("Satire [as opposed to the elegy and other literary forms] is all our own.")[2]

---

[1] *Satires*, I, 4, 6-7, trans. Fairclough, p. 49.
[2] *Institutio Oratoria*, x, i, 93, trans. H. E. Butler (London, 1920), IV, 53. Cf. Horace, *Satires*, I, 10, 65-66.

100

Old Comedy develops out of satiric improvisations; the first Roman satirist derives from the writers of Old Comedy; and satire is wholly a Roman form of art. The last statement, that of Quintilian, is the crucial one in this semantic nightmare.

For Quintilian the word *satura,* which we translate *satire,* had a sense quite different from that which we give it. It is impossible to think that the learned and judicious rhetorician displays either ignorance or patriotic partiality in his statement; he certainly knew the work of Aristophanes, for example, and the many Greek forms like the mime, the Bionean diatribe, etc., which we would call satirical, and his tendency is to depreciate, rather than to overvalue, Roman literary achievement. Quintilian means by *satura* something specific and definite which has been nearly submerged in our sense of the word *satire* today. When we speak of a satirical novel or a satirical play we probably have in mind a work of art which contains a sharp kind of irony or ridicule or even denunciation: John Osborne's *Look Back in Anger* is an example, or one of Mary McCarthy's novels. A satirical man is one whose tone is derisive or sarcastic—a wittily censorious man. For us, in short, satire has to do with tone and spirit (perhaps also purpose), but hardly with form. Irish and Arabic terms for satire comprehend our meaning, but also include the magical spells we have examined. For Quintilian, however, *satura* designates specifically a *form* of literature, a genus; and when he writes *satura . . . tota nostra est,* he means, as G. L. Hendrickson convincingly shows, "that the special type of literature created by Lucilius, dominated by a certain spirit, clothed in a certain metrical form, fixed by the usage of a series of canonical writers, and finally designated by a name specifically Latin, is Roman and not Greek."[3] This is not to say, of course, that Quintilian denies to the Greeks the satirical spirit which abounds in their literature (and which appears to be universal); it is simply that he has no single word like our *satire* to express that spirit, and he is talking about something else. We, however, have read into his *satura* the enormous inflation of meaning the term has suffered since late antiquity. We have been badly misled.

[3] "Satura tota nostra est," *CP,* XXII (1927), p. 58.

The confusion is neatly paralleled in English. Joseph Hall's famous boast in the Prologue to *Virgidemiarum* (1598):

> *I first aduenture: follow me who list,*
> *And be the second English Satyrist*

has been disallowed since Milton's scornful attack. But it seems likely that Hall, who knew Chaucer and Skelton among others, meant that he was the first in English to imitate systematically the satire of Rome. In this he was almost accurate.

It has seemed odd to scholars that the word *satura* appears so infrequently in Roman literature (Horace uses it only twice, and it then nearly drops out of currency until the time of Quintilian and Juvenal); whereas our word *satire* and its derivatives are among the most heavily worked of all literary terms. Hendrickson's explanation is convincing: until at least Quintilian's day *satura* meant only a fraction of what our *satire* means; no verbal or adjectival use (as in our *satirize, satirical*) had yet arisen; the signification was fixed and localized.[4] Gradually, however, *satura* came to be used in a metaphorical sense to indicate the spirit of Roman satire, at which point, as Hendrickson says, the word clamored for extension. "Here the Romans found ready at hand a Greek word of similar meaning and of almost identical form, σάτυρος [satyr], with a rich family of derivatives . . . and these they appropriated to add to the slender dower of their native *satura*." Thus the curious situation arises that our *satire* is derived from Latin *satura* (which had the original sense of *mixture* or *medley*), while our *satirize* and *satirical* come from the Greek word for satyr.

This etymological disentanglement was long in the making. In Renaissance England it was universally accepted that satire (*satyr* or *satyre*, it was spelled—the orthographic modification both reflected and contributed to the confusion) came from the ancient satyr plays. Puttenham, for example, wrote in the *Arte of English Poesie* (1588) that the ancients had a kind of poem called satyre, a bitter invective against vice and vicious men, named after the Satyrs, "these terrene and base gods being con-

---

[4] "Satura tota nostra est," pp. 56-59. It has also been pointed out that the Romans used generic literary terms infrequently. See J. Wight Duff, *Roman Satire: Its Outlook on Social Life* (Berkeley, California, 1936), p. 15.

uersant with mans affaires, and spiers out of all their secret faults. . . ."[5] Given such a rude and licentious source, it was thought appropriate that "satyre" should be harsh and rough and bold.[6] The effects on Elizabethan practice are clear enough:

> The *Satyre* should be like the *Porcupine*,
> That shoots sharpe quils out in each angry line,
> And wounds the blushing cheeke, and fiery eye,
> Of him that heares, and readeth guiltily.[7]

This temper dominates English satire until late in the seventeenth century, even though Isaac Casaubon's great *De satyrica Graecorum poesi et Romanorum satira* had exposed the fallacy of the satyr-satire relation as early as 1605. But the tradition was attractive: it was dramatic, it was "mythic," it provided admirable sanction for daring abuse; and so it lingered—and, indeed, lingers still. When Milton writes: "For a Satyr as it was borne out of a *Tragedy*, so ought to resemble his parentage, to strike high, and adventure dangerously . . . ," he is clearly thinking of the Greek satyr-play which followed after (was "borne

---

[5] George Puttenham, *The Arte of English Poesie*, ed. Gladys D. Willcock and Alice Walker (Cambridge, 1936), p. 31. For an account of Renaissance theories of satire, see Oscar James Campbell, *Comicall Satyre and Shakespeare's Troilus and Cressida* (San Marino, California, 1938), pp. 24 ff.; and Mary Claire Randolph, "The Medical Concept in English Renaissance Satiric Theory," SP, xxxviii (1941), pp. 125-57.

[6] One of the most curious and inexplicable ties between Renaissance satiric theory and the primitive background we have been concerned with occurs in a verse definition of satire by Thomas Drant, Archdeacon of Lewes, prefixed to his translation of Horace's satires in 1566. Drant connects satire with satyr and with the "writhled waspyshe" planet Saturn; but he also characterizes satire as a pinching, piercing instrument, well-named, he says, because the Arabic word for satire "doothe signifye a glave [sword]." As we saw in Chap. 1, 2, the Arabic word for satire, lampoon, magical curse is *hijá*; Mary Claire Randolph points out ("Thomas Drant's Definition of Satire, 1566," NQ, 180 [1941], pp. 417-18) that in its verbal form *hagg* the word carries the idea of severing, splitting, or cutting down, as with a sword. Or, another possibility, John Peter says (*Complaint and Satire in Early English Literature* [Oxford, 1956], p. 303) the Arabic word *sātūr* means a butcher's cleaver. Early Arabic satire, we have seen, is functionally very like Irish. Drant links these meanings with Roman and English satire in a couplet; but where he got the idea, and what it meant to him, is a mystery.

[7] Joseph Hall, *Virgidemiarum*, Bk. v, Satire 3, ll. 1-4; see his *Collected Poems*, ed. A. Davenport (Liverpool, 1949), p. 83.

out of") the tragic trilogy. Even in the twentieth century Gilbert Cannan writes of satire as "begotten by Pan, the goat-footed."[8]

The term *satura* puzzled even the ancients; and the literature, both ancient and modern, on its provenience is extensive and extraordinarily complex.[9] For our purposes it is sufficient to note that the sense of "medley" or "mixture" is consistently associated with the word, whether or not it applied originally to a rude, semi-dramatic musical performance (as Livy, in a disputed passage, has it). Juvenal's characterization of his own *saturae* admirably conveys the sense:

> quidquid agunt homines, votum timor ira voluptas
> gaudia discursus, nostri farrago libelli est.

(". . . all the doings of mankind, their vows, their fears, their angers and their pleasures, their joys and goings to and fro, shall form the motley subject of my page.")[10] By Quintilian's time, as we have seen, the form had become relatively fixed, and the tradition was established that Lucilius was the "inventor" of the form. Within severe limitations the tradition is probably correct. Although it is possible to find reflections of dozens of inchoate Greek forms in the developed satire of Rome, and although it has never been doubted that the satiric spirit is superbly manifest in Greek literature, it is still true that Lucilius and after him Horace and Juvenal, gave a structure to verse satire which was something new under the sun.

[8] Milton, "An Apology, &c., *Works* (New York, Columbia University edition, 1931), III, Pt. 1, p. 329. Cannan, *Satire* (London, 1914). See Hendrickson, "Satura tota nostra est," p. 60.

[9] I list some important studies: H. Nettleship, "The Original Form of the Roman Satura," reprinted in his *Lectures and Essays*, 2nd ser. (Oxford, 1895), pp. 24-43; G. L. Hendrickson, "The Dramatic Satura and the Old Comedy at Rome," *AJP*, xv (1894), pp. 1-30, and his "Satura—the Genesis of a Literary Form," *CP*, vi (1911), pp. 129-43; C. Knapp, "The Sceptical Assault on the Roman Tradition Concerning the Dramatic Satura," *AJP*, xxxiii (1912), pp. 125-48; A. L. Wheeler, "*Satura* as a Generic Term," *CP*, vii (1912), pp. 457-77; B. L. Ullman, "Satura and Satire," *CP*, viii (1913), pp. 172-94; B. L. Ullman, "The Present Status of the *Satura* Question," *SP*, xvii (1920), pp. 379-401; J. Wight Duff, *Roman Satire*, Chap. i, pp. 1-22.

[10] Satire i, 85-86, in *Juvenal and Persius*, trans. G. G. Ramsay (London, 1940), p. 9.

One of the major tasks of recent classical scholarship has been to elucidate the paradox that the new form was created almost entirely out of old materials. Roman satire goes back for its ethical and social premises to the Greek philosophies of conduct, cynicism and stoicism. Its dominant tone is a combination of Socratic irony and Old Comedy rigor. Almost every facet of its bewilderingly complex structure can be shown to have originated, directly or indirectly, in various popular Greek forms: among others, the Bionean diatribe, the *chria*, the mime, Atellan farce, the beast fable (which Archilochus used), and the Theophrastian character.[11] Aristophanic comedy, too, may have contributed structural principles to Roman satire, but its primary influence was unquestionably one of tone. Greek Old Comedy (on which Lucilius "wholly depended") was known for nothing so much as the extraordinary freedom and vigor with which the dramatists attacked their victims. Until restraining laws were finally passed, nothing was too harsh, or too obscene, for the playwright to say against his enemies (or those whom he adjudged enemies of the state), all in the name of morality. For Aristotle it was this "iambic" element which differentiated Old Comedy from the comedy of his own day; and in the *Nicomachean Ethics* he expresses unequivocally his disapproval of iambic abuse: he uses Old Comedy as the prime illustration of the "illiberal jest."[12] Lucilius, however, says Horace, is thoroughly in this established tradition of blunt, outspoken attack; that is why satire is feared and the satirist shunned as is a wild bull (*Satires*, I, 4, 33 ff.).

We have here a nexus of themes relating Roman satire with Old Comedy but also with the iambic poets Archilochus and Hipponax. Fear, we know, is inevitably associated with them, as is obscenity, violent personal attack, and general wild-bullishness.

[11] For the Greek background of Latin satire, see Paul Lejay, "Les origines et la nature de la satire d'Horace," the Intro. to his ed. of the *Satires* of Horace (Paris, 1911), pp. vii-lxxxii; George Converse Fiske, *Lucilius and Horace*, University of Wisconsin Studies in Language and Literature, No. 7 (Madison, Wisconsin, 1920), pp. 143-208.

[12] *Poetics*, v, 1449b; *Ethica Nicomachea*, IV, 1128a. G. L. Hendrickson points out that Aristotle's hostility to Old Comedy was by no means universally shared by later critics, many of whom recognized its "aggressive scurrility" but also attributed to it "a pleasing and liberal spirit of jest." "Horace, Serm. I, 4: a Protest and a Programme," *AJP*, xxi (1900), pp. 132, 141. Cf. Fiske, *Lucilius and Horace*, pp. 96 ff.

The great German scholar Friedrich Leo argued that there was
a direct line from the *Kampflust* of Archilochus and Hipponax
to the verse of Lucilius, even though Lucilius might not have
been aware of it; others believe that Lucilius was thoroughly
conscious of the relation.[13] In any event, Horace knew the tradition and in some moods identifies himself with it. In Epode vi
he writes of himself as an angry bull (probably a conventional
image for the satirist): "Beware, beware! For full fiercely do I
lift my ready horns against evil-doers, even as the slighted son-in-
law of perfidious Lycambes, or as Bupalus' keen foe. Or, if any
one with venomous tooth assail me, shall I forgo revenge and
whimper like a child?" Elsewhere he boasts of having been "the
first to show to Latium the iambics of Paros, following the
rhythms and spirit of Archilochus, not the themes or the words
that hounded Lycambes."[14]

Epode x is a direct imitation of Archilochus' poem against the
man "who was once my friend" (Frag. 97A), and a number of
the other Epodes follow Archilochus in spirit and tone. Numbers viii and xii are so gross in their abuse that editors invariably
apologize for Horace and blame Archilochus.

To be sure, these are Epodes, not *saturae*. While in general
the Epode is satirical in our sense, its structure and tone are distinct from those of the *sermones*, as Horace called his satires.
Epode ii with its sudden sardonic twist at the end may seem to
us a fine satire on a man who professes overwhelming love for
the simple life of the country, but cannot tear himself away from
the stockmarket ticker; yet neither Horace nor Quintilian would
have considered it a *satura*. For one thing, it is written in iambics
rather than in the conventional hexameter. Lejay says that the
Epode differs from the formal satire in its oratorical tone, in the
continuity of its invective, and in the varied and complex meters
in which it is composed.[15] The coarse invective of Horace's

[13] Leo, *Geschichte der römischen Literatur* (Berlin, 1913), p. 410;
Fiske, *Lucilius and Horace*, p. 201.
[14] *The Odes and Epodes*, trans. C. E. Bennett (London, 1930), p. 383;
Epistles, i, 19, 23-25, trans. Fairclough.
[15] "Les origines de la satire latine," p. lxxvii. It is interesting that Dryden in his "Essay on Satire" excludes Horace's Odes and Epodes from the
category satire, although, as he says, "Horace has written many of them
satirically against his private enemies"; *Works*, ed. Scott-Saintsbury
(Edinburgh, 1887), xiii, 82.

Epodes VIII and XII might be appropriate in iambics but would be out of place in *sermones*. Horace himself points to the problem of taste involved:

> carmine tu gaudes, hic delectatur iambis,
> ille Bioneis sermonibus et sale nigro.

("Lyric song is your delight, our neighbor here takes pleasure in iambics, the one yonder in Bion's satires, with their caustic wit.")[16] Still, although Horace's preference, and by and large his influence, is strongly for the *sermones* (and for wit gentler than the *sal niger*), it is perfectly apparent from the towering influence of Lucilius, from Horace's own theory and occasional practice (*Satires*, I, 2), and from the strength of his reaction to the established tradition, that Roman *satura* was closely linked to the mocking abuse of the Greek iambists.[17]

For over two thousand years satirists have shown a compulsive desire to justify on moral grounds their ungrateful art. With wearying iteration they have claimed (usually overtly, occasionally by implication) that they fight under the banners of truth, justice, and reason; that they attack none but the guilty, that their mission is a purifying one, undertaken almost against their will for the public benefit. Satire, in short, is, as Pope said, a moral weapon; and Juvenal's *facit indignatio versum* is the essential expression of the controlling attitude. The sanction of this moralistic concern has been, oddly enough, Greek Old Comedy. The crux of Horace's praise of the writers of Old Comedy is that they, like true poets, knew how to set their mark on wicked men; and Lucilius, says Horace, is in this respect a worthy follower. Old Comedy is good because it flays the wicked. Roman criticism throws great emphasis on the moral function of literature, but it was only following what had become indelibly established in Greek practice.

[16] *Epistles*, II, 2, 59-60, trans. Fairclough. Cf. Horace's statement that the *iambus* was the fitting weapon for the rage of Archilochus; *De Arte Poetica*, l. 79.

[17] G. G. Ramsay, following Livy, vii, 2, holds that *satura* was a name originally given to a "rough musical performance of a semi-dramatic kind . . . developed . . . from the rude banterings in extempore verse or otherwise of the Italian youth. . . ." Personal abuse, Ramsay says, "formed the essence of the first beginnings of *Satura*." Introduction to his translation of *Juvenal and Persius*, pp. xxxix-xl and note.

It is an intriguing paradox that Aristophanes, who recently has been considered so licentious as to threaten the purity of the United States mails, should have been the first to advance programmatically the thesis that poetry (specifically tragedy) should be judged by its ethical component.[18] However great the danger of lifting Aristophanes' aesthetic opinions out of the burlesque speeches of his characters, there is no doubt that *The Frogs*, for example, is a thesis play; it insists, through the mouth of the character Aeschylus, that the function of great poetry is to make great men, great patriots. So Aeschylus speaks in his underworld contest with Euripides:

> . . . we, the poets, are teachers of men.
> We are BOUND things honest and pure to speak. (1055-56)

Euripides is reviled for having corrupted the Athenians; he has taught them to doubt and mistrust; he has made chop-logics of them:

> to evil repute
> Your lessons have brought our youngsters. (1070)

Euripides' replies to the moralistic criticism of his dramatic art have their own cogency. Aristophanes has respected the complexity of the issue; this is no simple, black-and-white affair. But the dramatist's own position (argued, as Werner Jaeger says, with painful, almost tragic, seriousness) is unmistakable: poets are teachers and poetry must serve the ends of morality.[19] And we recall that even with Archilochus the sense of moral mission in the satirist is firmly, if not systematically, established.[20]

Aristophanes is, of course, a satirist—one of the greatest of all satirists; and although he is excluded from Quintilian's category,

[18] For a full discussion of Aristophanes' major role in this tradition, see Snell, "Aristophanes and Aesthetic Criticism" in *Discovery of the Mind*, pp. 113-35.

[19] For analogous passages, see *Wasps*, 1030 ff., where Aristophanes speaks of himself as a Heracles come forth "to grapple at once with the mightiest foes," and rid the land of them. Elsewhere, the purpose of "the holy Chorus" is to "exhort and teach the city"; it speaks "much in earnest, much in jest" (*Frogs*, 686, 390). Cf. Grant, *Ancient Rhetorical Theories of the Laughable*, p. 47. Jaeger's comment is in *Paedeia*, i, 365.

[20] See above, Chap. i, 1, and Jaeger, *Paedeia*, i, 121-24, who emphasizes the normative element in Archilochus' iambics and even in the popular lampoon.

it is interesting that the moral justification of *satura*—and the insistence of satirists ever since that theirs is a righteous enterprise—derives in large measure, whether legitimately or not, from him.

Another element in Aristophanes must be mentioned. The leading theme of *The Frogs* is a slashing attack on the intellectualism of Socrates and Euripides. In effect, the playwright accuses Socrates of being responsible for the downfall of tragedy; at the end of the play the chorus sings:

> Right it is and befitting
> Not, by Socrates sitting,
> Idle talk to pursue,
> Stripping tragedy-art of
> All things noble and true.

Euripides and the Sophists are lumped together in the same category with Socrates; Euripides is accused of being an irresponsible juggler of ideas, of turning the people into skeptical dissenters. He is guilty of the sin of rationalism. Opposed to these representatives of the new intellectualism is Aeschylus, irrational, unsophisticated, "mythic": the champion of the heroic tradition of the past. Aeschylus wins the contest with Euripides and is chosen to return from the underworld to save Athens. These ideas, of course, come dressed in motley; but the ideas are there, and Aristophanes' attitude toward them is dogmatic. The intellectuals are the villains. Like Juvenal and Swift, Aristophanes uses satire (in its sophisticated form a highly intellectual mode, claiming to depend strictly on the sanctions of reason) to undermine the cause of rationalism.[21] The three great satirists are all rationally anti-intellectual.

But to return to the achievement of the Roman poets: despite the welter of "influences"—influences of form, of spirit, tone, technique, purpose—there was established by the practice and the theory of Lucilius and Horace, Persius and Juvenal, a definite poetic genre, that of the formal verse satire. Actually, when we read the satires of these poets, we are likely to feel that they have remarkably little in common. To be sure, the satires are written in the hexameter, they share certain techniques and

---

[21] See Snell, *Discovery of the Mind*, p. 132.

avowed purposes, and so on; but the over-all impression is that the poems are so haphazardly organized, so willfully and randomly *individual* that there is little justification for speaking of them as members of a genus at all. Beneath the surface complexity, however, there exists, as Mary Claire Randolph has shown, a structural principle common to the satires of the Roman poets and their French and English followers.[22]

The formal verse satire has always a negative and a positive aspect, as it were. In what Miss Randolph calls Part A, the satire attacks a specific vice or folly (sometimes, to the pain of purists, vices or follies) and in Part B recommends an opposing virtue. The two parts are disproportionate in length and in importance, for the satirist has always been more disposed to castigate wickedness than to exhort to virtue. Still, the only obvious sanction of Part A is the promise of Part B; and while an attack on vice may be taken to imply a love of virtue, the satirist has not often dared rely on the inference, but has taken pains to align himself explicitly with the good.

Most verse satires are enclosed by a "frame." Just as a novel by Conrad may be framed by a situation in which his storyteller Marlow sits on an eastern veranda, telling his tale, stimulated into elaboration by the queries of his listeners, so the satire will be framed by a conflict of sorts between the satirist (or, more reasonably, his *persona*, the "I" of the poem) and an adversary. The adversary usually has a minor role, serving only to prod the "I" into extended comment on the issue (vice or folly) at hand; he may be sketchily defined, a completely shadowy figure, or he may be as effectively projected as Horace's Trebatius, or his awful bore, or his slave Davus, who turns the tables on his master. Similarly, the background against which the two talk may be barely suggested or it may form an integral part of the poem, as in the journey to Brundisium or in Juvenal's description of the Valley of Egeria, where Umbricius unforgettably pictures the turbulence and the decadence of Rome. In any event,

---

[22] "The Structural Design of the Formal Verse Satire," *PQ*, XXI (1942), pp. 368-84. Miss Randolph's unpublished doctoral dissertation, "The Neo-Classic Theory of the Formal Verse Satire" (University of North Carolina, 1939) is an extraordinarily rich survey of satiric theory and practice from the Romans through the eighteenth century.

the frame is usually there, providing a semi-dramatic situation in which vice and folly may reasonably be dissected.

Here is the heart of the satire, and here the latitude of the satirist is almost boundless. His avowed purpose is to expose some aspect of human behavior which seems to him foolish or vicious, to demonstrate clinically that the behavior in question is ridiculous or wicked or repulsive, and to try to stimulate in his reader (or in Roman times, his listener) the appropriate negative response which prepares the way to positive action. Miss Randolph summarizes the means at his disposal:

"To illustrate his thesis, win his case, and move his audience to thought and perhaps to psychological action, the Satirist utilizes miniature dramas, sententious proverbs and quotable maxims, compressed beast fables (often reduced to animal metaphors), brief sermons, sharp debates, series of vignettes, swiftly sketched but painstakingly built up satiric 'characters' or portraits, figure-processions, little fictions and apologues, visions, apostrophes and invocations to abstractions—anything and everything to push his argument forward to its philosophical and psychological conclusions in much the same manner as events might push action forward to a dénouement in drama or fiction. In addition to these structural devices, an innumerable variety of purely rhetorical devices is employed to give point, compactness, speed, climax, contrast, surprise, and a score more of the special effects so necessary to good satire."[23]

The extraordinary diversity of materials and the prevailing casualness of tone create the impression of haphazard organization. But ideally all the materials—all the devices and forms, however diverse they may be—should contribute to the analytical process, to the principal business of dissecting one phase of man's irrational behavior so that he may learn by negative example (as Horace claims he learned from his father) and come to live by the positive precept. Satire, says Pope (as all satirists have said), "heals with morals what it hurts with wit." There is no evidence that the claim has ever mollified their victims.

The formal verse satire thus does have (most of the time) a discriminable structure. The demands of relevance bind the poem internally, as it were, while the frame binds it externally.

[23] "The Structural Design of the Formal Verse Satire," p. 373.

So, at least, one thinks, it ought to be; and then one remembers the satires which do not fit the formula. As in almost any generalization about this protean form, we must qualify away from the schematic toward the nebulous. To redress the balance which has been upset by the over-schematization of this outline, we should keep in mind Lejay's statement, written in a similar context: ". . . qui dit satire latine, dit mélange."[24]

The Romans had definite, if conflicting, ideas about what the social function of satire should be. The conflict is best pointed up by Horace; his fourth satire of the first book is a reaction against an established satirical tradition and is, as Hendrickson says, "a criticism of literary theory put concretely," rather than, as it is often interpreted, a justification of his own work.[25] In his poem Horace identifies the function of Lucilian satire with the function of Old Comedy; both profess to scourge the wicked (who are attacked by name) in the interests of social reform, and both employ an aggressive, cutting, censorious wit. Like Old Comedy, satire, in its accepted function, hurts; and just as Aristophanes was feared and hated in his day, so the satirist is looked upon with suspicion and fear in Horace's time. Horace rebels against this dominant tradition. His praise of the freedom with which writers of Old Comedy set their mark upon wicked men, and of Lucilius for following their method, is undermined by his attack on Lucilius' style and by his characterization of his own satiric practice. In his deft and insinuating way Horace attempts no less than to change the character of satire, to give it a milder, less crusading nature. He is not a prosecutor (the function assumed by Lucilius), he claims; he is not armed with a writ against wicked men (1, 4, 70); if he sets up examples of folly, his interest is primarily in using them to correct his own faults, as his father taught him to do (ll. 103 ff.); he does not like to give pain (ll. 78-80); and if he laughs at various forms of nonsense, that does not mean that he is motivated by a dark and cutting malice (ll. 91-94); he swears to keep such malice from his pages completely (ll. 101-03). His purpose, that is, is

[24] "Les origines de la satire latine," p. lix.
[25] "Horace, Serm. 1, 4," *AJP*, xxi (1900), p. 124.

to disavow the *character Lucilianus* and to win the public over to a new conception of the true nature of satire.

Horace's strictures on style in the same poem and elsewhere are in keeping with this purpose. He makes no claim to being a true poet himself; rather, he writes conversations (*sermones*). His lines are mere prose given metrical form; they lack the inspiration and nobility of utterance of those who deserve the title poet.[26] Satire should aim only to versify the language of everyday life; its proper medium, then, is the plain style (I, 4, 38-62). Implied here is perhaps another disavowal of the tradition of the Greek iambic poets, the writers of Old Comedy, and Lucilius; for according to ancient rhetorical theory invective and abuse are associated with the grand style, not with the plain style.[27] In Horace, abusive language is likely to be an occasion for laughter rather than attack, as in the contest in reviling between the two buffoons in the "Journey to Brundisium" (*Satires*, I, 5, 51-69).

In a later poem (*Satires*, I, 10) Horace writes again of style: the sharpness of Lucilius is admirable and so is the ability to make a hearer laugh, but in addition the satirist must achieve brevity and a style flexible enough to vary from grave to gay. Ridicule, he adds, is often more effective in resolving serious issues than is severity (ll. 3-15).

Horace returns to some of the same themes in his famous *apologia* for satire, the delightful conversation with Trebatius (*Satires*, II, 1), but with his point of view somewhat altered. He writes satire, he says, because he can't help it; and when Trebatius points out that his verses inspire fear and hatred, even among those who have not been attacked (ll. 21-23), Horace throws up his hands: "What am I to do?" Tastes vary, he says: some like to drink, some play the horses, he likes to compose verse. Pope's admirable paraphrase is sharper than Horace but makes the point: "Fools rush into my head, and so I write." The great example of Lucilius is his sanction. Satire is a weapon,

---

[26] The profession of poetic incapacity, undoubtedly ironic in part, becomes a convention of the satirist's *apologia*. It has its serious side in its insistence on the division of styles.

[27] See Fiske, *Lucilius and Horace*, pp. 114 ff.; Grant, *Ancient Rhetorical Theories of the Laughable*, pp. 133 ff.

true; but, says Horace, it is a defensive weapon—one that he will never draw without provocation. Once he is provoked, however, his enemy had best beware, lest his name be sung up and down the town (ll. 39-46).

Generous as Horace is to Lucilius in this poem, and altered as his attitude toward satire seems to be, he has still not reverted to the old notion of satire as an indiscriminate social scourge. His practice is even further from that tradition than his theory, for Horace's example is (with few exceptions) toward the urbane, toward gentle mockery and mild ridicule, and away from the scarifying wit of Lucilius and his Greek forebears. The discrepancy between the gentleness of Horace's example and the intimations of severity in his theory is a notable feature of much later satiric writing.

Three-quarters of a century later Persius reverts to a number of the same themes in his first satire. He, too, has a compulsion to speak out; indeed, the folly he sees about him is so grotesque that, given his wayward wit, he must have his laugh out (i, 8-12). The theme is cleverly dramatized later in the poem as his "secret"—that all the world has asses' ears—bursts uncontrollably from him (i, 120-21). Like Horace, Persius is warned by his interlocutor that the biting truths of satire inevitably make enemies and that if he continues to write, he will find his great friends growing cool (ll. 107-10).[28] Bitterly ironic, Persius first promises to whitewash everything, then, in a change of tone, appeals to the authority of his illustrious predecessors: Lucilius flayed the city; Horace administered his satire so skillfully that even his victim laughed and became a friend.[29] May I then not mutter one word? he asks. The poem ends with praise of the withering boldness with which writers of Old Comedy told the truth. Persius seems then to admire equally the deft Horatian touch and the more aggressively censorious tone of an earlier

[28] In general, I follow G. G. Ramsay's edition and translation (*Juvenal and Persius*, pp. 317-31), in which there is a separate interlocutor. Hendrickson, however, believes that the poem is a mimetic monologue in which Persius in his own words reflects the objections of hostile criticism or friendly advice. "The First Satire of Persius," *CP*, xxiii (1928), pp. 102-07.

[29] I follow Hendrickson's rendering of lines 116-17 here, rather than Ramsay's. "The First Satire of Persius," p. 98, n. 1.

time. By implication satire may properly avail itself of both methods.

Juvenal displays no such even-handedness. His most characteristic posture is that of the upright man who looks with horror on the corruptions of his time, his heart consumed with anger and frustration. Horatian satire seeks to displace the social mask by the flick of laughter; Juvenalian satire would cleanse a rotten society in the fire of its hate. Juvenal's allegiance thus is to a more "primitive" satiric mode than that of Horace—to a mode the spirit and tone of which go back, in some respects, to the bitter wrath of Archilochus.

Like Horace and Persius (and probably Lucilius before them), Juvenal writes an *apologia* for satire and deals with the themes which by his time have become conventional.[30] Why does he write satire? Because tragedy and epic are irrelevant to his age. Viciousness and corruption so dominate Roman life that for an honest man it is difficult *not* to write satire (1, 30). He looks about him and his heart burns dry with rage; never has vice been more triumphant. How can he be silent?—*facit indignatio versum* (1, 45-89). But, warns the interlocutor of the poem, the freedom of the old days is gone; he who would attack the vicious by name today risks being burned in the arena. It was not so in the time of Lucilius: when he raged against evil-doers, the victim, conscious of sin in his cold soul, would turn red and sweat with terror. Hence wrath and tears. The interlocutor's warning has effect, and in a curious anticlimax, after the tribute to the power of Lucilius, Juvenal asserts that he will write only of the dead (1, 150-71).

The themes are conventional, but the perfervid tone is new—or, from another point of view, perhaps it is very old—and the images force themselves to our attention: the satirist burns, roars, rages, flails as with a sword; the victim cowers, blushes, sweats. Ancient beliefs are dead, however, and for Juvenal and his age rhetoric (in respect to satire, at least) has replaced magic: a blush is not a fatal blister, nor is trembling followed by self-

---

[30] His first satire contains the *apologia*. For a study of the convention, see Lucius R. Shero, "The Satirist's *Apologia*," *Classical Studies*, Series No. II, University of Wisconsin Studies in Language and Literature, No. 15 (Madison, Wisconsin, 1922), pp. 148-67.

destruction. But the imagery preserves a subterranean connection between sophisticated Rome and a dark cultural past—a past in which the verses of Archilochus caused death and Aithirne (whose "existence" was later in chronological time than Juvenal, but much earlier in cultural time) brought terror and destruction to his victims.

Juvenal's declamatory manner, the amplification and luxuriance of his invective, his grandiose flights into the grand style—these carry him far beyond the prescriptive bounds of the form as established by Horace.[31] At the end of the scabrous Sixth Satire, Juvenal deliberately flaunts his innovation: in this poem, he says, satire has taken to itself the lofty tone of tragedy; it has gone beyond the limits established by his Roman predecessors; it is Sophoclean (vi, 634-37).

These self-conscious efforts to escape the limitations of the *sermo pedestris* have had strange and confusing effects in the subsequent history of verse satire, as through the ages first Horace and then Juvenal has been elevated as *the* exemplar of *true* satire. In the Renaissance, for example, such eminent authorities as the elder Scaliger and Justus Lipsius held that Juvenal was the greatest of all satirists and the proper model, while Daniel Heinsius was one of many who argued for Horace. As John Dryden indignantly pointed out, Heinsius' definition of satire, which insisted that the form was characterized by "a low, familiar way of speech," automatically excluded Juvenal from the category. "Is the fault of Horace to be made the virtue and standing rule of this poem?" asks Dryden.[32]

Dryden's wandering, derivative, but thoroughly fascinating "Essay on Satire" is built around the theoretical problems resulting from the conflicting practices of Horace and Juvenal. Meticulously, reluctantly, as if dreading the necessity for final decision, Dryden balances off merit against merit, defect against defect in the two great ancients.[33] The process of evaluation itself forces him into considering problems of genre. The ancient

---

[31] See Gilbert Highet, *Juvenal the Satirist* (Oxford, 1954), pp. 173-74 and note 11; Inez G. Scott, *The Grand Style in the Satires of Juvenal* (Smith College Classical Studies, No. 8), 1927, throughout.

[32] John Dryden, "Essay on Satire," p. 108.

[33] Persius, whom Dryden considers out of deference to the authority of Casaubon, does not, in his view, seriously challenge their preeminence.

laws of satire, he says, paraphrasing Heinsius, held that satire's affiliations were with comedy rather than tragedy, that it should laugh at vices, not declaim against them. Persius and Juvenal were aware of the "law," for they knew Horace; but they also knew Lucilius and preferred to follow him. " 'They changed satire' "—Dryden quotes Barten Holyday approvingly—" 'but they changed it for the better; for the business being to reform great vices, chastisement goes further than admonition . . .' " (p. 96). For Dryden, Horace's deliberate choice of the *sermo pedestris* as the style most appropriate to the form was a mistake—or at least, if it was a good choice for Horace, given the conditions under which he wrote, it was a choice which enabled Juvenal to surpass him. Let Horace walk afoot, "but let not them be accounted no poets, who choose to mount, and show their horsemanship." The "sublimity" of Juvenal, his "majestic way," makes necessarily for greater poetry than the "low familiar way" of Horace (p. 108).

Roman satire has two kinds, says Dryden: comical satire and tragical satire. The poets in question excel in their respective kinds, but one kind is, for moral and sociological reasons, greater than another. Horace was at a disadvantage, as satirist, in the times in which he lived; the relatively moderate character of Augustan Rome demanded urbanity and good manners of a poet, and Horace quite properly tuned his verse accordingly. Folly was his quarry. Juvenal, less fortunate than Horace as a man, was more fortunate as a satirist in that he lived in a time of appalling corruption—a time that cried out for high indignation, vigorous wit, lofty expression. To the pressures of his age Juvenal responded appropriately; instead of laughing at folly, he was, as Dryden says, "wholly employed in lashing vices." Against Horace, a court poet and a temporizer, Juvenal looms large as a "zealous vindicator of Roman liberty" (pp. 86, 90). His mode is inherently more noble than that of his predecessor, and he is consequently the greater satirical poet.

Not even the final evaluation, however, is without equivocation: in Dryden's view all three ancients deserve the wreath of victory. Juvenal's victory is the greatest, Horace's next, but just barely next, and then Persius'. Dryden unquestionably had powerful precedent for his method of comparison and evaluation;

but it may be that the tortuous progress of the essay, the reluctance to come to judgment, betray a consciousness on his part of the aesthetic problems attendant on his enterprise. In any event, John Dennis, writing twenty years or so after the publication of Dryden's essay, raises the methodological problem in its most cogent form. No just comparison is possible, he argues, "between Authors whose Works are not *ejusdem generis,* and . . . the Works of those two Satirists [Horace and Juvenal] are not *ejusdem generis.*" Dennis develops Dryden's distinction:

"*Horace,* who wrote as *Lucilius* had done before him, in Imitation of the old Comedy, endeavours to correct the Follies and Errors, and epidemick Vices of his Readers, which is the Business of Comedy. *Juvenal* attacks the pernicious outragious Passions and the abominable monstrous Crimes of several of his Contemporaries, or of those who liv'd in the Age before him, which is the Business of Tragedy, at least of imperfect Tragedy. *Horace* argues, insinuates, engages, rallies, smiles; *Juvenal* exclaims, apostrophizes, exaggerates, lashes, stabbs. There is in *Horace* almost every where an agreeable Mixture of good Sense, and of true Pleasantry, so that he has every where the principal Qualities of an excellent Comick Poet. And there is almost every where in *Juvenal,* Anger, Indignation, Rage, Disdain, and the violent Emotions and vehement Style of Tragedy."[34]

"Can there . . . be," Dennis asks, "A just Comparison made between these two Satirists, any more than there can be between a Tragick and a Comick Poet?" In the formulation of the question may be seen the problem which has plagued critics and historians of satire since Roman times: what *is* satire, if the two greatest satirists diverge so completely in theory and intent, in subject and style, as to be incommensurable? Answers generally take two forms. The first is that of Dennis: *true* Roman satire is "of the Comick kind" and was perfected by Horace; Juvenal's innovation—satire "of the Tragick kind"—was late and (presumably) inferior. The method works perfectly for critics who simply reverse his evaluation. The second popular answer has been that of critics who ignore the radical difference between the two

[34] John Dennis, "To Matthew Prior, Esq; upon the Roman Satirists," *Critical Works,* ed. Edward Niles Hooker (Baltimore, Maryland, 1943), II, 218-19.

writers, who pay lip-service to both as though Roman satire were one thing, and recommend the manner of the poet who is more congenial to them.[35] Satirists who follow Juvenal face the occupational hazard of seeing their works damned because they are not Horatian in tone; conversely, followers of Horace are just as likely to be accused of lacking high seriousness.

The contradictions built into the establishment of verse satire as a literary genre are of great historical interest; but the significant fact is that this kind of satire, as the result of the achievement of Horace and Juvenal, *did* become a literary form whose order and whose values were to be determined by reference to their practice. Quintilian's *satura tota nostra est* is accurate, and verse satire has a safe, if ambiguous, position within the hierarchy of literary kinds.

If we think back for a moment to the theme which has been of primary concern in this book so far, it would seem that by Quintilian's day satire has broken cleanly from its remote past. Its magical encumbrances have been cast off. Whatever "primitive" elements may have gone into its making have been thoroughly assimilated, and satire has entered upon an essentially literary mode of being. This is of course true and it would be folly to suggest otherwise. But it is a question whether assimilated materials of the kind we have discussed ever completely lose their original character. In any event, one or two historical threads linking developed satire with its magical background remain to be followed briefly.

Literary as Roman satire may be, it comes from and flourishes in a society in which magical beliefs were very widespread, despite the opposition of the state.[36] The Romans, like all other

---

[35] In some instances (e.g., in *l'Art Poétique* of Vauquelin de la Fresnaye) the differences in style and tone between the Roman satirists are not recognized and (in Vauquelin's case) Juvenal is made over into a second Horace. See J. A. Hild, "Quelques Observations à propos de Juvenal au XVIIe Siècle," in *Mélanges Boissier* (Paris, 1903), pp. 287-89.

[36] For discussion of these matters see W. Warde Fowler, *The Religious Experience of the Roman People* (London, 1911), Lectures II, III; H. J. Rose, *Primitive Culture in Italy*, throughout; Cyril Bailey, *Phases in the Religion of Ancient Rome* (Berkeley, California, 1932), Chap. I; Eugene Tavenner, *Studies in Magic from Latin Literature* (New York, 1916), Chap. I.

peoples, had their indigenous magic which thrived in the coun-
tryside and among the populace of the city, and they had as well
beliefs imported from Greece and from the East. Magic was a
powerful enough concomitant of Augustan life to attract the
interest of the most sophisticated poets. Horace, for example, in
the eighth Satire of the first book and again in Epode 5, describes in grisly detail the activities of the witch Canidia. In the
latter poem she is shown as about to bury a young boy up to his
neck in earth. Food will be placed just beyond his reach; he will
be left to starve so that from his marrow may be extracted a love-
philter which will instill a desire for the lover as strong as the
boy's desire for the food. All this is accompanied by rites so
standardized in magic lore that the witches of *Macbeth* could
have performed them perfectly. Horace's attitude toward such
matters is equivocal (although he indicates thorough skepticism
in Epode 17, for example, where he ridicules the activities of the
same Canidia), but there can be no doubt that the Roman
people believed in the efficacy of rites such as these. Virgil's
position is like that of Horace: in Eclogue 8 he winds an elaborate love-spell in the fashion of Theocritus and in the *Aeneid*
describes the magical rites of Dido in fine and knowledgeable
detail; but what he believed about magic we do not know.[37]

More imposing than the abundant literary evidence of the
hold of magic on men's minds is the unremitting effort of the
state to stamp out magical activities, some of which were illegal
from earliest times. The first Roman legal records of which we
know are the XII Tables, dating (so tradition has it, at least)
from the middle of the fifth century B.C.; they invoke the death
penalty for two specific practices: for using magical rites to en-
tice a neighbor's crops into one's own fields, and for chanting
an evil charm against an individual.[38] This latter prohibition is

[37] See J. F. D'Alton, "Horace and Popular Beliefs," *Horace and his Age*
(London, 1917), pp. 198-249; Cyril Bailey, "Magic, Omen, and Prophecy," *Religion in Virgil* (Oxford, 1935), pp. 5-28.

[38] For the restored text of the XII Tables, see *Fontes Iuris Romani
Antiqui*, ed. C. G. Bruns, 7th ed. (Tübingen, 1909); a translation by
J. H. Wigmore appears in *Sources of Ancient and Primitive Law*, ed.
Albert Kocourek and J. H. Wigmore (Boston, 1915), I, 465-68. A. S.
Diamond, *Primitive Law* (London, 1935), pp. 134-43, discusses the date
and authenticity of the Tables.

of particular interest to us and will be considered below. At various periods up to the time of Augustus it is recorded that magicians and astrologers were banished from Italy in fruitless efforts of the government to do away with that which can hardly be effectively prohibited. When Augustus himself ordered that all books having traffic in the occult be burned, 2,000 volumes went up in flame. Later, the laws against magic became much more stringent and great numbers of people were executed merely for believing in magic.[39]

All this is general enough and certainly not surprising; but in thinking about satire, one wonders whether any specific remnants of old beliefs in the malign efficacy of invective or ridicule survived. One wonders, for example, how literally the widely-known legend of Archilochus was regarded. G. L. Hendrickson has called attention to a passage in Cicero which bears on the problem.[40] In Book III of Cicero's *De natura deorum*, Cotta, the Academic, attacks the Stoic conception of the gods which has been propounded in the preceding book: "those who were injured by the iambics of Hipponax [says Cotta] or wounded by the verses of Archilochus did not nurse a hurt visited upon them by supernatural power, but rather one derived from themselves."[41] On this passage the editor of the *De natura deorum* has the following note: "Cicero has cut down his original so much as to obscure the force of his illustrations. Apparently the deaths of the offenders against Archilochus and Hipponax must have been attributed by some Stoic to the vengeance of the gods. Cotta argues that no external cause is needed; they are sufficiently explained by wounded feeling."[42]

The point is of course that Cicero saw nothing odd or anachronistic about discussing the supernatural powers attributed to the iambics of Archilochus; the subject was an appropriate one

---

[39] Tavenner, *Studies in Magic from Latin Literature*, pp. 12-17.

[40] "Archilochus and the Victims of his Iambics," *AJP*, XLVI (1925), p. 119.

[41] Hendrickson's translation of *De natura deorum*, III, 91. Cotta places the iambics of Archilochus and Hipponax in the context of the curses of mythology. See his comments, in the same passage, on the dying curse of Myrtilus.

[42] Joseph B. Mayor, ed., M. Tullii Ciceronis, *De natura deorum* (Cambridge, 1885), III, 189.

for intellectual consideration. Cotta, the rationalist, accepts the basic terms of the story—i.e., that Lycambes and his daughter died as a result of Archilochus' verses—as thoroughly as have the Stoics; they differ only in their analysis of cause. For the Stoics the cause is supernatural: the intervention of vengeful gods; for Cotta it is rational, scientific, "modern"—a psychosomatic cause, we would say.[43] "Whether the poets by such stories have led the Stoics astray," continues Cotta, speaking of the effect of curses, "or whether the Stoics have merely lent their sanction to the poets, it would be hard to say; in any case both are talking non-sense." It is clear that much such "nonsense" was talked in Cicero's time—talked and believed in.

As to the XII Tables mentioned above: Pliny the Elder reports (*Natural History*, xxviii, 4, 18) that of the two kinds of magic prohibited in the laws, one had to do with the chanting of evil charms (*malum carmen incantare*). The phrase is interesting and has given rise to considerable speculation among scholars because of the ambiguity of the word *carmen*, which of course means song or poem, but also incantation. In earliest usage *carmen* referred to a rhythmical concatenation of words employed to constrain supernatural powers. The XII Tables (insofar as we know them) record the beliefs of a society in a very early stage of development; there is little doubt that the law forbidding the singing of a *malum carmen* was in fact, as H. J. Rose says, "a prohibition of private, anti-social magic used for evil ends."[44]

Cicero makes an important reference to the same laws: ". . . our Twelve Tables," he writes, "though they provided the death penalty for only a few crimes, did provide it for any person who sang or composed a song which contained a slander or insult to anyone else" (*nostrae contra duodecim tabulae cum perpaucas res capite sanxissent, in his hanc quoque sanciendam putaverunt, si quis occentavisset sive carmen condidisset, quod infamiam*

[43] Plato hints at an equally modern explanation of the effects of sorcery and incantation. See *Laws*, Bk. xi, 933.

[44] For full discussion, see Paul Huvelin, "La Notion de l' 'Iniuria' dans le très ancien Droit Romain," *Mélanges Ch. Appleton* (Lyon and Paris, 1903), p. 404. Rose, *Primitive Culture in Italy*, p. 77.

faceret flagitiumve alteri).[45] Scholars are thoroughly divided on how to read this passage. The traditional interpretation is that the law had to do with slander or verbal injury, that it was the earliest of the Roman laws against libel. *Occentare* in this view referred to utterances which inflict ill repute or insult upon another; *carmen* was a song or poem; the phrase had no relation to magic. Others believe, however, that this interpretation fails to account for the extraordinary severity of the penalty attached to verbal injury. Over the past fifty years many scholars, following Huvelin, have held that the original sense of *occentare* had to do with a magical attack; that, like the *malum carmen*, it was an incantation.[46]

According to this interpretation a violent verbal assault on an individual by name, uttered by a man specially qualified by personality or position, would in the early culture of Rome have had malign efficacy. The elements of magic here are familiar: the insult, the direct statement of ill will, the rhythmical form of expression, the use of the name; and with these elements we are back once more in a world in which satire (in its extended sense) has magical power. Naevius, Rome's first epic poet (third century B.C.) was imprisoned (and later died in exile) for satirizing the powerful family of the Metelli by name. He may have been punished under the statute forbidding the *malum carmen*, but, if he was, the ambiguity of the phrase makes it impossible to know whether he was held to be guilty of simple defamation of character or of a more recondite offense.[47]

Huvelin speculates (p. 448) that personal attacks motivated by sheer ill will may long have been punished by death as mag-

---

[45] *De republica*, IV, x, 12, trans. Clinton Walker Keyes (London, 1948), p. 241.

[46] Huvelin summarizes a forty-five page discussion: "Les textes qui parlent des *carmina* et de l'*occentatio* des Douze Tables sont relatif, non à l'injure au sens moderne du mot, mais à certains rites de caractère magique destinés à nuire." "La notion de l' 'Iniuria,' " p. 448. Lejay agrees with Huvelin that Cicero misinterpreted the language of the XII Tables; see his edition of Horace, *Satires*, p. 286. Cf. R. E. Smith, "The Law of Libel at Rome," *CQ*, XLV (1951), pp. 169-70; G. L. Hendrickson, "Verbal Injury, Magic, or Erotic Comus?" *CP*, XX (1925), pp. 289 ff.; Eduard Fraenkel's review of Franz Beckmann, *Zauberei und Recht in Roms Frühzeit*, *Gnomon*, I (1925), pp. 194 ff.

[47] See H. J. Rose, A *Handbook of Latin Literature* (London, 1936), pp. 27-28.

ical, but that attacks motivated by a sense of justice may gradually have lost their religious (or magical) significance, and, as
the power of the state strengthened, have entered the realm of
law—or perhaps, one might add, of literature. These speculations
are attractive, but unproved. Any magical significance that *occentare* may once have conveyed unquestionably dropped out
in the course of time.

These matters are given particular point by a curious, and
amusing, play on words in Horace's *apologia* for satire, the
famous dialogue with the lawyer Trebatius (*Satires*, II, 1). Horace has come to Trebatius for advice about the dangers and the
legal complications attendant upon writing satire. Give up writing, as Trebatius would have him do, he cannot; and he must
write satire, rather than epic or panegyric. His pen is his sword,
which he will keep sheathed unless attacked. "But if one stir
me up ('Better not touch me!' I shout) he shall smart for it
and have his name sung up and down the town" (ll. 44-46).
The lines parallel closely the portion of a poem by Archilochus
reconstructed by Hendrickson: "What god pray, or in anger at
what, has kindled you [Lycambes] to stir up a creature garrulous like me, looking for nothing better than themes for his
iambics? You have seized in fact a cicada by the wing, which
shrills by nature and without occasion, and when touched shrills
the louder. What do you mean? Do you desire to become notorious at any cost?"[48] Horace's verses seem almost a compressed,
less aggressive version of Archilochus; it is surely not rash to think
that he had Archilochus in mind when he wrote them.

To go on with Horace's poem: Trebatius reverts to his warning. Beware, he says, lest "ignorance of our sacred laws bring
you into trouble. If a man write ill verses against another (*si
mala condiderit in quem quis carmina*), there is a right of action
and redress by law" (ll. 80-83). Horace agrees about the ill
verses, but asks what would happen if one composed good verses
(*bona* [*carmina*]) of which Caesar approved. Then all would
be well, says Trebatius gaily, and the poem ends.

The primary interest here is Horace's conscious play with the
ambiguity of the *mala-bona carmina* phrase. There is clearly a

[48] Hendrickson, "Archilochus and Catullus," *CP*, xx (1925), pp. 155-
57. See Chap. I, 1, above.

smile in his exploitation of the aesthetic sense of *mala-bona*; but beneath the smile, qualifying it strongly, is a serious implication. One cannot doubt that Horace deliberately uses the language of the XII Tables. The death penalty, he knew, was once exacted for *mala carmina*, which presumably he interpreted as slanderous attacks on individuals by name.[49] Even in his own time the poet who named his victim ran a grave risk and was always liable to be taken before the pretor.[50] Horace had real reason for anxiety. Was there awareness beneath this level of meaning of a magical implication to *mala carmina*? It is impossible to say. The earlier lines in which the poet seems deliberately to associate himself with Archilochus perhaps support such a possibility. Speaking now on quite inadequate evidence, I should not be surprised if in the mind of even the most sophisticated Roman poet there lingered an impression that a poetic assault on an individual by name was somehow related to magical injury. The question whether the satirist should attack his victims by name has been a lively one from the beginning to the present. It may well have originated in the magical context we have been discussing.

Belief in the power of name-magic was still widely prevalent in Horace's day, as the curse tablets, which rely for their efficacy on the manipulation of the name, indicate; and at least one extremely sophisticated Roman poet wrote a literary curse against

[49] Horace reverts to the matter in another context. In the first Epistle of the second Book he is describing the development of Roman drama from its rude beginnings in the Fescennine verses. These were abusive and ribald verses whose freedom, "welcomed each returning year, was innocently gay, till jest, now growing cruel, turned to open frenzy, and stalked amid the homes of honest folk, fearless in its threatening. Stung to the quick were they who were bitten by a tooth that drew blood; even those untouched felt concern for the common cause, and at last a law was carried with a penalty, forbidding the portrayal of any in abusive strain" (*quin etiam lex/poenaque lata, malo quae nollet carmine quemquam/describi*). *Epistles*, II, 1, 152-54, trans. Fairclough.

[50] Lejay in his ed. of Horace, *Satires*, p. 287. Juvenal had greater cause for caution; hence his elaborate disclaimer in the first Satire, in which he announces that he will write only of the dead. Highet (*Juvenal*, pp. 289-94) believes, however, that Juvenal attacked living contemporaries under metrically correspondent cover-names: Cluvienus for (possibly) Decianus in 1, 80, for example.

an individual which absolutely reeks of magical devices. In the bulk of his work Ovid seems to have little use for love-philters, sorcery, and the general hocus-pocus of magic, yet his poem *Ibis* might have been written by an adept, so fully does it draw on the great underground tradition of magical practice.[51]

The *Ibis* is a mighty blast made up of curses, invective, mal-ediction, imprecation, spelled out with tireless and pedantic in-genuity against an enemy whom Ovid refuses to name but calls Ibis (the ibis was a bird of spectacularly filthy habits; it was said to administer enemas to itself by means of its beak). The poem opens with an apology: this is the first time, says Ovid, that he has written injurious verse. The attack to follow can be justified only by the incredible perfidy of his enemy. Harsh as it is, how-ever, the attack is only a skirmish compared to what will ensue, for Ovid writes now in the elegiac measure, not in the measure in which warfare ought to be waged, i.e., the iambic. He will not strike now at his enemy's hated head, nor will he use his enemy's right name. The intention to omit the name is repeated several times.[52] If the Ibis persists in his ways, "my satire unre-strained shall hurl at thee missiles tinged by Lycambean blood" (ll. 53-54). There follows then for several hundred lines an erup-tion of the most grotesque curses, calling down upon Ibis every conceivable torture, these to be inflicted upon every joint, every bone, every sinew of the wretch. Invoking the aid of the high gods and the low to give efficacy to his verses, Ovid utilizes all the linguistic devices (except absolute unintelligibility) em-ployed by the professional maker of curses. At the end, after myth and literature have been ransacked for examples of evil fortune and painful demise, the original threat is reinforced: "Thou shalt read more anon, bearing thine own true name, and writ in a measure wherein bitter wars rightly should be waged" (ll. 643-44).

[51] See Hermann Fränkel, *Ovid: a Poet between Two Worlds* (Berke-ley, California, 1945), p. 203, note 27.

[52] *Ibis*, ll. 1-52, in *The Art of Love and other Poems*, trans. J. H. Mozley (London, 1929). Ovid's earlier *Tristia*, iv, 9, is also a threat against an enemy, presumably Ibis. Here Ovid characterizes himself as a bull whose horns (verses) are weapons of defence (cf. Archilochus and Horace), and threatens to use the enemy's right name. The repetition of the threat in *Ibis* is evidence that Ovid uses magical formulas primarily in a fictional way. See Fränkel's discussion, *Ovid*, pp. 245-46, notes 5 and 6.

Centuries later Ben Jonson drew the Ovidian themes into clear and direct relation with the conventional apology for satire. The Epilogue to *Poetaster* contains nearly every major element of the *apologia*: *Poetaster*, says Jonson, speaking in his own right, is an innocent and inoffensive response to a long series of unprovoked assaults, which have left him unmoved; it is intended to shame his attackers into better ways; it lashes vice but spares individuals and institutions; it is not mere railing but follows the tradition of Aristophanes, Persius, and Juvenal.[53] Nothing could be more conventional than this; each justification comes directly from the stock established by Horace and his followers. But interspersed between Jonson's claims to virtue are outbursts of the grossest intemperance, recalling themes of more ancient provenience. It is unnecessary to detail the garbage and excrement that Jonson flings at his enemies, even as he professes to be unmoved. But two passages are important. We are familiar with the one in which Jonson claims Archilochus' powers to "make the desperate lashers hang themselues," his threat to rhyme his enemies to death like Irish rats. Again, in a final salute to his detractors he addresses them as "these vile *Ibides*, these vncleane birds, / That make their mouthes their clysters. . . ." Jonson undoubtedly had Ovid's *Ibis* in mind here (Ovid, we recall, is a major character in *Poetaster*); and, like Ovid, Jonson claims to have tempered the power of his attack: "I vs'd no name." Without Ovid's poem in mind, the significance of this in context is equivocal; but when we know the background, the phrase inevitably pulls with it the magical meaning behind Ovid's use of the same words. Jonson, we cannot doubt, is consciously bringing the magical themes under the rubric of the formal *apologia* for satire.

But to return to Ovid: in the *Ibis* we find the full panoply of the magical tradition—a feigned exploitation of power as it resides in the form of words and in their content, in the character of man and the will of the gods, in the mystery of that great talisman, the true name. What precisely Ovid believed about these matters we do not know, any more than we know his actual motives in writing the poem. He is admittedly imitating a work (now lost) of the same name by Callimachus. Despite a scholi-

[53] *Jonson*, ed. Herford and Simpson, IV, 317-24.

ast's comment that Callimachus' invective brought about the death of his enemy, and that Ovid's intention is the same, we need not think that either poet actually believed in the power of his verses to effect harm. Ovid's poem is too literary for that.[54] It seems reasonable to assume with most scholars that he had an individual enemy in mind and that he chose this Hellenistic form as the one best fitted to give literary expression to his hatred. But "literary expression" hardly exhausts the question of intention or belief; and it is also reasonable to assume that anyone (even a poet like Ovid) steeped so thoroughly in magical lore will stand in a complex relation to his material. However literary his intentions, we can safely attribute to Ovid some ambivalence toward his magic.

The *Ibis*, to be sure, has nothing directly to do with the developed satire of Rome; its relations are most self-consciously with the broader sense of satire which has concerned us earlier. I cite the *Ibis*, not to suggest that Ovid thought he could wield the power of Archilochus, but to show how completely the tradition of the malign power of the word was available to him for his own purposes. Horace used the Archilochean threat freely, but, as with Ovid, we do not know what it "really" meant to him. On the public, conscious level he certainly did not intend the threats to be taken literally. If he was aware of the intimations of forbidden power in the *malum carmen* phrase, he was content to exploit them as a metaphor for poetry. The ancient reference remained obscure, a faint but persistent buzz of implication in the background.

The purpose of this chapter has been to trace briefly the establishment of verse satire as a literary genre with some attention to its sources, its structure, its function. This is what the Western world has agreed to call "true" satire; and although the word *satire* itself has expanded in meaning almost beyond recognition, usually at the bottom of the word, so to speak, is a

---

[54] See Hendrickson, "Archilochus and the Victims of his Iambics," *AJP*, XLVI (1925), pp. 110-12. This is not to say, as W. Sherwood Fox does, that Ovid was far above such "plebeian superstition" and that "the whole piece is a burlesque," a source of humor like Ernulphus' curse in *Tristram Shandy*. See "Cursing as a Fine Art," *Sewanee Review*, XXVII (1919), p. 475.

sense of reference to the urbane mockery of Horace or the lashing denunciation of Juvenal. What may lie behind *those* characteristics, it has been the intent of the earlier chapters to suggest. In such a sophisticated literary genre there is small place for the kinds of power wielded by an Archilochus or an Aithirne. When Horace or Juvenal hurls threats in Archilochean terms, we understand the threats in a special sense: language which was once believed capable of magically inflicting death, now kills in a metaphorical sense only. The age of myth-making was over. Still, for Roman poets and their audience, the myths were there, primarily as material for literature, it is true, but (in another dimension) living on in their memories, coloring their beliefs, affecting them in obscure and impalpable ways. Sophisticated as Roman satire is, it still retains a connection, enigmatic though it be, with its primitive past.

CHAPTER IV

THE SATIRIST SATIRIZED: STUDIES OF
THE GREAT MISANTHROPES

Upon this great foundation of misanthropy, though not in
Timon's manner, the whole building of my Travels is erected.
—JONATHAN SWIFT TO ALEXANDER POPE

1. THE RAILER

AT ONE of the most critical moments in the fortunes of the
Greeks on the windy plains before Troy, Homer introduces a
kind of buffoon—the lame, hump-backed, warped-headed Thersites. The Greeks are about to board their aging ships and to
abandon the siege. Agamemnon's trial of their steadfastness has
got out of hand; Ulysses has barely been able to persuade them
to return for a final council. The great debate opens, not, as one
might expect, with the measured oratory of one of the heroes,
but with the shrill scurrilities of the ugliest of all the Achaians.
One wonders how Thersites has stayed alive so long; the favorite
targets of his railing, Homer tells us, are Achilles and Ulysses;
and on this occasion his diatribe is aimed at his king, at Agamemnon himself. It is a puzzling scene, memorable because of
its incongruity. To be sure, Thersites gets as good as he has given;
although Agamemnon remains silent, Ulysses reviles Thersites
and threatens to strip and beat him and drive him away with
blows of shame. He lays the golden sceptre across Thersites'
back, raising a bloody welt. The Greeks roar with laughter at the
railer's discomfiture, at the tears which burst from his eyes.
Ulysses has never done a better thing, they say, than stopping
the tongue of this scurrilous rascal (*Iliad*, II, 211ff.).[1]

[1] An amusing coda to the episode is provided by Lucian. In A *True
Story*, II, the shade of Thersites sues the shade of Homer for libel, be-

Thersites is an archetypal figure, his characteristic lineaments appearing with remarkable regularity in Western heroic literature. In Norse legend, for example, the god Loki's role is that of slanderous troublemaker. The *Lokasenna*, a poem probably dating from the tenth century, shows him engaged in flytings with the gods as he attacks them one by one with foul-mouthed insinuation and insult. This episode in the tangled history of the god takes place after his outrageous behavior has caused him to be ejected from a feast; but because Othin is afraid that Loki may speak evil of them, the gods allow him to return to the banquet. Bragi even tries to bribe Loki to keep him from stirring up trouble. But Loki is ruthless:

> Bale and hatred I bring to the gods
> And their mead with venom I mix.

His vicious attacks on the banqueters, his accusations of adultery, incest, and cowardice (many of them justified, it must be said, by the history of those concerned) are delivered with such force that individually the gods seem helpless before him. Even Othin and Thor suffer the lash of his tongue, and although Thor threatens him with his hammer, nothing stops the flood of abuse. Gefjun speaks with a note of despair:

> Loki is famed for his mockery foul,
> And the dwellers in heaven he hates.

The hate pours out until "the slanderer of the AEsir" has said what he has to say. He then stalks away, unharmed, in an evil triumph.[2]

Old Irish saga has a Thersites-figure in Bricriu Poison-tongue, who is as venomous as Loki although somewhat less straightforward. Bricriu invites the heroes of Ulster to attend a banquet, but Fergus and the other nobles refuse: "No; for if we go our dead will outnumber our living, when Bricriu has incensed us against each other."[3] But when Bricriu threatens to stir up strife

---

cause Homer had ridiculed him. With Ulysses as counsel, Homer wins. *Lucian,* trans. Harmon, i, 325.

[2] *Lokasenna* in *The Poetic Edda,* trans. Henry Adams Bellows (New York, 1923), pp. 151-73.

[3] *The Feast of Bricriu,* trans. George Henderson (Irish Texts Society, 1899), p. 5; Cross and Slover, *Ancient Irish Tales,* p. 255.

between kings and heroes, between mothers and daughters, and among all the women of Ulster, the nobles yield and the banquet is held. Bricriu is driven out of his own feast by men with drawn swords; nevertheless, his tongue does remarkable damage: the heroes are set to fighting each other, and their ladies egged on to compete for precedence of place. The latter contest (in a magnificently comic scene) turns into a surreptitious foot race to see which lady can enter the palace first. It nearly ends disastrously. "The amount of confusion then occasioned by the competition to enter the hall first was as it were the noise of fifty chariots approaching. The whole palace shook and the warriors sprang to their arms and made essay to kill one another within."[4] But Sencha realizes that it is Bricriu Poison-tongue who is responsible for the melée, and peace is restored. On a later occasion Bricriu, like Thersites, taunted once too often. A jibe so angered Fergus, who had been playing chess, that he struck Bricriu Poison-tongue in the head with the five chessmen he had been holding in his hand. The blow was powerful enough to sink the chessmen deep into Bricriu's skull. This, says the story, was a lasting hurt to him.[5]

Bricriu has been linked not only with Thersites, but with Conan (a crop-eared, spiteful railer of the Ossianic cycle, the object of both fear and ridicule) and with Sir Kaye of the Arthurian romances (the "shamefullyst knyght of your tunge that now ys lyvynge," according to Sir Trystramys).[6] It is possible that Unferth (his name means mar-peace) who "unbinds a battle-rune" against Beowulf in the Anglo-Saxon epic may also belong to the type. And then one thinks, in a different context, of the malcontents of Elizabethan drama—superb railers, many

[4] *The Feast of Bricriu*, p. 21; Cross and Slover, p. 260.

[5] "The Adventures of Nera," trans. Kuno Meyer, *RC*, x (1899), p. 227; Cross and Slover, p. 253. As for Thersites' death: according to the *Aethiopis*, Thersites mocked at Achilles' remorse for having slain the Amazon, Penthesilea. Achilles, stung beyond bearing, killed the railer.

[6] George Henderson, Introduction, *The Feast of Bricriu*, p. xi. Dorothy M. Hoare characterizes Bricriu as a railer *par excellence*, notes the relation with Thersites, and suggests that the railer may be "a stock character in heroic poetry, the delineation of which never alters." *The Works of Morris and of Yeats in Relation to Early Saga Literature* (Cambridge, 1937), pp. 19-20. The reference to Sir Kaye is from Sir Thomas Malory, *Works*, ed. Eugène Vinaver (Oxford, 1947), ii, 488.

of them—and of later characters who fit the pattern more or less precisely.

These are all literary representations of the Thersites figure. It seems, however, that the careers of various real persons have, by the assimilating powers of history, been made part of the stereotype. The historical man, that is to say, is mythologized into a type whose lineaments pre-exist and, as it were, await his coming. Some of Archilochus' legend lends itself to this kind of identification.[7] Actually, very little is known of his character and his career; evidence from the existing fragments of his poetry is conflicting and confused and, in any strict sense, highly unreliable. But the whole weight of ancient tradition from Pindar to the Church Fathers enforces the idea that Archilochus was a man in a perpetual rage, always ready "à blâmer, à médire et à mordre."[8] His career has been set in history by the type. Hipponax, who lived a century or so later, is made to fit the pattern even more perfectly. Like Thersites, he was physically misshapen, and like Thersites and Archilochus, his wrath was bitter and unrestrained: "Go quietly by the tomb, lest ye awake the malignant wasp that lies asleep; for only just has it been laid to rest, the spite of Hipponax that snarled even at his parents. Have a care then; for his verses, red from the fire, have power to hurt even in Hades."[9] From this point of view the accounts of the actual persons Archilochus and Hipponax are as "literary" as the story of Loki.[10] The figure of the railer, however, gains depth and resonance from its assimilation of historical figures, particularly when to their poetry has been attributed the malign efficacy of which we know.

One wonders whether an obscure association of magic with

[7] The legend of Archilochus incorporates conflicting elements. One image of him is that of the railer; but another has him as a favorite of the gods, an archaic poet-priest whose words are divinely inspired and magically potent.

[8] Amédée Hauvette, *Archiloque* (Paris, 1905), p. 201.

[9] Sepulchral epigram of Leonidas, *Greek Anthology*, Bk. VII, 408, trans. Paton, II, 221.

[10] A comparable development occurs in the story of the Cynic philosopher Diogenes, who, according to Plutarch, tells Alexander to stand out of the sun. In later elaborations (e.g., John Lyly's *Campaspe* [1584]) Diogenes becomes a licensed critic of kings and quite of a kind with the railers of literature.

railing and invective may help to account for the frequency with which the railer-figure appears in literature. Under certain circumstances, clearly, abuse can be harmful indeed; but in other licensed situations, as we saw in the discussion of ridicule, it brings good luck; that is, it is good luck to be abused and mocked and cursed. The Thonga kings of Africa keep (or kept) a "public vituperator," a licensed court jester "who may hurl the most offensive insults at anyone in the country, from the king down. He may wantonly accuse his countrymen of incest and snatch food from the hands of the king himself."[11] Not many years ago in the neighborhood of Berlin if you wished a hunter to have good luck, instead of saying so, you would tell him that you hoped he would break his neck, or both his neck and his legs. The wish was expressed, as Frazer says, with pregnant brevity in the phrase, "Now then, neck and leg!"[12] We see an aspect of the notion today among people who dislike being wished good luck—actors, for example, who resent being wished well before a performance. Somehow, the idea is, this is tempting fate. But there is much evidence of the positive luck in curses. According to Frazer, brothers and sisters in certain parts of India abuse each other fulsomely on a given holiday in the belief that their lives will be prolonged thereby and their fortunes improved. Esthonian fishermen believe that the best thing that can happen to them is to have someone so angry that he will curse them; each curse will bring at least three fish into the net. Various other peoples take elaborate pains to get themselves soundly cursed in the interests of good fortune. In short, it is lucky in certain circumstances to have a railer around. This belief may help explain the prevalence of the literary type and the fact that his abuse provokes relatively little resentment in proportion to its offensiveness.

Other more or less obscure explanations of the popularity of the figure seem possible. Railing and invective were important, as we have seen, in the Phallic Songs of ancient Greece. In his edition of Pausanias, Frazer cites a number of fertility rituals from Greece and elsewhere in which abuse and vituperation are

[11] Robert H. Lowie, *Primitive Society* (New York, 1920), p. 373.
[12] *The Golden Bough*, Vol. 1: *The Magic Art*, 1, 278-82. Cf. J. H. Mozley, "On Cursing in Ancient Times," Appendix to his trans. of Ovid, *Art of Love*, p. 362.

an essential part of the rite; he confesses to being puzzled at the connection between abuse and fertility, although he is sure there is one.[13] But Cornford and others have hit upon the explanation: railing has an apotropaic function; it drives away evil. He who rails, then (in the appropriate circumstances), will be cherished. On the other hand, railing and ridicule and invective can be dangerous and he who uses them may have to be punished, perhaps ritually punished in such a way that he will bear on his own shoulders the bad luck of the group. In effect, the railer who drives away evil may at the same time be made to take upon himself the accumulated evil of his people. He may be singled out as a *pharmakos*, a scapegoat, and be ceremonially beaten and exiled, if not slain. This is precisely the threat that in the *Iliad* Ulysses makes to Thersites. On the basis of this circumstance and the physical description of Thersites (so characteristic of the *pharmakos*-type), some scholars have identified Thersites as a scapegoat figure.[14]

Such identifications can only be conjectural and to push them further is risky. But it is interesting to speculate on the degree to which the scapegoat theme may be attached to the archetype we have been considering. Probably the best approach to the matter is by way of a firm if partial identification of the railer with the fool. Thersites fits well into the tradition of dwarf fools of antiquity and later, and in some respects Loki and Bricriu and others of their kind in heroic literature have fool-like characteristics. For example, it has been suggested that the function of the sharp-tongued Unferth at King Hrothgar's court in *Beowulf* may have been something like that of the later court fool.[15] But the figure of the malcontent in Elizabethan drama provides the clearest tie.[16] The malcontent has many character-

[13] *Pausanias's Description of Greece* (London, 1898), II, 492; III, 266-68.

[14] Hermann Usener, *Kleine Schriften* (Leipzig, 1913), IV, 239 ff.; Gilbert Murray, *Rise of the Greek Epic* (Oxford, 1907), pp. 185-87.

[15] Joseph Bosworth, *An Anglo-Saxon Dictionary*, ed. T. Northcote Toller (Oxford, 1882): see "þyle"; Blanche Colton Williams in her ed. of *Gnomic Poetry in Anglo-Saxon* (New York, 1914), p. 78, n. See Miss Welsford's discussion, *The Fool*, pp. 84-88.

[16] For discussions of the malcontent, see Elmer Edgar Stoll, "Shakspere, Marston, and the Malcontent Type," *MP*, III (1905-06), pp. 281-303; Oscar James Campbell, "Jaques," *Huntington Library Bulletin*, VIII

istics of the fool and at the same time is the very type of the railer. "Come down," says Pietro to Malevole in Marston's *The Malcontent*, "Come down, thou rugged cur, and snarl here; I give thy dogged sullenness free liberty: trot about and bespurtle whom thou pleasest"; and Malevole, whose highest pleasure "is to procure others vexation," trots about obediently, stirring up trouble wherever possible. "Discord to malcontents is very manna," he snarls.[17] Bricriu Poison-tongue could say no better. Yet with all his savagery of utterance and notwithstanding his major role in the plot, Malevole has scenes in which his japery and extravagant witticisms are indistinguishable from those of Passarello, the true fool of the play (I, iii; III, i, etc.). Further, Malevole is a feigned malcontent; he is putting on the role, and so is extraordinarily careful to get it right.

Unquestionably the greatest master of scurrilous abuse among characters of this type is Shakespeare's Thersites in *Troilus and Cressida*. To one who knows his genius, Thersites' threat to Ajax is appalling: "If thou use to beat me, I will begin at thy heel and tell what thou art by inches, thou thing of no bowels, thou!" A good example of Thersites' eloquence is his exchange with Patroclus:

THER. Thou art thought to be Achilles' male varlet.

PATR. Male varlet, you rogue? What's that?

THER. Why, his masculine whore. Now the rotten diseases of the South, the guts-griping, ruptures, catarrhs, loads o' gravel i' th' back, lethargies, cold palsies, raw eyes, dirt-rotten livers, whissing lungs, bladders full of imposthume, sciaticas, lime-kilns i' th' palm, incurable boneache, and the rivelled fee simple of the tetter, take and take again such preposterous discoveries!

PATR. Why, thou damnable box of envy, thou, what means't thou to curse thus?

THER. Do I curse thee?

PATR. Why, no, thou ruinous butt! You whoreson indistinguish-able cur, no!

(1935), pp. 71-102. In this chapter and elsewhere I have benefited from Professor Campbell's *Comicall Satyre.*

[17] I, i. All quotations from Marston are from the edition of his *Works* by A. H. Bullen, 3 vol. (London, 1887).

THER. No? Why art thou then exasperate, thou idle immaterial skein of sleave silk, thou green sarcenet flap for a sore eye, thou tassel of a prodigal's purse, thou? Ah, how the poor world is pest'red with such waterflies—diminutives of nature! (v, i, 17-39)

Thersites' hideously nimble tongue inevitably gets him into trouble: Ajax beats him and he faces threats of greater violence. Still, when Patroclus appears ready to lose his temper completely under the sting of Thersites' jibes, Achilles breaks in with a warning: "He is a privileg'd man" (II, iii, 61). Throughout the play Thersites is called on as messenger and go-between, he quite consciously plays the fool at the end, and he is repeatedly addressed directly as "fool" (II, i) or spoken of in the third person as "the fool" ("I'll send the fool to Ajax . . ." [III, iii, 235], or "Achilles hath inveigled his fool [Thersites] from him" [II, iii, 100]).

The fool's license in speech throughout history needs no discussion here. He has always had prerogative to say what other men dare not say. As Erasmus' Folly has it, what would be a hanging matter in the mouth of a wise man will bring delight if spoken by a fool.[18] Jaques (a thoroughgoing malcontent) puts it thus in *As You Like It*:

> . . . they that are most galled with my folly,
> They most must laugh. . . .

"There is no slander in an allowed fool," says Olivia to Malvolio, "though he do nothing but rail"; and railers like Marston's Malevole, Jonson's Carlo Buffone in *Every Man Out of His Humour*,[19] Thersites, and others share fully in the fool's privilege. A malcontent "is as free as air; he blows over every man," Pietro says of Malevole; and Malevole, speaking to the audience of his feigned role as malcontent, elaborates:

[18] Desiderius Erasmus, *The Praise of Folly*, trans. Hoyt H. Hudson (Princeton, N.J., 1941), p. 50.

[19] Jonson's characterization of Carlo Buffone is significant: "A *Publike, scurrilous, and prophane Iester; that* (more swift then Circe) *with absurd simile's will transforme any person into deformity. . . . His religion his rayling, and his discourse ribaldry*." Prefatory to *Every Man Out of His Humour*, in *Jonson*, ed. Herford and Simpson, III, 423-24.

> . . . this disguise doth yet afford me that
> Which kings do seldom hear, or great men use,—
> Free speech: and though my state's usurp'd,
> Yet this affected strain gives me a tongue
> As fetterless as is an emperor's.
> I may speak foolishly, ay, knavishly,
> Always carelessly, yet no one thinks it fashion
> To poise my breath. . . . (*Malcontent*, i, i)

But, like the fool, the railer must sometimes pay for his privilege.

Enid Welsford has a chapter in her fine book *The Fool* in which she attempts tentatively to trace the origins of that odd institution, the court-fool. Her complex argument (which might have been strengthened had she considered the role of Thersites) draws upon material from Egypt, India, China, ancient Rome, and much of Christian Europe, and concludes with something like the following: there is good reason to believe that in the great periodic ritual which called for the death and rebirth of the priest-king, a mock-king was eventually substituted for the actual king. In places, it seems, the role of the mock-king was taken by a *pharmakos*, a mocking, jeering buffoon—a fool, in fact—who had been ritually delegated to take upon himself the evils of the community and who would be slain in place of the king, or, in a modification of the original rite, would be beaten and driven from the village. This "festival-fool" is a ritual character, says Miss Welsford, and may be distinct from the fool "who blusters about the royal court." On the other hand, the two figures may have had a common origin in the "lucky-un-lucky creature [who] would be valuable as a permanent inmate of a household, and particularly in request as a safeguard for the King"—as a lightning rod to deflect the King's ill-luck on to himself, as it were.

"He would also be very much in request to ward off the Evil Eye from the priests who were performing important ritual acts by parodying their rites and ridiculing their sacred persons. But here he would be on very dangerous ground. He might have to do this as a duty and yet have to be punished for his irreverence, or again, if the central rite was the solemn slaying of the King himself, he might prove a very convenient substitute. At this point he would be drawn into the ritual and so become the type of scapegoat who was periodically excommunicated or put to death. Some such evolution would explain the anomalous position of the festival fool, who is so essentially a being apart from his fellows, detached from his surroundings, and yet bears unmistakable traces of ancient sacrificial rites, and appears at times as the central figure of festival performances. If this hypothesis is true, the court-fool and the festival-fool are quite distinct from one another, but both originate in the notion that a grotesque fool can be used as an abusive scapegoat, a kind of living mascot." (p. 74)

Against this background it is plausible to suggest that the railer figure we have been considering may be thought of as constituting a species of the genus *fool*. "Twenty to one this fool's some satirist," says the interlocutor in one of the poems of *Micro-cynicon*, and one is inclined to agree with the odds.[20] The railer is not a half-wit, he does not wear cap and bells, he need not be physically deformed (although I should think that Thersites makes a bridge here), but he is a kind of fool, nevertheless. His special license and his special function may in part be accounted for by an early (hypothetical) association with our most ancient life-giving rituals, wherein he was called upon as a magical protector against evil forces, but might also be rejected as a loathsome sacrifice.[21]

This hypothesis may help to account for the peculiarly ambivalent attitudes toward the railers exhibited by other characters in the works in which they have their lives—an ambivalence perhaps experienced by us as readers. It may help to explain, for example, the complexity of our response to Jimmy Porter in John Osborne's recent *Look Back in Anger* (and, in the play, the response of Alison and Helena). To be sure, intemperate abuse is often mere verbal fireworks, material for humor. "Good Thersites, come in and rail," says Patroclus (*Troilus and Cressida*, II, iii, 26); and Thersites obliges, to our reluctant delight.

[20] T. M. *Gent.*, Satire VI, *Micro-cynicon: Sixe Snarling Satyres* (1599) in Thomas Middleton, *Works*, ed. A. H. Bullen (London, 1886), VIII, 134.
[21] Cf. C. L. Barber's treatment of Falstaff as a scapegoat figure, "From Ritual to Comedy," *English Stage Comedy*, ed. W. K. Wimsatt, Jr., English Institute Essays, 1954 (New York, 1955), pp. 22-51.

But much railing is hardly of this character, and a possible comic effect seems inadequate motivation for the extraordinary interest shown in the railer by authors (anonymous or otherwise), characters, and audiences.

One other suggestion—equally conjectural and this time in psychological terms—toward accounting for the special characteristics of this figure. Perhaps in his many manifestations from Thersites on, the railer is privileged to abuse whom he will because he affords author and audience vicarious satisfaction as he attacks figures of authority. Momentarily, perhaps unconsciously, we identify with him and so gain release of frustrated aggressive feelings with which we are charged. The demands of reality see to it that the railer is sometimes punished, but basically he is quite unrealistically privileged in legend and literature because he represents our own (and presumably the author's) suppressed aggressive impulses. An Ashanti tribesman hurls invective at his friend in the presence of the real target, the chief; and the Ashanti's soul is cooled thereby. We read of Thersites inveighing scornfully against Agamemnon and in an odd way (for, Thersites *is* despicable) our souls are cooled too. It is rare that one has a chance to strike out at the Agamemnons (to say nothing of the Ulysseses and the Ajaxes) of the world. Thersites must be our proxy.

Homer's treatment of the Thersites scene entails a significant complication. Hauvette describes it thus: "Thersites serves a double function: popular orator and indefatigable railer, he represents well in Homeric society the spirit of satire and of vilification which will animate iambic poetry; and, on the other hand, described by Homer as an odious and ridiculous character, he is made the object of a most felicitous satirical portrait."[22] The satirist satirized: here is precisely the theme that we discovered in the Irish tale, *The Great Visitation to Guaire*. And, as we shall see, it is a powerful theme in the three works to be discussed in the remainder of this chapter: *Timon of Athens*, *Le Misanthrope*, and *Gulliver's Travels*.

[22] *Archiloque*, pp. 209-10.

2. TIMON OF ATHENS

The great misanthropes of literature—Timon, Alceste, Gulliver of the last voyage—are mighty railers at man, but it is a question whether they belong strictly to the type discussed in the previous section. The affiliations are obvious, the differences more difficult to specify. The misanthropes move in a different world from that of Thersites, Bricriu, and the rest, outside the peculiar ambiance of courts and heroes and ritualistic behavior. Their diatribes are likely to be directed at Man rather than at individual men, and they have no special license. Actually, there is no reason that a misanthrope, generally speaking, need rail at all. One of the first references to Timon of Athens—that of the hero of Phrynicus' comedy *The Misanthrope* (415 B.C.)—implies that Timon was silent: "I live like Timon. I have no wife, no servant, I am irritable and hard to get on with. I never laugh, I never talk, and my opinions are all my own."[1] But over the centuries, as the Timon story takes on its unique form, the convention develops that the misanthrope shall be frantically voluble in expressing his hatred of man. Whether he is a true "railer" or not, the fact is that he rails superbly.

Timon of Athens, Timon the Misanthrope, seems to have been an actual person who lived in the fifth century B.C. References to him in Greek Old and Middle Comedy establish that his singular fame rested on his reputation as a hater of man and the gods. As Plutarch says, the comedians "mocked him, calling him a vyper, and malicious man unto mankind, to shunne all other mens companies. . . ."[2] Plutarch's account of Timon in the life of Mark Antony is one of two classical sources chiefly responsible for the proliferation of the legend. It is brief, "factual," contains a number of essential elements of the story. According to Plutarch, Timon's misanthropy resulted from "the unthankefulnes of those he had done good unto, and whom he tooke to be his frendes. . . ." Timon would suffer only one companion, the "bolde and insolent" Alcibiades, whom he made much of because, as Timon said, "one day he shall do great mischiefe unto

[1] Cited in Ernest Hunter Wright, *The Authorship of Timon of Athens* (New York, 1910), p. 8.

[2] *Plutarch's Lives*, Englished by Sir Thomas North, Introd. George Wyndham, The Tudor Translations (London, 1896), VI, 73.

the Athenians." Plutarch tells two anecdotes involving Timon's bitter jokes and then says matter of factly that he died in the city of Hales (there is no mention of how he died) and was buried near the sea. He records two epitaphs, one allegedly written by the misanthrope himself, the other by the poet Callimachus. Elsewhere, in the life of Alcibiades, Plutarch elaborates the story of the relationship between Timon and the brilliant soldier (*Lives*, II, 107-08). In this account Alcibiades has just received new honor as the result of an eloquent oration. Timon, breaking his custom, went straight to Alcibiades, took him by the hand and said: "O, thou dost well my sonne, I can thee thancke, that thou goest on, and climest up still: for if ever thou be in authoritie, woe be unto those that followe thee, for they are utterly undone."

I go into this detail because Shakespeare, in his treatment of the Timon legend, used Plutarch freely. In just what way he used Lucian's *Timon, or the Misanthrope*, the second major source of the story, is not entirely clear. Lucian's dialogue did not exist in English in Shakespeare's lifetime, although there were Italian and French translations. Further, Lucian was certainly the source of an anonymous Elizabethan academic play, *Timon*, which probably antedates Shakespeare's version and which he may or may not have known. In any event, Shakespeare's *Timon* contains material that appears in Lucian but not in Plutarch, and material that appears in the anonymous *Timon* and in neither of the classical sources. It seems reasonable to suppose that Shakespeare knew Lucian's version of the story either directly or through an intermediate source.[3]

Lucian's dialogue, the earliest literary treatment of the Timon story we have, makes Timon a comic figure. To be sure, he is unmistakably the misanthrope; he rails at men and gods with remarkable abandon, but the violent diatribes are consistently undercut by Lucian's wit and by comments of other characters in the work. While we sympathize with Timon in his denunciations of the parasites who haunt him, we are never allowed to

[3] See E. K. Chambers, *William Shakespeare: A Study of Facts and Problems* (Oxford, 1930), I, 483-84; George Lyman Kittredge, ed., *The Complete Works of Shakespeare* (Boston, 1936), pp. 1045-46. All quotations from Shakespeare are from this edition.

identify with him completely. We see him always from the angle of vision given by comedy.

The dialogue opens with a long, mocking diatribe against Zeus uttered by the impoverished Timon, now so low in fortune that he is dressed in filthy skins and earns a living as a ditch-digger: You! he shouts, you who are supposed to be so powerful, where is your vaunted thunderbolt now? "You neither hear perjurers nor see wrong-doers; you are short-sighted and purblind to all that goes on and have grown as hard of hearing as a man in his dotage." When will you punish all the wickedness in the world? Come, you marvellous ruler, take my case: "After raising so many Athenians to high station and making them rich when they were wretchedly poor before and helping all who were in want, nay more, pouring out my wealth in floods to benefit my friends, now that I have become poor thereby I am no longer recognized or even looked at by the men who formerly cringed and kowtowed and hung upon my nod."[4] Timon's statement of his case elicits sympathy until we overhear Hermes, a voice of reason throughout the dialogue, explaining Timon's situation to Zeus: "Well, you might say that he was ruined by kind-hearted-ness and philanthropy and compassion on all those who were in want; but in reality it was senselessness and folly and lack of discrimination in regard to his friends. He did not perceive that he was showing kindness to ravens and wolves, and while so many birds of prey were tearing his liver, the unhappy man thought they were his friends. . . . But when they had thoroughly stripped his bones and gnawed them clean . . . they went away and left him like a dry tree with severed roots . . ." (p. 335). Nevertheless, Zeus remembers fondly Timon's former sacrifices to him and orders Hermes to escort Riches and Treasure down to the unfortunate man who is causing the commotion on earth. Timon greets them with snarls of rage: "I hate all alike, both gods and men. . . . I should be content if I could bring sorrow to the whole world, young and old. . . ."

"Don't say that, my friend," says Hermes reasonably, "they do not all deserve sorrow."

Timon threatens to break Riches' head with his pick, for he blames all his own misfortunes on him. But Riches rather plain-

4 *Lucian*, trans. Harmon, II, 327-31.

tively observes: "It is I who brought you everything that is de-lightful,—honour, precedence, civic crowns, and every form of luxury; and you were admired and puffed and courted, thanks to me. On the other hand, if you have suffered any cruel treat-ment at the hands of the toadies, I am not to blame; rather have I myself been wronged by you because you so basely put me at the mercy of scoundrels who praised you and bewitched you and intrigued against me in every way" (p. 369). Bowing to the power of the gods, Timon is finally constrained to accept Treas-ure. He digs and lo! there is gold. The discovery, which he wel-comes with comic alacrity, is the occasion for Timon's most ex-tended outburst of man-hatred. He resolves to "associate with no one, recognize no one and scorn everyone. Friends, guests, comrades and Altars of Mercy shall be matter for boundless mockery." His favorite name shall be the Misanthrope and the character traits he will cultivate are "testiness, acerbity, rudeness, wrathfulness and inhumanity. If I see anyone perishing in a fire and begging to have it put out, I am to put it out with pitch and oil; and if anyone is being swept off his feet by the river in winter and stretches out his hands, begging me to take hold, I am to push him in head-foremost . . ." (pp. 373-75).

It is an impressive paean to hatred. But even this cannot be taken very seriously, for Timon's manner of expression insulates the statement of hatred from connection with the real world. Framing the utterance is a rhetorical flourish of Timon's own devising: although he is quite alone he pretends to be addressing a body of lawmakers. "Be it resolved and enacted into law," he begins, "to be binding for the rest of my life, that I shall as-sociate with no one, recognize no one and scorn everyone." And after he has sworn to push drowning persons in deeper, the extraordinary outburst ends: "Moved by Timon, son of Echecra-tides, of Collytus; motion submitted to the assembly by the aforesaid Timon" (p. 375). The device is one of make-believe, removing the passage from the context of day-to-day reality. It requires us to discount the literal significance of what are, after all, appalling sentiments. Timon is not allowed to escape from the comic frame.

In the last scene of the dialogue Timon abandons railing in favor of swinging his pick and hurling stones at the swarm of parasites who gather at the whiff of gold. His one sustained speech (pp. 387-89) is not misanthropy but a deft satirical character of Thrasycles in the best Theophrastian manner. At the end our sympathies are with Timon as he drives off his tormenters.

This is excellent comedy; and, as so often in Lucian, it makes its point fairly explicitly. We are asked to recognize that wholesale prodigality is as foolish as extreme miserliness. (I have praise, says Riches "only for those who . . . observe moderation . . . neither holding hands off altogether nor throwing me away outright" [pp. 343-45]). We understand that generosity is admirable, but that Timon was a fool in his failure to discriminate between the worthy and the unworthy, between true friends and jackals. And finally, as Hermes puts it (p. 365), it is reasonable for Timon to hate those who have treated him horribly. But beyond this, the whole weight of the dialogue demonstrates that Timon's indiscriminate rage and hatred make for comical folly. The railer, like Thersites and like Senchán in the Irish tale, is mocked.

The point of view of Shakespeare's *Timon* is far less easy to stipulate. For every interpretation, a dozen counter-readings are possible and have been advanced; yet it, too, falls, I believe, roughly within the same pattern.[5]

The editors of the First Folio (the only source of our text) included *Timon of Athens* among the tragedies, probably as a last-minute substitution for *Troilus and Cressida*; and most critics have considered it as a tragedy. Professor Sisson's comment in his recent edition of *Timon* is characteristic. The play, he says, is a "powerful and tragic study of character." Shakespeare "made Timon himself a noble, generous idealist, whose misanthropy is one with his highmindedness, who, like Hamlet, is a true prince among men." Timon has been compared in various contexts to Lear, Othello, Macbeth, Coriolanus; his fall has been said to equal theirs in tragic grandeur. The most extreme presentation

[5] Professor Oscar J. Campbell has urged something like this interpretation of the play against the majority of critics. My reading differs from his, however, in a number of ways. See his *Shakespeare's Satire* (New York, 1943), pp. 168-97.

of this tragic Timon (and one of the most brilliant) is that of G. Wilson Knight, whose "prince-hearted, love-crucified" misanthrope is famous.[6]

These interpretations are based directly on the text of the play and particularly on the first scene or two. "In no play of Shakespeare is the opening more significant," says Mr. Knight, and unquestionably the early scenes are laced with eloquent testimony to Timon's noble (and potentially tragic) character. The Poet, the Painter, the Jeweller, the Merchant, the Lords, various followers—all ring changes on the same tune:

> The noblest mind he carries
> That ever govern'd man

says the First Lord (i, i, 291-92); and only Apemantus dissents.

If we put ourselves, as Mr. Knight and others seem to do, in Timon's position—see everything through his eyes, hear everything through his ears—we will then accept at face value every such speech and every such character. In this cloudless world exact correspondence will hold between word and concept; language will once again be performing its ancient creative function: what it states, by virtue of being stated, is. Here is no room for ambiguity, irony, misapprehension, doubt—to say nothing of deliberate deceit. In the world Timon creates for himself, as in the world of Gulliver's Houyhnhnms, to say the thing which is not is inconceivable. But unlike Timon, we cannot remain part of such a world, being uncomfortably aware of the perplexing possibilities in language and behavior. Unlike Mr. Knight, we are reluctant to accept the Poet, the Painter, the Jeweller, and the Merchant as pure representatives of art, wealth, and trade (as he puts it), as the symbols of progress, civilization, and happiness. We listen to their language and note its ambiguities; we are aware of discordant effects beneath the opulent surface of the dialogue. We hear Apemantus. Even without the evidence of later scenes, this should be enough to show us the falseness of Timon's court, a falseness by which Timon is tainted and to which he contributes.

[6] C. J. Sisson in his edition of Shakespeare, *Complete Works* (London, 1954), p. 910; Knight's interpretation is advanced at length in *The Wheel of Fire* (Oxford, 1930), pp. 227-62, although the quoted phrase comes from *The Shakespearian Tempest* (London, 1953), p. 206.

Our problem is to decide what, in the ways appropriate to literature, the play *Timon of Athens* means; this may be reduced, in effect, to the problem of identifying Timon: who is he? what is he? If Timon is indeed "prince-hearted, love-crucified," we will be forced to consider his self-exile, his man-hatred, his suicide (or willed death, or however one interprets it) as tragic, and to conceive the play in tragic terms. If, on the other hand, we think of Timon as a "naked gull," as one of the characters speaks of him, our conception will be quite different. The only evidence is language on the printed page: what the words say the characters say—and our uncertain sense that beyond, behind, between the interstices of words lies a truth: the truth of the play, which the language of the characters sometimes catches whole and pure, but sometimes obscures.

In criticizing a play we are hypothetically directing it; at least we are making a sketch for a production. Our interpretation will be the image of the production as we see it in our "mind's eye." Theoretically, we will see the production whole; our reading of any particular line will have behind it the weight of the entire five acts of the play. In this respect we are god-like in comparison to the characters: we know how things come out; they do not. Our interpretation of events in Act i will differ from theirs. Furthermore, as critics we have faith that a great dramatist will have made his play so that in the end will be the beginning; and in the beginning, the end.

It seems necessary to restate some of these platitudes because of the curious way critics have approached the opening scenes of *Timon*, as though those scenes had no connection with what comes later, as though a character in Act v is somehow discontinuous with the same character in Act i. In Act v, Scene i, the Poet and the Painter whose words had opened the play reappear, magnetically drawn to Timon's cave by the rumor that he is again "full of gold." They have a brief colloquy (overheard by Timon) in which they make totally explicit the shameless hypocrisy of their natures:

POET. Then this breaking of his has been but a try for his
  friends?
PAINT. Nothing else. You shall see him a palm in Athens again,

and flourish with the highest. Therefore 'tis not amiss we tender our loves to him in this suppos'd distress of his. It will show honestly in us. . . .

POET. What have you now to present unto him?

PAINT. Nothing at this time but my visitation. Only I will promise him an excellent piece.

POET. I must serve him so too. . . .

PAINT. Good as the best. Promising is the very air o' th' time. . . . To promise is most courtly and fashionable; performance is a kind of will or testament which argues a great sickness in his judgment that makes it. . . .

POET. I am thinking what I shall say I have provided for him. It must be a personating of himself; a satire against the softness of prosperity, with a discovery of the infinite flatteries that follow youth and opulency.

TIM. [aside] Must thou needs stand for a villain in thine own work? Wilt thou whip thine own faults in other men?

Now, unless Shakespeare has taken monstrous liberties with characterization, the essential elements of these cardboard characters should have appeared in the opening scene of the play.[7] They do in fact appear. There is no open confession of villainy. But consider the hints for a sensitive director in the first lines. The Poet and the Painter greet each other; the Poet asks if there is anything new in the world, anything not matched by "manifold record." "See," he cries, pointing to the Jeweller, the Merchant, the Mercer—to all, including himself and the Painter, who throng at Timon's door: "See,"

> Magic of bounty, all these spirits thy power
> Hath conjur'd to attend!

The implication is that bounty's magic is an old one whose conjuring power is well attested in manifold record. The tone is

---

[7] The deplorable state of the text raises problems. Most scholars today accept E. K. Chambers' hypothesis that the entire play is Shakespeare's but that it was left unfinished. This at least allows us to consider the play as one thing, even if flawed, and does away with the gambit which dismisses contradictory or awkward passages by reference to an assumed interpolation by an unknown hand. The Poet and Painter scene in Act v has been so dismissed; see, e.g., Kenneth Muir, "In Defence of Timon's Poet," *Essays in Criticism*, III (1953), pp. 120-21.

ironic. It is important in fixing the range of our attitudes toward
what follows. "I know the Merchant," continues the Poet, in-
tending perhaps simple identification but implying also that he
knows his character, sees his motives in dancing attendance. The
Merchant and the Jeweller exchange praise of Timon:

> A most incomparable man; breath'd, as it were,
> To an untirable and continuate goodness,

says the Merchant. "I have a jewel here—" responds his companion, firmly encompassing the praise with avidity of personal
gain. As early as line 15 the Poet introduces a theme to which he
continually reverts—that of hypocritical praising:

> 'When we for recompense have prais'd the vile,
> It stains the glory in that happy verse
> Which aptly sings the good.'

Later he speaks of "glib and slipp'ry creatures," the "glass-fac'd
flatterer," those who fill Timon's lobby with tendance,

> Rain sacrificial whisperings in his ear,
> Make sacred even his stirrup, and through him
> Drink the free air. (1, i, 81-83)

These are the hangers-on against whom he will warn Timon in
his poetic allegory of the hill of Fortune. The Poet's tactics are
among the oldest in the annals of rascality; he attacks in others
the vice he bears in himself. The passage already cited from Act
v, which hammers home this crucial point, is full commentary.

   Timon's entrance reveals him in his most characteristic stance:
distributing largesse, buying love, like Lear, at so much per talent. He rescues Ventidius from creditors:

> I am not of that feather to shake off
> My friend when he most needs me (1, i, 100-01)

—the tone of complacency jars. He endows his servant Lucilius
so that he may marry the daughter of a very thrifty Athenian:

> To build his fortune I will strain a little,
> For 'tis a bond in men.

He promises money to Poet, Painter, and Jeweller, and affably bears their commendation. The scene closes with a brief dialogue between two Lords, sometimes cited by critics as establishing beyond cavil Timon's essential nobility:

1. LORD.   Come, shall we in
And taste Lord Timon's bounty? He outgoes
The very heart of kindness.

2. LORD.   He pours it out. Plutus, the god of gold,
Is but his steward. No meed but he repays
Sevenfold above itself. No gift to him
But breeds the giver a return exceeding
All use of quittance.

1. LORD.   The noblest mind he carries
That ever govern'd man.

2. LORD.   Long may he live
In fortunes!

Unquestionably the words of the first Lord are a superb tribute; in a different context they would certify to Timon's towering virtues. But the second Lord's comments act so powerfully as a gloss on the simple attribution of virtue that the gloss assimilates the text. Throughout the first part of the play this grotesque metamorphosis operates consistently: nobility *becomes* the disgorgement of gold. The Lords who use the language of virtue so perversely are native to the world which flourishes around Timon; they are flat figures, have no characters, and because they are alone on the stage, they have no motive to flatter. Their tone is one of heightened adulation and wonder, like the tone of the Poet and the Painter as they praise extravagantly each other's works. Except for Apemantus, this is the only tone heard at Timon's court. Everyone talks alike. It is a disease, brought on by a superfluity of gold, and it is presented as a disease. No Jacobean audience could have missed the point: the deliberately trite hill of Fortune allegory of the Poet; the insistent emphasis on prodigality; the fawning and flattering and the reiterated hope that good fortune will last (the fortune-equals-money equation constantly present)—all this could presage nothing but disaster.

The one exception to the pervasive tone is important. Apemantus' corrosive words cut cleanly through the treacle of adulation to the rottenness beneath. This cynic, this "churlish

philosopher," is a perfect type of the railer-fool. He hates everyone, is "ever angry," as Timon says. His grotesque wit converts
all experience into ugliness—but reveals much truth thereby. His
license to rail is absolute:

TIMON.   Look who comes here.
              Will you be chid?
JEWELLER.   We'll bear, with your lordship.
MERCHANT.   He'll spare none. (i, i, 175-77)

Apemantus' railing is, in one sense, a performance, a kind of
game; various characters egg him on, feed him lines, to see the
clown perform (". . . here comes the fool with Apemantus. Let's
ha' some sport with 'em" [ii, ii, 47]); but, in another sense,
his railing peels off layer after layer of fraudulence, as it cuts
its way to the core of things. Outrageous as Apemantus is, bitter,
cynical, snarling, his view of the reality at Timon's court is
healthy by comparison with what prevails. Thou liest, he says
to the Poet, because "in thy last work . . . thou hast feign'd him
[Timon] a worthy fellow."

POET. That's not feign'd; he is so.
APEMANTUS. Yes, he is worthy of thee, and to pay thee for thy
   labour. He that loves to be flattered is worthy o' th' flatterer.
   (i, i, 228-33)

Apemantus has an eye for the thing itself and, like other malcontents who brood on degeneration, the moral bias of the
idealist manqué. Appalled at the ceremoniousness he sees about
him—a ceremoniousness divorced from the moral order which
might give it meaning—he bursts out:

That there should be small love amongst these sweet
      knaves,
And all this courtesy! The strain of man's bred out
Into baboon and monkey. (i, i, 258-60)

Even for him there had once been a true strain of man. But it is
easy to exaggerate: Apemantus can carry little moral authority;
his hatred is as general and indiscriminate as Timon's easy love,
and his chief function here is to set counter-currents working.
   The second scene continues and elaborates themes already es-

tablished. Timon's generosity reaches fabulous heights as he dispenses money, jewels, horses, and hospitality in boundless profusion. The more he gives, the more he is praised, although one may occasionally detect a faint note of irony (i, ii, 21). The munificence of Timon so far has been almost mechanical; that is, it has not been related to an inner life, but in this scene we see something more of what moves him. He refuses on principle Ventidius' offer to repay the recently-provided money:

> there's none
> Can truly say he gives, if he receives. (i, ii, 10)

In practice, Timon insists on maintaining the one-way flow of friendship. In theory, as he shows a few lines later, he is willing to entertain contradictory possibilities: "O you gods, think I, what need we have any friends if we should ne'er have need of 'em? . . . We are born to do benefits; and what better or properer can we call our own than the riches of our friends? O, what a precious comfort 'tis to have so many like brothers commanding one another's fortunes!" The sentiment in more austere circumstances would be noble; here, as must be apparent to the audience, it is fatuous. "Why, I have often wish'd myself poorer, that I might come nearer to you," cries Timon and weeps at the joy he envisions in such a possibility. "I promise you, my lord, you mov'd me much," says the third Lord. "Much!" says Apemantus.

In the course of the scene, Flavius, the faithful servant (who along with Apemantus recognizes the falseness of the friends [i, ii, 209-10]), indicates that the great flow of Timon's generosity comes out of an empty coffer. His master has been inaccessible to warning, is still ignorant that the fabulous estate has been dissipated in the "flow of riot" (ii, ii, 3). The irony of the munificence is sharpened:

> Methinks I could deal kingdoms to my friends
> And ne'er be weary,

cries Timon, emphasizing strongly his removal from reality; and warnings, ironic and direct, come thick but are unheeded.

Thus by the end of the first Act an image of Timon in prosperity has been firmly established. He is a man so victimized by the excess of a good quality, generosity, so blinded by his in-

discriminate love of all humanity, that he is incapable of seeing
the reality about him. His hallucinatory vision metamorphoses
flatterers into friends and sycophants into brothers. Material
wealth, in Timon's view, is inexhaustibly magical, the act of dis-
pensing it enough to convert evil into good. Timon plays god in
these scenes, but his love lacks humility, and his "worshipers"
basely serve their own ends.[8] The many references to Timon's
nobility must be discounted by our awareness of who utters them
and why, and Timon himself must seem more gullible than
heroic. The audience waits for the inevitable crash, and, knowing
it well-deserved, waits, I should think, without much sympathy
for the man whom Apemantus calls, at the best, an "honest
fool."

This, our earliest impression of Timon, is most important; but
it is qualified—or, more accurately, in the curious way of this
play, it is contradicted—by later evidence which tends to build
Timon's character in retrospect. In Act III, Scene ii, after Timon
has been denied by his friends, a Stranger, over-hearing, speaks:

> For mine own part,
> I never tasted Timon in my life,
> Nor came any of his bounties over me
> To mark me for his friend; yet I protest,
> For his right noble mind, illustrious virtue,
> And honourable carriage,
> Had his necessity made use of me,
> I would have put my wealth into donation. . . .

One might question why, if his admiration is sincere, he does
not proffer aid of his own accord; but then one understands that
the Stranger too has been tainted by the corruption of the times:

> I perceive,
> Men must learn now with pity to dispense;
> For policy sits above conscience.

[8] A Senator, one of Timon's creditors, professes to love and honor him
but makes his actual contempt explicit:
> Still in motion
> Of raging waste? It cannot hold; it will not.
> if I want gold, steal but a beggar's dog
> And give it Timon—why, the dog coins gold. (II, i, 3-6)

Timon's servants are remarkably steadfast: "Yet do our hearts wear Timon's livery" (IV, ii, 17); and Flavius, after his early irritation with his blind master, consistently gives him a good character:

> Poor honest lord, brought low by his own heart,
> Undone by goodness! (IV, ii, 37-38)

The special quality here is that of loyal, uncritical devotion, revealing rather more of Flavius than of Timon.[9] Finally, the last words of the play, Alcibiades' elegiac utterance, must be put into the balance; Alcibiades speaks of Timon's grave hard by the sea:

> . . . rich conceit
> Taught thee to make vast Neptune weep for aye
> On thy low grave, on faults forgiven. Dead
> Is noble Timon, of whose memory
> Hereafter more.

It is difficult to know what to make of Alcibiades. The Emperor Hadrian's remark in the fictional *Memoirs* by Marguerite Yourcenar is apt: "Alcibiades had seduced everyone and everything, even History herself. . . ."[10] Shakespeare's characterization may in part be an example. In Plutarch's *Life* Shakespeare found a portrait of a man dazzlingly brilliant but fatally unstable. Plutarch has high praise for Alcibiades' eloquence, his wit and courage, his talents in general; but he is consistently severe on Alcibiades' dishonesty, his licentiousness, his chameleon-like qualities: "the unconstancie of his life, and waywardnes of his nature and conditions."[11] Alcibiades is even spoken of as having been corrupted by money (II, 192). It is worth quoting again Plutarch's version of an encounter between Alcibiades and Timon. The misanthrope took the brilliant young orator by the

---

[9] The same quality appears in Laches, the servant of the anonymous Elizabethan *Timon* which Shakespeare may or may not have known. (There is no comparable character in Plutarch or Lucian.) In that play Timon is introduced as a monster of foolish pride, wallowing in adulation. When Laches remonstrates about his prodigality, Timon threatens to cut out his tongue and turns him out of doors. But Laches remains uncritically faithful. See *Timon*, ed. Rev. Alexander Dyce (London, for The Shakespeare Society, 1842).

[10] *Memoirs of Hadrian*, trans. Grace Frick (New York, 1955), p. 166.

[11] *Lives*, trans. North, II, 108.

hand and said: "O, thou dost well my sonne, I can thee thancke, that thou goest on, and climest up still: for if ever thou be in authoritie, woe be unto those that followe thee, for they are utterly undone." Plutarch continues: "When they had heard these wordes, those that stoode by fell a laughing: other reviled Timon, other againe marked well his wordes and thought of them many a time after . . ." (II, 108).

This is the portrait with which Shakespeare presumably worked. Clearly he altered it in important respects. At the end of the play, at least, Alcibiades seems closer to Fortinbras than to Plutarch's character. Still, he is a contradictory Fortinbras: noble and war-like, surely, and steadfast in defense of his friend, but extraordinarily bloodthirsty as his first words (beyond those of formal greeting) show. Timon has remarked: "You had rather be at a breakfast of enemies than a dinner of friends." Alcibiades answers: "So they were bleeding new, my lord, there's no meat like 'em" (I, ii, 78-81), thus partaking of the cannibal theme, the imagery of which is pervasive in the play. He is prompted to war against Athens by the unfeeling harshness of the corrupt Senators, yet is pleased to be able to strike at his native city in a cause he thinks worthy his spleen and fury. The most discreditable blot on Alcibiades, however, is that with no qualms he enjoys the company of two of Shakespeare's foulest women, the whores Phrynia and Timandra. "Thy lips rot off!" is Phrynia's first utterance; and after Timon has urged them (in a monstrous tirade) to "Be strong in whore" so that they will infect the entire race, the women raise their aprons at his bidding and call for more counsel with more gold: "Believe't that we'll do anything for gold" (IV, iii, 63-167). Alcibiades departs in their company for Athens, that "coward and lascivious town," he calls it (V, iv, 1), lashing in others the vice that consumes him. I may have pushed this dubious matter further than it warrants—nothing could be more statesmanlike, we must recognize, than Alcibiades' final speech—but the unresolved character of the man is puzzling, and it is a question whether we are justified in taking without reservation the "noble Timon" of his obituary.[12]

[12] J. C. Maxwell in his perceptive " 'Timon of Athens,' " *Scrutiny*, xv (1947-48), p. 206, n. 16, expresses puzzlement at the appearance of Phrynia and Timandra with Alcibiades. "I should be reluctant to regard

In any event, the Stranger, the servants, Flavius, and Alcibiades—all relatively disinterested witnesses—testify to the nobility of Timon's character. An odd feature of this evidence is that it comes late in the play, is strangely abstract compared to the concreteness of early impressions, and contradicts rather than modifies the image we have of Timon from the first Act. A general disposition for good in him we can recognize at that point, the disposition vitiated, however, by his lack of humility and the failure of his intelligence. As we observe Timon's acts, listen to his voice, and overhear those who smother him with flattery, it is impossible to think of this man, so willfully unaware of the evil to which he contributes, as truly noble.

Timon's abrupt plunge into misanthropy is psychologically and dramatically sound. He is a man of excess; from his cave he repeats the excesses of his court, substituting hate for love, but dealing out gold as lavishly as before. The most powerful commentary on his early imbalance is the extreme to which his disillusionment brings him. Dr. Johnson speaks of Timon's "malignant dignity" as he utters his hatred. He has that quality, but not consistently. After the transition scene of the mock banquet comes the first great rolling curse, an invocation of the anarchy against which the willed order of Ulysses' speech in *Troilus* is arrayed:

> Matrons, turn incontinent!
> Obedience fail in children! Slaves and fools,
> Pluck the grave wrinkled Senate from the bench
> And minister in their steads! To general filths
> Convert o' th' instant, green virginity!
> Do't in your parents' eyes! Bankrupts, hold fast!
> Rather than render back, out with your knives
> And cut your trusters' throats! Bound servants, steal!
> Large-handed robbers your grave masters are
> And pill by law. Maid, to thy master's bed!
> Thy mistress is o' th' brothel. Son of sixteen,
> Pluck the lin'd crutch from thy old limping sire;
> With it beat out his brains! Piety and fear,

---

it as intended to indicate that the claims of Alcibiades . . . to regenerate Athens are to be taken cynically." See also the Introduction to his ed. of *Timon* (Cambridge, 1957). I have profited from both essays.

Religion to the gods, peace, justice, truth,
Domestic awe, night-rest and neighborhood,
Instruction, manners, mysteries and trades,
Degrees, observances, customs and laws,
Decline to your confounding contraries
And let confusion live! (IV, i, 3-21)

The long list of imperatives ends, almost as an afterthought, with an invocation to the gods—"you good gods all"—to confound the Athenians and allow Timon's hate to grow.

There is dignity here, if only in the grandeur of the demonic conception and in the attempted resuscitation of atavistic powers. Curse follows on curse as Timon fixes the range of his misanthropy; his hate is as all-embracing and indiscriminate as was his love:

All's obliquy;
There's nothing level in our cursed natures
But direct villainy. Therefore be abhorr'd
All feasts, societies, and throngs of men!
His semblable, yea, himself, Timon disdains.
Destruction fang mankind! (IV, iii, 18-23)

A procession of visitors to his cave feeds his rage. Alcibiades is exhorted to universal slaughter in Athens: Spare not old age, mothers, virgins, Timon urges; the dimpled babe: "mince it sans remorse." The soldier is then cursed himself. The harlots are dipped in the most spectacular horrors of their trade in language brutal beyond belief; but they emerge untouched, their sensibilities assuaged by gold. Apemantus, the bandits, Flavius, the Senators—all are subjected to a flood of vituperation that must finally seem mad in its excess. But by the end the dignity has gone and Timon is an object of derision.

The crucial scene is that between him and Apemantus, between the new misanthrope and the old railer, who seems jealous of his prerogative. Apemantus' insight into Timon's condition is as sharp after the fall from prosperity as it has been before:

Men report
Thou dost affect my manners and dost use them

. . . .

This is in thee a nature but infected,
A poor unmanly melancholy sprung
From change of fortune. (IV, iii, 198-204)

(Earlier, Alcibiades had explained to "sweet Timandra" that Timon's wits are drowned; later the first Bandit reports that "The mere want of gold and the falling-from of his friends drove him into this melancholy" [IV, iii, 401-03].) "Shame not these woods," says Apemantus, "By putting on the cunning of a carper." My willing misery, he argues, brings more content and is more worthy than your enforced misery. Timon debates with Apemantus the question of which one has the best title to hate men: he who had the world as his confectionary, or he who was born a rogue. For a moment Apemantus seems softened by the power of Timon's claims; he offers him food. But Timon will not soften reciprocally—he will no more accept food now than earlier he would accept repayment of money—and he wishes for poison to sauce his fellow's dishes.[13] Apemantus' comment is to the point: "The middle of humanity thou never knewest, but the extremity of both ends."

The dialectic of man-hatred continues, developing a curious self-congratulatory air. Apemantus would turn the world over to the beasts and would become one himself. Timon is at such ingenious pains to explain what a beastly ambition this is that Apemantus seems delighted: the pupil is surpassing the master. The mutual self-indulgence is unmistakable. But as Apemantus prepares to leave, the tone shifts significantly.

TIM. I had rather be a beggar's dog than Apemantus.
APEM. Thou art the cap of all the fools alive.
TIM. Would thou wert clean enough to spit upon!
APEM. A plague on thee! Thou art too bad to curse.
TIM. All villains that do stand by thee are pure.
APEM. There is no leprosy but what thou speak'st.
TIM. If I name thee.

[13] William Empson points to the reversal of roles here. In his first speech in the play, Apemantus has said he will not be gentle until Timon becomes a dog (the common Renaissance epithet for "cynic,") and the knaves honest. The knaves are "honest" only in that they have revealed their villainy; but Timon snarls like a cynic and Apemantus offers charity. See *The Structure of Complex Words* (London, 1951), pp. 177-78.

I'll beat thee—but I should infect my hands.
APEM. I would my tongue could rot them off!
TIM. Away, thou issue of a mangy dog!
    Choler does kill me that thou art alive;
    I swoond to see thee.
APEM.   Would thou wouldst burst!
TIM.   Away,
    Thou tedious rogue! I am sorry I shall lose
    A stone by thee. [*Throws a stone at him.*]
APEM.   Beast!
TIM.   Slave!
APEM.   Toad!
TIM.   Rogue, rogue, rogue!

The form, the content, the tone of this are familiar. It is a
conventional wit-combat in invective, much like that described
by Horace in the "Journey to Brundisium": the contest in scurrility between Sarmentus and Messius at which Horace and
Maecenas and Virgil laughed.[14] The rapid tempo, the give and
take of abusive epithet, the element of contest as one tries to
outdo the other, the total lack of dignity—these are characteristics of stichomythia, of a flyting, a performance. The participants are for the moment buffoons, *scurrae*; they would not be
greatly out of their element in a drum-match among the Eskimos. After the grandiose intemperance of language in this Act,
the final inarticulate sputters ("Beast!" "Slave!" "Toad!"
"Rogue, rogue, rogue!") and the throwing of the stone can
only be grotesquely comic. The scene is past rage and into the
ridiculous. There is a clear sense in which Apemantus' characterization of Timon, "A madman so long, now a fool," is precise.

The episode colors indelibly the rest of the play; for, while
the lost dignity is reasserted, the curses sound a different tone.
What moral authority Timon brought into misanthropy he has
forfeited by making himself an object of ridicule. Still, he main-
tains his bitter course to the end. Although he can ask forgive-
ness for his "general and exceptless rashness" and recognize
that one honest man ("Mistake me not—but one!") exists, his
advice to Flavius is of a piece with his rigidly undiscriminating
temper:

[14] *Satires*, 1, 5, ll. 51-69.

> Hate all, curse all, show charity to none,
> But let the famish'd flesh slide from the bone
> Ere thou relieve the beggar. (IV, iii, 534-36)

Lear's disillusionment brings insight: "They told me I was everything. 'Tis a lie—I am not ague-proof" (IV, vi, 107). Timon's does not; he is incapable of breaking out of the circle of hatred he has drawn about himself. There are flashes of self-recognition, as when he says he is worthy only of the venal Senators who come for his aid, and they worthy of him (almost the words of Apemantus in I, i, when he said that Timon was worthy of the flatterer, and the flatterer of him). But his last utterance issues from passionate pride:

> Sun, hide thy beams! Timon hath done his reign.
> (V, i, 226)

Mr. J. C. Maxwell speaks of the "intangible and mysterious consummation" which is Timon's end, and it is true that a new tone in his utterance leads one to think in lyrical terms: ". . . say to Athens," he tells the Senators,—

> Timon hath made his everlasting mansion
> Upon the beached verge of the salt flood,
> Who once a day with his embossed froth
> The turbulent surge shall cover. Thither come
> And let my gravestone be your oracle. (V, i, 217-222)

But the grandeur of the rhetoric belies the sentiment, and the consummation is flawed. The oracle is Timon's grotesque epitaph:

> Here lies a wretched corse, of wretched soul bereft.
> Seek not my name. A plague consume you wicked
>   caitiffs left!
> Here lie I, Timon, who alive all living men did hate.
> Pass by, and curse thy fill; but pass, and stay not
>   here thy gait.[15]

Timon's last words from out the nothingness he coveted are a snarl.

[15] Shakespeare here joins the contradictory epitaphs recorded in North's Plutarch: the one said to be by Timon himself, the other by Callimachus.

They are not, however, the last words about him. These, as we have seen, come from Alcibiades, who before the walls of Athens speaks of "noble Timon" and of "faults forgiven." Alcibiades' march on the city has been halted and his bloody purpose blunted by the arguments of certain Senators. Critics have neglected these arguments, mistakenly, I think, for they seem to me to constitute a choral commentary on the theme of the play. The Senators plead for the concreteness of individual moral responsibility as opposed to the abstraction of mass guilt. They ask for rational discrimination between those who deserve punishment and those who do not:

> We were not all unkind, nor all deserve
> The common stroke of war. (v, iv, 21-22)

(We recall Hermes in the *Timon* of 1500 years earlier: when the misanthrope wanted to bring sorrow to the whole world, Hermes quietly spoke, "Don't say that, my friend, they do not all deserve sorrow.") Some of the guilty have already paid, we learn; the Senators responsible for Alcibiades' banishment have died of shame—a remarkable touch! But, "All have not offended," argues a senator:

> Like a shepherd,
> Approach the fold and cull th' infected forth,
> But kill not all together.

The Senators plead, in short, for precisely the virtues that Timon lacked; for Timon was never, from beginning to end, able to discriminate between the healthy and the infected.

Whatever our misgivings about Alcibiades, he speaks at this moment as one aware of heroic responsibilities; he accedes to the Senators' plea: the guilty will be "set out" from the innocent, and only they shall fall.

> Bring me into your city,
> And I will use the olive, with my sword,
> Make war breed peace, make peace stint war, make each
> Prescribe to other, as each other's leech.

Alcibiades' tone helps create a sense of reasserted sanity. The money-madness which has corrupted Athens has been purged in

Timon's wild excesses. The fabric of Athenian society is being rewoven.

Although *Timon of Athens* ends in a manner appropriate to tragedy, Professor Campbell's denomination of it as a tragical satire is just; the play is entangled in the most complicated ways with problems of satirical theory and practice. A Jacobean audience, for example, would have associated both Timon and Apemantus with satirists; or, at least, they would have recognized in the misanthropic utterances a tone that had become conventional for satirists of the period. Renaissance usage having to do with satire was no more strict than our own. For Puttenham, *Piers Ploughman* was a "Satyr" and its author "a malcontent of that time," whom Puttenham places in the tradition of Lucilius, Juvenal, and Persius, characterizing them all by their "rough and bitter speaches, and their inuectiues." Skelton also was a "sharpe Satirist, but with more rayling and scoffery then became a Poet Lawreat"; he was, in fact, says Puttenham, a buffoon.[16]

Throughout the period the over-riding influence of Juvenal sanctioned the satirist in the most extravagant flights of invective and general intemperance of language. Marston is an excellent example. In one of his formal satires, after a noxious description of sexual perversion in London, he gropes for authority. Shall I, he asks,

> Halter my hate, and cease to curse and ban
> Such brutish filth?

Shall I, he continues to question over seventy-five perfervid lines, be silent in the face of such enormities? The answer:

> No, gloomy Juvenal,
> Though to thy fortunes I disastrous fall.[17]

As for style, like Juvenal he will violate convention, hurl his invective at the top of his bent:

> O how on tip-toes proudly mounts my muse!
> Stalking a loftier gait than satires use.

[16] *The Arte of English Poesie*, ed. Willcock and Walker, pp. 62, 26.
[17] Satire III, ll. 126-27, 195-96, *The Scourge of Villainy* in *Works*, ed. Bullen, III, 322-25.

Methinks some sacred rage warms all my veins,
Making my sprite mount up to higher strains
Than well beseems a rough-tongu'd satire's
   part. . . . (*Scourge*, IX, 5-9)

Almost without question Marston patterned the lines after Juvenal's similar declamation at the end of his Sixth Satire.[18] Invective and vituperation were the stock-in-trade of the satirists of the 1590's (Marston was a "rugged Timon," according to Bullen); and their subjects—lust, hypocrisy, miserliness, usury, greed—covered an astonishing range of man's vice as well as his folly. True, they rarely attack man as such, as Timon does; but when Timon inveighs against lust and gold and hypocrisy, his voice, though grander than theirs, is well within their key.

Timon even adopts as an occasional tactic the satirists' mocking, bitter humor. In Act V, Scene i, the Senators plead with him to intervene against Alcibiades' savage approach to the city. Timon answers:

If Alcibiades kill my countrymen,
Let Alcibiades know this of Timon,
That Timon cares not. But if he sack fair Athens
And take our goodly aged men by th' beards,
Giving our holy virgins to the stain
Of contumelious, beastly, mad-brain'd war,
Then let him know (and tell him Timon speaks it
In pity of our aged and our youth)
I cannot choose but tell him that I care not. . . .

His rhetoric is palpably designed to tantalize the Senators, to raise their hopes and keep them up, delicately balanced, through several lines of verbiage—then to bring them crashing down in a derisive anti-climax. Precisely the same technique is employed in the bitter joke about the tree which immediately follows:

[18] See Chap. III above and cf. Joseph Hall, Prologue, *Virgidemiarum*, ll. 19-23.

   Goe daring Muse on with thy thanklesse taske,
   And do the vgly face of vice vnmaske:
   And if thou canst not thine high flight remit,
   So as it mought a lowly Satyre fit,
   Let lowly Satyres rise aloft to thee. . . .
Collected Poems, ed. A. Davenport (Liverpool, 1949), p. 11.

the tree will cure all afflictions, says Timon, and Athenians high and low are welcome to hang themselves from it. These are tricks of the snarling satirist.

Now, what of Apemantus? Like Carlo Buffone, Malevole, Thersites, and others, he is a buffoon, a scurrilous railer and detractor; the only question is whether in Shakespeare's day a railer could be considered a satirist. To be sure, there is considerable frowning on buffoonery in the period. Puttenham feels that Skelton's scurrilities assort ill with his Laureateship, although he does call Skelton a satirist. The formal satirists themselves attack cynics and railers and detractors.

> Who cannot rail?—what dog but dare to bark
> 'Gainst Phoebe's brightness in the silent dark?
>
> .   .   .   .
>
> Vain envious detractor from the good,
> What cynic spirit rageth in thy blood?

asks Marston contemptuously, and the same attitudes are echoed by various contemporaries.[19] Such evidence leads Professor Campbell to say that the formal satirists distinguish "true satire from raillery [railing?] and mere detraction. . . . The cynic's spirit, they knew, was a metempsychosis of a snarling dog and utterly unsuited to satire."[20] But the satirists had many moods. They often arrogate to themselves the license (particularly in obscenity of expression) which in literature and legend had been the privilege of the railer; and for some moods nothing seemed more appropriate than the snarl of a dog. Marston frequently refers to himself as a barking or a sharp-fang'd satirist;[21] he boasts of his "respectless rude satiric hand," swears to "rail upon / This fusty world."[22] He writes a "Cynic Satire" (*Scourge*, VII) in which the interlocutor, tired of the Cynic's detraction, says he will stop "thy currish, barking chops (l. 102)." But the interlocutor is an *ingénu*, a butt; the Cynic is the satirist and is thus

[19] Satire IV, ll. 9-10, 25-26 in *Works*, III, 280-81.
[20] *Comicall Satyre*, p. 67. See above, Chap. I, 3, n. 9, where both Greek and Irish satirists are associated with wrathful dogs.
[21] See "The Author in praise of his precedent Poem [Pygmalion]," l. 46; *The Scourge of Villainy*, Sat. II, l. 8; Sat. IV, l. 4 (*Works*, III, 262, 312, 362).
[22] *Scourge*, Sat. VIII, 48; Sat. II, 12-13 (*Works*, III, 355, 312).

identified throughout (ll. 50, 92). T. M. *Gent's Micro-cynicon: Sixe Snarling Satyres* (1599) snarls more fiercely than it bites; but it is apparent from this and other work that in the 1590's the posture was conventional. In *Timon of Athens*, "dog" is the epithet most frequently applied to Apemantus. His *is* the role that is projected by many young satirists of the period. If it would be naïve to identify unequivocally the poets with the surly *personae* they adopt,[23] it is impossible to ignore the fact that satire is, in part, at least, precisely the kind of thing that Apemantus utters. His fine, edged speech on flatterers (IV, iii, 205 ff.) has clear counterparts in Donne, Marston, and others; and his cynical comments may be matched many times over in the formal satires of Shakespeare's contemporaries.

To identify both Timon and Apemantus as satirists is by no means, of course, to imply that they are identical. Occasionally, it is true, they speak alike, particularly when Timon is being least himself. In the buffoon scene examined above, their rhetoric is indistinguishable. Again, when Phrynia spits at Timon: "Thy lips rot off!" his response is worthy Apemantus:

> I will not kiss thee; then the rot returns
> To thine own lips again. (IV, iii, 64-65)

But by and large the resemblance is smothered beneath the weight of difference. It is enough to reiterate that Apemantus has all the characteristics of the railer, a type we have examined. We have also seen in earlier chapters the prototypes of Timon. After his fall from prosperity Timon's language takes on the incantatory tone of a prophet. He tries to preempt the full power of the archaic curse, calling on the gods, the heavens, the earth—and, as it were, the demonic power within himself—to confound the hated creature man. It is as though Timon were reenacting an ancient role, attempting to change the world through the power of language. He is a magician manqué, a

---

[23] The authors sometimes make the distinction explicit. T. M. *Gent.* writes "His Defiance to Envy" (in imitation of Hall) as a preface to *Micro-cynicon.* The last couplet of the "Defiance" reads:

> I, but the author's mouth, bid thee avaunt!
> He more defies thy hate, thy hunt, thy haunt.

Here "I" is the *persona*, "He" the poet himself. See Middleton, *Works*, ed. Bullen, VIII, 114.

primitive satirist ages out of his time. Part of his frustration, part of his ultimate humiliation, is the fact that magic is no longer viable. The Irish poet Laidcenn satirized and cursed the men of Leinster "so that neither grass nor corn grew with them, nor a leaf, to the end of a year." Timon calls upon the sun to "draw from the earth/ Rotten humidity" and infect the air. He commands the earth: "Dry up thy marrows, vines, and plough-torn leas," commands it to go great with tigers, to teem with new monsters. But Timon's words break on the cold substantiality of a world from which magic has vanished, and the only monster he can conjure up is man.[24] Still, the awful words affect us; in obscure ways we are moved by Timon's efforts to manipulate atavistic powers. Even in our revulsion we are attracted, as was Yeats:

> Myself must I remake
> Till I am Timon and Lear
> Or that William Blake
> Who beat upon the wall
> Till Truth obeyed his call.[25]

If Apemantus is a satirist-railer in the tradition of Thersites, Timon is a satirist-curser in the tradition of Aithirne and others of his kind. The distinction is pointed up in the play by their debate and made a question of class. Apemantus was "bred a dog," as Timon says, never knew Fortune's tender clasps:

> Why shouldst thou hate men?
> They never flatter'd thee. . . .
> If thou wilt curse, thy father (that poor rag)
> Must be thy subject, who in spite put stuff
> To some she-beggar and compounded thee
> Poor rogue hereditary. (IV, iii, 269-74)

Apemantus, in short, is the poor man's misanthrope. Timon, who had the world as his confectionary,

> The mouths, the tongues, the eyes, and hearts of men
> At duty. . . .

[24] For the power of Laidcenn and other Irish satirists, see Chap. I, 3, above. The references to *Timon* are from IV, iii, 1-3, 189-93.
[25] "An Acre of Grass," *Collected Poems* (New York, 1957), p. 299.

is entitled to curse until the heavens crack; but his words, un-like those of Lear, which find an echo in nature, seem mere madness to his auditors.

The words cannot, however, be dismissed easily. The denun-ciation of man has a hideous kind of cogency. It is so powerfully stated that many critics have been led to identify Timon's words with Shakespeare's psyche, to speak of black periods in the dramatist's life and of mental breakdowns. This seems unneces-sary. The full horror is there, of course, its statement about man ineradicable. That in one sense it is Shakespeare's statement is clearly true. But in the full literary sense the Timon view of man is qualified, contradicted, by the structure of the play. There is, in fine, a third satirist: Shakespeare himself. Again we have the ancient complication: the created character, hurling curses and invective, using language as a magical instrument, functioning in effect as a primitive satirist—he being satirized, in the sophisticated sense of the term, by his creator. Timon's in-discriminate love and his indiscriminate hate are shown dramat-ically to be folly. The denunciation of man is frightfully power-ful and it stands; but Shakespeare sharply undercuts its effect by pulling Timon down from heights of vatic eloquence to the mud, where he plays the buffoon with Apemantus.

The play can hardly be said to argue *for* anything, except by implication. It argues most clearly against excess: the excess, first, of Timon's "love," with its lack of humility, its flaccid refusal to discriminate, its abstractness; then against the excess of his liberality, which perverts into destructive folly a disposi-tion originally virtuous; finally, against the excess of his hate. It argues against the abstraction that would hold all Athenians (all men) worthy and against that which would hold them all vicious. To say that the play argues implicitly for moderation, for rational discrimination in judging the ways of men, while at the same time it takes full cognizance of the dreadful power of the extreme, is to sound almost trivial; for the virtues of mod-eration are not in great demand in the twentieth century, dom-inated as it is by the *exigence d'absolu*. Yet such is the burden of the satirist-satirized theme as it appears in Lucian and in Shakespeare's *Timon*.

3. *LE MISANTHROPE*

In the course of his fine essay on Molière's *Misanthrope*, Martin Turnell remarks that the play is "pre-eminently a comedy; it is not a *tragédie bourgeoise* in the manner of *l'Education sentimentale*."[1] The opinion seems reasonable; but as anyone who has wandered in the jungle of Molière criticism knows, these words are a challenge to battle. In the Widener Library copy of *The Classical Moment*, alongside Turnell's comment, is printed in pencil a large HELL! The play, which is concerned with the problem of moral violence, provokes its own problem. If Molière, like Troilus, looks down on "this litel spot of erthe" from the eighth sphere, he must be amused.

The issue which divides critics is simply stated: Does Molière wish us to take the side of Alceste or the side of Philinte? asks M. Brunetière. "Who . . . represents Molière?" asks E. B. O. Borgerhoff.[2] To most people the meaning of the play has seemed inextricably bound up in the question, although not everyone has agreed that an answer is possible. M. Michaut has an admirable summary of the enormous critical literature, which can be divided without undue distortion, he says, into three principal schools.[3] First (the largest group) are those who think Molière intended Alceste to be the sympathetic character of the play, a model to be admired and followed—an intemperate model, perhaps, but noble compared to the temporizing man of the world, Philinte. Second is a smaller group (including Michaut himself) which takes exactly the opposite position: Philinte, the urbane and reasonable gentleman, is the model, as opposed to the outrageous malcontent, Alceste. A still smaller third group, plumping for the *juste-milieu*, is itself split: most think that neither Alceste nor Philinte is a model, but that one must put together the best qualities of each, avoiding their respective extremes; and one critic holds that the opposed principles of both characters must be equally rejected. M. René Bray's recent *Molière: Homme de Theatre* (1954) established

[1] *The Classical Moment* (London, 1947), p. 96.
[2] Ferdinand Brunetière, "Les époques de la comédie de Molière," *Etudes critiques* (Paris, 1910), VIII, 101; E. B. O. Borgerhoff, *The Freedom of French Classicism* (Princeton, N.J., 1950), p. 159.
[3] G. Michaut, *Les Luttes de Molière* (Paris, 1925), pp. 207 ff.

a new category: that which, insisting on the radical distinction between the life of the theatre and real life, calls such moral problems irrelevant and absurd. *Le Misanthrope* is a comedy; and comedy exists only to please, to make us laugh.

But whether the play is characterized as a comedy or as something else depends in large part on which of the "sides" the critic is committed to. For Goethe, who thinks of Alceste as a pure and noble spirit doing battle against a corrupt society, the play is a tragedy ("The theme of *Timon* seems comic in comparison," he wrote). So it is for Brunetière: *Le Misanthrope* and *Tartuffe* are *tragédies bourgeoises* which Molière vainly tried to force into the framework of comedy. Most of Brunetière's nineteenth-century colleagues concur, particularly the Romantics, who, like Rousseau, saw themselves in Alceste.[4] On the other hand, critics who decide that Philinte speaks with Molière's voice, that he stands for the familiar certitudes of Molière's world, tend to see the play as an amusing comedy in which Alceste is a kind of humour character whose excess is laughable. Others characterize it as a satiric onslaught on society. The permutations are endless.

There is no harm in this. It is folly to think that only one "real" interpretation of so richly ambiguous a play as *Le Misanthrope* is possible, although unquestionably, as in Orwell, some interpretations are more real than others. "Nous portons beaucoup d'hommes en nous, et il en va de même pour les personnages inventés," writes M. Mauriac of unorthodox theatrical conceptions of Alceste's role.[5] One must agree; and the conflict of responsible interpretations is simply irrefragable testimony to the continuing generative power of a major work of art. The reading to follow acquires its form and its special emphasis from the satirist-satirized theme which has concerned us.

As with *Timon* it is imperative to weigh every nuance of the opening scene of *The Misanthrope*—a scene almost unparalleled in the skill with which the dramatist establishes the basic themes, sets the dominant tones. The play opens with Alceste, disgruntled, willfully rude, railing at Philinte:[6]

[4] Michaut, *Luttes de Molière*, p. 208, n. 1; p. 210, n. 1; p. 242.
[5] François Mauriac, *Journal* (Paris, 1937), II, 146.
[6] Quotations are from Molière's *The Misanthrope*, translated by Rich-

My God, you ought to die of self-disgust.
I call your conduct inexcusable, Sir,
And every man of honor will concur.
I see you almost hug a man to death,
Exclaim for joy until you're out of breath,
And supplement these loving demonstrations
With endless offers, vows, and protestations;
Then when I ask you, "Who was that?" I find
That you can barely bring his name to mind!
Once the man's back is turned, you cease to love him,
And speak with absolute indifference of him!
My God, I say it's base and scandalous
To falsify the heart's affections thus;
If I caught myself behaving in such a way,
I'd hang myself for shame, without delay. (i, i, pp. 6-7)

Philinte deflects the extraordinary outburst with a mild joke, then asks, genuinely curious, "How else are people to behave?" Alceste answers:

I'd have them be sincere, and never part
With any word that isn't from the heart.

Philinte pleads social custom, politeness, but Alceste bursts out again:

No, no, this formula you'd have me follow,
However fashionable, is false and hollow,
And I despise the frenzied operations
Of all these barterers of protestations . . .
Who court and flatter everyone on earth
And praise the fool no less than the man of worth.
. . . no self-respecting heart would dream
Of prizing so promiscuous an esteem;
However high the praise, there's nothing worse
Than sharing honors with the universe.
Esteem is founded on comparison:
To honor all men is to honor none. . . .
I spurn the easy tribute of a heart

Which will not set the worthy man apart:
I choose, Sir, to be chosen; and in fine,
The friend of mankind is no friend of mine.

Already an image of the man forms in our minds: he argues for truth and sincerity; he hates hypocrisy and affectation. Excellent! But Alceste's reaction does seem over-determined, disproportionate. "Base," "scandalous," "vice," "crime"—these are terms appropriate to the kiss of Judas, as Michaut says, rather than to a silly social affectation which led Philinte to embrace overeffusively a man he hardly knew. To balance this, we find another quality to admire in Alceste: he insists vigorously on moral discrimination; he loathes the lax obliteration of moral distinction—the kind of thing so characteristic of Timon's court. "To honor all men is to honor none." Yet we have to anticipate less than thirty lines to find Alceste making the most indiscriminate condemnations of humanity. No matter where he looks, he says, he finds nothing, nothing, but the basest flattery, injustice, dishonesty, self-interest, treachery; he is ready to wash his hands of the whole race.

Once again Philinte wards off the violence of this with a flick of wit, but then, changing tone, he warns his friend that his intemperance has become a disease, that he is making himself ridiculous. All the better, says Alceste; he despises mankind (tous les hommes) so thoroughly that he would loathe being thought wise. The lines that follow are particularly significant:

PHIL. Your hatred's very sweeping, is it not?
ALC.   Quite right: I hate the whole degraded lot.
PHIL. Must all poor human creatures be embraced,
    Without distinction, by your vast distaste?
    Even in these bad times, there are surely a few . . .
ALC.   No, I include all men. . . .

Here is the theme of Lucian's *Timon* once again, with Philinte as Hermes, quietly exposing the irrationality of Alceste—Timon's unqualified denunciation. Philinte's insistent query: With no exception? works hard against Alceste's earlier demand for discrimination. The link with Timon is strengthened as Alceste justifies his misanthropy:

> Some men I hate for being rogues; the others
> I hate because they treat the rogues like brothers.

The lines are almost a direct translation of sentiments attributed to Timon of Athens by Erasmus.[7]

From Alceste's frenzied account we learn of his lawsuit and of his disposition toward it. He will take none of the ordinary steps prompted by prudence to increase his chances of winning the case. His cause is just, his opponent is a villain. "I'm either right, or wrong." If politics interfere adversely, so much the worse. Or rather, so much the better!

> I'll discover by this case
> Whether or not men are sufficiently base
> And impudent and villainous and perverse
> To do me wrong before the universe.
>
> . . . .
>
> Oh, I could wish, whatever the cost,
> Just for the beauty of it, that my trial were lost.
>
> (i, i, p. 16).

His extravagance has reached another peak, and Philinte reiterates his warning, his threat, really, of a sanction as powerful as anything his society could wield:

> If people heard you talking so, Alceste,
> They'd split their sides. Your name would be a jest.

People do hear, of course—those of the audience, and their cue, I should think, *is* to laugh; at least, to reject. Alceste is willfully ridiculous and remains impervious to warning: "So much the worse for jesters."

Although Alceste's criticism of society has thus far been rational enough (who can deny its basic thrust?), his terms are so extravagant as almost to nullify his premises. His inflexibility of mind is reflected in his inability to modulate his discourse; for, as Turnell shows, whatever Alceste discusses, from the important to the trivial, his tone remains uniform.[8] He demands the most

---

[7] *Apophthegms*, Bk. VI, liv, in *Opera Omnia* (Lugduni Batavorum, 1703), IV, 318. Almost the same words appear in the third Dialogue of Lilio Giraldi's *Historiam Poetarum Graecorum et Latinorum*; see his *Opera Omnia*, 2 vol. in 1 (Lugduni Batavorum, 1696), II, 132.

[8] *Classical Moment*, p. 97.

acute moral discriminations of his friends, yet lacks the quality
he requires in others. His incapacity is revealed in both the content and the form of what he says. Such rigidity is repellent.
But by the end of the scene a counter-motion is under way:
Alceste is in love—irrationally, foolishly in love with Célimène,
a coquette who represents all that his reason causes him to despise. He knows his own folly, realizes that the good-hearted
Eliante would be a far wiser choice for him:

> each day my reason tells me so;
> But reason doesn't rule in love. . . . (i, i, p. 19)

With that, as M. Mauriac writes, "Alceste se rapproche de
chacun de nous et nous devient fraternel. . . ."[9] The intransigence
of his attitude toward man is belied by the irrationality of his
love.

Meanwhile, in reaction to his friend, Philinte has established
his own position vis-à-vis man and society. "Come," he says at
the end of a violent tirade:

> Come, let's forget the follies of the times
> And pardon mankind for its petty crimes;
> Let's have an end of rantings and of railings,
> And show some leniency toward human failings.
> This world requires a pliant rectitude;
> Too stern a virtue makes one stiff and rude;
> Good sense views all extremes with detestation,
> And bids us to be noble in moderation.
> The rigid virtues of the ancient days
> Are not for us; they jar with all our ways
> And ask of us too lofty a perfection.
> Wise men accept their times without objection,
> And there's no greater folly, if you ask me,
> Than trying to reform society.
> Like you, I see each day a hundred and one
> Unhandsome deeds that might be better done,
> But still, for all the faults that meet my view,
> I'm never known to storm and rave like you.
> I take men as they are, or let them be,
> And teach my soul to bear their frailty;

[9] *Journal*, ii, 149.

And whether in court or town, whatever the scene,
My phlegm's as philosophic as your spleen. (i, i, p. 13)

Nothing could be more moderate, more civilized, more representative of the *honnête homme* who often speaks for Molière.
As with many such statements of neo-classic moderation, we
must be careful not to dismiss Philinte's argument as a tissue
of cold abstractions. Behind the key terms lie the great positive
values of a high civilization; and in "La parfaite raison fuit toute
extremité" is implicit centuries of honored precept. "We may
grasp virtue in such a manner that she will become vicious, if
we embrace her with too violent and fierce a desire," wrote
Montaigne, citing Horace and St. Paul to similar effect.[10] In no
case was paradox intended.

But moderation itself enrages Alceste. Wouldn't you be furious, he demands, if someone you trusted conspired to rob you
of property and reputation? No, answers Philinte:

> These faults of which you so complain
> Are part of human nature, I maintain,
> And it's no more a matter for disgust
> That men are knavish, selfish and unjust,
> Than that the vulture dines upon the dead,
> And wolves are furious, and apes ill-bred.[11]

Alceste and Philinte clearly have in common an extremely low
opinion of man, but they differ radically in how they dispose
that opinion. Two ways of life, two schemes of value, are in conflict. The audience cannot but be implicated.

Scene ii tests the opposing schemes in action. At first, curiously, Alceste's role is that of moderation. Oronte's praises of

---

[10] "Of Moderation," *Essays*, trans. E. J. Trechmann (New York, 1946),
p. 169. For a different interpretation of Philinte's speech, see Borgerhoff,
Freedom of French Classicism, p. 158.

[11] It is interesting to see Swift, in certain moods, expressing similar
sentiments: "I tell you after all, that I do not hate mankind:" he wrote
to Pope in 1725, "it is *vous autres* who hate them, because you would
have them reasonable animals, and are angry for being disappointed. . . .
I am no more angry with [Walpole] than I was with the kite that last
week flew away with one of my chickens. . . ." *Correspondence*, ed. F.
Elrington Ball (London, 1912), III, 293. In *Gulliver's Travels*, the
Houynhnhnms hate the Yahoos, but they do not blame them for their
odious qualities, any more than they blame a bird of prey for being cruel.

him are of course fantastic, but he bears them with relative equanimity, and his deflection of the proffered friendship displays a courtier's skill. Oronte's fatuousness becomes insistent, however, and his vanity intolerable. No man of Alceste's temperament and principles could remain silent. The sonnet finally provokes the explosion as Alceste is obliged by Oronte's importunities to tell him, first indirectly, then directly, what trash he thinks it is. Our sympathies are with Alceste.

Philinte, meanwhile, has also commented on the sonnet: ". . . the style's delightful"; "How handsomely you phrase it!"; "The close is exquisite"; "I can't remember a poem I've liked so well" (I, ii, pp. 25-26). The interjections are gratuitous; Philinte was not being addressed nor was his opinion asked. The best construction one can put on this nonsense is that Philinte is trying to compensate for what he knows will be his friend's reaction. Even at that, one squirms at the brazenness of the flattery. In its way it is as bad as the worst flourishes of Oronte.

At the end of Scene ii we have this situation: the man who is extreme on principle has attempted moderation but has been forced into verbal violence, while the man who is moderate on principle has somewhat immoderately indulged himself in social hypocrisy. Insofar as the scene constitutes a test of values in action, Alceste emerges with most honor. We may dislike the extravagance of his language in Scene i, but against the pusillanimity of Philinte, his deeds show well. The initial imbalance between the two, weighted in favor of Philinte, has at least partially been redressed.

Alceste is characteristically blunt in his first scene with Célimène, the charming coquette whom he loves.

> Shall I speak plainly, Madame? I confess
> Your conduct gives me infinite distress,
> And my resentment's grown too hot to smother.
> Soon, I foresee, we'll break with one another. (II, i, p. 39)

Like Pope's Belinda, Célimène smiles on all alike. Alceste, who loathes to share honors with the universe, is hurt by her failure to discriminate; he feels himself inadequately distinguished. He rages helplessly against the folly of his love, swears that it is the greatest love man ever felt for woman, then lapses into sullenness under the inundation of suitors.

It is not easy to characterize precisely the special quality of the scene that follows. Célimène has an audience for which she quite deliberately performs and from which, at the end, she receives the applause due a performer. The assembled fops "feed" her one by one the names of absent members of their circle, and one by one she demolishes them by superbly turned satiric characterizations. Within the highly stylized pattern of the play, the scene has its own stylization. It is a performance within the larger performance; and while it contributes to the more inclusive order, it seems almost to have an independent life of its own. In part this is a result of the self-consciousness of Célimène's activity. All pretense of true conversation is dropped. Célimène is simply given cues: "Tell us about Géralde"; "Now for Adraste"; "What about young Cléon?" To each cue the response is the same: an essential characteristic grasped, turned, elaborated upon (although often briefly), until the finished portrait is there, perfect in its destructive integrity:

> That tiresome ass.
> He mixes only with the titled class,
> And fawns on dukes and princes, and is bored
> With anyone who's not at least a lord.
> The man's obsessed with rank, and his discourses
> Are all of hounds and carriages and horses;
> He uses Christian names with all the great,
> And the word Milord, with him, is out of date. (ii, v, p. 52)

To compare Célimène with a railer-fool like Shakespeare's Thersites may seem absurd, but only at first glance. Their formal situations are thoroughly comparable. "Come, what's Agamemnon?" demands Achilles of Thersites; Patroclus, daring, asks for a characterization of himself and is infuriated with what he elicits.[12] Thersites performs on demand, like other fools, partly because it is expected of him, and partly, one feels, because of the sadistic joy he takes in his own performance. Similarly, Célimène responds to the demands of her entourage, yet also pleases herself. The two represent, of course, enormously differ-

---

[12] *Troilus and Cressida*, ii, iii, 46 ff.

ent worlds, as their language reflects. Invective has given way to the greater indirections of wit, and uninhibited railing to the polite assassinations of the drawing room. The deaths are metaphorical, but serious, and we think again of Pope's Belinda: "At every word a reputation dies."

Célimène's genius for this kind of thing shows brilliantly again in her contest with Arsinoé. The portrait of the prude is unforgettable:

> Your affectation of a grave demeanor,
> Your endless talk of virtue and of honor,
> The aptitude of your suspicious mind
> For finding sin where there is none to find,
> Your towering self-esteem, that pitying face
> With which you contemplate the human race,
> Your sermonizings and your sharp aspersions
> On people's pure and innocent diversions—
> All these were mentioned, Madam, and, in fact,
> Were roundly and concertedly attacked.
> "What good," they said, "are all these outward shows,
> When everything belies her pious pose?
> She prays incessantly; but then, they say,
> She beats her maids and cheats them of their pay;
> She shows her zeal in every holy place,
> But still she's vain enough to paint her face;
> She holds that naked statues are immoral,
> But with a naked *man* she'd have no quarrel." (III, v, p. 80)

Perhaps even more pitiless is the self-portrait that follows. Célimène admits that once her beauty has faded, she may find it expedient to become a prude herself:

> When all one's charms are gone, it is, I'm sure,
> Good strategy to be devout and pure. . . .

This is in part a rhetorical move in the wit combat, a cruel reference to Arsinoé's age and condition. But the satiric thrust has a second edge, turned, by Molière, against Célimène herself. It is clear that although she speaks to attack, she believes as she speaks, thus revealing the poverty of her soul. Célimène's words open a vista into the hell of her future—this kind of hell:

> See how the World its Veterans rewards!
> A Youth of Frolics, an old Age of Cards,
> Fair to no purpose, artful to no end,
> Young without Lovers, old without a Friend,
> A Fop their Passion, but their Prize a Sot,
> Alive, ridiculous, and dead, forgot![13]

The last two acts of the play, far from resolving earlier complexities, only deepen our sense of the equivocal nature of Molière's themes. Alceste's talent for the extreme is given full scope and leads him quickly enough into absurdity; but at the same time the play demands that, in part, at least, he be regarded as a heroic figure. The strongest explicit evidence of this comes from Eliante. She is the one character in the work who is universally respected. Molière himself appears to have no ironic reservation whatever about her. She is an apostle of frankness (she praises frankness on three separate occasions), she loves Alceste, and her characterization of him is crucial:

> His conduct has been very singular lately;
> Still, I confess that I respect him greatly.
> The honesty in which he takes such pride
> Has—to my mind—its noble, heroic side.
> In this false age, such candor seems outrageous;
> But I could wish that it were more contagious. (IV, i, p. 94)

The speech builds powerfully our feeling that in some sense Alceste represents the positives of his dramatic world. We associate it with his justified contempt for the shallowness and hypocrisy of his society; with his earlier conduct with Arsinoé when he scornfully rejects the possibility of a courtier's career, and when, in a moment of astonishing humility, he says, on being warned that Célimène is unfaithful:

> You may be right; who knows another's heart? (III, vii, p. 89)

We may perhaps associate it with a final belated dignity as in the closing moments of the play Alceste rejects Célimène, pays tribute to Eliante, and stalks off into voluntary exile.

But strong as this movement of the play is, it by no means

[13] Pope, "To a Lady," *Moral Essays*, Epistle II, ll. 239-48.

predominates; superimposed over the image of Alceste as hero
is an image of Alceste as butt. The extravagance of principle and
the intemperance of behavior that we saw in Act I culminate in
absurdity under the more stringent tests of the final scenes. Consider Alceste's reaction to the letter furnished him by Arsinoé.
He accepts it as proof that Célimène is false. He is deeply
wounded, as any lover would be. But it is characteristic of
Alceste that he should leap from personal hurt to cosmic implication, that in his mind a coquette's unfaithfulness should be
equivalent to "le déchaînement de toute la nature." Célimène
suddenly becomes the most evil creature ever produced by
Heaven or Hell. It is as though Lear had suddenly been set
down in a Parisian salon. The incongruity is heightened as
Alceste rather despicably seeks revenge on Célimène by offering
his heart to Eliante. He vows never to think of Célimène further,
yet within a hundred lines is struggling helplessly within the
bonds of his "unrewarded, mad, and bitter love." Doubtless
there is something touching about this, but there is surely rather
more of the ridiculous. Alceste's own pride and pretensions make
it so.

As an ultimate expression of his love, Alceste lays a wish at
Célimène's feet:

> I wish you were in such distress
> That I might show my deep devotedness.
> Yes, I could wish that you were wretchedly poor,
> Unloved, uncherished, utterly obscure;
> That fate had set you down upon the earth
> Without possessions, rank, or gentle birth;
> Then, by the offer of my heart, I might
> Repair the great injustice of your plight;
> I'd raise you from the dust, and proudly prove
> The purity and vastness of my love. (iv, iii, pp. 108-09)

Like Timon, Alceste would play god, and Célimène with some
justice scorns him. As though to point up the equivocal character
of the situation, a scene of pure farce, that between Alceste and
his valet Dubois, follows.

Alceste is confirmed in his misanthropy when the universe
deals him a final blow: he loses his lawsuit. If injustice has been

done to him, then the world is a jungle and a jackal's lair and he will abandon it forever. Again it is his extravagance that undermines him, not his general position. Philinte can agree that theirs is a "low, conniving age," that only trickery prospers, but as a reasonable man he will not allow that opinion to justify abandoning society. For Alceste, however, only the absolute has meaning; in his compulsive quest for the extreme he hails the legal verdict:

> I wouldn't have it changed for anything.
> It shows the times' injustice with such clarity
> That I shall pass it down to our posterity
> As a great proof and signal demonstration
> Of the black wickedness of this generation.
> It may cost twenty thousand francs; but I
> Shall pay their twenty thousand, and gain thereby
> The right to storm and rage at human evil,
> And send the race of mankind to the devil. (v, i, pp. 119-20)

This verges on the paranoid, which in some circumstances can still be comic. Alceste takes pains to supply the circumstances as in his last speech of the scene he caricatures himself:

> . . . leave me with my gloom
> Here in the darkened corner of this room.

Philinte's rejoinder is wry: "C'est une compagnie étrange. . . ."

Without Timon's mad eloquence, Alceste could hardly push these sentiments further. His reaction during the exposé of Célimène is strangely subdued. Still infatuated, he makes his final offer: he will forgive all her treachery on condition that she fly with him

> To that wild, trackless, solitary place
> In which I shall forget the human race.

Célimène's horror and her counter-offer of marriage disgust him: "No, I detest you now"; and his last gesture, that of self-exile, is made with dignity.

Thus the end has an effect like that of *Timon* in that it adds a last level of complication to our feelings about the central character. The dignified exit by no means cancels out Alceste's absurdity, any more than Timon's folly is cancelled out by Alcibiades' last speech. It is simply that "taking sides" in the either-or sense is impossible, as it often is in situations in which a major satirical character is himself satirized by his creator.

Voltaire thought *Le Misanthrope* a wiser and finer satire than any written by Horace or Boileau.[14] We may share his enthusiasm, but we have still to distinguish more precisely who is satirist and who and what are satirized. A principal target of course is the foppish crew dancing attendance on Célimène. One of the particular delights of the play is that some of the sharpest satire directed at the group comes from within the group itself; that is, from Célimène with the support of her suitors. None of them recognizes that Célimène's portraits are, in a sense, of themselves. All that is required for any given etching is the absence of the individual concerned. Eliante remarks:

> The conversation takes its usual turn,
> And all our dear friends' ears will shortly burn. (ɪɪ, v, p. 51)

This society pillories itself; its high priestess is chief executioner, and, as in the dialogue with Arsinoé, numbers herself among her victims. Célimène is a splendid, if spiteful, satirist ("en François," wrote Dacier, "qui dit *satire*, dit *médisance*");[15] but she is engulfed in the more sweeping, more powerful satire of Molière.

In his important critique of the *Misanthrope*, Rousseau claims that Molière uses the performance of Célimène to distinguish sharply between the (ignoble) *Médisant* and the (noble) *Misantrope*, who, in his "fierce and mordant bitterness, abhors calumny and detests satire."[16] It is not quite that simple. To be sure, Alceste is disgusted at Célimène's satiric performance, largely because she and her collaborators are hypocritical about it. Earlier, however, in conversation with Célimène, he has neatly equated the human worth of the fop Clitandre with "the

[14] See Molière, *Oeuvres*, ed. E. Despois and P. Mesnard (Paris, 1880), v, 428.

[15] André Dacier, "Preface sur les Satires d'Horace," in his edition of *Oeuvres d'Horace* (Amsterdam, 1727), vɪ, xvii.

[16] J.-J. Rousseau, *Lettre a Mr. d'Alembert sur les Spectacles*, ed. M. Fuchs (Lille, 1948), p. 59.

splendidly long nail of his little finger" (II, i, p. 40). As Alceste develops his conceit, Clitandre as a person disappears until there is left only a congeries of blonde wig, embroidered hose, ribbons, and vast German breeches. Alceste has considerable talent in Célimène's own vein.

But his major importance is as a satirist in the larger sense of the term. With Juvenalian fervor he hurls his invective against the vice and folly which he sees inundating his society. It is as though by naming the evils, imposing the order of language upon them, he could somehow control them; but of course he cannot, and his outbursts, like those of Timon, are mere denunciation, outrageous in the extravagance of their pretension.

Alceste has the compulsion endemic among satirists to strip the mask of appearance and illusion from the reality beneath, to penetrate to the thing itself and bring it to light:

> . . . we should condemn with all our force
> Such false and artificial intercourse.
> Let men behave like men; let them display
> Their inmost hearts in everything they say;
> Let the heart speak, and let our sentiments
> Not mask themselves in silly compliments. (I, i, pp. 8-9)

Part of the reason for his rage against society is that it blandly accepts the mask behind which the villainous opponent of his lawsuit hides (I, i, p. 12). In a way the conflict between Alceste and Philinte can be seen as a conflict over the social utility of satire. Both see the same unpleasant reality beneath the mask. Emilie, who paints and coquettes in her old age, is just as ugly to Philinte as to Alceste. Alceste would expose her, Philinte would not:

> there's no greater folly . . .
> Than trying to reform society. (I, i, p. 13)

For him, as for Erasmus' Folly, the social mask has positive value; to strip it off in the service of some exaggerated sense of honesty would be ridiculous (I, i, p. 9).[17]

---

[17] While Alceste and Philinte differ over the value of the mask, they agree in distinguishing between it and the truth. In *Tartuffe* Orgon's great folly is that he cannot make the basic distinction. See Cléante's outraged query: "What? will you not make any distinction between

Thirty years later Swift wrote a brilliant fantasia on the same theme. In the "Digression on Madness" in A *Tale of a Tub* two ways of life are opposed: that which follows reason as it cuts and pierces and mangles below the surface of things, to come back gravely with the information "that in the inside they are good for nothing"; and that which, "truly wise," is content with the outside, with the mask—content to "cream off Nature, leaving the Sower and the Dregs, for Philosophy and Reason to lap up." Alceste's way, in Swift's terms, is bloody and cruel: "Last Week I saw a Woman *flay'd*, and you will hardly believe, how much it altered her Person for the worse." Philinte's way leads to "the sublime and refined Point of Felicity, called, *the Possession of being well deceived*; The Serene Peaceful State of being a Fool among Knaves."[18]

There is no such shocking resolution (if it is a resolution) in Molière, although similar pressures are exerted. Alceste's "primitive," slashing mode of life, containing its own power and its own truth, is still shown to be inadequate as a solution to the problem of how one is to live as a man among mankind. The self-exile to which Alceste's reason leads him is defeat, not solution. Philinte's mode, reasonable in a very different sense, moderate, tolerant, is still tepid and temporizing to the point of repugnance. By the end of the play it is apparent that, faced with any given wickedness, Philinte would shrug his shoulders, maintaining that the existence of such evil is necessary for the exercise of the virtue of patience:

> each human frailty,
> Provides occasion for philosophy,
> And that is virtue's noblest exercise. (v, i, p. 120)

An impeccable argument in the abstract, as Alceste sees, but

---

hypocrisy and sincerity? Will you speak of them in the same words, and render the same homage to the mask as to the face, put artifice on a level with sincerity, confound the appearance with the reality, value the shadow as much as the substance . . . ?" (I, v, ll. 331-37), trans. A. R. Waller in *Plays of Molière* (Edinburgh, 1926), IV, 23.

[18] A *Tale of a Tub*, ed. A. C. Guthkelch and D. Nichol Smith (Oxford, 1920), pp. 171-74. For a fuller discussion of Swift's treatment of the theme, see Robert C. Elliott, "Swift's *Tale of a Tub*: an Essay in Problems of Structure," *PMLA*, LXVI (1951), pp. 450-55.

shoddy in a concrete human situation. Outrageous as he is, Alceste is the heroic one of the play, not Philinte. Or, in other terms, he is a satirist, while Philinte is one of the many Trebatiuses of the world who will always counsel swimming the Tiber as a means of getting human folly out of one's head.

It would be tedious at this point to insist on Molière's role. His satire incorporates and transcends that of Célimène and Alceste. He rejects Célimène, as we must, however reluctantly; but he demands toward Alceste a complex response, composed, as Turnell suggests, of apparently contradictory elements. It is Alceste, after all, who has the *either-or* mentality: "J'ai tort, ou j'ai raison"; and that is his failure. Molière's satire of his satirist is much less exclusive; and our response must be *both-and*, balanced between our sense of Alceste as hero (his moral integrity, his attack on social folly are superb) and our sense of him as butt (his intransigence and intemperance and lack of proportion are absurd). Molière's demands are far from unique; writers have always known that the law of contradiction does not apply to human character. In what other terms can one possibly experience *Don Quixote?*—or, as the following discussion indicates, *Gulliver's Travels?*

4. GULLIVER'S TRAVELS

For a number of reasons Swift's *Gulliver* is more difficult to come to terms with than *Timon* or *The Misanthrope*, even from the limited point of view which defines our special interest in the works. The most immediate problem is that of genre. *Timon* and *The Misanthrope* are plays; no matter how much satire and how many satirists may be involved, the plays conform to well-established dramatic conventions. We know the conventions, know in general what to expect in the way of structure, characterization, etc. But what of *Gulliver's Travels?* It is a fiction; it is written in prose; it is an "imaginary voyage." So much one can say, but to say this is to say very little. The imaginary voyage has taken such an astonishing variety of forms that it seems impossible to define it as a genre, to say nothing of systematizing its conventions.[1] Is *Gulliver* a novel? Probably not, although it

[1] See Part One of Philip B. Gove, *The Imaginary Voyage in Prose Fiction* (New York, 1941).

is not easy to say (except by arbitrary stipulation) why it is not. Clearly it is satire; but that is not to say that it is *a* satire. Arthur E. Case, for example, thinks that it is not: ". . . it would be more accurate and more illuminating to call it a politico-sociological treatise much of which is couched in the medium of satire."[2] We shy from using the category "a satire" today, at least when we are trying to speak precisely, because the term has lost for us any sense of formal specification.

Why worry about genre? one might ask. Every work is entitled to its own *donnée*. Why not consider *Gulliver* in its own terms, *sui generis*, working out from the text its own presuppositions, its own assumptions? Theoretically the method is feasible, practically very difficult. As the history of Swift criticism shows, the temptation has been overpowering to slip from considering the *Travels* as a thing in itself, to considering it as a kind of confession (Swift's confession), as a children's tale, as a novel, as a curse, as comedy, as tragedy, as evidence of Swift's lunacy, his coprophilia, whatnot. Some of these uses are doubtless legitimate enough for special purposes; but if we are interested in critical evaluation of *Gulliver's Travels* as a literary work, then we must judge it by the laws of its own conventions, not by the laws of a country to which it owes no allegiance. For this reason we must try to "place" *Gulliver* as best we can.

Lucian tells an amusing parable of how Dionysus, Pan, Silenus, the satyrs, and the maenads invaded India. The Hindus with their massive armies, their elephants, their towers on top of the elephants, thought the invasion absurd. Scouts brought word that the enemy army consisted largely of young clodhoppers with tails and horns, given to dancing about naked, and crazy women who rushed around shouting "Evoe!" The two principal lieutenants were an old man with a gross belly and big ears, and an odd creature built below like a goat. It was impossible not to laugh at them. But when the Indians were finally forced to do battle with the invaders and encountered the whirling, shrieking frenzy of Dionysus' troops, their ponderous array of elephants broke and fled in terror. Lucian makes his point: ". . . most people are in the same state of mind as the Hindoos when they encounter literary novelties, like mine for example.

[2] *Four Essays on Gulliver's Travels* (Princeton, N.J., 1945), p. 105.

Thinking that what they hear from me will smack of Satyrs and of jokes, in short, of comedy . . . some of them do not come at all, believing it unseemly to come off their elephants and give their attention to the revels of women and the skipping of Satyrs, while others apparently come for something of that kind, and when they find steel instead of ivy, are even then slow to applaud, confused by the unexpectedness of the thing."[3]

In his recent *Anatomy of Criticism* Northrop Frye deals brilliantly with the "steel instead of ivy" puzzle, insofar as it concerns works like *Gulliver's Travels, Candide, Erewhon, Brave New World*—all prose fictions but all dubiously attached to the rubric of the novel.[4] These works Frye calls Menippean satires. The term requires explanation. Menippus was a pugnacious Greek Cynic (third century B.C.) who wrote satires in a mixture of prose and verse. His works have been lost, and most of what we know of him comes from his admirer and professed imitator, Lucian. Menippus figures as a character in several of Lucian's satires, in, for example, the *Icaromennipus* which almost unquestionably influenced Swift. Another imitator of Menippus was Marcus Terentius Varro, the most learned of all the Romans, whose *Saturae Menippeae* were extremely influential but survive today only in fragments. The Menippean (or Varronian, as it is sometimes called) tradition was continued by Seneca (*Apocolocyntosis: The Pumpkinification of Claudius*), Petronius (*Satyricon*), and Apuleius (*The Golden Ass*).[5] Quintilian describes the Menippean as an older kind of satire than that written by Lucilius and characterizes it by its mixture of prose and verse.[6] Since his time little has been done to give the form (if it is a form) more precise lineaments.[7] Dryden, for example, uses the term in much the same way as Quintilian used it.

[3] "Dionysus," in *Lucian*, trans. Harmon, I, 49-55.
[4] (Princeton, N.J., 1957), pp. 305 ff.
[5] For various reasons Frye later abandons *Menippean* in favor of the term *anatomy*, as in Burton's *Anatomy of Melancholy*.
[6] *Institutio Oratoria*, x, 95, trans. Butler, IV, 55.
[7] After a considerable discussion J. Wight Duff concludes that Varro's *Menippeae*, Seneca's *Apocolocyntosis*, and Petronius' *Satyricon* are properly in the Menippean tradition; they resemble each other in "their blend of prose and verse, in their borrowings from the common speech and proverbial lore, in their introduction of parodies on the grand style, and in their use of irony at the expense of gods and mythology." *The Golden*

Frye is more ambitious. He attempts to work out the characteristics of a form strict enough to incorporate its own conventions, but flexible enough to include the works mentioned above
together with other great mavericks: *The Praise of Folly, Gargantua and Pantagruel, The Anatomy of Melancholy,* the Alice
books, etc. He describes the form thus (the prose-verse mixture
has, somewhat awkwardly, been dropped as a *differentia*):

"The Menippean satire deals less with people as such than
with mental attitudes. Pedants, bigots, cranks, parvenus, vir-
tuosi, enthusiasts, rapacious and incompetent professional men
of all kinds, are handled in terms of their occupational approach
to life as distinct from their social behavior. The Menippean
satire thus resembles the confession in its ability to handle abstract ideas and theories, and differs from the novel in its characterization, which is stylized rather than naturalistic, and presents people as mouthpieces of the ideas they represent. Here
again no sharp boundary lines can or should be drawn, but if
we compare a character in Jane Austen with a similar character
in Peacock we can immediately feel the differences between the
two forms. Squire Western belongs to the novel, but Thwackum
and Square have Menippean blood in them. . . .

"Petronius, Apuleius, Rabelais, Swift, and Voltaire all use a
loose-jointed narrative form . . . [that] relies on the free play
of intellectual fancy and the kind of humorous observation that
produces caricature. It differs . . . from the picaresque form,
which has the novel's interest in the actual structure of society.
At its most concentrated the Menippean satire presents us with
a vision of the world in terms of a single intellectual pattern.
The intellectual structure built up from the story makes for
violent dislocations in the customary logic of narrative, though
the appearance of carelessness that results reflects only the carelessness of the reader or his tendency to judge by a novel-centered
conception of fiction."[8]

We are all novel-centered, I suspect, in our dealings with
fiction of every kind; it is a difficult orientation to overcome.
Still, our expectations when we read Petronius or *Candide* are

---

Ass, he feels, contains too little verse to be "strictly" Menippean. See
Roman Satire, pp. 33-38, 84-105.
   [8] *Anatomy of Criticism,* pp. 309-10.

by no means the same as when we read George Eliot. It would be absurd to criticize Lucian's *True Story* because "Lucian" (the "I" of the narrative) does not grow into a rounded character. It is in the nature of the enterprise that he shall remain the same stolid, deadpan recorder of incredible adventures. The adventures may have significance for author and reader, but not for the adventurer, to whom things happen only so that he can record them. He is a true innocent, totally untouched by experience, has no inner life, no character at all. To maintain the innocence of Encolpius, the narrator of the *Satyricon*, would be over-paradoxical, and he is more complex than "Lucian"; but he is not essentially different. Twenty more dinners, fifty more seductions, weeks more of discussion (perhaps they were all recorded in the complete work) would leave him as he was, and, one might add, as he should be. Encolpius and his companions exist in a timeless, causeless atmosphere which lacks the substance to nourish change and growth. *The Golden Ass*, to be sure, is different; here change is crucial. Lucius, the narrator, becomes an ass; and, like Gulliver (who at least tries to become a horse), is grateful for the experience. Both Lucius and Gulliver undergo conversions: Lucius into the cult of Isis, Gulliver into the cult of misanthropy. But, radical as these changes are, they accord with the logic of Menippean satire, not with the logic of the novel.

Swift's major satires lack the admixture of verse which is usually taken to be an essential characteristic of the Menippean mode, but in most other respects fit admirably to the pattern. Even that wild farrago *A Tale of a Tub* may be thought of as Menippean satire, a kind of intellectual odyssey, held together by the fact that the narrative portions of the *Tale* (the story of the three brothers) and the Digressions are all part of the intellectual experience of the tale-teller, who remains at the end of his narrative as he was at the beginning. *Gulliver's Travels* conforms to the tradition even more obviously, although treatment of Gulliver's character raises problems which bear on the satirist-satirized theme we have been following.

If we ask who is the satirist of *Gulliver's Travels*, the answer obviously is Swift—or, if he is not "of" *Gulliver's Travels*, he is the satirist who creates the satire of *Gulliver's Travels*. But in the extended sense of the term we are familiar with Gulliver is also a satirist, different from Timon, but in his own way as devastating:

"[I assured his Honour] That, our young *Noblemen* are bred from their Childhood in Idleness and Luxury; that, as soon as Years will permit, they consume their Vigour, and contract odious Diseases among Lewd Females; and when their Fortunes are almost ruined, they marry some Woman of mean Birth, disagreeable Person, and unsound Constitution, merely for the sake of Money, whom they hate and despise. That, the Productions of such Marriages are generally scrophulous, rickety or deformed Children; by which Means the Family seldom continues above three Generations, unless the Wife take Care to provide a healthy Father among her Neighbours, or Domesticks, in order to improve and continue the Breed. That, a weak diseased Body, a meager Countenance, and sallow Complexion, are the true Marks of *noble Blood*; and a healthy robust Appearance is so disgraceful in a Man of Quality, that the World concludes his real Father to have been a Groom or a Coachman. The Imperfections of his Mind run parallel with those of his Body; being a Composition of Spleen, Dulness, Ignorance, Caprice, Sensuality and Pride."[9]

This of course is the Gulliver of the Fourth Voyage, worlds removed from the ship's surgeon who was charmed with the Lilliputians and quick with praise of "my own dear native Country." That Gulliver, he of the early voyages, is so far from being a satirist that he is often the butt *par excellence* of satire: Swift's satire, of course, and, within the work, the King of Brobdingnag's; but also, in a sense, of his own—his, that is, when he is an old man, sitting down to unaccustomed literary labors to compose his memoirs.

We must look at some of the formal relations governing the work. Swift gives us little "outside" information about how or when Gulliver wrote the account of his travels. Richard Sympson, the fictive publisher, said to be a relative of Gulliver on his mother's side, writes that he corrected the Captain's papers; and

---

[9] *Gulliver's Travels*, ed. Harold Williams (Oxford, 1941), pp. 240-41. This edition, which is Vol. xi of the *Prose Works* under the general editorship of Herbert Davis, is the source of all references to the *Travels*.

Gulliver himself complains that his manuscript has been tampered with. That is all we know. Within the work itself, however, is evidence that Gulliver composed his memoirs as an elderly man, after he had retired from his unfortunate life on the sea. Several times in the narrative Gulliver looks back in chronological time to previous voyages, bringing his experience from them to bear on a "present" predicament; but he never looks forward specifically to "future" adventures as commentary on what is happening at the moment. Still, it is apparent from casual comments in the early voyages that a whole realm of "future" experience is available to the writer. For example, at the end of Part 1 Gulliver describes his preparations for shipping out again: "My Daughter *Betty* (who is now well married, and has Children) was then at her Needle-Work" (p. 64). Between "now"—at the time of writing—and "then" lie the years of Gulliver's three subsequent voyages, plus five years which elapse between his final return to England and the composition of the work.

The Gulliver who writes, then, is Gulliver the misanthrope who stuffs his nose with tobacco leaves and keeps a long table between himself and his wife. It is he who "creates" the ship's surgeon—a man capable of longing for the tongue of Demosthenes so that he may celebrate his country in a style equal to its unparalleled merits. Given the emotional and intellectual imbalance of the old seaman, he is remarkably successful in producing an objective portrait of himself as he was in time long past.

The actual, as opposed to the fictive, situation, of course, is that Swift has created two dominant points of view to control the materials of the *Travels*: that of his favorite *ingénu* (the younger Gulliver) and that of the misanthrope. The technique has obvious advantages. An *ingénu* is a superb agent of indirect satire as he roams the world uncritically recording or even embracing the folly which it is the satirist's business to undermine: "*Flimnap*, the Treasurer, is allowed to cut a Caper on the strait Rope, at least an Inch higher than any other Lord in the whole Empire" (p. 22). On the other hand, a misanthrope can develop all the great power of direct, hyperbolic criticism. By allowing Gulliver, an uncritical lover of man, to become an uncritical hater of man, Swift has it both ways.

The technique is not that of the novelist, however. Swift pays little regard to psychological consistency; Gulliver's character can hardly be said to develop; it simply changes. If one takes seriously the premise that Gulliver writes his memoirs after his rebirth, then many passages in the early voyages turn out to be inconsistent and out of character. "There are," says Gulliver of Lilliput, "some Laws and Customs in this Empire very peculiar; and if they were not so directly contrary to those of my own dear Country, I should be tempted to say a little in their Justification" (p. 42). (The laws from Swift's point of view, from the point of view of reason, are excellent.) Here Gulliver is trapped in a conflict between his patriotism and his reason; as he is an *ingénu* his patriotism wins. But note the tense: "I should be tempted"; that is, now—at the time of writing. Given this tense, and given the logic of the controlling situation, it must follow that this is the utterance of Gulliver as he composes the work. At the time he writes, however, Gulliver is committed so irrevocably to the claims of reason that the appeal of patriotism could not possibly have meaning for him—could not, that is, if we assume general consistency in Gulliver's character.

Similar examples of what in novels would be called inconsistency in characterization can be found in nearly all Menippean satires. The first surviving sequence of the *Satyricon* is a direct, serious attack on current abuses in the teaching of oratory; the sentiments are, presumably, those of Petronius, but they are incongruously delivered through the mouth of Encolpius. Two minutes after delivering the attack, Encolpius is racing through a bawdy house where he is unquestionably more at home. There is an amusing passage in Apuleius where Lucius, still in the form of an ass, delivers a diatribe against the venality of judges: "Well, then, you lowest of the low, yes, I am referring to the whole legal profession, all you cattle-like law-clerks and vulture-like barristers—are you really surprised that modern judges are corrupt . . . ?" But then, after some ransacking of history and myth, he breaks off. "Forgive this outburst! I can hear my readers protesting: 'Hey, what's all this about? Are we going to let an ass lecture us in philosophy?' Yes, I dare say I had best return to my story."[10] Many of the tales of *The Golden Ass*,

[10] *The Golden Ass*, trans. Robert Graves (New York, 1951), pp. 259-60.

charming in themselves, are told by the most inappropriate persons. Finally, one does not, after all, read *Brave New World* or Nathaniel West's *A Cool Million* for insight into individual human character. In all these works characters may be amusing, likable, touching—even "consistent"—but almost as by-products of their primary function. They are first of all agents of satire, and the ordinary criteria by which we judge character in novels do not apply.

On the other hand, as though to contradict the above, Menippean satire may employ techniques that we are accustomed to associate only with the most sophisticated novelists. I propose to follow Professor Auerbach's analysis of one such technique as Petronius uses it. The scene is the fantastic banquet given by the parvenu Trimalchio. Encolpius, the narrator of the *Satyricon*, asks his neighbor at the table to identify the woman who is busily running up and down the banquet hall. He obliges:

"That's Trimalchio's wife. Fortunata they call her. She measures money by the bushel. Yet not so long ago, not so long ago, what was she? I hope you won't mind my putting it that way, but you wouldn't have accepted a piece of bread from her hands. Now she sits on top of the world and is Trimalchio's one and only. . . . He can't keep track of what he owns; he's so filthy rich. But that bitch looks out for everything, even where you'd least expect it. She doesn't drink; she's level-headed; her advice is good. But she has a nasty tongue and gossips like a magpie once she gets settled on her cushion. When she likes a person, she really likes him. When she hates one, she certainly hates him. Trimalchio's estates reach as far as a falcon flies. And some money he has! There's more silver in his porter's lodge than any one man's whole estate. And the number of slaves he's got! O my God, I don't think one out of ten knows his master even by sight. Believe me, he could stick any of these louts here in his pocket. . . . But his fellow freedmen are not to be despised either. They aren't badly off. Look at the one sitting all the way back there. Today he is worth eight hundred thousand, and when he started out he had nothing. Not so long ago he carried wood around on his back. But they say—of course I don't know, except that I have heard people talk about it—they say he stole a goblin's magic cap and then found a treasure. Well I won't begrudge a fellow what God has given him. . . . That one there sitting with the freedmen—he used to have a nicely feathered nest too. I don't want to say anything against him. He had a cool million. But somehow he slipped badly. . . ."[11]

The response is remarkable in its circumstantiality, depicting as it does not only Fortunata and Trimalchio and his fellow freedmen, but the values of a whole society and, indeed, of the speaker himself. His language, full of jargon and cliché, throws a light inward, as it were, for it reveals the speaker for what he is: one completely and unselfconsciously at home in the milieu he describes. His wistful awe in the face of all that money places him perfectly. Society and speaker are finely rendered, objectified, for our view. Petronius, however, has not simply set down an objective description of a society of freedmen, as if to say: this is the way it was. Instead, writes Auerbach, he has given us a subjective image of the society as it exists in the mind of a man who is himself a member of the society.

"[Petronius] lets an 'I' who is identical neither with himself nor yet with the feigned narrator Encolpius, turn the spotlight of his perception on the company at table—a highly artful procedure in perspective, a sort of twofold mirroring, which I dare not say is unique in antique literature as it has come down to us, but which is most unusual there. . . . Nowhere, except in this passage from Petronius, do we have, on the one hand, the most intense subjectivity, which is even heightened by individuality of language, and, on the other hand, an objective intent—for the aim is an objective description of the company at table, including the speaker, through a subjective procedure. This procedure leads to a more meaningful and more concrete illusion of life. Inasmuch as the guest describes a company to which he himself belongs both by inner convictions and outward circumstances, the viewpoint is transferred to a point within the picture, the picture thus gains in depth, and the light which illuminates it seems to come from within it."[12]

The scene is an artistic triumph of the highest order and marks Petronius, says Auerbach, as a creative genius. Modern

[11] The translation is by Willard R. Trask; it appears in his translation of Erich Auerbach, *Mimesis* (Princeton, N.J., 1953), pp. 25-26.
[12] *Ibid.*, p. 27.

novelists, Proust, for example, use exactly the same technique.

A passage in Part 1 of *Gulliver's Travels* leads to similar considerations. Gulliver has established himself in Lilliput; he has captured the enemy fleet, been created a *Nardac*, has extinguished a fire in the royal palace. At the height of his fortunes he receives a secret visit from a friend, a considerable person at court, who comes with a warning of impeachment proceedings already undertaken against him:

"In the several Debates upon this Impeachment, it must be confessed that his Majesty gave many Marks of his great *Lenity*. . . . The Treasurer and Admiral insisted that you should be put to the most painful and ignominious Death. . . . Some of your Servants were to have private Orders to strew a poisonous Juice on your Shirts and Sheets, which would soon make you tear your own Flesh, and die in the utmost Torture. . . .

"*Reldresal* . . . justified the good Thoughts you have of him. He allowed your Crimes to be great; but that . . . if his Majesty, in Consideration of your Services, and pursuant to his own merciful Disposition, would please to spare your Life, and only give order to put out both your Eyes . . . Justice might in some measure be satisfied. . . . [As to the Treasurer's objections to the cost of feeding you, that evil might be provided against, said Reldresal] by gradually lessening your Establishment; by which, for want of sufficient Food, you would grow weak and faint, and lose your Appetite, and consequently decay and consume in a few Months; neither would the Stench of your Carcass be then so dangerous, when it should become more than half diminished; and immediately upon your Death, five or six Thousand of his Majesty's Subjects might, in two or three Days, cut your Flesh from your Bones, take it away by Cart-loads, and bury it in distant Parts to prevent Infection; leaving the Skeleton as a Monument of Admiration to Posterity.

"Thus by the great Friendship of the Secretary [i.e., Reldresal], the whole Affair was compromised." (pp. 53-55)

No warning could be more explicit, and no objective description more convincing. As in the episode from the *Satyricon*, the presentation is entirely subjective. Swift is many removes away: Gulliver as an old man is reporting what he as a much younger man was told by a courtier; the courtier in turn paraphrases or quotes what his Majesty or Skyris Bolgolam or Reldresal said. Even Conrad seldom gets further "inside" an affair than that. We are convinced of the "truth" of the courtier's report precisely because we know he belongs, heart and soul, to what he describes. Friendship may prompt his warning Gulliver, but his rhetoric betrays the identity of his values with those of the persons against whom the warning is given. "Thus by the great Friendship of the Secretary, the whole Affair was compromised." The cool objectivity of the speaker's tone as he details the fate in store for Gulliver is a magnificent commentary on himself and what he represents. The Lilliputian court, like that of Trimalchio, is measured by its own standards.

Petronius allows his scene to carry its own judgment; Encolpius' only comment, when his companion's flow of commentary is interrupted by Trimalchio, is that these have been delightful tales. But Swift adds a further twist or two. It is not enough that the Lilliputian court be damned by the report of one of its own. Gulliver comments:

"Yet, as to myself, I must confess, having never been designed for a Courtier, either by my Birth or Education, I was so ill a Judge of Things, that I could not discover the *Lenity* and Favour of this Sentence; but conceived it (perhaps erroneously) rather to be rigorous than gentle. I sometimes thought of standing my Tryal; for although I could not deny the Facts alledged in the several Articles, yet I hoped they would admit of some Extenuations. But having in my Life perused many State-Tryals, which I ever observed to terminate as the Judges saw fit to direct; I durst not rely on so dangerous a Decision. . . .

"At last I fixed upon a Resolution, for which it is probable I may incur some Censure, and not unjustly; for I confess I owe the preserving mine Eyes, and consequently my Liberty, to my own great Rashness and Want of Experience: Because if I had then known the Nature of Princes and Ministers, which I have since observed in many other Courts, and their Methods of treating Criminals less obnoxious than myself; I should with great Alacrity and Readiness have submitted to so *easy* a Punishment." (pp. 56-57)

The satire spreads like the shock wave from an explosion: from local viciousness to world-wide inhumanity, from the Lilliputian target to the centers of power throughout Europe. Gulliver's bitterness points forward to his later immersion in misanthropy.

Similar as the management of perspective is in the passages from the *Satyricon* and from *Gulliver,* and successful as they both are in achieving the illusion of objective reality, there is still a great difference in their respective tones. The difference is wholly a matter of style. Petronius manages brilliantly to capture the accent and intonation of the speaker himself. The rhythm of the speech, the syntax, the vocabulary—all bespeak the amiable vulgarian who is part of what he describes. Unquestionably here the style is the man. Not so with Swift. His concerns when dealing with human beings are characteristically more abstract. Oddly, the conversation with the courtier is one of the few in the *Travels* presented as direct quotation; conversations are normally reported in Gulliver's hurried, summarizing way as indirect discourse: I informed him that. . . . I dwellt long upon. . . . I computed. . . . He asked what. . . . He then desired to know. . . . It is as though Swift deliberately avoided the direct confrontation in which individuals would speak with their own voices. But the passage under consideration is in direct discourse: "You are to know, said he, that several Committees of Council have been lately called in the most private Manner on your Account. . . ."; the monologue continues for several pages. Still, we have no real sense that what is said represents a *personal* voice at all. One reason is that the bulk of what the friend reports is something between summary and quotation of what other people have said:

"*Bolgolam,* the Admiral, could not preserve his Temper; but rising up in Fury, said, he wondered how the Secretary durst presume to give his Opinion for preserving the Life of a Traytor: That the Services you had performed, were, by all true Reasons of State, the great Aggravation of your Crimes; that you, who were able to extinguish the Fire, by discharge of Urine in her Majesty's Apartment (which he mentioned with Horror) might, at another time, raise an Inundation by the same Means, to drown the whole Palace. . . ." (p. 54)

These are the rhythms that Gulliver as author habitually employs in recording conversation. The speaker is allowed almost no individual tone, as a consequence of which our sense of him as a person is vague. Yet we know unmistakably his relation to certain ideas and moral attitudes. Through him we are shown the motivation of admirals, the "magnanimity" of princes, the objectivity of friends in discussing one's own demise. Insubstantial as he may be, he is an excellent conductor of satire.

But if the characters Gulliver meets on his travels lack individuality, if their voices lack the kind of realism we find in the voice of Encolpius' nameless companion, how different the texture of most of the rest of the work! Swift claims in a letter to Pope that a Bishop in Dublin had read the *Travels* and decided it was full of improbable lies—he hardly believed a word of it; it is as good testimony as any to the extraordinary illusion of verisimilitude Swift imparts to the narrative.[13] "There is an Air of Truth apparent through the whole," says Richard Sympson, the "publisher," attributing it to the circumstantiality of the "plain and simple" style, to which he condescends a little, and of which Gulliver is proud. Gulliver can hardly be conceived of apart from his style; he defines himself by the way he writes, particularly at the beginning:

"My Father had a small Estate in *Nottinghamshire*; I was the Third of five Sons. He sent me to *Emanuel-College* in *Cambridge*, at Fourteen Years old, where I resided three Years, and applied my self close to my Studies. . . . I was bound Apprentice to Mr. *James Bates*, an eminent Surgeon in *London*, with whom I continued four Years. . . . I took Part of a small House in the *Old Jury*; and being advised to alter my Condition, I married Mrs. *Mary Burton*, second Daughter to Mr. *Edmond Burton*, Hosier, in *Newgatestreet*, with whom I received four Hundred Pounds for a Portion." (pp. 3-4)

To define one's life, one enumerates the solid, unproblematic facts that have gone to make it, and one uses solid, unproblematic sentences—simple and straightforward as one's own character.

[13] *Correspondence*, ed. Ball, III, 368. A story is told that John Bell, author of *Travels from St. Petersburg* . . . (1763), applied to William Robertson, the eminent Scottish historian, for advice on the style most appropriate for an account of the travels he had made into Asia. "Take Gulliver's Travels for your model," said Robertson, "and you cannot go wrong." *Quarterly Review*, XVII (1817), p. 464 n.

As the account proceeds the factual texture is thickened:

"By an Observation, we found ourselves in the Latitude of 30 degrees 2 Minutes South. Twelve of our Crew were dead by immoderate Labour, and ill Food; the rest were in a very weak Condition. On the fifth of *November*, which was the beginning of Summer in those Parts, the Weather being very hazy, the Seamen spyed a Rock, within half a Cable's length of the Ship; but the Wind was so strong, that we were driven directly upon it, and immediately split. Six of the crew, of whom I was one, having let down the Boat into the Sea, made a Shift to get clear of the Ship, and the Rock. . . . In about half an Hour the Boat was overset by a sudden Flurry from the North. What became of my Companions in the Boat, as well as of those who escaped on the Rock, or were left in the Vessel, I cannot tell; but conclude they were all lost. For my own Part, I swam as Fortune directed me. . . ." (pp. 4-5)

The lack of modulation is striking. The predominately declarative sentences set out the things that happen in their concrete particularity, piling them up but making no differentiation among them. There is something monstrous in the way that Gulliver can describe the taking of a geographical fix, the deaths of twelve seamen, the wreck of the ship, the loss of his companions, his inability to sit up after his sleep ashore—all in sentences similar in structure and identical in tone. Ordinarily, by his style a writer judges his material, places it for his reader in the context of moral experience. Here, the lack of modulation in the style is a moral commentary on the writer—on Gulliver. Even the King of Brobdingnag is struck by this aspect of Gulliver's style: "He was amazed how so impotent and groveling an Insect as I (these were his Expressions) could entertain such inhuman Ideas, and in so familiar a Manner as to appear wholly unmoved at all the Scenes of Blood and Desolation, which I had painted. . . ." (pp. 118-19)

But while we may equate the impassivity of tone with an impassivity of sensibility, we are overwhelmed by the impression of Gulliver's commitment to hard, undeniable fact. Dr. Johnson speaks finely of Swift's "vigilance of minute attention"; we see it most impressively as Gulliver records his reaction to the Lilliputians. The pages are peppered with citations of numbers, figures, dimensions: I count over thirty such citations in the last three paragraphs of Chapter One, each figure increasing our sense of the reality of the scene; for nothing, we tend to think, is so real as number. Gulliver's style approximates an ideal of seventeenth-century scientists: "the marriage of words and things," the deliverance, as Thomas Sprat puts it in a famous passage, of "so many *things*, almost in an equal number of words."[14] Swift (not Gulliver, now) is parodying the life-style that finds its only meaning in things, that lives entirely in the particularity of externals, without being able to discriminate among them. This explains in part the function of the scatological passages of Parts I and II which have been found so offensive.[15] The style also helps prepare for the satire on language theory in Part III. But, parody or no, Gulliver's style is a marvellous instrument for narration, building easily and with increasing fluidity the substantiality of his world.

Gulliver, then, succeeds in the novelist's great task of creating the illusion of reality.[16] But again we must recall that he is not a novelist. The reality he creates is one of externals only. He does not create a sense of reality about himself—or rather, to

[14] *History of the Royal Society* (London, 1667), p. 113.

[15] "I hope, the gentle Reader will excuse me for dwelling on these and the like Particulars; which however insignificant they may appear to grovelling vulgar Minds, yet will certainly help a Philosopher to enlarge his Thoughts and Imagination, and apply them to the Benefit of publick as well as private Life; which was my sole Design in presenting this and other Accounts of my Travels to the World; wherein I have been chiefly studious of Truth, without affecting any Ornaments of Learning, or of Style. But the whole Scene of this Voyage made so strong an Impression on my Mind, and is so deeply fixed in my Memory, that in committing it to Paper, I did not omit one material Circumstance: However, upon a strict Review, I blotted out several Passages of less Moment which were in my first Copy, for fear of being censured as tedious and trifling, whereof Travellers are often, perhaps not without Justice, accused." (p. 78)

[16] "I may . . . venture to say," writes Henry James, "that the air of reality (solidity of specification) seems to me the supreme virtue of a novel—the merit on which all its other merits (including . . . conscious moral purpose . . .) helplessly and submissively depend. If it be not there they are all as nothing, and if these be there, they owe their effect to the success with which the author has produced the illusion of life." "The Art of Fiction," in *The Future of the Novel*, ed. Leon Edel (New York, 1956), p. 14.

step now outside the framework of the *Travels*, Swift does not create a sense of reality about Gulliver. Gulliver is not a character in the sense that Tom Jones, say, is a character. He has the most minimal subjective life; even his passion at the end is hardly rooted in personality. He is, in fact, an abstraction, manipulated in the service of satire. To say this of the principal character of a novel would be damning; but to say it of a work written according to the conventions of Lucian's *A True Story*, the *Satyricon, Gargantua* is simply to describe.

The paucity of Gulliver's inner life needs little documentation. To be sure, he is shown as decent and kindly and honorable at the beginning: we are delighted with his stalwart vindication of the honor of the Treasurer's wife, whom malicious gossip accused of having an affair with him. But his life is primarily of the senses. He sees—how superbly he sees!——he hears, smells, feels. Poke him and he twitches; but there is little evidence of rational activity. The *leaping* and *creeping* contest at the Lilliputian court is a diversion for him, nothing more; he sees no resemblance between it and practices in any other court in the world. Except for an occasional (dramatically inconsistent) episode where he is startled into an expression of bitterness, Gulliver's is a life without nuance. The nuances are there, of course, everywhere, but must be supplied by the reader.

In the second voyage Gulliver is even more obviously a mouthpiece for ideas (usually absurd or despicable ideas set up to be subverted by the satire) than a character in his own right. True, he is occasionally reflective: "Undoubtedly Philosophers are in the Right," he muses, as he cowers in fear of being squashed under the foot of the Brobdingnagian, "when they tell us, that nothing is great or little otherwise than by Comparison" (p. 71). And his own thoughts may even reflect satiric insight. On one occasion the King of Brobdingnag remarks on how human (i.e., Brobdingnagian) grandeur can be mimicked by insects like Gulliver. Gulliver is furious; but the King's mockery works insidiously, and Gulliver begins to wonder whether he has been injured or not: ". . . if I had then beheld a Company of *English* Lords and Ladies in their Finery and Birth-day Cloaths, acting their several Parts in the most courtly Manner of Strutting, and Bowing and Prating; to say the Truth, I should have been strongly tempted to laugh as much at them as this King and his Grandees did at me." (p. 91; cf. p. 108)

Most of the time, however, Gulliver either is impenetrably innocent or embraces the pride and the folly of European civilization with insatiable zeal—all in the interest of the most mordant satire. We can best see how this works by looking at the climactic series of dialogues with the King. The scene is projected with a fine sense of dramatic value: by the King's order Gulliver's box is carried into the royal closet and set upon the table; Gulliver brings one of his chairs out of the box, settles himself on a level with the King's head. The two sit there gravely discussing politics and government and morality. What an opportunity for Gulliver! "IMAGINE with thy self, courteous Reader, how often I then wished for the Tongue of *Demosthenes* or *Cicero* that might have enabled me to celebrate the Praise of my own dear native Country in a Style equal to its Merits and Felicity" (p. 111). As he writes his memoirs, Gulliver reports the substance of the conversations (there were at least seven of them) rather than the conversations themselves: "I then spoke at large upon the Constitution of an *English* Parliament, partly made up of an illustrious Body called the House of Peers, Persons of the noblest Blood, and of the most ancient and ample Patrimonies." The picture he draws of England's history and political institutions is roseate, innocent, abstract—a fat target for the wickedly acute questions of the King. These (still in indirect discourse) are at first simple statements in interrogatory form of abuses in the institutions Gulliver has described: "He asked . . . What Qualifications were necessary in those who are to be created new Lords: Whether the Humour of the Prince, a sum of Money to a Court-Lady, or a Prime Minister; or a Design of strengthening a Party opposite to the publick Interest, ever happened to be Motives in these Advancements." No indication of the King's own attitude is given (nor does Gulliver think it either prudent or convenient to repeat his answers) but the cumulative effect of the long series of queries, all in the same form, is powerful. As the questions continue to probe into weaknesses both institutional and moral, the interrogatives become overt accusations: the King was at a loss . . . he wondered to hear . . . he was amazed . . . he laughed at . . . he was perfectly astonished. Under the implacable pounding Gulliver's flimsy structure is reduced to rubble, and we are prepared for the terrible climax. It gains much effectiveness by a shift into direct discourse:

"My little Friend *Grildrig*; you have made a most admirable Panegyrick upon your Country. You have clearly proved that Ignorance, Idleness, and Vice are the proper Ingredients for qualifying a Legislator. That Laws are best explained, interpreted, and applied by those whose Interest and Abilities lie in perverting, confounding, and eluding them. I observe among you some Lines of an Institution, which in its Original might have been tolerable; but these half erased, and the rest wholly blurred and blotted by Corruptions. It doth not appear from all you have said, how any one Perfection is required towards the Procurement of any one Station among you; much less that Men are ennobled on Account of their Virtue, that Priests are advanced for their Piety or Learning, Soldiers for their Conduct or Valour, Judges for their Integrity, Senators for the Love of their Country, or Councellors for their Wisdom. . . . By what I have gathered from your own Relation, and the Answers I have with much Pains wringed and extorted from you; I cannot but conclude the Bulk of your Natives, to be the most pernicious Race of little odious Vermin that Nature ever suffered to crawl upon the Surface of the Earth." (p. 116)

It is a stunning culmination to a scene constructed on the principles of the formal verse satire. Here the "frame" is provided by the controlling fiction and given dramatic cogency by all the brilliantly elaborated narrative which has led up to the encounter. The "I" of the scene—Gulliver—presents the thesis: the institutions of England are perfection itself; the *adversarius* —the King—demolishes the thesis by his questions and pushes on from institutional criticism to the shrivelling condemnation of man. The destructive power of his analysis is overwhelming, but even as he delivers it the "positives" of his world (Part B of the formal verse satire according to Miss Randolph's schematization)[17] are made clear. Sometimes they appear in the question itself: The King asked, "whether a private Man's House might not better be defended by himself, his Children, and

[17] See Chap. III above.

Family; than by half a Dozen Rascals picked up at a Venture in the Streets, for small Wages, who might get an Hundred Times more by cutting their Throats." Sometimes the King makes them explicit: "He said, he knew no Reason, why those who entertain Opinions prejudicial to the Publick, should be obliged to change, or should not be obliged to conceal them." In any event the positive and the negative aspects of the satire confront each other in bold relief; it is rare in Swift to find the positives of the text in such unequivocal accord with what are manifestly his own positives.

But Swift is not content to leave the scene there. He adds a coda, hammering home the themes and warping Gulliver's character around in the service of his aim. Gulliver's reaction to the King's judgment of man is an embarrassed apology; he is sorry that his noble and most beloved country has been subjected to such treatment, and he is apologetic also about his Majesty:

". . . great Allowances should be given to a King who lives wholly secluded from the rest of the World, and must therefore be altogether unacquainted with the Manners and Customs that most prevail in other Nations: The want of which Knowledge will ever produce many *Prejudices,* and a certain *Narrowness of Thinking*; from which we and the politer Countries of *Europe* are wholly exempted. And it would be hard indeed, if so remote a Prince's Notions of Virtue and Vice were to be offered as a Standard for all Mankind." (p. 117). (It is not always possible simply to invert Gulliver's statement so as to arrive at Swift's point; witness the fine ambiguity of "it would be hard indeed" in the last sentence.) To ingratiate himself with the King, Gulliver describes (now in indirect discourse but with great graphic power) the destruction wrought by gunpowder and offers him the secret of its manufacture—a secret which would make him "absolute Master of the Lives, the Liberties, and the Fortunes of his People." The King's horror Gulliver can shrug off: "A STRANGE Effect of *narrow Principles* and *short Views*!" From a simple *ingénu,* uncritically bemused by patriotic fervor, Gulliver is made to become an immoralist, advocating doctrines that earlier he has loathed. (In Lilliput he had indignantly refused to be an "Instrument of bringing a free and brave People into

Slavery.") Where Gulliver's standards had once represented the satirical positives, here, with the same issue in view, his position is reversed. The satire is consistent, but the characterization is not.

Once again the positives are blocked out with great explicitness. When Gulliver speaks in his own person only the most obvious reversal is required: "The Learning of this People is very defective; consisting only in Morality, History, Poetry and Mathematicks; wherein they must be allowed to excel. But, the last of these is wholly applied to what may be useful in Life; to the Improvement of Agriculture and all mechanical Arts; so that among us it would be little esteemed. And as to Ideas, Entities, Abstractions and Transcendentals, I could never drive the least Conception into their Heads" (p. 120). When Gulliver expounds the King's sentiments, the positives are quite unproblematic: "He confined the Knowledge of governing within very *narrow Bounds*; to common Sense and Reason, to Justice and Lenity, to the speedy Determination of Civil and criminal Causes; with some other obvious Topicks which are not worth considering. And, he gave it for his Opinion; that whoever could make two Ears of Corn, or two Blades of Grass to grow upon a Spot of Ground where only one grew before; would deserve better of Mankind, and do more essential Service to his Country, than the whole Race of Politicians put together" (pp. 119-20). We look in vain for ironic undercutting. Swift might well be speaking in his own voice.

I see no virtue in demonstrating in detail what is universally agreed to: that the third voyage is the weakest of the four. Coleridge called it "a wretched abortion";[18] and while not everyone shares either the grounds of his dislike or its violence, still one would be hard put to make a case for the uniform literary success of Part III. It has, to be sure, its own excellencies. Swift uses satirical techniques here, familiar in his earlier work, that are quite unlike the prevailing methods of the *Travels*. In *A Tale of a Tub* and elsewhere one of his favorite devices is to take literally a metaphorical statement of likeness between two things, then to push the implications of the statement into the gro-

---

[18] *Coleridge's Miscellaneous Criticism*, ed. Thomas M. Raysor (Cambridge, Mass., 1936), p. 130.

tesque. An ingenious projector in the Academy of Lagado wants to cure the diseases and corruptions of government. He starts with the commonplace notion on which "all Writers and Reasoners have agreed, that there is a strict universal Resemblance between the natural and the political Body" (p. 172). What, then, could be more logical than to treat the peccant humours of a Senate—its tendency to "Spleen, Flatus, Vertigoes and Deliriums—" as one would treat these ailments in individuals? Apothecaries are the answer to good government, and for the body politic there is nothing like a good laxative. If not a laxative, then "Lenitives, Aperitives, Abstersives, Corrosives, Restringents, Palliatives, . . . Cephalalgicks, Ictericks, Apophlegmaticks, Acousticks." The spirit, in this grotesque world, still operates mechanically.

Again, Gulliver's account of eighteenth-century McCarthyism is superb:

"I told him, that in the Kingdom of *Tribnia,* by the Natives called *Langden,* where I had long sojourned, the Bulk of the People consisted wholly of Discoverers, Witnesses, Informers, Accusers, Prosecutors, Evidences, Swearers. . . . It is first agreed and settled among them, what suspected Persons shall be accused of a Plot: Then, effectual Care is taken to secure all their Letters and other Papers, and put the Owners in Chains. These Papers are delivered to a Set of Artists very dextrous in finding out the mysterious Meanings of Words, Syllables and Letters. For Instance, they can decypher a Close-stool to signify a Privy-Council; a Flock of Geese, a Senate; a lame Dog, an Invader; the Plague, a standing Army; a Buzard, a Minister; the Gout, a High Priest; a Gibbet, a Secretary of State; a Chamber pot, a Committee of Grandees; a Sieve a Court Lady; a Broom, a Revolution: a Mouse-trap, an Employment; a bottomless Pit, the Treasury; a Sink, a C——t; a Cap and Bells, a Favourite; a broken Reed, a Court of Justice; an empty Tun, a General; a running Sore, the Administration." (p. 175)

But clearly this goes beyond McCarthyism. The first target is the interpreters who wrench and distort language for their own infamous purposes; to say that when a man has written the word *gibbet* he intended to signify the Secretary of State is absurd and vicious. Then the satire coils around itself: these grossly unjust distortions of language are, from one point of view, accurate. The Administration *is* a running sore, and its minions are best qualified to make the full identification. Their ingenuity is not yet exhausted: "By transposing the Letters of the Alphabet, in any suspected Paper, they can lay open the deepest Designs of a discontented Party. So for Example, if I should say in a Letter to a Friend, *Our Brother* Tom *hath just got the Piles*; a Man of Skill in this Art would discover how the same Letters which compose that Sentence, may be analysed into the following Words; *Resist, a Plot is brought home—The Tour.* And this is the Anagrammatick Method" (pp. 175-76). For benefit of the curious: La Tour was the pseudonym adopted by Swift's friend Bolingbroke during his exile in France; and the anagram almost works.

Such passages, together with the Juvenalian horror of the Struldbrugg episode, are successful in themselves, but fit into no coherent pattern. Gulliver travels too much in his third voyage, his experience is too diffuse, and there is a noticeable lapse in the control of materials. One does not have to be inordinately novel-centered to feel that the haphazard shifts in point of view are confusing and ineffective. For pages Gulliver can condemn everything he sees on the fantastic Flying Island, then in the next breath declare it "the most delicious Spot of Ground in the World." He spins between extreme bitterness and extreme naïveté as though he had lost a rudder. His gyrations disperse the power of the satire.

Still, the drift of Gulliver's attitude is clearly toward the misanthropic; and when in the last voyage he finds himself caught between the fixed positions of the Yahoos and the Houyhnhnms, he is quick to make his unnaturally extreme choice. There is logic to his change. Like Tennyson's Ulysses, he is part of all that he has known: he has heard the King of Brobdingnag, he has learned the dirty secrets of modern history at Glubbdubdrib, he has suffered at the hands of the most abandoned criminals—those who composed his crew. In a way his misanthropy has been earned. But this is really beside the point; for Gulliver's change comes about, not in any psychologically plausible way, but because the final, desperate, internal demands of the satire force him to change.

Part IV of the *Travels* is schematically so like Part II that comparison is inevitable. The intellectual climaxes of the voyages come in conversations between Gulliver and his host of the moment: The King in Brobdingnag, the grey steed in Houyhnhnm-land. In Part II, as we have seen, Swift prepared the scene carefully, giving it a dramatic setting and structure like that of the formal verse satire. The conversations in Part IV are less sharply dramatized, the climactic chapters five and six hardly being set apart from other talks in which Gulliver has explained to his Master who and what he is. Gulliver discourses on war, law, commerce, medicine, ministers-of-state, the nobility—the subjects of his rhapsody in Part II—but this time in a flood of vituperation rarely matched in literature. The Houyhnhnm has little role in this onslaught except to ask an occasional question. He is as shadowy an interlocutor as some of Juvenal's. The whole tremendous force of these dozen pages is carried by Gulliver's diatribe. For comparison one thinks of Shakespeare's Timon; yet the difference in tone between the two modes of utterance is enormous. Timon vents personal rage; his hatred comes boiling forth in a mighty, prolonged curse. Gulliver here expresses no hatred; he professes simply to be laying before his Master "the whole State of Europe," as he says. His vein is cold, analytic, impersonal. He speaks of the law:

"I SAID there was a Society of Men among us, bred up from their Youth in the Art of proving by Words multiplied for the Purpose, that *White* is *Black* and *Black* is *White*, according as they are paid. To this Society all the rest of the People are Slaves.

"For Example. If my Neighbor hath a Mind to my *Cow*, he hires a Lawyer to prove that he ought to have my *Cow* from me. I must then hire another to defend my Right; it being against all Rules of *Law* that any Man should be allowed to speak for himself. Now in this Case, I who am the true Owner lie under two great Disadvantages. First, my Lawyer being practiced almost from his Cradle in defending Falshood; is quite out of his Element when he would be an Advocate for Justice, which as an Office unnatural, he always attempts with great Awkwardness, if not with Ill-will. The second Disadvantage is, that my Lawyer must proceed with great Caution: Or else he will be reprimanded by the Judges, and abhorred by his Brethren, as one who would lessen the Practice of the Law. And therefore I have but two Methods to preserve my *Cow*. The first is, to gain over my Adversary's Lawyer with a double Fee; who will then betray his Client, by insinuating that he hath Justice on his Side. The second Way is for my Lawyer to make my Cause appear as unjust as he can; by allowing the *Cow* to belong to my Adversary; and this if it be skilfully done, will certainly bespeak the Favour of the Bench.

"Now, your Honour is to know, that these Judges are Persons . . . picked out from the most dextrous Lawyers who are grown old or lazy: And having been byassed all their Lives against Truth and Equity, lie under . . . a fatal Necessity of favouring Fraud, Perjury and Oppression. . . . It is a Maxim among these Lawyers, that whatever hath been done before, may legally be done again: And therefore they take special Care to record all the Decisions formerly made against common Justice and the general Reason of Mankind. . . . under the Name of *Precedents*. . . ." (pp. 232-33)

This goes on for paragraphs.

The two chapters of unimpassioned tirade (one can speak of this style only in terms of paradox) slide imperceptibly between indirect and direct discourse, between the imperfect and the historical present tense, producing sometimes a feeling of dramatic immediacy, sometimes a feeling of rapid survey. As one "fact" is coldly and neatly balanced upon another, there is little modulation in tone, no attempt at climax, no dramatic shift into direct discourse as in Part II; it is as though Swift, here at the apogee of Gulliver's progress, scorned such rhetorical tricks, as Gulliver himself claims to do, content to let his "plain Matter of Fact" carry the burden. In its impassive efficiency the style reminds one in some respects of an official Air Force report of a successful bombing raid on a large city.

But this is overstated. The most obvious rhetorical device used here is the exaggeration which pushes Gulliver's account into the realm of the grotesque. We can no more believe in the reality of Gulliver's lawyers than we can believe in Falstaff's tales of his prowess at Gadshill: the two passages have something in common. These lawyers are superhuman, true giants of duplicity. They belong in a far more ideal world than any we know; we can even (unless we are too shocked, or unless we are lawyers) laugh. For obscure reasons, the exaggeration makes our pleasure possible, while it in no way weakens the destructive force of the satiric attack.[19]

Swift uses another favorite stylistic maneuver here—the incongruous catalogue: ". . . vast Numbers of our People are compelled to seek their Livelihood by Begging, Robbing, Stealing, Cheating, Pimping, Forswearing, Flattering, Suborning, Forging, Gaming, Lying, Fawning, Hectoring, Voting, Scribling, Stargazing, Poysoning, Whoring, Canting, Libelling, Free-thinking, and the like Occupations: Every one of which Terms, I was at much Pains to make him understand" (p. 236). It is a noxious enumeration, saved from mere ranting by the incongruity. Syntactical equivalence in a list of this kind obviously implies moral equivalence. Thus star-gazing and canting come to equal murder. At first sight the conjunction is amusing (as is the picture of Gulliver spending days in the intricate job of translation); but the final satiric insinuation is that in a sense the equivalence holds: common to all the "Occupations" is a perversion of reason and morality which can lead only to disaster. Precisely this is the burden of the great satire contemporary with *Gulliver's Travels*, Pope's *Dunciad*.[20]

Such rhetorical flourishes are rare in the climactic two chapters of the fourth voyage, however. Their over-riding function is to develop with cold implacability the horror of English civilization as Gulliver sees it. Like Timon and like Alceste, Gulliver has assumed the role of satirist, and from this point on he broadens his target to include humanity itself: "When I thought of

[19] It is as difficult to account for our pleasure in vituperation as for our pleasure in tragedy. But the pleasure is there. A Victorian clergyman (T. E. Brown, the Manx poet) wrote of *A Tale of a Tub*: "The hearty cursing . . . goes straight to my midriff—so satisfying, the best of tonics." *Letters of Thomas Edward Brown*, ed. Sidney T. Irwin (New York, 1900), I, 173.
[20] One passage from Chapter v seems strangely out of key: "Differences in Opinions hath cost many Millions of Lives: For Instance, whether *Flesh* be *Bread*, or *Bread* be *Flesh*: Whether the Juice of a certain *Berry* be *Blood* or *Wine*: Whether *Whistling* be a Vice or a Virtue . . ." (p. 230). The technique and the imagery come from Swift's youth, from *A Tale of a Tub*, rather than from Gulliver in any of his manifestations.

my Family, my Friends, my Countrymen, or human Race in general, I considered them as they really were, *Yahoos* in Shape and Disposition" (p. 262).[21]

Against the destructiveness of Gulliver's onslaught, we look for the kind of positives that are evident in the episode of the Brobdingnagian King. We naturally turn to the Houyhnhnms who represent to Gulliver (and surely in some sense to Swift) one pole of an antinomy: "The Perfection of Nature" over against the repulsiveness of Yahoo-man. Both Gulliver and the Houyhnhnms are at pains to point out wherein Houyhnhnm perfection lies. It is first physical: Gulliver is lost in awe of the "Strength, Comeliness and Speed" of the horses, whereas he can view his own person only with detestation. The Houyhnhnms themselves are emphatic on the deficiencies of the human physique: Gulliver's hands are too soft to walk on, his nails too short to claw with, his face flat, nose prominent, eyes misplaced, etc. (pp. 226-27). Houyhnhnm perfection is next mental: the horses' lives are "wholly governed" by reason, an infallible faculty, at least to the degree that there is nothing "problematical" about it; reason strikes them with immediate conviction, so that opinion and controversy are unknown. Their perfection is finally moral. They lead austere lives devoted to temperance, industry, and cleanliness; they have no idea of what is evil in a rational creature, have no vice, no lusts, and their passions are firmly controlled by the rational faculty. Their principal virtues are friendship and benevolence, which extend to the whole race; and love as we understand it is unknown. For Gulliver the Houyhnhnms are the repository of all that is good.

Here are positives in abundance, the only question being whether they are unqualifiedly Swift's positives. Most critics have felt that they are and that *Gulliver's Travels* (to say nothing of Swift's character) suffers thereby. Coleridge, for example, writes: ". . . the defect of the work is its inconsistency; the Houyhnhnms are not rational creatures, *i.e.*, creatures of perfect

---

[21] Gulliver is even capable of a macabre wit: "And, to set forth the Valour of my own dear Countrymen, I assured him, that I had seen them blow up a Hundred Enemies at once in a Siege . . . and beheld the dead Bodies drop down in Pieces from the Clouds, to the great Diversion of all the Spectators" (p. 231).

reason; they are not progressive. . . . they, *i.e.*, Swift himself—has a perpetual affectation of being wiser than his Maker . . . and of eradicating what God gave to be subordinated and used; *ex. gr.*, the maternal and paternal affection. . . . In short, critics in general complain of the Yahoos; I complain of the Houy-hnhnms."[22] F. R. Leavis writes that the Houyhnhnms "stand for Reason, Truth, and Nature, the Augustan positives, and it was in deadly earnest that Swift appealed to these"—ineffectually appealed, according to Leavis. For G. Wilson Knight, Swift "has none of any *emotional* power" in presenting his positives. "His Hellenic sympathies are all castrated before fit for use. His Utopia is as coldly rational as Milton's Christ." Most recently, Middleton Murry, writing in the same vein, finds the Houyhnhnms "ludicrously inadequate" as symbols of goodness.[23] So, in a carefully qualified sense, they are; and so they were designed to be.

It seems likely that a close reading of Gulliver's fourth voyage is such a shocking experience as to anesthetize the feeling for the ludicrous of even the most sensitive readers (perhaps *particularly* the most sensitive readers). I do not mean to deny the horror of the work, which is radical; but the horror is ringed, as it were, by Swift's mocking laughter. For example, Coleridge is outraged at the way "the horse discourses on the human frame with the grossest prejudices that could possibly be inspired by vanity and self-opinion." Human limbs, Coleridge stoutly insists, are much better suited for climbing and for managing tools than are fetlocks. Swift lacks "reverence for the original frame of man." True, Swift did lack reverence for human clay; but he also wrote the scene of the Houyhnhnm's denigration of the human body as comedy. It is very funny. It is a kind of parody of the eighteenth century's concern over man's coveting various attributes of the animals, "the strength of bulls, the fur of bears." It is even connected, as we shall see, with the theme of man's coveting supra-human reason. It has the same satirical function as the parallel passage in the second voyage, where the

[22] *Coleridge's Miscellaneous Criticism*, ed. Raysor, pp. 128-30.
[23] Leavis, "The Irony of Swift," in his edition of *Determinations* (London, 1934), pp. 101-02; Knight, *The Burning Oracle* (London, 1939), p. 129; John Middleton Murry, *Jonathan Swift* (London, 1954), p. 345.

Brobdingnagian philosophers determine after close examination of his form that Gulliver is incapable of preserving his life "either by Swiftness, or climbing of Trees, or digging Holes in the Earth" and must be a *Lusus Naturae*—this kind of determination being "to the unspeakable Advancement of human Knowledge" (pp. 87-88). The equine chauvinism of the Houyhnhnms, amusing as it is, undercuts their authority; it must raise doubts in our minds about their adequacy as guides to *human* excellence, to say nothing of the adequacy of Gulliver, who wants to become a horse and whose capacities in matters requiring moral and intellectual discrimination have not been such as to inspire confidence.

Our dubieties are likely to be strengthened by a careful reading of the last part of the voyage. Although Gulliver presumes to doubt the reasonableness of the Houyhnhnm decision to banish him, he builds his canoe of Yahoo skins and prepares, brokenhearted, to sail into exile. His Master condescends to lift his hoof to Gulliver's mouth; and with this accolade ("Detractors are pleased to think it improbable, that so illustrious a Person should descend to give so great a Mark of Distinction to a Creature so inferior as I") he pushes off in search of an uninhabited island: "so horrible was the Idea I conceived of returning to live in the Society and under the Government of Yahoos." He reaches an island, where he is the victim of an unprovoked attack by savages who wound him with an arrow, and is then picked up, against his will, by Portuguese sailors.[24] An odd situation arises here if we remember that it is the misanthropic Gulliver who is writing his memoirs. It is he who in describing the Portuguese insists on their admirable qualities. The common sailors are "honest"; they address Gulliver with "great Humanity." Captain Pedro de Mendez "was a very courteous and generous Person"; in his dealings with Gulliver he is shown consistently to be a wise and compassionate man. Yet Gulliver is

[24] The first critic I know to have considered systematically the importance of the Portuguese sailors to the meaning of the fourth voyage is John F. Ross, "The Final Comedy of Lemuel Gulliver," in *Studies in the Comic*, University of California Publications in English, Vol. 8, No. 2 (Berkeley, Calif., 1941), pp. 175-96. Since the publication of this article a number of American critics have argued against the identification of Swift's positives with the Houyhnhnm world.

unable to distinguish morally between the savages who had wounded him and this human being whose benevolence is worthy Houyhnhnm-land. Because the Captain is a man (a Yahoo in Gulliver's terms), Gulliver is perpetually on the verge of fainting at his mere presence; the best he can say of Don Pedro is, "at last I descended to treat him like an Animal which had some little Portion of Reason" (p. 271). Such is the attitude of Gulliver aboard ship. But the Gulliver who is writing (five years, he says, after his return to England) is of precisely the same mind. He shows not the slightest compunction at his earlier fierce denial of spiritual kinship with the Portuguese; he still stuffs his nose against the hated smell of humanity, keeps a long table between his wife and himself, and talks willingly only to horses.

The violence of Gulliver's alienation, his demand (like that of Timon and Alceste) for the absolute, incapacitate him for what Lionel Trilling calls the "common routine" of life—that feeling for the ordinary, the elemental, the enduring which validates all tragic art.[25] Each of Gulliver's voyages begins with a departure from the common routine, each ends with a return to it—to his wife "Mrs. *Mary Burton*, second Daughter to Mr. *Edmond Burton*, Hosier" and their children. This commonplace family represents a fixed point of stability and calm in Gulliver's life, a kind of norm of humble though enduring human values. Gulliver comes from this life, his early literary style is an emblem of it; and it is against the background given by the common routine that his wild rejection shows so startlingly. His first sight of his family after the years of absence produce in him only "Hatred, Disgust and Contempt. . . . As soon as I entered the House, my Wife took me in her Arms, and kissed me; at which, not having been used to the Touch of that odious Animal for so many Years, I fell in a Swoon for almost an Hour" (p. 273).

In short, Gulliver's *idée fixe* is tested in the world of human experience. The notion that all men are Yahoos cannot accommodate a Don Pedro de Mendez any more than it can accommodate the long-suffering family at Redriff. But this is our own

[25] Lionel Trilling, "Wordsworth and the Iron Time," *Kenyon Review*, XII (1950), p. 495, reprinted as "Wordsworth and the Rabbis," in *The Opposing Self* (New York, 1955).

ironic insight, unavailable to Gulliver, who has never been capable of evaluating the significance of his own experience. Gulliver persistently moulds the world according to his idea of it, instead of moulding his idea according to the reality of things—which must include the Portuguese. Such behavior defines comic absurdity as Bergson expounds it. In other contexts this kind of "inversion of common sense" is characteristic of insanity.[26]

The circumstances of Swift's haunted life have been an open invitation to those who would identify him with Gulliver's obsessive and undiscriminating hatred of man—this despite Swift's famous disclaimer: "I have ever hated all nations, professions, and communities," he wrote to Pope, as he was finishing *Gulliver*, "and all my love is toward individuals: for instance, I hate the tribe of lawyers, but I love Counsellor Such-a-one, and Judge Such-a-one: so with physicians—I will not speak of my own trade—soldiers, English, Scotch, French, and the rest. But principally I hate and detest that animal called man, although I heartily love John, Peter, Thomas, and so forth. . . . I have got materials toward a treatise, proving the falsity of that definition *animal rationale*, and to show it would be only *rationis capax*. Upon this great foundation of misanthropy, though not in Timon's manner, the whole building of my Travels is erected."[27]

Gulliver's hatred *is* in Timon's manner, for John, Peter, and Thomas are precisely as odious to him as the worst Yahoo alive. So far removed is he from Swift.

The last words of Gulliver's memoir are part of the complex process of discrediting his vision of the world. He ends with a virulent diatribe against pride, a sin of which he himself is conspicuously guilty. Like the Poet in *Timon*, he whips his own faults in other men. We recall his absurd condescension to Don Pedro: ". . . at last I descend to treat him like an Animal which had some little Portion of Reason"; his reluctance to exchange the Yahoo skins he wears for Don Pedro's shirts, lest he be de-

[26] Henri Bergson, *Laughter*, trans. Cloudesley Brereton and Fred Rothwell (London, 1911), pp. 183-85. Cf. Joseph Conrad's remark in *Nostromo* about Charles Gould: "A man haunted by a fixed idea is insane. He is dangerous even if that idea is an idea of justice; for may he not bring the heavens down pitilessly upon a loved head?" (Modern Library ed. [1951]), p. 422.

[27] *Correspondence*, ed. Ball, III, 277.

filed. Other manifestations of his pride are charmingly ingenuous. In the last chapter he writes: "I AM not a little pleased that this Work of mine can possibly meet with no Censurers. . . . I write for the noblest End, to inform and instruct Mankind, over whom I may, without Breach of Modesty, pretend to some Superiority. . . . I hope, I may with Justice pronounce myself an Author perfectly blameless. . ." (pp. 276-77). We smile at the vision of Gulliver trotting around like a horse, proclaiming his superiority in a whinny.[28]

But Gulliver's pride has more important implications. His is the pride of reason, the belief that man can and should conduct his life entirely in accord with reason, as do the Houyhnhnms. Reason for them, it will be recalled, is not the faculty of ratiocination, but an innate power: "Neither is *Reason* among them a Point problematical as with us, where Men can argue with Plausibility on both Sides of a Question; but strikes you with immediate Conviction; as it must needs do where it is not mingled, obscured, or discoloured by Passion and Interest" (p. 251). The faculty is unmistakably supra-human. Swift makes the point explicit when he has Gulliver condescend to Don Pedro's "very good *human* Understanding" (p. 272). The italics are Swift's. Houyhnhnm reason reminds one of the faculty innate in the gods of Stoic theology, as they are described in Cicero's *De natura deorum*. Above the vegetable kingdom, above the animals, above man, says the Stoic speaker, is another level of existence: "But the fourth and highest grade is that of beings born by nature good and wise, and endowed from the outset with the innate attributes of right reason and consistency; this must be held to be above the level of man. . . ."[29] Houyhnhnm reason is very close to this—close, that is, to the attributes of the gods: far from those of man. In aspiring to this reason, Gulliver is like the philosopher in *The Mechanical Op-*

---

[28] Swift (as Professor Sherburn reminds me) has another amusing joke at the expense of Gulliver, and perhaps the reader. As warrant for his own truthfulness, Gulliver quotes the lines from Virgil in which the Greek Sinon proclaims *his* truthfulness: Sinon, the greatest liar of antiquity, the man who talked the Trojans into bringing the wooden horse inside the city gates. See *Gulliver's Travels*, p. 276.

[29] Cicero, *De natura deorum academica*, II, xxi, 34, trans. H. Rackham (London, 1933), p. 155.

eration of the Spirit who, his eyes fixed on the stars, allowed his lower parts to be seduced into the ditch. Swift's intense moral realism prompted him always to work for the attainable.

Again, although the Houyhnhnms have emotions and are said to have passions, their emotional life is firmly controlled by reason: their "grand Maxim is, to cultivate Reason, and to be wholly governed by it." We have no impression that the horses must struggle, as men have struggled, to achieve this state of affairs. Compare Stoic doctrine: "Wipe out imagination," wrote Marcus Aurelius, "check impulse: quench desire: keep the governing self [Reason] in its own power."[30] Stoic exaltation of the reason at the expense of the passions represented to many eighteenth-century writers a particularly virulent form of pride. It was a denial of man's nature, of his middle state—that state explored so fully in spatial terms in the first two voyages of *Gulliver*. It was man's effort to rise above himself in the scale of created things. "To be a *Stoic*," wrote Sir William Temple, ". . . one must be perhaps something more or less than a man. . . ." To try to live by reason alone was, as Lovejoy puts it, "an attempt to be unnaturally good and immoderately virtuous."[31] We have "too much weakness for the Stoic's pride," wrote Pope; and a good deal of the *Essay on Man* is devoted to showing the constitutive role of the passions in the nature of man. By advocating for humanity a reason explicitly supra-human, Gulliver exemplifies well the folly of Stoic pride. His moral overstrain is symbolized in his galloping gait and his whinnying tone; his pride is presented dramatically, as, scorning the good about him, he compounds for the shadow of a shadow: two horses and the smell of a stable.

Gulliver, in trying to be a Houyhnhnm, violates the great principle of order:

[30] *The Meditations of the Emperor Marcus Antoninus*, IX, 7, ed. and trans. A. S. L. Farquharson (Oxford, 1944), I, 175. Swift states his opinion of quenching desire in *Thoughts on Various Subjects*: "The Stoical Scheme of supplying our Wants, by lopping off our Desires, is like cutting off our Feet when we want Shoes."

[31] Temple, "Of Health and Long Life," *Works* (Edinburgh, 1754), II, 395; Arthur O. Lovejoy, *Essays in the History of Ideas* (Baltimore, Md., 1948), p. 67.

In Pride, in reas'ning Pride, our error lies;
All quit their sphere, and rush into the skies.
Pride still is aiming at the blest abodes,
Men would be Angels, Angels would be Gods.

. . . .

All this dread ORDER break—for whom? for thee?
Vile worm!—oh Madness, Pride, Impiety![32]

Pope's tone is fervent, for the passages adumbrate catastrophe. Gulliver's venture into the same madness leads not to cosmic disaster but to the ridiculous.

"Oh! if the world had but a dozen Arbuthnots in it, I would burn my Travels," Swift wrote to Pope in the letter cited above. Middleton Murry suggests plausibly that Swift had Arbuthnot in mind as a model for Don Pedro de Mendez; in any event, the two men, one in life and one in fiction, redeem mankind from the charge of total Yahooism. In the character of Don Pedro— slender reed!—Swift makes the strongest statement of his positives in this final part of the *Travels*. To be sure, the destructive criticism—the satire—often carries its own implied standard of excellence. It seems folly to expect a satirist who attacks war to say overtly that he favors peace. But Swift makes a further gesture. Insofar as Gulliver's positives are defined by the *exigence d'absolu* represented by the Houyhnhnms, they are largely discredited as unavailable to man; but by a neat ironic twist Swift has Gulliver, in the Letter to Captain Sympson, voice standards more or less viable in human terms.[33] It is a feature of Gulliver's absurdity that he thinks seven months ample time for Yahoos to have been reformed by his book. Yet,

"I cannot learn that my Book hath produced one single Effect according to my Intentions: I desired you would let me know by a Letter, when Party and Faction were extinguished; Judges

[32] Pope, *Essay on Man*, I, 124-27, 257-58.
[33] "A Letter from Capt. *Gulliver*, to his Cousin *Sympson*" first appeared in the Faulkner edition of the *Travels* published in 1735. The Letter serves a number of extra-literary purposes; but it may also be that Swift felt a need, which he could here satisfy, to state explicitly the conventional reforming intent of satire. Compare the inverted statement of positives at the end of *A Modest Proposal*.

learned and upright; Pleaders honest and modest, with some Tincture of common Sense; and *Smithfield* blazing with Pyramids of Law-Books; the young Nobility's Education entirely changed; the Physicians banished; the Female *Yahoos* abounding in Virtue, Honour, Truth, and good Sense: Courts and Levees of great Ministers thoroughly weeded and swept; Wit, Merit and Learning rewarded; all Disgracers of the Press in Prose and Verse, condemned to eat nothing but their own Cotten, and quench their Thirst with their own Ink. These, and a Thousand other Reformations, I firmly counted upon by your Encouragement; as indeed they were plainly deducible from the Precepts delivered in my Book."

The normative urgency in Swift rarely finds distinguished utterance, and the positives here are perfunctorily stated. Doubtless they are as unattainable in a literal sense as those of the Houyhnhnms, but one does not have to neigh to utter them.

As to the satirists in the work: The King of Brobdingnag functions as one, we know, in the scene we have discussed and again when he takes Gulliver up in his right hand, strokes him, laughs, and asks whether Gulliver is Whig or Tory. It is a splendid passage, reducing in a gesture the folly of party faction to the level of High-Heels versus Low-Heels in Lilliput. The King speaks from standards indistinguishable from those of Swift; and the Brobdingnagian "mixed" government probably represents Swift's notion of an ideal not entirely beyond man's capacity to achieve. The rarefied atmosphere of Houyhnhnm-land could hardly support satire, although Gulliver once accuses his Master of a "malicious Insinuation, which debased human Understanding below the Sagacity of a common *Hound*" (p. 247); but the satirist of Part iv is not a horse, it is Gulliver. Occasionally he displays a satirical technique of great sophistication, as when he wishes that a number of Houyhnhnms could be sent to Europe to teach "the first Principles of Honour, Justice, Truth, Temperance, publick Spirit, Fortitude, Chastity, Friendship, Benevolence, and Fidelity. The *Names* of all which Virtues are still retained among us in most Languages, and are to be met with in modern as well as ancient Authors; which I am able to assert from my own small Reading" (p. 278).

But this is rare. Gulliver's great function is to lay bare the rottenness at the core of human institutions and to show man what, in Gulliver's view, he is: an animal cursed with enough reason to make him more repulsive and more dangerous than the Yahoos. Satirists have always used the transforming power of language to reduce man to the level of the beast, but few have debased man as systematically and as ruthlessly as does Gulliver. To find parallels one must go to the theologians. John Donne describes man's mortal condition in one of his Lincoln Inn sermons: "Between that excremental jelly that thy body is made of at first, and that jelly which thy body dissolves to at last; there is not so noisome, so putrid a thing in nature." "What is man," asks Jeremie Taylor, "but a vessel of dung, a stink of corruption, and, by birth, a slave of the devil?"[34] It may be, as Mr. Roland Frye contends, that Swift's image of the Yahoo was adapted from the vast body of Christian symbolism which emphasizes the loathsome degradation of man's state. It would be possible in that case to think of Gulliver as a satirist of man within the Christian tradition. But *Swift*, as this essay has tried to show, writes as a humanist, not as a theologian. *His* satire undercuts Gulliver's vision of man, which is shown dramatically, concretely, to be incommensurate with man's total experience. The vision, to be sure, has a certain abstract cogency, and in Houyhnhnm-land it carries conviction; but Gulliver (like Timon and Alceste) fails to assume the human burden of discriminating morally between man in the abstract and John, Peter, Thomas, and Don Pedro de Mendez. Swift, in life and in this work, insists upon that responsibility.

This reading of *Gulliver's Travels* dissolves a logical paradox. Insofar as Gulliver's vision of man obtains, Swift is implicated: if all men are Yahoos, the creator of Gulliver is a Yahoo among the rest, and *Gulliver's Travels* (and all literary works whatsoever) are no more than the noisome braying of an odious beast. As a clergyman, there is a sense in which Swift might have accepted those implications; but as a humanist and an author he could not. He could accept his own involvement in the great range of human folly which Gulliver avidly depicts, but he could not accept the total Yahoodom of man.

[34] Donne, *Works* (London, 1839), IV, 231; Taylor, *The Whole Works* (London, 1880), I, 396; both cited in Roland M. Frye, "Swift's Yahoo and the Christian Symbols for Sin," *JHI*, xv (1954), pp. 210-11.

One or two things remain to be said on the significance of the satirist-satirized theme. In the terms of this book the primitive satirist is one who wields the mysterious powers of language simply to further his own dominion over man and nature. He is subject to the restraints attendant upon magical utterance, but otherwise is a law unto himself. His "satire," like that of Aithirne the Importunate, is properly thought of as magic—black magic. When, however, the poet breaks out of the magic circle of mythical consciousness, he finds himself free of the restraints of magical discourse, but bound, in a quite different way, by the heavy aesthetic and moral responsibilities entailed by art.

By only a moderate stretch of our imaginations we can conceive of the three literary works just discussed as representing a kind of paradigm of this situation. Timon, Alceste, Gulliver—those satirist-railers *par excellence*—wield their extraordinary powers of language in almost demonic fashion. Assuming god-like prerogatives, they damn all men; and because they cannot thrust the world into outer darkness, they exile themselves: Timon to his cave and then his grave by the sea, Alceste to the desert, Gulliver to the stable. Their invective develops all the force of the primitive; we, the readers, feel the magic and show it by becoming obsessed with their incantatory denunciations. One result is that we partially misread; we forget that these are works of art, not magic; that the superb invective is incorporated in artistic structures. The most common misreading takes the form of a facile identification of the fictive railer (the "primitive satirist") with the actual author, of a reading from literature directly to life: Timon *is* Shakespeare, Alceste *is* Molière, Gulliver *is* Swift. The equation appears scores of times in the critical literature.

Doubtless many explanations of this romantic fallacy are possible: let me suggest one that fits into the interests of this book. May it not be that the power of the satirist-railer archetype is such that we feel it must be given a status in real life? Is it not somehow necessary that we make *our* Archilochuses fit the pre-existent pattern?[35] Do we not feel reluctant to admit that the magic of denunciation may be a literary construct, a product of imagination, rather than a "real" expression of completely "real"

[35] See the discussion of the railer, Chap. iv, 1, above.

feelings? Our instinct may be in a way correct: the author rails (with what "sincerity" we cannot know) through the mouth of his character. Presumably, like the Ashanti who stages a quarrel before the chief, he experiences release of aggressive emotions. His soul is cooled, but with a difference; for the expression of emotion in art must be patterned and objectified in accord with the formal demands of the medium. In the works we have been considering the objective control of the three writers is most clearly seen in their ultimate rejection of the primitive satirists they have set in motion. This is not to say that the works are thereby softened. Shakespeare, Molière, Swift—each, it seems clear, looked full into the abyss of despair. What that meant in biographical terms we can only surmise. But we have the literary evidence that somehow in the act of creating the image of despair, each artist transcended the abyss. The primitive satirists of their work are, in the total literary sense, satirized. Their creators, rejecting the irresponsibility of the primitive mode, assume the plenary responsibilities of art.

This process may be seen more clearly in a further ramification of the satirist-satirized theme: that in which the work is presented in the first person, through the mouth of an "I," as in Horace's satires, the Irish *Vision of MacConglinne, The Canterbury Tales, A Modest Proposal*, etc. Horace's Satire vii of Book II, for example, consists of a dialogue between "Horace" and his slave Davus. It is the time of the Saturnalia; Horace, full of good will, gives Davus the customary freedom to speak his mind. The slave takes his advantage more keenly than had been expected. He launches sharp criticism of Horace's laziness, his fickleness, the fact that (according to the Stoic paradox) he, the free man, is a slave of his passions. Horace is disconcerted, loses his temper; at the end calls for a stone to throw at Davus and threatens to ship him off to the Sabine farm. "Horace," the *persona*, is a butt of Horace's satire; and although the relationship between *persona* and writer is ambiguous, there is a sense in which the satirist draws himself, knowingly, into the orbit of his own ridicule.

The dubious relation between "I" and author is often much more problematic than this. The "I" of *A Tale of a Tub*, that egregious modern, avid after conquests and systems, is removed from Swift by the whole great range of the irony. Similarly, the "I" of *A Modest Proposal* is a horrible parody of Jonathan Swift, Dean of St. Patrick's. These are Swift's anti-selves. But in a way the anti-self implies complement; and the folly, even the cannibalism, of the projector of the *Modest Proposal* are symbolically the folly and cannibalism of Swift himself (and of ourselves insofar as we read properly): "Madame Bovary, c'est moi," said Flaubert.[36] There is a sense (not Thackeray's sense or the unearned sense of most such identifications) in which "I" is I and, to revert to the *Travels*, Swift is Gulliver: giant and pigmy, bemused admirer and victim of scientific idiocy, lover and hater of man—purveyor and target of satire.

Ordinarily, we are reluctant to accept the conventional pose of the satirist: the self-appointed censor who seems to delight in telling us, derisively, of our sins. But it is a measure of the greatest satirists (perhaps the greatest men) that they recognize their own involvement in the folly of human life and willingly see themselves as victims, in obscure ways, of their own art. Swift mockingly accuses himself:

> . . . you alone of all the Race
> Disclaim the *Human Name*, and Face,
> And with the *Virtues* pant to wear
> (May Heav'n Indulgent hear your Pray'r!)
> The *Proof* of your high *Origine*,
> The *Horses's Countenance Divine*.[37]

He was intensely aware of being human.

[36] Compare Kenneth Burke: "A tragedy is not profound unless the poet *imagines* the crime—and in thus imagining it, he symbolically commits it. Similarly, insofar as the audience participates in the imaginings, it also participates in the offense. So we get Mann's 'sympathy with the abyss,' Gide's suggestion that in 'Thou shalt not' there is implicit 'what would happen if . . . ,' Hopkins' 'tykishness,' or Goethe's statement that the poet contains the capacity for all crime. . . . Mann contains within his work all the errors to which the Nazis are prone . . . *but encompasses them within a wider frame—and as so encompassed, they act entirely differently than they would if 'efficiently' isolated in their 'purity.'* " *Philosophy of Literary Form*, pp. 48-49.

[37] "A Panegyric on Dean Swift," *Poems*, ed. Harold Williams (Oxford, 1937), II, 498.

CHAPTER V

TWENTIETH-CENTURY MAGIC

. . . his [Shakespeare's] laughter had not the metallic bark that kills.—HORACE ZAGREUS IN WYNDHAM LEWIS' *The Apes of God*

1. WYNDHAM LEWIS: THEORY

IN MANY RESPECTS ours is a satirical age; yet while a number of our writers have stiffened their work with satire, one could hardly call the twentieth century an age of great satire, or think of its leading authors as preeminently satirists. To be sure, a great deal depends on terminology: Proust has been called the greatest satirist of our time; and Wyndham Lewis writes of Hemingway, Faulkner, and Eliot as satirists. Hemingway, he says, "is, as it were, a proletarian clown; he satirises *himself*—but . . . not his private self." Faulkner is "a satirist with a corn-cob . . . a fierce moralist, who operates upon the satiric plane, armed with corn-cobs and such like sardonic weapons of aggression, to insult the victims of his ethical rage." And Mr. Eliot's Sweeney, the enigmatic Mrs. Porter, Prufrock, Klipstein, and Burbank are "authentic figures of Satire, and nothing else." But even for Lewis this is by the way, for the only fictionist deliberately dealing in satire of sufficient importance for him to take seriously is—himself.[1]

In the United States one of the most consistent cries of our troubled times is the cry for a great satirist: Why have we no Swift? The British cry less fervently; for in Lewis they have had a Swift—at least he has often been compared to Swift, even by men of the eminence of Yeats, and they have had Roy Campbell, whose affinities with Byron have been frequently noticed. It can-

[1] *Men without Art* (London, 1934), pp. 12-13.

not be said that the work of Lewis and Campbell brought comfort to much of English society; but that is hardly the way they conceived their roles, and there can be no question that, whatever else they were, they were authentic satirists. Despite the bathos involved in moving from Shakespeare and Molière and Swift to Roy Campbell (and despite the leap in chronology), I propose to discuss Campbell's work and that of Lewis—the theory of Lewis and the practice of Campbell—not because I think them necessarily representative of our time, or our greatest satirists, but because of those writing satirically in English today, they seem to me the most consciously within the tradition we have been following. Campbell, strenuously Byronic, presents an image of himself as a lonely, alienated bard, gifted with strange knowledge and strange power, fated from the beginning

> To wear his liver on his sleeve,
> To snarl, and be an angry man.[2]

As for Lewis, he conducted BLAST (a periodical consecrated to cursing and blessing) in a magically-charged prose worthy of an archaic prophet. In another guise, that of the Enemy in "If So the Man You Are," he spits, "and a small green flame darts up from the gothic parquet."[3]

Time and again throughout his long career Lewis reverted to problems presented by the theory and practice of satire. Characters in his fiction frequently talk about satire, sometimes satirically (the discussion of satire being itself satiric), often as though with the voice of their creator. But the best way to see Lewis' position is to look at the more or less systematic discussions in his philosophical-polemical-autobiographical-critical works, *Men without Art* (1934) and *Rude Assignment* (1950). These books incorporate much of the material from Enemy Pamphlet No. 1, from *Satire and Fiction*, a joint production of Lewis and Campbell, from Lewis' "Studies in the Art of Laughter," from various essays in *The Diabolical Principle* and elsewhere. Lewis' theory, it should be said, is neither consistent nor

---

[2] "Poets in Africa," *Collected Poems* (London, 1955), p. 192. Cf. Byron's "I was born for opposition."

[3] *One-Way Song* (London, 1933), p. 72.

viable; but it is the theory of a first-rate satirist, it provides valuable commentary on his own work, and it has no competitors in the field.

Lewis wrote *Men without Art,* he claims, to provide the theoretical foundations for the great period of imaginative satire which, in the 1930's, he confidently anticipated (pp. 10, 160). He finds satire everywhere: most people are satirists (often malicious ones) in conversation, and nearly every major writer Lewis can think of is at least a part-time satirist. As harbingers of the satiric renaissance he cites (in addition to himself) the most brilliant young poet of the thirties, Auden, who "is above all a satirist," and Roy Campbell, whose *Georgiad* is "a masterpiece of the satiric art, which may be placed beside the eighteenth-century pieces without its suffering by that proximity" (p. 160). These, one gathers, are "true" satirists in the conventional dictionary meaning of the term.[4]

Throughout most of *Men without Art,* however, Lewis ignores conventional meanings and assigns his own. The book is a defense of satire, he says, but: "to 'Satire' I have given a meaning so wide as to confound it with 'Art.' So this book may be said to be nothing short of a defence of art—as art is understood in the most 'highbrow' quarters today" (p. 10). Justification of this usage is complex and is rooted in Lewis' theory of the "external" in art. No theme is more insistent in his work, or more consistently held, than that the true subject of art is the external, the plastic surface of things.[5] He loathes the art of the inside: the internal monologue of Joyce and Woolf, the Stein-stutter, the squishiness of Proust and Lawrence. "Dogmatically . . . I am for the Great Without, for the method of *external* approach—for the wisdom of the eye rather than that of the ear." The rigid, articulated skeleton as opposed to the moil and mess of the in-

[4] *Rude Assignment* (London [1950]), p. 46. Lewis attempts by a kind of typographical agility to differentiate among various meanings of the central term here; he writes: satire, Satire, "Satire," *satire,* and so on, but the usage is inconsistent and confusing. I shall continue to write *satire* (except when quoting him), trusting to context to indicate a broad or restricted sense.

[5] For discussion of Lewis' theory, see Geoffrey Wagner, *Wyndham Lewis* (New Haven, 1957), pp. 269 ff.; Hugh Kenner, *Wyndham Lewis* (Norfolk, Conn., 1954), pp. 86 ff.

side. Satire is preeminently an art of the outside, according to Lewis, and for him an art of the outside may easily be extended to "Art." "The *external* approach to things belongs to the 'classical' manner of apprehending. . . . as for pure satire—there the eye is supreme." The way of satire is the way of art—the best way to achieve "those polished and resistant surfaces of a great *externalist* art. . . ."[6]

The medium of satire is laughter, says Lewis—not the laughter of *Punch* or gentle parody or the characteristic English sense of humor; these Lewis loathes—but a bitter, cold, *tragic* laughter in accord with satire's cruelty and its destructiveness. Lewis sometimes speaks of satire as a hybrid form, standing midway between tragedy and comedy: a "*grinning* tragedy, as it were. Or . . . a comedy full of dangerous electrical action, and shattered with outbursts of tears."[7] But the emphasis is on the tragic. "The wind that blows through satire is as bitter as that that predominates in the pages of *Timon* or *King Lear*. Indeed, the former *is* a satire. And *Hamlet*, for instance, is very much that too—a central satire—developing now into comedy, now into tragedy."[8] Satire is *cold*; it is the grotesque; it is found in everything good; in short, "Satire is good!" (p. 121)

But even more: satire is also the truth of natural science. "That objective, non-emotional truth of the scientific intelligence sometimes takes on the exuberant sensuous quality of creative art: then it is very apt to be called 'Satire,' for it has been bent not so much upon pleasing as upon being true" (p. 121). The confusion evident here between satire as truth, and the truth, because it is unpleasant, being *called* satire, reappears as Lewis later reverts to the theme. In *Rude Assignment* he writes that the portrait of Squire Western in *Tom Jones* is that of a kind of man who actually existed; it is realistic (true) and would have been thought so in the eighteenth century; but today, because it does not refine the truth, it is called satire. Similarly, although the Dublin scene in *Ulysses* is an accurate presentation of life as it is, it too is called satire (p. 45). The difficulty is in our notion of

[6] *Men without Art,* pp. 128, 126-27, 121.
[7] "Studies in the Art of Laughter," *London Mercury,* xxx (1934), p. 515.
[8] *Men without Art,* p. 113.

what truth is. Lewis can deduce from the examples above the axiom: "*wherever there is objective truth there is satire*"; that is because "for us *the true* must (1) always be emotional, must (2) be favourable to the object" (p. 48). There are two truths: the truth of the intellect, i.e., satire, and the truth of the beauty-doctor. Whenever the artist presents a picture of objective reality that has the least unpleasantness about it, it will be called satire because of our prevailing tender-minded, rose-colored vision. Whether or not this objective reality *should* be called satire is never apparent, despite Lewis' dextrous juggling with terms. Clearly, though, if the plain, naked truth is called satire (man being what he is, that truth is likely to be disagreeable), the writer who sets out to satirize in the usual critical, denigrating sense of the term will be regarded as the agent of the Fiend himself (p. 51).

Lewis' equation of satire with art and truth is quite arbitrary, but, in a final justification, eloquent: " 'Satire,' as I have suggested that word should be used in this essay (applying to *all* the art of the present time of any force at all) refers to an 'expressionist' universe which is reeling a little, a little drunken with an overdose of the 'ridiculous'—where everything is not only tipped but *steeped* in a philosophic solution of the material, not of mirth, but of the intense and even painful sense of the absurd. It is a time, evidently, in which *homo animal ridens* is accentuating . . . his dangerous, philosophic, 'god-like' prerogative—that wild nihilism that is a function of reason and of which his laughter is the characteristic expression. [The art of Picasso, Henry Moore, Joyce, Eliot expresses this tendency.] And that is why, by stretching a point, no more, we can without exaggeration write *satire* for *art*—not the moralist satire directed at a given society, but a metaphysical satire occupied with mankind."[9]

The disclaimer of moral purpose in the last sentence, at such variance with the claims of most satirists, points to a key difficulty in Lewis' theory. Time and again he has reversed himself on the question whether or not satire is an agent of the ethical will. Writing of Shakespeare in 1927 he conceives of satire as "essentially ethical"—at least, "it is difficult for it not to be . . ."; and in his earliest work he thinks of satire as a weapon in the

[9] *Ibid.*, pp. 288-89.

war against the stupidity and folly of the *Zeitgeist*.[10] But in *Men Without Art* the position is turned about. Admittedly, says Lewis, most satire gets by with the public on the assumption that the writer is a moralist; he is willing to concede that some of the greatest satirists have written in the name of morality and may even have been moralists as well. But not all. A major purpose of his book is to "join issue . . . with the moralist, who regards satire as belonging pre-eminently to his domain. . . . I am a satirist. . . . But I am not a moralist" (p. 106). He suggests that "the greatest satire *cannot* be moralistic at all; if for no other reason, because no mind of the first order, expressing itself in art, has ever itself been taken in, nor consented to take in others, by the crude injunctions of any purely moral code." Manipulate these terms as he will, however, Lewis is utterly incapable of disguising the intense moral urgency underlying his whole literary enterprise. Mr. Geoffrey Wagner is probably right in suggesting that Lewis goes to these self-contradictory lengths to avoid seeming "edifying."[11] Lewis' favorite stance is that of detachment, of being above the battle, above commitment; to have allied himself overtly with "the crude injunctions of any purely moral code" would have been to destroy this image. In *Rude Assignment*, however, after a discussion of the preponderance of the intellectual over the moral passion in Flaubert, Lewis writes: "When (we could assert) a very strong moral element is present, as in the pictures of Hogarth, where it is *vice* rather than *folly* that is the target, or folly so noxious as to amount to vice—and provoking reactions that vice engenders but not mere folly—we are in the presence of Satire." (pp. 46-47)

Despite this last comment, which contradicts the contradiction, Lewis most of the time tries to avoid the moralist's label. (This is rather like his position on politics; while proclaiming over and over his unique impartiality, his independence of political affiliation, he made many public statements which, at the least, gave aid and comfort to the fascists.) He will not be the champion of Mrs. Grundy, any more than he will go through the ritual prescribed for the satirist in more sophisticated circles: "a short prayer for absolution regarding the blood he was about to

[10] *The Lion and the Fox* (New York, n.d.), p. 168.
[11] *Wyndham Lewis*, p. 213.

spill, or if the god had the features of Demos, an invocation to his bloody fist—a brief class-war-dance, with a 'more power to my elbow incantation!' And so forward to battle, the Geneva Bible in the breast-pocket."[12]

With moral purpose abandoned, there is, Lewis confesses, some difficulty in finding a sanction for satire. Neither Persius nor Dante had any such problem: the Stoic philosophy of the one and the Christian principles of the other provided ample justification for roasting their enemies, in whom they could easily detect vice. Today it is another matter. "How does a cartoonist like Mr. Low square it with his conscience, for the blood-thirsty life he has led—driving his *banderillas* into so many hides, year after year? Or Mr. H. G. Wells, or Mr. Maugham, or . . . M. Gide?" Lewis answers for Low, Wells, and himself.[13] They produce political satire, which is the same as social satire; and this, apparently, is self-justificatory. His own *Apes of God* is political. "If anyone smarted because of it (and it seems that they did, for although the personal identifications may have been unfounded, the class identification was probably accurate) they smarted for a political reason. As a class, they had outstayed their usefulness and had grown to be preposterous parasites."[14] One needs no justification for blasting parasites. Mr. Maugham's case is, embarrassingly, forced back to morality for its sanction. *Cakes and Ale* was morally justified because the victim deserved it. "It all depends, in a case of that nature, whether you think it is a *good thing* or not." Much depends upon the author's motivation. Irresponsible lampooning of individuals for the malicious pleasure of the thing, or to acquire a sense of power over them, is detestable. This, says Lewis, echoing Pope and many others, is not satire at all.[15]

[12] *Men without Art*, p. 107.

[13] David Low has since written his own interesting, if conventional, justification of his activities in his *Autobiography* (London, 1956). He admits to being disrespectful and irreverent, but these qualities, he claims, are the very essence of satire, which functions in the service of reason and morality, not of accepted shibboleths. "Truth and the Good remained unimpaired by ridicule. Only humbug died" (pp. 191-94).

[14] *Rude Assignment*, pp. 52-53.

[15] Cf. Pope's comment in the Advertisement prefatory to his *Satires and Epistles of Horace Imitated*: ". . . *there is not in the world a greater Error, than that which Fools are so apt to fall into, and Knaves with good*

Lewis justifies his satire in polemics that are often satirical themselves and have in turn to be justified. Many of his arguments are taken from the conventional stock that has been at the disposal of the satirist since Horace. Controversy, for which he has no love, says Lewis, has been forced upon him by the nature of the times and by the malice of enemies. He is finally forced to defend his character against the distortions they have made current. "It is not any one particular thing: it is a small mountain of ever-increasing nonsense, which has to be shovelled away—deposited by many hands, for a great number of petty reasons." Because in a servile society he has spoken out frankly in defense of himself and his art, he has now "the obligation of a cleansing operation on the grand scale."[16] This is Pope to the life: *"This Paper is a Sort of Bill of Complaint, begun many years since, and drawn up by snatches, as the several Occasions offer'd. I had no thoughts of publishing it, till it pleas'd some Persons of Rank and Fortune . . . to attack in a very extraordinary manner, not only my Writings . . . but my* Person, Morals, *and* Family, *whereof to those who know me not, a truer Information may be requisite."*[17]

Like Pope, Lewis feels obliged to deal with the charge that the objects of his satire are hardly worth the powerful ammunition expended on them. (T. S. Eliot, who has called Lewis the greatest prose writer of his generation, makes this charge.) Pope's "defense" of his dunces is well known; Lewis, speaking of his own case, exploits the paradox: "Here is the satirist, at last compelled to defend his victims against the contemptuous aspersions of the rest of the world! A situation of the finest comedy."[18] But these targets, the argument runs, are not insignificant; they do great harm, and he is obliged, for the good of society, to expose

---

reason to incourage, the mistaking a Satyrist *for a* Libeller; *whereas to a* true Satyrist *nothing is so odious as a* Libeller, *for the same reason as to a man* truly Virtuous *nothing is so hateful as a* Hypocrite." *Imitations of Horace,* ed. John Butt, 2nd ed. (London, 1953), p. 3.

[16] *Rude Assignment,* p. 11.

[17] Advertisement prefatory to the *Epistle to Dr. Arbuthnot,* in *Imitations of Horace,* ed. Butt, p. 95. Cf. "A Letter to the Publisher" in the prolegomena to the *Dunciad;* this is signed by William Cleland but is very probably by Pope.

[18] *Men without Art,* pp. 140-41.

them: ". . . in defending myself I play a not unuseful part, and defend many, many other people. I am a sort of public body-guard."[19]

Lewis concludes his *apologia* in *Rude Assignment* with a significant comparison: "As once upon a time, according to English law, it was the duty of any man, observing another rustling a horse, to apprehend him (if he could) and to hang him (if he had a rope) to the nearest tree (if there were one thereabouts): so it was incumbent upon all good citizens to turn satirists on the spot, at the sight of such as those exhibited in 'The Apes of God'—if they had any Satire in them, of which I happened to have an adequate supply" (p. 53). In this image the satirist is a hangman, as elsewhere in Lewis he is a dissector, a surgeon, an executioner, a prophet—his function being in each case that which from the beginning satirists have arrogated to themselves.

As to the power of satire to effect change in the world, Lewis is, like many others, ambivalent. Low, he remarks, is said to have killed a statesman by his satirical portraits; but although he is in no way disposed to deny the power in Low's extraordinary art, he dismisses the story as probably a "pleasant exaggeration."[20] Lewis himself claims to have "paralyzed" by the violence of his pamphleteering attacks the most troublesome "Apes" in his neighborhood, thereby making possible the writing of the *Apes of God*.[21] But these are only incidental remarks, linking him with the tradition we are interested in, to be sure, but not consciously at the heart of his enterprise.

On the other hand, Lewis feels that, for a number of reasons, satire can do little to correct the abuses of his time. In the *Apes of God*, Horace Zagreus, who speaks for Lewis, paraphrases Swift's famous complaint: *"Satyr is a sort of* Glass, *wherein Beholders do generally discover every body's Face but their Own; which is the chief Reason for that kind Reception it meets in the World, and that so very few are offended with it."*[22] Zagreus is talking to Lionel and Isabel Kein who profess to be such admirers of Proust that they would be delighted to figure as characters in a work of his. Zagreus savagely exposes the hypocrisy,

---

[19] *Rude Assignment*, p. 201.   [20] *Ibid.*, p. 45.
[21] *The Diabolical Principle* (London, 1931), pp. viii-ix.
[22] Preface to *The Battle of the Books*.

indeed the *impossibility*, of their profession: " 'How is it that no one ever sees *himself* in the public mirror—in official Fiction? . . . Everybody gazes into the public mirror. No one sees himself! What is the use of a mirror then if it reflects a World, always, without the principal person—the Me? Let us put it in this way. You would not like to look into such a mirror and suddenly find *yourself* there. Not so cunningly sucked in and eternally fixed as happens with a master like Proust. . . . I do not wish to be disobliging or rude—but flesh and blood will not stand *that*!' "

But Isabel persists: " 'I believe I regard myself just as objective-ly as Proust could.'

" 'Then why—how shall I put it—are you not *different*? . . . Why do you never *change* . . . ?' " Zagreus answers his own ques-tion: " 'People feel themselves under the special protection of the author when they read a satire on their circle—am I right! It is always the *other fellows* (never them) that their accredited romancer is depicting, for their sport. Or is it that the Veneerings and the Verdurins read about themselves, see themselves right enough—*and are unabashed*?' "

Zagreus looks to see whether this wicked implication has pene-trated. It has not. He thrusts the knife in deeper: " 'At all events nothing happens. It would seem that it is impossible to devise anything sufficiently cruel for the rhinoceros hides grown by a civilised man and a civilised woman. . . . The satirist merely seems to put them on their mettle. . . . It is almost as if, when they saw him approaching, they exclaimed: *"Here comes a good satirist! We'll give him some sport. We are just the sort of animals he loves."* Then the official satirist fills his pages with monsters and a sprinkling of rather sentimental "personnages sympathiques," and everybody is perfectly happy. The satirist is, of course, quite as insensitive as his subjects, as a rule. Nothing really disgusts him.' "[23]

It is a brilliant scene—perhaps, in a way, more brilliant than Lewis knew, suggesting, as it does, certain self-reflexive implica-tions. But the skill with which Lewis builds the scene so that it embodies concretely the thesis under discussion is masterful.

Very rarely can the satirist know that his professed aims have

[23] *The Apes of God* (New York, 1932), pp. 255-56.

actually been achieved: his victims no longer develop blisters or hang themselves, and social folly is too amorphous to measure. Swift's temporary success with the *Drapier's Letters* is usually cited as one example of an occasion on which satire demonstrably affected the course of human affairs; but satirists have long recognized that such spectacular achievements are necessarily rare, and that the effects of their own work, when there are any, will be much less tangible. "Perhaps neither Pope nor Boileau," wrote Dr. Johnson, "has made the world much better than he found it. . . ." Wyndham Lewis may indeed have believed that his satire was ineffectual, or he may simply have been following a convention; in any event, lack of visible effect did not deter him. Yeats remarked to him that it would be amusing to see how London society would alter under the impact of the *Apes*. Yeats was wrong, said Lewis years later. "Nothing could change the kind of people of whom I wrote—they had not the necessary vitality for that."[24] Even the confession of defeat is an attack.

Lewis claims that, except for verse, the only work of his that can be called "pure" satire is the *Apes of God*. That extraordinary novel conforms admirably to his dicta on what satire should be, even to the confusion about morality. Its subject, says Lewis, is the "social decay of the insanitary trough between the two great wars."[25] To characterize a subject thus is automatically to sanction the most thorough destructive operation. Bloomsbury individuals and types, with their decadence, frivolity, dilettantism, sexual perversions—these are the main targets—deserve their fate; and the satirist is a public benefactor, as is a surgeon, an executioner, or even, as Lewis says of himself, a "dropper of molten iron" on the victims below. The savage brilliance of the book provoked a violent reaction. Richard Aldington called it, admiringly, "the most impressive display of Schrecklichkeit ever witnessed in literature" and "the most brilliantly witty piece of writing, merely as writing, which I have ever read." Naomi Mitchison wrote that Lewis "hates more thoroughly and efficiently than any writer living, and is probably effective in destroying what he hates."[26] The extravagance of these statements seems

[24] *Rude Assignment*, p. 201.   [25] *Ibid.*, p. 199.
[26] Cited in Lewis, *Satire and Fiction*, Enemy Pamphlets, No. 1 (London [1930]), pp. 23, 32-33.

appropriate. In the second of his major discourses on satire in the *Apes*, Zagreus (who repeats by rote the ideas of the enigmatic Pierpoint, and therefore, presumably, the ideas of Lewis)[27] asserts that " 'True satire must be vicious. . . . the venom of Pope is what is needed.' " (Shakespeare's laughter was too good-natured, Zagreus says, to be satire; it " 'had not the metallic bark that kills' " [pp. 450-52].) The *Apes* has venom in plenty. It is notoriously a *roman à clef*, with identifications of some of the more repulsive characters an open scandal. Lewis, of course, repeatedly denied the identifications: the subject of his book, he claims, is "magnified and stylised. It is not portraiture. A new world is created out of the shoddy material of everyday, and nothing does or could, go over into that as it appeared in nature." Again, the figures of the *Apes* are, "by reason of their scale and their vitality, remote from the photographic reality of life . . . and in this satiristic dimension . . . are most unlike the beings we meet with every day."[28] His art in the *Apes*, Lewis asserts, is like the art of Vicky, the famous English cartoonist, whose caricatures do not "hurt" because they are fanciful, far removed from reality. In this they differ from the style of Low, whose *lifelikeness* is extraordinary and whose caricatures are far more personal. ("If I were a politician, planning the slaughter of a rival, I should pick Low," writes Lewis.)

This is an effective defense, rhetorically speaking, and if the *Apes* is read a hundred years from now it may be that Lewis'

[27] According to Kenner, *Wyndham Lewis*, p. 100, the name of the public executioner in England was Pierpoint. The literal signification of the name ("peer," "point"), together with the association with the executioner's office, would clearly be attractive to Lewis. Despite the fictional Pierpoint's embarrassing political beliefs, Kenner identifies Lewis with him.

[28] *Rude Assignment*, pp. 199-200. Roy Campbell supports this thesis in his review of the *Apes* ("The History of a Rejected Review," *Satire and Fiction*, p. 15); cf. this comment of Augustus John, which Lewis reprints in two or three places: "In your 'Apes of God' you have, as it were, suspended upon magical wires colossal puppets, whose enlarged and distorted features may be attributed to those of not a few contemporary figures known to fame, infamy, and myself. Some of these you, from your own superabundance, have endowed with unexpected intelligence; others, by an ingenious operation of trepanning, you have bereft of what wits they had or could lay claim to.—These grandiose toys you manipulate with a gargantuan and salutary art unexampled in our or any other time I know of." Cited in *Rude Assignment*, p. 200.

claims about his method will be granted. To grant them today is more difficult. Lewis worked deliberately from known persons, seizing upon salient "humours," exaggerating them, treating the figures like puppets, but manipulating them in such a way that their human prototypes are clearly recognizable. It is as though Lewis were to a degree deliberately violating in the act of writing the book the injunctions laid down in the work by Zagreus-Pierpoint-Lewis. Zagreus says:

" '. . . the world created by Art—Fiction, Drama, Poetry etc.— must be sufficiently removed from the real world so that no character from the one could under any circumstances enter the other (the situation imagined by Pirandello), without the anomaly being apparent at once. . . . But there is a further, a supreme, reason, why these two worlds should not be fused into one. It is precisely that truth . . . cannot exist in the midst of the hot and immediate interests of 'real' everyday social life. . . . Used as a weapon only, it must lose its significance. The creation resulting from such a mixture must daily become more utilitarian. *The works of literature resulting can be nothing but weapons of the vanity. . . .*' " (pp. 265-66)

Whatever defense Lewis can make, it is a fact that the *Apes* is inextricably involved in the hot interests of the real world, as the game of establishing identifications still goes on—although, because of libel laws, not in public. Questions of historical fact constantly intrude themselves in discussions of the work: Was X really like that?—as do questions of morality: Was it ethical to put Y into the book? These extra-literary problems are so compulsive upon the imagination as to have obscured for many people the artistic merits of the work. In a hundred years such questions may seem as irrelevant as the complaint of the eighteenth-century writer who, admitting Dryden's wit in *Mac Flecknoe*, still raised the major question: "Whether *Shadwell* had not as much Wit and Humour as ought to have preserved him from the Ridicule."[29] The *Apes of God* requires from the reader as much distance as did *Mac Flecknoe*.

This is not to say that Lewis was all out for the kill. A final

[29] "To the Author of the *Dunciad*," prefacing *A Compleat Collection of all the Verses, Essays, etc. . . . Occasioned by . . . Miscellanies, by Pope and Company* (London, 1728), p. xi.

word from Zagreus indicates something of what might have been in store had Lewis deliberately set out to be Low: " 'What I really am trying to say is that none of us are able in fact, in the matter of quite naked truth, to support that [Proustian] magnifying glass, focussed upon us, any more than the best complexion could support such examination. Were we mercilessly transposed into Fiction, by the eye of a Swift, for instance, the picture would be intolerable, both for Fiction and for us.' " (p. 257)

Lewis has no intention of demonstrating this thesis in the *Apes*; true, he uses the microscope from time to time to create brief static scenes of Brobdingnagian disgust, but the over-all effect of the work (one deliberately aimed at) is that of a giant puppet show. The characters are flat, inhuman, animated masks, and are so referred to countless times; in their two-dimensional way they embody the vices and follies of a "moronic inferno of insipidity and decay," and they might have been created by a man intent on illustrating the effects of the predominance of, say, black bile in the physiology of Bloomsbury. But my intention is not to go further with the *Apes*, which we have been considering less as a work of art than as a document in the statement and elucidation of Lewis' theory of satire. Its status as art is still, in the public view, in question, although it would take a dull eye not to see the great talent that went into its making. The book has been highly praised—placed by responsible persons on a level with *Ulysses* and *Remembrance of Things Past*, for example; and it has been as authoritatively damned. To become entangled in "reality" and all the welter of extra-literary considerations annexed thereunto is an occupational hazard of the satirist. He must perforce take the long view.

Lewis' literary success in manipulating his automata had curious consequences. Hugh Kenner points out that in *Time and Western Man* Lewis had argued against the behaviorists, who, he said, insulted the human race by reducing people to a set of mechanical gestures. In his fiction of this period Lewis employed the same reductionism, originally for satirical purposes. But the satire turned back on itself as Lewis came increasingly to believe that human beings in fact amounted to no more than the behaviorists said: a complex system of predictable twitches.[30] What

[30] Kenner, *Wyndham Lewis*, p. 107.

began as satirical strategy ended by convincing the strategist, as though Swift had turned cannibal. The contradiction in Lewis' thought issues in a remarkable variation on the theme of the satirist satirized.

2. ROY CAMPBELL: PRACTICE

Roy Campbell, the South African poet, bull-fighter, cowboy, fisherman, soldier, sailor, dog-stealer, director of literature for the BBC Third Program, whip-wielding bully-boy, was killed in an automobile accident in Portugal in spring 1957, just when interest in his poetry and his legend was reaching new heights. The critical boycott from which he had suffered for years in England was beginning to relax, and in the United States the imprimature of the New Conservatives had been placed on his life and works by Russell Kirk, who in the *Sewanee Review* had hailed Campbell as the last of the hero-poets.

Extravagant himself, Campbell has always provoked extravagance in others. John Ciardi, writing of Campbell, speaks of storm-trooper arrogance, Sieg Heil piety, Nietzschean rant, and magnificent poetry. Richard Aldington thinks Campbell "our greatest satirist since Dryden." Dylan Thomas called him a poetic genius. Edith Sitwell spoke of him as a "poetic tornado" and of his "extreme and lovely skill" with language. Eliot, Tate, Geoffrey Grigson, G. S. Frazer, less flamboyant, have had high praise for Campbell's poetic talent. Let me add my own opinion that Campbell wrote some beautiful lyrics, some superb translations of St. John of the Cross and Baudelaire, and some of the most accomplished English verse satire of our time.

I want to register this impression strongly because of the unpleasantness to follow. Campbell always claimed, doubtless with justice, that his works were refused notice in England because of his opinions, political and otherwise. It is impossible to write of Campbell without taking notice of those opinions: he flaunted them whenever possible; his poetry is shot through with them; they form the core of his public being. Campbell vociferously supported (although apparently he did not fight for) Franco in the Spanish war in order to defend his Church (he was a convert to Roman Catholicism) but also out of his admiration for fascism and his disgust with democracy:

> . . . style and unity and emulation
> Inform each clean rejuvenated Nation,
> Wherever there's a Leader to rebel
> Against the outworn democratic Hell,
> And weld our people under one bright star—
> A Franco, Mussolini, Salazar. . . .[1]

Praises of fascism and Hitlerism are scattered throughout *Flowering Rifle* and the first of his two autobiographies, *Broken Record*. He exults at being able to bring

> The tidings that Democracy is dead,
> And that where'er he strives with the New Man
> The Charlie still must be an Also Ran. . . .

(For Campbell, "Charlie" is Charley Chaplin's tramp and his "disastrous shuffling pedestrian civilisation"; he is a tragic symbol of the decline of the West: "Down with him forever!")[2] Campbell's anti-semitism is so violent and pervasive as to seem pathological. "I am no pogromite myself," he writes, "but I fail to see how a man like Hitler makes any 'mistake' in expelling a race that is intellectually subversive as far as we are concerned: that has none of our visual sense. . . ." This, with its absurd trailing echo of Wyndham Lewis' theories, was written, to be sure, in 1934; but it is as close as he comes to a "rational" expression of his prejudice. Most other expressions of it are obscene. His aggressive Catholicism leads him to characterize Bolshevism as "The Reformation come to roost," to defend wildly the Inquisition:

> Which slew less Jews with its protecting hand
> Than Cecil's Ogpu made them rich and grand
> By murdering Christians for their wealth and land. . . .

and to write the most vulgar attacks on dignitaries of the Church of England.

---

[1] *Flowering Rifle* (London, 1939), pp. 124-25. Campbell revised this poem extensively for the second volume of his *Collected Poems* (London, 1957), issued shortly after his death. The revisions do not affect the thesis of this essay, and my quotations, unless otherwise noted, are from the first edition.

[2] *Flowering Rifle*, p. 125; cf. pp. 35, 58, 109, 116-18; *Broken Record* (London, 1934), pp. 170, 207, 42.

On the subject of intellectual freedom, Campbell writes that newly discovered facts should be kept as secrets in the hands of a priesthood or an intellectual aristocracy; the crime of the nineteenth century was that such "secrets" were allowed to fall into the hands of irresponsible agitators.[3] As a natural corollary to this he despises attempts to spread literacy among the ignorant, recommending instead the crudest kind of primitivistic notions. His anti-intellectualism is everywhere. Campbell was born in South Africa and in some of his early verse attacked the exploitation of the Negro there, a venture into liberalism he was later to deplore: "I am all on the side of the natural human relationship of slave and master. No colour feeling ever existed until slavery was abolished."[4] In *Flowering Rifle* (p. 93) Campbell justifies the killing by Falangists of the great Spanish poet Garcia Lorca, although later he expressed the opinion that the murder resulted from a personal grudge and was in no way politically motivated.[5]

The list of Campbell's hatreds is impressive: communism, of course, in every manifestation; left-wing poets, humanitarians, homosexuals, the League of Nations ("That sheeny club of communists and masons"); he is anti-Labor, anti-Freud ("It is natural that gluttons and cowards should take him up"), anti-progress, anti-almost everything that Wyndham Lewis is anti-—except the Sitwells. Some of his pronouncements are grotesquely irresponsible enough to have a kind of charm. Writing of Bloomsbury, he says that beyond a doubt the book *Peter Pan* "has exerted more influence on the English mind than any other work, including the Bible. There are hundreds of Peters in modern literature; at least a dozen poets, and all fairies, as far as I know."[6] And of the attitude that allegedly holds illness and disease to be the normal state of London (an image of a sick society that he probably picked up from Auden): "This idea is

[3] *Broken Record*, p. 47.

[4] *Ibid.*, p. 144.

[5] *Lorca* (Cambridge, Eng., 1952), p. 7. Mr. Charles David Ley states in a letter to *TLS* (Aug. 30, 1957), p. 519, that Campbell admitted to him the possibility that the "private grudge" theory was quite wrong. In a footnote to the revised version of *Flowering Rifle* (*Collected Poems*, II, 199) Campbell calls Lorca cowardly and cites with approval the opinion of the South American critic Borges that Campbell is a better poet than Lorca.

[6] *Broken Record*, p. 158.

generally spread by Jews or Quakers who accept the idea of original sin, and uncleanness, physically, morally, and intellectually, as far as it concerns the white man."[7] It is not clear how many of the above sentiments Mr. Russell Kirk had in mind when, in a review of several volumes by Campbell, he wrote with unstinting admiration of the poet's work and his career, characterizing him as "curiously innocent," and speaking of the "real lovable naïveté that suffuses his autobiography."[8]

Wyndham Lewis, whose anti-semitism and authoritarian views in general are unpleasant enough, cannot be held responsible for the outrages of his followers, although his influence on Campbell was strong. Campbell speaks of Lewis as having more "intelligence, wisdom and skill" than he, and regards himself as "only a banderillero in the cuadrilla of that great matador." Later he writes of how he came increasingly under the spell of Lewis, "till I started generating ideas of my own, and he went 'cosmic.' "[9] One would be hard put to find the ideas of his own that Campbell refers to. When he flails away at ideas of progress, at Bergsonian ideas of time and flux, and so on, he is simply echoing faintly the much more cogent polemics of Lewis. Otherwise, Campbell can hardly be said to have displayed a mind in his writing at all. The kind of trash cited above records his prejudices and his passions; there is no evidence of ratiocination whatever.

So much for this. Many of the opinions of Campbell must be loathsome to any civilized mind. It will not do, as several writers of elegiac reviews have done, to ignore the opinions and to praise Campbell for his lyrical gifts and his talent for Homeric friendships. If the opinions are not evidence of derangement, if Campbell is to be held morally responsible for them, then our conclusion is inescapable: the opinions are stupid and evil and insofar as they inform the poetry, the poetry must suffer thereby.[10]

[7] *Ibid.*, p. 155.
[8] "The Last of the Scalds," *Sewanee Review*, LXIV (1956), p. 164. The second phrase refers to *Light on a Dark Horse* (Chicago, 1952), a less extravagant book than *Broken Record*.
[9] *Light on a Dark Horse*, p. 203.
[10] Campbell's work, like some of Ezra Pound's, raises an ancient dilemma: to what degree does a poet's advocacy in a poem of stupid or evil sentiments affect the *artistic* value of the poem? The case of the *Pisan*

Granting all this, however, we must face the extraordinary fact emphasized at the beginning of this discussion: Campbell has written, amid a good deal that is shoddy, some excellent poetry. We shall be concerned only with his satire and with his conception of his own role as satirist.

In 1930 Campbell wrote a vigorous defense of Lewis' *Apes of God*: "The fact is that the present age is so inimical to satire that there is no depth of grovelling to which its representatives will not descend, both to conceal the success of such a book as 'The Apes' and to dissimulate their uneasiness. . . . The art of Satire, one of the chief glories of English literature, has been dead for a hundred years. . . . What we like to call 'satire' is the gentle ping-pong of the Bloomsburies played over a table of fifty years against a dead and dying generation. But the traditional satire (real satire) of the Romans, the English, and the French has always been directed by fearless individuals, at close range, against powerful groups, prominent contemporary figures, and against the follies and shams which they represent. . . ."[11]

This has a Miltonic ring: "Satyr . . . ought . . . to strike high, and adventure dangerously. . . ." Campbell thinks of Lewis' work and of his own as in this tradition and perhaps in an even older one. He projects an image of himself as the *vates*, the seer, alienated from society by reason of his prophetic gifts and by the powers annexed to his calling. No matter what the forces arrayed against him, he will win through to fame: "The English language is an almost supernatural weapon, and the flame of poetry will fuse locks, bars, and stone walls."[12] It is *his* weapon, magnificently suited to a satirist who is "doubly cursed with second sight," one who seeks out "the cold infernal hates / Whose company I love the best."[13]

In 1926, together with William Plomer, Campbell conducted a magazine in Durban, South Africa, called *Voorslag*, which

---

Cantos was heatedly argued at the time of the Bollingen award to Pound. I have no intention of entering into the ramifications of the problem here. The statement in the text expresses my conviction.

[11] "The History of a Rejected Review," in Lewis' *Satire and Fiction*, pp. 13-14.

[12] *Light on a Dark Horse*, p. 219.

[13] *Selected Poems* (Chicago, 1955), pp. 193, 190. Unless otherwise noted, page numbers in the text will refer to this volume.

means "whiplash." It was intended, according to Plomer, to "sting with satire the mental hindquarters, so to speak, of the bovine citizenry of the Union."[14] Campbell is characteristically more frenetic; he and Plomer are poets,

> Each with a blister on his tongue,
> Each with a crater in his tooth,
> Our nerves are fire: we have been stung
> By the tarantulas of truth. (p. 192)

In varying contexts Campbell describes himself as a restive steer, a centaur's foal, a guerrilla at home in the Wasteland, a lighthouse, an angry whale. On one page he is Samson among the Philistines and a monstrous changeling "Lashing his laughter like a knotted scourge" (p. 15). He is, in a final metamorphosis, a cobra:

> I too can hiss the hair of men erect
> Because my lips are venomous with truth. (p. 31)

Many of these images can be looked upon as changes rung on the motif associated strongly with Archilochus: "And he drank the bitter wrath of the dog and the sharp sting of the wasp: from both of these comes the poison of his mouth."[15]

Out of his early experience with *Voorslag* came Campbell's first long poem, *The Wayzgoose*, a mock-heroic work modelled loosely on the *Dunciad*. It is a slashing, intermittently amusing, attack on the stupidity of South African literary life, limited in its effectiveness by many passages of careless writing in the Byronic vein, and by the same kind of provinciality that Campbell attacks in his enemies. Campbell's characteristic truculence is everywhere, as is his obsessive concern with the magic power of language:

> Be warned by me . . .
> Sooner with your own pens a lion assail
> Or prick a sleeping mamba in the tail . . .
> Than dare, though journalists you be, our curse,
> Which still can turn you into something *worse*. (pp. 254-55)

If language has this power, then it is wit—"Wit, the irreverent,

---

[14] *Double Lives* (London, 1943), p. 166.
[15] Frag. 37a in *Callimachus and Lycophron*, trans. Mair, p. 239.

wit, the profane"—that provides the efficacy. Without wit the anger of Campbell's enemies has no point; their attempts to blister, like Balaam's curse, anoint instead. The true function of wit in Campbell's view, is precisely that which Renaissance theory, and earlier, Old Irish belief, gave to satire:[16]

> It scalds like fire, it pierces every pore,
> It bites as hard as Bolitho can bore.
> It burns like small-pox, it inflames the eyes,
> And wipes out even journalists like flies. (p. 249)

These are metaphors, of course, and used humorously; but their affinities with the primitive tradition (whether conscious or not) are strikingly clear.

South African writing, according to Campbell, lacks this power completely. The pen is no longer a weapon in his enemies' hands: a harpoon as Marvell used it, or a boomerang

> that Dryden threw
> To crumple Flecknoe as I crumple you. (p. 251)

Instead,

> . . . wrapped around it like a woollen bib,
> Lo! Jubb's soft hand, perspiring, plies the nib.

It is a fine couplet, deriving from Pope and worthy him; the smothering vowels of the first line and the nibbling consonants of the second are beautifully congruent with the images of flaccidity. Jubb, a literary figure of local prominence, is a principal target in the *Wayzgoose*, his name a god-send to a poet of Campbell's proclivities. When by the end of the poem we read of what is disgorged from Jubb's pockets:

> The work of poets altered in the proofs
> And trampled by a thousand donkeys' hoofs,
> Dismembered manuscripts, reduced to splinters,
> Bejubbified before they reached the printers;
> Broken agreements, fragments of a play,
> A bunch of lentils and a wisp of hay. . . . (pp. 266-67)

---

[16] See Chap. 1, 3, above, and Mary Claire Randolph, "The Medical Concept in English Renaissance Satiric Theory: its Possible Relationships and Implications," *SP*, xxxviii (1941), pp. 125-57.

the man has been transformed from a stupid editor with an unlikely name to a wantonly destructive process. Jubb himself has
been bejubbified.

The power of poetic language extends far beyond Durban's
provincial limits. Campbell's enemies may be strong there—

> But out beyond—the World will laugh enough!
> My words, O Durban, round the World are blown
> Where I, alone, of all your sons am known:
> I circle Tellus with an airy robe—
> Thou art the smear I leave upon the globe!
> Cobham outsoared, I sail on Satire's wings—
> Satire, who dares to box the ears of kings . . .
> In vain you'll strive to minimize my powers
> Whose laughter will outlast your tallest towers.
> I mock to last: you scold poor rats! to die
> Save in my verse where you immortal lie. (pp. 251-52)

Satire has always conveyed its dubious immortality upon the vermin who are transfixed forever in the amber of its verse.

The *Georgiad*, published in 1931, has obvious affinities with
the *Wayzgoose*; it is a long satire, over sixty pages, again written
in heroic couplets and strung loosely on a fictional framework.
Again Campbell attacks his contemporaries violently, many of
them by name. But the contemporaries are no longer South
Africans; they are the literati of London: Georgian poets and
major philosophers, Bloomsburyites and writers for reviews, Fa-
bians and Freudians and suffragettes, and all the literary hangers-on who scratch each other's backs and offend major poets like
Roy Campbell either because they praise his verse or because
they fail to praise it. The *Georgiad* is a more successful poem
than the *Wayzgoose*, in part, no doubt, because of subject matter and locale, but in good measure because the verse here is
more assured, more controlled, and the incidence of wit is high.
There is little blustering about the powers of wit or the magic
of language in the poem, although an occasional warning is
bluntly stated:

> For if one scribbles in the cause of Cash
> To praise a satirist is wildly rash;

And so be warned by me, you Bulls and Bears,
And in your literary stocks and shares,
Don't gamble with satirical affairs:
And all you Nicolsons and Arnold Bennetts
Be circumspect with Satire, even when it's
To show you have the taste (which you have not)
To know true poetry from Tommy Rot:
For thus your tails before my boot to stick—
It's hardly worth the pleasure of a kick. . . . (p. 217)

The "plot" of the poem is negligible: its hero is Androgyno, a young poet who has merged with his Muse and become a hermaphrodite, a new Orlando,

Able to lisp as sweetly as a man,
Or roll far down into as deep a bass
As any lady-writer in the place.
It was a voice of 1930 model
And in a Bloomsbury accent it could yodel
Between its tonsils drawling out long O's
Along its draughty, supercilious nose. . . . (p. 203)

Androgyno goes to a week-end house-party at Georgianna's Summer School of Love, where most of London's literary society has assembled. The young poet is remarkably, if ambiguously, equipped for conquest, and the climax of the poem comes in a wild burst of grotesque fancy as his encounters with litterateurs of both sexes are described. After an orgiastic night, Androgyno leaves, sadly disillusioned, and ends up in London editing a posh review. The adventures are amusing, have their own satiric point; but probably less than a quarter of the poem has anything to do with Androgyno's affairs, which serve only as a base-camp for Campbell's incursions into enemy territory.

Like Wyndham Lewis, Campbell bags small game with his heavy bore. Among other things, he despises the English cult of dog-worship (he is extremely proud of once having belonged to a gang of dog thieves), and the notorious Georgian sentimentality about dogs sends him into a frenzy. Pages of the *Georgiad* are devoted to burlesquing these and similar attitudes. The poet John Squire, who was later knighted, is a favorite target; he is

pictured weeping beside a bulldog for a "vanished Lycidas," a
dog named Willie:

> And both together mix the mutual moan
> Squire for the dead, and Fido for a bone.
> Partners in grief, in watery tourney vie
> The rheumy jowl and the poetic eye,
> While with its tail for baton, keeping time,
> The poet wags his mangy stump of rhyme. (p. 211)

From this Campbell moves into a broader attack on Squire's
poetry:

> Nor at his football match is Squire more gay—
> Heart-rending verse describes funereal play;
> While swarming adjectives in idle ranks,
> As dumb spectators load the groaning planks,
> See the fat nouns, like porky forwards, sprawl
> Into a scrum that never heels the ball—
> A mass of moving bottoms like a sea,
> All fatter than his head, if that could be;
> While still attentive at their clumsy calves
> The adverbs pine away, dejected halves,
> The verbs hang useless by, like unfed threes
> With trousers idly flapping in the breeze,
> And while they strike their arm-pits for some heat
> Or idly stamp their splayed trochaic feet,
> The two full-backs of alternating rhyme
> Walk sadly up and down to kill the time. (p. 212)

Campbell's satire is often effective in destruction but feeble
in providing intellectual and moral sanction for his attacks. His
positives usually entail excessively romantic exaltation of the
senses (see "What I Love," pp. 218-19) or revoltingly authoritarian principles (there is much less of this in the *Georgiad* than
in later satires) or flatly anti-intellectual grunts. The assault on
a contemporary philosopher (probably Bertrand Russell, although
Campbell cleverly avoids the technical identification) is a good
illustration:

> Searching through life with crooked intellect
> For things to which his conscience may object,

And, with a more than mathematic skill,
For causes against which to pit his will . . .
First of earth's protestants, his single voice,
When Eden heard the morning stars rejoice,
Was lifted in complaint: in that loud vote
He struck the first meek English Liberal note:
And in his sluggish vegetarian veins
The spirit of objection still remains,
That sees no fun save in progressive change
Even if it be from normal health to mange.
He roars with agony at Venus' thrill
And takes his pleasures as a bitter pill
Or social duty, much against his will;
And when he leaps enthroned in stallion state,
Less with hot flame, than pedantry, elate,
Ponders the physiology of birth,
And strives, of sex, "the meaning" to unearth:
And, if he found it, would not stop to breathe
But straight the sex of meaning would unsheathe,
And, even that discovered, would not wait,
But work out its relation to "the State"—(pp. 222-23)

This is excellent; but the positives advanced to provide intellectual reference are crudely bathetic:

But happiness to a true man will come,
Sometimes, for merely sitting on his bum.

Against doubt and complexity, Campbell offers "the Obvious."
"Philosophy?" he wrote in another poem, "He is an ass / Who
tries to fish in such a stream" (p. 274).

At Georgianna's week-end party are gathered representatives
of all that Campbell despises: "literary nancies," grim suffragettes, the cliques and cults of London's artistic world. Some
are named outright; others are easily-recognizable caricatures of
actual persons. Campbell's attack is cruel, often offensive, and,
given enough distance, very funny. In his own defense he claims
that the *Georgiad* was the sortie of a mason wasp against spiders.
He had been provoked. All satirists have said this, but few have
dared Campbell's extraordinary assurance: "It is within the

bounds of the very strictest chivalry to retaliate as I did."[17] In any event, the poisonous crew of his poem is gathered for the kind of ritual festivities:

> Where knife and fork dissect the latest plays
> And criticism serves for mayonnaise;
> Where of the Hawthornden the latest winner
> Is served as joint or sirloin of the dinner,
> And, succulent to busy tongues as pork,
> Suffers the martyrdom of knife and fork:
> Where the last novel, in a salver set,
> Is masticated, à la vinaigrette,
> By hungry cannibals till naught remains
> Of the poor calf that wrote it, or his brains,
> All his fine feelings and his tender fancies
> Ruthlessly ravened by his fellow-nancies. . . . (p. 232)

They are frantically busy, clattering and clacking and tearing reputations to bits, busy as fowls in a barnyard. But if they chance to look up

> . . . and see whose shadow cuts the ray
> In those clear heights of intellectual day
> Where eagles mate, who only stoop to slay:
> Perhaps some Lewis, winged with laughter, soars
> And in his wake the laughing thunder roars
> To see the fear he scatters as he goes
> And hear the cackle of his dunghill foes—(p. 233)

Instead of Wyndham Lewis comes Androgyno, whose monstrous vitality let loose among this desiccated gathering gives rise to strange and wonderful things. Campbell closes the poem with a kind of commentary: he denies (probably following Lewis) any moral purpose in writing. Why has he taken all this trouble? He has simply been indulging a pleasant hobby: this has been inno-cent pleasure—like Ovid's *Ibis*, in no way as destructive as it might have been.

The *Georgiad* is too long, it contains careless passages, lacks a coherent center; but if the reader can get outside the extra-literary judgments imposed by the subject, he is bound to recog-

---

[17] *Broken Record*, pp. 162-63.

nize the fine facility with language displayed here: images startlingly witty and exuberant, rhymes clever and genuinely creative, whole passages alive with the vitality of satire in the tradition of Byron. Campbell unquestionably had major gifts.

In the first of his autobiographies, *Broken Record*, Campbell boasts that he has been used as a character and put to violent and harrowing deaths in nine novels and stories, to say nothing of the hundred-odd squibs raised by the *Georgiad*. He explains this extraordinary phenomenon by reference to Frazer's *Golden Bough*. "It is a return to ritual; an instinctive sacrifice of the individual . . . by the atheistical priests of democracy, performed in pantomime upon a dummy image as people burn that of Hitler . . . (pp. 9-10). One has to use similar terms to characterize Campbell's own *Flowering Rifle*, a 150-page roar of rage from the battlefields of Spain. The book can best be understood, I think, as a magical document, as a satire (Campbell calls it both satire and epic) written to kill. Between it and the works Campbell refers to in *Broken Record*, however, there is this somewhat harrowing difference: Campbell, as far as one can tell, believes, literally believes, in his own magic. Laidcenn in Irish saga could dry up corn with his curses; Timon, with all his demonic eloquence, tried to perform similar feats and failed; but with Campbell we are back once more in a world charged with magic potency, where the poet's word brings Nature to heel and the future is at his command.

Let me illustrate. We are familiar with Campbell's reiterated claim to be a prophet; he is "cursed with second sight," and in *Flowering Rifle* he writes of "my pen / Which never yet in prophecy has failed" (p. 16). Repeatedly he seeks to substantiate the claim by reference to a "prophecy" made in a poem in *Mithraic Emblems* (1936) and later "fulfilled" in the Spanish war. In the "Dedication to Mary Campbell" included in *Mithraic Emblems*, Campbell snipes at the "pink Tommies," a "legion of the lost," and asks rhetorically how they are to be rounded up. "No need to hurry," he answers himself, "with an easy mind / We catch them—where they left themselves behind!"

> To find a red-neck cheap upon this day
> You do not need to wander far away—

> Each comes with his pink halter to your hand
> And noosing one you seem to noose the band.[18]

During the Spanish war a group of British fighting with the International Brigade were captured at San Mateo. This, says Campbell in *Flowering Rifle*, was the direct result of his prophecy:

> But let these prisoners speak for my precision
> And answer for my range and drive of Vision
> . . . [He quotes some lines from the earlier poem] . . .
> Surrendering without a single blow
> For nothing, save that I foretold it so . . .
> To see them act down to its quaintest antic
> The verse they dared to dream of as "Romantic,"
> When (ere they dreamed of it) I had portrayed
> The British International Brigade,
> And twice predicted clearly in advance
> Lest any fool should foist it on to chance
> If only once I'd whirled the whistling line
> To get them hog-tied with iambic twine,
> Preventing all suggestions of coincidence
> When the live words should burgeon into incidents. . . .

> (pp. 22-23)

There is a great deal more of this throughout the poem with, as far as I can tell, no hint of irony.

The world of *Flowering Rifle* is totally responsive to magic and miracle; it is an animistic world in which Nature "knows," like Campbell, the difference between right and wrong and accordingly fights with Franco. Repeatedly, the point is made that

> Grass hates to grow on communistic fields!
> The plains and valleys fought upon our side
> And rivers to our Victory were allied. . . . (p. 15)

Where "they" were, famine and desolation followed; where "we" were, magically came plenty. To be sure, the imagery is familiar and the "pathetic" one of the oldest and best esteemed of our "fallacies." But it is a different matter surely when the phrase "grass hates to grow" is intended not as metaphor but as an

[18] *Selected Poems*, pp. 178-79.

affirmation of truth. Nature's awareness extends to brute matter, which, as Campbell writes, "has opinions of its own"; during battle enemy machinery rebelled, and Falangists

> with our Pater nosters and Hail Marys
> Were liming Aeroplanes like tame canaries:
> They came down singing to the left and right
> And on our very doorsteps seemed to light.

So with tanks, which, "as if they knew the road," wheeled in, "quite of their own volition," to be captured, like bakers' vans on order (pp. 56-57). In the animistic world the magician is supreme, and Campbell feels his power: "I've got the future in my bag."

Campbell once wrote that "Faith or disillusion are extraneous to poetry, just as literary considerations are to painting. . . ."[19] It would be hard to think of a poem which violates this precept more thoroughly than *Flowering Rifle*. For 157 pages it screams its demand for faith, faith in the magic of the poet, faith in the righteousness of his cause. Without the antecedent faith there is no poetry. *Flowering Rifle* reverses the process we have traced earlier in this book in which primitive satire breaks out of the restrictive bonds of magic to become art. Here art retreats into magic as the poet tries literally to wield supernatural power. Poetic form and order collapse; coherence is lost; even the rhymes, which ordinarily Campbell manages imaginatively, become forced and mechanical. We find ourselves in an altogether different mode of discourse from that of art. In no other way can one account for the insane fury of the language in this poem, for the incantatory ferocity of the invective. The poet is no longer a maker of art; he is the instrumentality of his own rage which pours from him in a cascade of violence designed only to annihilate. I cite only one example; here is Campbell on "the pink Mitred Globs of Guts and Suet," that is, the bishops of the Church of England:

> These Pickwickoid buffoons will smell you roses
> Where even dunghill rats would hold their noses,

---

[19] "Contemporary Poetry," in *Scrutinies*, ed. Edgell Rickword (London, 1928), p. 176.

And though divorce was their first end and source
Though Onanism's now their next resource,
And next, who knows, to keep the same proportion
These canting thugs will sanctify abortion? (p. 97)

The tone is reproduced on dozens of pages: Reds, Jews, democrats, liberals, humanitarians, Freudians—all are made indistinguishable by the shrieks of this imagery. Ernst Kris writes of the art of the insane that it "has deteriorated from communication to sorcery," as it tries to transform the external world.[20] There is a sense in which the phrase is strictly applicable to *Flowering Rifle*.

Campbell's work after *Flowering Rifle* is never again so overwhelmed by raw emotion, although certain passages in *Talking Bronco* (1946) balance precariously on the edge of hysteria. The title poem (the epithet was bestowed upon him by a left-wing poet, says Campbell, wearing it proudly) is still embedded in the experience of the Spanish war, still written out of hate, still violent and vindictive. It is unquestionably a libel, if not in the legal, then in the literary and moral sense. When his own feelings were engaged, Campbell was unable to differentiate between himself as an outraged human being and himself as a poet. We usually think of Alexander Pope as our most personal, most vindictive, satirist; yet Maynard Mack has shown how skillfully Pope utilized the fictional characteristics of the formal satire, how adroitly he manipulated the *persona*, the "I" of his poems, for dramatic and rhetorical purposes; and how mistaken we are to read directly from the poetic statement to the psyche of the poet.[21] With Campbell, even outside *Flowering Rifle*, the case is different. In passage after passage one sees no element of fictionality, no dramatic handling of the "I" whatever, only the rage of the man himself. Yet if we disregard the distinction between libel and satire which satirists often make in theory and ignore in practice, then "Talking Bronco" is effective satire. Its

[20] *Psychoanalytic Explorations in Art*, p. 61. Cf. Hugh MacDiarmid's equally violent attack on Campbell, *The Battle Continues*, cited above, Chap. 1, 3.
[21] "The Muse of Satire," *Yale Rev.*, XLI (1951-52), pp. 80-92; reprinted in *Studies in the Literature of the Augustan Age*, ed. R. C. Boys (Ann Arbor, Michigan, 1952).

affirmations, the moral reference it provides against which to judge the evil it attacks, are negligible as before, going little beyond glorification of the lonely hero Roy Campbell. But most of the time the poem's destructive force is managed with artistic control.

The principal target is "joint MacSpaunday," the name a conflation of the names of four leading British poets. Campbell makes no attempt to fictionalize the character: this is a murderous attack on recognizable individuals who are accused of greed, cowardice, hypocrisy, opportunism, and of boycotting Roy Campbell. The attacks vary from a gutter-brawling kind of vituperation to excellent examples of "the sword play of the wits," as Campbell calls his satire. Encompassing the unmediated rage are passages in which Campbell manages to distance himself sufficiently to laugh, even at himself; or at least to present a picture of the poet as warrior grotesque enough to evoke amusement:

> A Talking Bronco, sharked from ear to ear
> With laughter, like a running bandolier,
> With teeth, like bullets fastened in their clips,
> To chew the thunder and to spit the pips,
> Ejecting from the breech, in perfect time,
> The shells of meter and the shucks of rhyme. . . .[22]

In a companion passage he works out an image of the poet as magically invulnerable, armed with a deadly art:

> The "salted" horse that never need the vet see
> Owes his inoculation to the tsetse:
> Via the cobra's bite we get the serum,
> And, further still, to illustrate my theorem,
> Mythologers anticipated science
> Applying homeopathy to giants;
> The hydra is inherent to the hero:
> In Fafnir's blood they douche the Herculero:
> Achilles from the Styx his temper took,
> With frothy gargle hissing in the brook,
> Like a hot sword, whose handle was his heel,

[22] *Talking Bronco* (London, 1946), p. 77. Page numbers in the text refer to this source.

Acquiring thus the properties of steel;
So I, in Lethe ducked a thousand times
By wishful critics, make a float of rhymes,
Deriving buoyancy from leaden spite
And like a pearly nautilus, or light
"Portuguese-man-of-war's" more airy kite,
Go sailing with a six-yard thread of sting—
And woe to him who mixes with the thing! (p. 84)

There is excellent control here, an objectivity completely lacking in *Flowering Rifle*. Campbell makes the image and masters the tone; the advance is marked over the earlier self-indulgence.

"Talking Bronco" contains still more versions of the poet-as-prophet theme:

My verse was nourished by Toledo's sun
In whose clear light Ray, Sword, and Pen are one,
One in her soldier-poets of the past,
And here again united in her last:
The Pen a sword, prophetic in advance,
Deriding probability or chance,
That with unerring skill and biting scorn
Can sack a dud republic ere it's born! (p. 85)

The poem ends with a last tiresome complaint of how Roy Campbell has had to stand alone against a "strange rout of Briddishers and Yitons" and with a final (confused) image, which gathers together the rage, the bloodthirstiness, the magic: the poet is a lion ensconced on the breaking spine of a giraffe, raking the beast's side with his claws, forcing him headlong to the ground in a pool of blood:

So will my verse propel you to your doom,
And give you to the vultures for a tomb!

These echoes of an ancient power sound sadly hollow. They remind me irresistibly of an Irish poem, written in the seventeenth century after the devastation of the land and the destruction of the bardic order. The Celtic scholar Robin Flower provides the context and the translation: "They [the poets] had been proud and wanton, and presumed often upon the privileges of their order. But now all that was gone and no man regarded them. They fell back in their despair on the one weapon left to them, that gift of satire and effective cursing inherited from the old enchanters, before which in the ancient days kings had trembled. One Peadar O'Mulconry writes a poem against a farmer in whose service he was, who had mocked his art of poetry:

> Were not the Gael fallen from their high estate
> And Fola's warrior kings cast down by fate
> And learning mocked in Eire's evil day,
> I were no servant, Edmond, in thy pay.
>
> .   .   .   .
>
> Edmond, I give good counsel. Heed it thou!
> Leave mocking at my holy labours now,
> Or such a rain of venomed shafts I'll send
> That never a man shall save thee nor defend.
>
> A tale I've heard that well may tame thy mood.
> A gamesome chief of Gascony's best blood
> Refused a poet once. The satire sped
> And the man withered, strengthless, leprous, dead.[23]

I find the juxtaposition of this with "Talking Bronco" remarkably instructive. Given its historical context, the Irish poem has genuine pathos, I believe; but when Roy Campbell attempts overtly to exploit atavistic powers, he is merely absurd, the threat pure bombast. The Irish poet's pathos is not available to the twentieth century.

In Wyndham Lewis' *Apes of God* Horace Zagreus laments that no one ever sees *himself* in the mirror of satire. It has been recently said of Lewis that his greatest weakness as a satirist was that "the mirror . . . he held up to the world was without the most important Me of all—Percy Wyndham Lewis." His satire "does not include itself among its subjects."[24] The point is easily illustrated. Lewis writes in "Studies in the Art of Laughter" that no layman can be expected to love satire. It is different for the artist: ". . . *we*, who are writers, do not give a damn whether it be god or a sewer-rat that comes out of the hat, provided that

---

[23] *The Irish Tradition* (Oxford, 1947), pp. 171-72.
[24] An anonymous reviewer in *TLS* (Aug. 2, 1957), pp. 465-66.

the man who elicits it be a superlative conjurer. . . ." But as for the man of the great public: ". . . *your* face, *your* character, *your* behaviour—all that is most intimately *you*—is what the satirist takes for his target. And you do not thank him for it."[25] Between the "we" (which really means "I") and the "you" is an unbridgeable gulf. Neither Lewis nor Campbell can conceive of entering into the circle of his own critique. They are gods, magically set apart from the world of folly and error, each infallible in prophecy and invulnerable to criticism. One sees this most clearly in *Flowering Rifle* where the distance between "we" and "they" is absolute: *we* are all Christs in uniform; *they* are all

> pure Evil, flawless and unmixed
> Save for their bodies like swelled bugs affixed. (p. 56)

Life, for Campbell, is that incredibly simple, and from this stance it is impossible that the trajectory of the satire should include "us" or "me."

Campbell reverses what we have come to think of as the great role of the satirist in modern times, the role of a Swift or a Pope, who out of a profound sense of civilized order could expose with devastating brilliance the threatening encroachment of the powers of disorder:

> Lo! thy dread Empire, CHAOS! is restor'd;
> Light dies before thy uncreating word:
> Thy hand, great Anarch! lets the curtain fall;
> And Universal Darkness buries All.

As against this, Campbell, who deliberately assumed the ancient role of prophet, surgeon, and executioner, expressed, rather than opposed, the most demonically potent disorders of his time. Unquestionably, many of the follies and evils—many even of the individuals—he attacked were targets worthy of a satirist's attention. But his successes are tangential, against the grain; for Campbell worked from a rotten center. As a poet he rejected the austere demands of art by retreating into the irresponsibilities of magic. Against the chaos of a disintegrating society he could oppose only the madness of totalitarian violence. To paraphrase a famous epigram of the Austrian satirist Karl Kraus, Campbell is the disease he pretends to cure.

[25] *London Mercury*, xxx (1934), p. 509.

CHAPTER VI

THE SATIRIST AND SOCIETY

—————————=✠=—————————

It is not for euery one to rellish a true and naturall Satyre. . . .
—JOSEPH HALL, *Virgidemiarum*, "A Post-script to the Reader"

—————————=✠=—————————

Two CRIPPLES, characters in Yeats's play *The King's Threshold* (1904), speak:

SECOND CRIPPLE. If I were the King I wouldn't meddle with him [Senchán, chief poet of Ireland in the seventh century]; there is something queer about a man that makes rhymes. I knew a man that would be making rhymes year in and year out under a thorn at the crossing of three roads, and he was no sooner dead than every thorn-tree from Inchy to Kiltartan withered, and he a ragged man like ourselves.

FIRST CRIPPLE. Those that make rhymes have a power from beyond the world.

The ancient belief that the poet has magical powers is so compelling that it survives in certain distorted ways today. "People speak with justice," says Freud, "of the 'magic of art' and compare artists with magicians. . . ." In early European culture the association led directly into the realms of the forbidden; the artist was regarded as the heritor of the mythical beings whose "creativity" was rebellion and who were punished for their awful audacity: Daedalus, who was imprisoned; Wieland and Hephaestus, both crippled; Prometheus, the great prototype, chained to his rock. For man to create—a statue, a building, a painting, a poem—has always been in some sense to encroach on divine prerogative. Mann's *Dr. Faustus* is a late variation on a perennial theme. Today, writes Ernst Kris, creative personalities still bear part of their ancient heritage, for good and ill. Like their mythical ancestors, they are "to some extent beyond the pale of society, beyond the dictates which normally rule it and hold it together. They enjoy special prerogatives—e.g., the prerogative of greater sexual freedom—but the radius of their lives extends only from Parnassus to bohème; they are the objects of our admiration and the targets of our ambivalence."[1]

The power from beyond the world that the character in Yeats' play speaks of is the power associated with this theme, but the passage has even more direct relevance to our enterprise. Senchán, of whom the cripples speak, is the Senchán of *The Great Visitation to Guaire*, the curious tale we examined above. Yeats here treats him as a symbolic figure: he is The Artist, heroically prepared to die in defense of the ancient right of the poets.[2] In the original tale, however, Senchán was, as we know, a satirist-magician, his power somewhat declined, it is true, as he is mocked by his creator, but "real" enough and inferior only to the power of the saints and the demons. If poets in real life were thought to have such powers, they must as a consequence have stood in a very special relation to their respective societies.

The magician has always and everywhere been the focus of conflict reflecting the double-edged cultural role of magic. On the one hand, says Malinowski, magic "has exercised a profound positive function in organizing enterprise, in inspiring hope and confidence in the individual." It is, he says elsewhere, "one of the means of carrying on the established order [and] is in its turn strengthened by [that order]."[3] Insofar as the magician uses his great powers to enhance the well-being of society—defending it from its enemies, coercing the powers of nature into favorable performance, enriching the inner life of society through ritual performance—he is honored and revered. On the other hand, magic on its dark and fearsome side exerts "disturbing and subversive influences."[4] The very fact that the socially approved practices of the magician are made possible by the exercise of supernatural power implies a complementary danger, for the

---

[1] *Psychoanalytic Explorations in Art*, pp. 78-80.

[2] Yeats says that he "twisted [the tale] about and revised its moral that the poet might have the best of it." *Collected Works* (Stratford-on-Avon, 1908), II, 255.

[3] *Coral Gardens and their Magic*, II, 240; *Argonauts of the Western Pacific*, p. 76.

[4] Malinowski, *Coral Gardens*, II, 240.

powers of the magician are not always amenable to social control. In them is potentiality for benefit, but also for danger, both social and personal. The magician is at once prop and threat to the social order; his relation to society is always colored by the ambivalent emotional attitudes generated by this knowledge.[5]

The situation of the satirist-magician is similar. His satire may contribute to the richness and coherence of his culture by virtue of its being a constitutive element of ritual, as in the Greek Phallic Songs. Or it may be employed in straightforward and warlike defense of his tribe against threat from without. Archilochus cursed the enemy Sapaeans. Arabic satirists were preeminently warriors, their lethal verses their weapons. Irish satire caused the enemy to melt away before it. The satirist may even partake of a partial divinity, as did Archilochus, of whom it was foretold that he would be immortal.[6] In these situations the satirist-magician unquestionably inspires emotions of adulation and respect and awe. But in other, and possibly more characteristic, roles, he becomes the object of hate and fear. Again, Archilochus serves as example. Tributes from classical times to his poetic achievement are nearly rapturous: he is second only to Homer in some pantheons, and he was worshipped after his death; yet the dominant image that has come down through history is that of the implacable foe whose verses, steeped in poison, brought death to Lycambes and his daughter. Similarly, Irish poets were honored and loved in their positive roles, but hated and feared because of their oppressiveness and their power to do harm. Cormac's false etymology of the word for poet reflects well the doubleness of the image. *File* is derived, says Cormac, "from poison (*fi*) in satire and splendour (*li*) in praise."

These attitudes toward poet-magicians are reflected in ancient

[5] Paul Radin (*The World of Primitive Man* [New York, 1953], pp. 137-50) emphasizes the crucial economic significance of magical practices and institutions in both simple and complex cultures. Old Irish satirist-magicians, according to the tales, often exert their magical powers blatantly in the interests of economic exploitation. Later satirists have behaved similarly; the most notorious example is Pietro Aretino, the scourge of princes, whose satire is said to have caused the death of Antonio Broccardo and who extorted money from nobles by threatening them with his verse. See P. L. Ginguené, *Histoire Littéraire d'Italie* (Paris, 1824), IX, 216.

[6] See *Elegy and Iambus*, ed. Edmonds, II, 93.

law. The Roman Twelve Tables, as we have seen, threaten with death anyone who would "chant an evil charm" (*qui malum carmen incantassit*), and Plato's *Laws* recommend extremely severe penalties against similar activity. Old Irish law undertakes zealously to regulate the activity of satirists, making provision for the reward of "good" satire (satire directed, that is, toward socially sanctioned ends), but laying down heavy penalties for "bad" satire, that which wantonly injures.[7] Here in the old legal formulas are codified the ambivalent attitudes of a society toward its poet-magicians.

As conscious belief in magic drops away, the role of the satirist changes: he is no longer a medicine-man, half in society and half out, as he mediates between his people and higher powers; his mantic function is preempted by the priest, and interest in his poetic utterance is on aesthetic value rather than on magical potency. Only in this way can the magic invective of an heroic folk society develop into literary art.[8] Cassirer's statement, in the final chapter of *Language and Myth,* is precisely to this point, although he happens here to be speaking of pictorial art: "The image . . . achieves its purely representative, specifically 'aesthetic' function only as the magic circle with which mythical consciousness surrounds it is broken, and it is recognized not as a mythico-magical form, but as a particular sort of *formulation.*"[9] In short, the satirist becomes, instead of a prophet, a "mere" poet, writing, as he frequently confesses, in an inferior genre. The distinction is well pointed up by contrasting a statement on the function of the poet in a heroic society with a comparable statement of Horace. Carpre, the Irish poet, is asked in one of the sagas what he will do in battle. "Not hard to say," quoth Carpre. "I will make a *glám dícind* on them. And I will satirize them and shame them, so that through the spell of my art they will not resist warriors." The heroic tone, the magnificent sense of power belong (in Cassirer's phrase) to a mythically bound society. Horace, in his account to Augustus of the poet's function, writes: "Though a poor soldier and slow in the field, the poet is of use to the State, if you

[7] See Chap. I, 3, above.
[8] See Chap. II, 3, above.
[9] Ernst Cassirer, *Language and Myth,* trans. S. K. Langer (New York, 1946), p. 98.

grant that even by small things great ends are helped."[10] However the characteristic wry understatement discounts the literal
meaning, it is a mighty falling off. But even granting the changed
modes of belief and the relatively inferior status of the poet, it
is still possible to see in the relationship of the satirist to a more
sophisticated society some reflection of the ambiguities we have
been considering.

The law continued to pay close heed to the satirist as bans on
magical utterance gave way to bans on libel. From the beginning
the satirical poet has skated on the thin edge of censorship and
legal retribution. Archilochus' poetry was barred from Sparta,
according to Valerius Maximus, on thoroughly modern grounds:
because of its indecency and because of the savagery of the poet's
"obscenis maledictis" against Lycambes and his family.[11] Athens,
it is true, allowed its poets almost complete freedom to attack
both institutions and individuals. Attempts to censor comedy in
general and personal abuse in particular were either abortive or
successful for short periods only. Cleon had the young Aristophanes brought before the council on charges of slandering the
state, but within a year Aristophanes had his revenge with the
performance of the *Knights*, surely one of the most unrestrained
assaults on a man in power ever made. But Athens was unique.[12]
We know that Horace in his gingerly consciousness of the delicate line he had to draw was justifiably worried over legal retribution. Juvenal's situation was more precarious; his fear of legal
sanctions may be taken to account for the extraordinary anti-
climax of his first satire in which he announces, after an im-
passioned outburst, that he will write only of the dead.

In England in 1599 the Archbishop of Canterbury and the
Bishop of London issued an order prohibiting the printing of
any satires thereafter and requiring that works of Hall, Marston,
Nashe, and others be burned.[13] Ben Jonson complains that the

[10] *The Second Battle of Moytura*, trans. Stokes, RC, xii (1891), pp.
91-93; Cross and Slover, p. 41; Horace, *Epistles*, ii, 1, ll. 124-25.
[11] *Factorum et Dictorum Memorabilium*, Lib. vi, 3, Ext. 1; see the
edition of Carolus Kempf (Lipsiae, 1888), p. 291.
[12] See Max Radin, "Freedom of Speech in Ancient Athens," *AJP*,
xlviii (1927), pp. 215 ff.; Victor Ehrenberg, *The People of Aristophanes*
(Cambridge, Mass., 1951), pp. 25-26.
[13] The order is reprinted in *A Transcript of the Registers of the Com-*

"apologeticall Dialogue" which he wrote as an Epilogue to *Poetaster* (the Epilogue containing the Archilochean threat) was spoken only once from the stage and was then forbidden by authority. When the play was published in quarto in the same year (1601) the apology was again forbidden; it did not appear in print until the Folio edition of 1616.[14] What seems to be a covert reference to these matters appears in the play itself. Jonson added a scene (III, v) for the Folio. The scene consists entirely of a dialogue between Horace (who stands for Jonson himself) and Trebatius; it is, in fact, a direct, if expansive, translation of Horace's famous *apologia* (*Satires*, II, i). In Horace's poem, we recall, Trebatius warns Horace against writing satire. Horace persists: "whether . . . rich or poor, in Rome, or, if chance so bid, in exile, whatever the colour of my life, write I must" (*quisquis erit vitae scribam color*). Jonson's version is somewhat more pointed; he presents the same alternatives, then:

> What hiew soeuer, my whole state shall beare,
> I will write satyres still, in spight of feare.

The greater concreteness of this line probably has autobiographical significance and is specifically related to the prohibition of satire in 1599. It should be added, however, that the censorship was not notably effective, and verse satires continued to be published under some desultory harassment. Still, this episode in Elizabethan literary history provides a forceful reminder of the abiding legal interest in satiric ventures.

The satirist faces comparable problems today. In democratic countries he attacks individuals only at the risk of grave financial loss to himself and his publisher; in totalitarian countries the satirist risks death. No matter how carefully he may choose his target, a shift in governmental policy may undo him completely: what one day seemed worthy the most extreme denunciation may the next day be sacrosanct. It is a harrowing occupational hazard. Under extreme conditions satire against the reigning order is out of the question; so canonical is this rule that political analysts use the amount and character of satire permitted in the Soviet Union as an indication of the relative intensity or relax-

---

pany of Stationers of London, ed. Edward Arber (London, 1876), III, 316.
[14] *Jonson*, ed. Herford and Simpson, IV, 317, 193.

ation of pressures there at any given time. Isaac Deutscher, for example, interprets the increasing amount of Soviet satire against internal abuses since Stalin's death as a favorable sign.[15]

The relation of satire to the law has had considerable importance in determining the forms satire takes and the methods it uses. When verse satires were banned in Elizabethan England, the poets immediately found a new form in which the satiric impulse might be incorporated. Under the leadership of Ben Jonson and Marston, a new dramatic "kind" was inaugurated: the "comicall satyre," a coinage that Jonson applies to his own *Every Man Out of his Humour, Cynthias Revels*, and *Poetaster*.[16] Professor Campbell shows convincingly that Shakespeare's *Troilus and Cressida* is best thought of as an example of the new form, an offspring, as it were, of satire's perennial conflict with the law.

Such historically demonstrable effects of social pressures on satiric form are impressive, but it seems likely that over the course of history the pressures have worked also in more subtle and more pervasive ways. Freud perhaps throws some light here: from the childhood of civilization, he says, society has subjected our impulses of hostility (and our sexual impulses) to progressive restrictions and repressions, just as it restricts similar impulses in us as we grow older as individuals. The hostility remains, of course; but the physical violence that in archaic times might have resulted from it comes to be forbidden by law and is gradually replaced by verbal invectives. Later, even that kind of weapon is rendered inappropriate; as we grow more civilized we realize that to use abusive language is undignified and improper. From prohibitions of this kind, says Freud, developed wit, an effective, if often indirect, agent of hostility.

[15] "Russia in Transition," *Dissent*, II (Winter, 1955), p. 27. Cf. Clifton Daniel's story in the *New York Times* (Jan. 30, 1955), p. 19, on Arkadi Raikin, who gave a popular nightly review in Leningrad in which he satirized "everything from nepotism in the state apparatus to inefficiency in the retail trade network," but not the principles of Communism or the leaders of the party.

[16] This is the thesis of Professor Campbell's *Comicall Satyre*. Miss Mary Claire Randolph arrived independently at a similar conclusion in her unpublished dissertation, "The Neo-Classic Theory of the Formal Verse Satire," University of North Carolina (1939).

"Society . . . prevents us from expressing our hostile feelings in action; and hence, as in sexual aggression, there has developed a new technique of invectives, the aim of which is to enlist . . . [society] against our enemy. By belittling and humbling our enemy, by scorning and ridiculing him, we indirectly obtain the pleasure of his defeat by the laughter of the third person [i.e., society]. . . .

"Wit permits us to make our enemy ridiculous through that which we could not utter loudly or consciously on account of existing hindrances. . . ."[17]

Once wit has been brought into the service of the satiric spirit, then all the rhetorical maneuvers by which the literary satirist achieves his end become available: irony, innuendo, burlesque, parody, allegory—all the devices of indirection which help make palatable an originally unacceptable impulse. It is a nice complication, however, that the devices which make satire acceptable to polite society at the same time sharpen its point. "Abuse is not so dangerous," said Dr. Johnson, "when there is no vehicle of wit or delicacy, no subtle conveyance." The conveyances are born out of prohibition.

The Earl of Shaftesbury, writing in the eighteenth century, recognized the "creative" significance of legal and other repressions on the writing of satire. He explains the prevalence of irony, raillery, and writing in disguise as resulting from the weight of censorship. " 'Tis the persecuting spirit has raised the bantering one," he says. "The greater the weight [of constraint] is, the bitterer will be the satire. The higher the slavery, the more exquisite the buffoonery."[18] Shaftesbury's insight requires the qualification made above. Under a massively efficient tyranny, satire of the forms, institutions, or personalities of that tyranny is impossible. But under the more relaxed authoritarianism of an easier-going day, remarkable things could be done. Max Radin writes of how satirical journals in Germany before the First World War, even in the face of a severe and rigorously enforced law against *Majestätsbeleidigung*, vied with each other to see

[17] *Wit and its Relation to the Unconscious*, trans. A. A. Brill (New York, 1916), pp. 148-50.
[18] Anthony Earl of Shaftesbury, *Characteristics*, ed. J. M. Robertson (London, 1900), I, 50-51.

how close they could come to caricatures of the Kaiser without actually producing them.[19] Kenneth Burke sums up this paradoxical aspect of satire's relation with the law by suggesting that "the conditions are 'more favorable' to satire under censorship than under liberalism—for the most inventive satire arises when the artist is seeking simultaneously to take risks and escape punishment for his boldness, and is never quite certain himself whether he will be acclaimed or punished."[20] Voltaire's whole career is an excellent case in point. Bigots and tyrants may have turned pale at his name, as Macaulay's hyperbole has it; but Voltaire's life was a long series of niggling subterfuges to avoid the penalties of the law and to escape the wrath of those he had angered. The acclaim showered on him was a product of a kind of illegality, and the praise accorded him had as its concomitant the fear and the hatred which his work inspired. The satirist's status with respect to society is like that of the magician: it is necessarily problematic.

We have an excellent opportunity to examine the satirist's claims for social approval largely by reason of the literary convention which decrees that he must justify his ungrateful art. From the times of Horace, Persius, and Juvenal, down to Boileau, Swift, and Pope, and into our own day with men like Wyndham Lewis, the satirist has felt compelled to write an *apologia*, whether formal or informal, in verse or prose. The *apologiae* are remarkably similar in their protestations (Mr. Lewis dissenting in part); from them we get an ideal image which the satirist projects of himself and his art. According to the image the satirist is a public servant fighting the good fight against vice and folly wherever he meets it; he is honest, brave, protected by the rectitude of his motives; he attacks only the wicked and then seldom or never by name; he is, in short, a moral man appalled by the evil he sees around him, and he is forced by his conscience to write satire. Juvenal's *facit indignatio versum* is the prototype.[21]

[19] "Freedom of Speech in Ancient Athens," *AJP*, XLVIII (1927), p. 226.
[20] *The Philosophy of Literary Form*, pp. 231-32.
[21] The image is not always so solemn. Samuel Butler writes: "A Satyr is a kinde of Knight Errant that goe's upon Adventures, to Relieve the Distressed Damsel Virtue, and Redeeme Honor out of Inchanted Castles, And opprest Truth, and Reason out of the Captivity of Gyants or Magitians." *Characters*, ed. A. R. Waller (Cambridge, 1908), p. 469.

The satirist claims, with much justification, to be a true conservative. Usually (but not always—there are significant exceptions) he operates within the established framework of society, accepting its norms, appealing to reason (or to what his society accepts as rational) as the standard against which to judge the folly he sees. He is the preserver of tradition, the true tradition from which there has been grievous falling away.

Society, quite naturally, is dubious. On the most obvious level it points to the inevitable discrepancy between the ideal image, projected by rhetorical convention, and what it takes to be the actual fact. Swift, or Pope—so goes the reasoning—was a wicked man; therefore we may dismiss his satire. The *non sequitur* is comforting. But the problem on other levels is more complex. Despite society's doubts about the character of the satirist, there may develop a feeling that in its general application his work has some truth in it—or the feeling that other people may *think* that it has some truth in it. Individuals who recognize characteristics of themselves in the objects of attack cannot afford to acknowledge the identity even privately. So they may reward the satirist as proof of piety, while inwardly they fear him. *"Satyr,"* says Swift in a passage quoted earlier, *"is a sort of Glass, wherein Beholders do generally discover every body's Face but their Own; which is the chief Reason for that kind Reception it meets in the World, and that so very few are offended with it."* "Publicly offended," one might add. Publicly the satirist may be honored, but privately he will be feared.

From the beginning satirists have been uneasily explicit about the antagonism they arouse. Each of the three major classical *apologiae* (Horace, II, 1; Persius, 1; Juvenal, 1) contains a warning from the interlocutor on the animosities stirred up by satire and on the dangers the satirist risks. The dangers are unquestionably real: satirists have always attacked vice and viciousness and stupidity as they exist in the real world, and they have had to face the antagonism that inevitably accompanies such activity. Countless satirists in all lands have been beaten, imprisoned, tortured, even executed as a result of their daring. During James I's reign a Pole named Stercovius wrote a harsh satire on the Scots. King James was furious. In 1609 he had passed an act with the consent of Parliament rigorously forbidding the issuance of "pasquillis, lybellis, rymes, cokalanis, commedies, and siclyk occasionis." Somehow, even though Stercovius was in Poland, James arranged to have him executed. The cost to the British government was six hundred pounds.[22]

Even in periods when satire has flourished, opposition to it on moral and pragmatic grounds has been vigorous and outspoken. Gabriel Harvey, for example, writhing under the ridicule of Greene, Nashe, and others, wrote in furious indignation against the outrage of satire: "Inuectiues by fauour haue bene too bolde: and Satyres by vsurpation too-presumptuous: I ouerpasse *Archilochus, Aristophanes, Lucian, Iulian, Aretine*, and that whole venomous and viperous brood, of old & new Raylers: euen *Tully*, and *Horace* otherwhiles ouerreched. . . ."[23] Yet in a bow to his enemies' abuse, Harvey says he will try to amend any defects with which he has justly been charged.

Sir William Temple felt that the popular vein of satire and ridicule (he uses the terms synonymously) was "the Itch of our Age and Clymat" and thoroughly noxious in effect. He cites with at least partial approval the theory of an ingenious Spaniard who held that *Don Quixote*, by subjecting the Spanish romantic attitudes toward love and valor to ridicule, had brought about the ruin of the Spanish monarchy. In England, Temple says, ridicule has "helpt to Corrupt our modern Poesy"; and while he can praise Rabelais and Cervantes, the great masters in this kind of writing, his final attitude is uncompromising: "But let the Execution be what it will, the Design, the Custom, and Example [of satire] are very pernicious to Poetry, and indeed to all Virtue and Good Qualities among Men, which must be disheartened by finding how unjustly and undistinguish't they fall under the lash of Raillery, and this Vein of Ridiculing the Good as well as the Ill, the Guilty and the Innocent together."[24]

The most strenuously articulate of all those who have written against satire on whatever grounds was Pierre Bayle, author of the influential *Dictionnaire historique et critique* (Rotterdam,

[22] James Maidment in his ed. of *A Book of Scottish Pasquils, 1568-1715* (Edinburgh, 1868), pp. ix-xiii, 421.
[23] *Fovre Letters and Certeine Sonnets* (1592), ed. G. B. Harrison (London, 1922), p. 15.
[24] "An Essay upon the Ancient and Modern Learning" and "Of Poetry"; see Spingarn's edition of these *Essays*, pp. 41-42, 71-72.

1697). For Bayle satire was the Art of Poisoning; in hundreds of passages in the *Dictionary* he lashes out at the immorality, the untruthfulness, the cruelty of satire, which, despite its protestations, he says, neither prevents crime nor effects reform. Bayle is clearly fascinated by what horrifies him. In the article on Hipponax he writes: "He was neither the first, nor the only person who have forced people to make away with themselves by their invectives." Then follows a long, long list of historical examples of those who are said to have died as a result of ridicule, vituperation, or reproach. Satire, libel, lampoon, defamation, slander, ridicule—all are one to Bayle, and the satirist no better than a "mad dog," whose motive is to kill: ". . . a satirist who attempts upon the honour of his enemy with libels, would attempt upon their life with sword or poison, if he had the same opportunity."[25]

Bayle's arguments furnished ammunition for dozens of writers in the eighteenth century. Satirists were widely read and publicly applauded, but at the same time the distaste and fear which they inspired are plainly evident in the large body of literature directed against their mode. ". . . whence this Lust to Laugh?" queried William Whitehead lugubriously in his rhymed *Essay on Ridicule* (1743)—a plea for the demise of satire—and answered himself:

> Why, Shaftsb'ry tells us,
>   Mirth's the Test of Sense . . .
> Not so, fair Truth. . . .

Many echoed his "Not so."[26] Dr. Johnson had no love for satire. In an allegorical essay in the *Rambler* he wrote that Satire, who was born of an unholy cohabitation of Wit and Malice, carried poisoned arrows which could never be extracted from his victims. Earlier, in a similar allegory, Addison had expressed his disapproval by characterizing satire as a woman with a smile on her face and a dagger concealed under her garment. William Cowper questioned satire's efficacy:

[25] *Dictionary*, trans. des Maizeaux, v, 746, 765. See Mary Claire Randolph, "Pierre Bayle's Case against Satire and Satirists," *NQ*, 181 (1941), pp. 310-11.
[26] See Chap. II, 2, n. 35, above.

Yet what can satire, whether grave or gay?
It may correct a foible, may chastise
The freaks of fashion, regulate the dress,
Retrench a sword-blade, or displace a patch;
But where are its sublimer trophies found?
What vice has it subdu'd? Whose heart reclaim'd
By rigour, or whom laugh'd into reform?
Alas! Leviathan is not so tam'd.[27]

Even Voltaire (who had himself been victimized by libellers) harshly condemned his favorite mode in arguments drawn from Bayle: "If I followed my taste, I would speak of satire only in order to inspire abhorrence and to arm virtue against this dangerous form of writing. Satire is almost always unjust, and that is its least defect. . . . It is a trade, like selling adulterated wine. One must admit that there is hardly a trade more unworthy, more cowardly, and more punishable."[28]

By the early nineteenth century the word *satire* had acquired in the popular mind a wide range of generally unpleasant associations. Lady Middleton, in Jane Austen's *Sense and Sensibility* (1811), dislikes Elinor and Marianne Dashwood: ". . . because they were fond of reading, she fancied them satirical: perhaps without exactly knowing what it was to be satirical; but *that* did not signify. It was censure in common use, and easily given."[29] Thackeray's defense of satire in mid-century is totally revealing. He has been deploring the savagery of the caricaturists Gilray and Rowlandson: "We cannot afford to lose Satyr with his pipe and dances and gambols. But we have washed, combed, clothed, and taught the rogue good manners: or rather, let us say, he has learned them himself; for he is of nature soft and kindly, and he has put aside his mad pranks and tipsy habits; and frolicsome

[27] Johnson, *Rambler*, No. 22; Addison, *Spectator*, No. 63; Cowper, *The Task*, II, ll. 315-22, and cf. "Charity," ll. 491-556.

[28] "Satire" (1749), *Oeuvres complètes* (Paris, 1879), XXIII, 414-17. Cf. his earlier comments on Boileau: "What did his satires accomplish? they raised laughter at the expense of ten or twelve men of letters; they caused two men who had never harmed him to die of shame; they aroused enemies who followed him almost to the grave, and who would have ruined him more than once if he had not had the protection of Louis XIV." "Mémoire sur la satire," *ibid.*, XXIII, 53.

[29] Chap. XXXVI (Oxford World's Classics, 1950), p. 233.

always, has become gentle and harmless, smitten into shame by the pure presence of our women and the sweet confiding smiles of our children."[30] Shame, the instrument by which the satirist once killed, and later purported to bring about moral reform, has, in this view, tamed the satirist himself—perhaps a final variation on the satirist-satirized theme. The fear and the hatred have disappeared: but so, clearly, has the satire.

The whole theme of the satirist's ambiguous relation to society is neatly encapsulated, I think, at the end of Juvenal's first satire. The full-blown description of Rome's insanely abandoned ways comes to a climax as Juvenal considers the situation of the poet. No time has ever needed him more, he proclaims: all vice is at its acme, and Juvenal exhorts the poet to spread his sails, to shake out every stitch of canvas. But then the recollection of danger intervenes. Where is the freedom our heroic forefathers had to attack the wicked, to name the evildoer? Anyone who today dared describe Nero's master in debauchery, Tigellinus, would be burned at the stake in the arena. It was not always so: ". . . when Lucilius roars and rages as if with sword in hand, the hearer, whose soul is cold with crime, grows red; he sweats with the secret consciousness of sin. Hence wrath and tears."[31] The image of the satirist projected here is that of a hero; but, "inde ira et lacrimae"—he is a hated hero. The wrath is that of the victim for the satirist; as the context indicates, he may be capable of doing the poet great harm. But the victim also turns red and sweats in his consciousness of guilt. The tears are his as well as the anger. The satire, heroically issued, has aroused wrath and fear; yet it has also performed its moral function. In the phrase "inde ira et lacrimae" is epitomized the purported function of satire and, by implication, the ambiguous situation of the satirist in relation to his contemporaries.

Society has many grounds for its dislike and distrust of satire. No matter what abuses it may expose, no matter what lofty motives the satirist may profess, he has no *right* (so goes the chief moral argument) to take the honor and reputation of other men into his hands or to set himself up as a censor of established

[30] "John Leech's Pictures of Life and Character" (1854), *Works* (New York, 1903), xxv, 484.
[31] I, 149-68, trans. Ramsay.

institutions or modes of behavior. Further, for all the pain he causes, the satirist never actually brings about reform.[32] These are the objections most often stated. But society has other reasons for dubiety. The pressure of the satirist's art inevitably comes athwart society's efforts to maintain its equilibrium. The satirist usually claims that he does not attack institutions; he attacks perversions of institutions. When, for example, he ridicules a corrupt judge he intends no reflection on the law as such; he is attacking a corruption which has crept into the law. Ben Jonson's Cordatus, the "Moderator" of *Every Man Out of his Humour*, speaks precisely to this point. The innocent will not be injured in this play, he says; to claim injury would be "to affirme, that a man, writing of NERO, should meane all Emperors: or speaking of MACHIAVEL, comprehend all States-men; or in our SORDIDO, all Farmars; and so of the rest: then which, nothing can be vtter'd more malicious, or absurd."[33] In large measure, of course, Cordatus is right. As Northrop Frye says, the satirist attacks primarily neither the man nor the institution; he attacks an evil man who is given gigantic stature and protected by the prestige of the institution. "The cowl might make the monk if it were not for the satirist."[34]

But there is another sense in which Cordatus is wrong, for an attack by a powerful satirist on a local phenomenon seems to be capable of indefinite extension in the reader's mind into an attack on the whole structure of which that phenomenon is part. Significantly, I think, this imaginative process is magical; it functions by synecdoche, which is one of the foundations of magic. In "mythico-linguistic thought," to use Cassirer's phrase, the part does not merely represent the whole, it *is* the whole; by the magical process of identification the nail paring or the lock of hair

---

[32] The sociologist Frederick E. Lumley considers the problem of whether satire accomplishes its purported end. He quotes authors on both sides of the question, then concludes that until "hundreds of testimonies of satire's effectiveness" be collected, "the proposition that satire is an effective instrument of control must be left in the air." *Means of Social Control* (New York, 1925), pp. 251-55.

[33] II, vi, 166-70. See *Jonson*, ed. Herford and Simpson, III, 494-95.

[34] "The Nature of Satire," *University of Toronto Quarterly*, XIV (1944-45), pp. 79-80. Cf. Dryden's "A satirical poet is the check of the laymen on bad priests." "Preface to the Fables," *Essays*, ed. W. P. Ker (Oxford, 1926), II, 260.

from an enemy *is* the enemy, and whoever controls the part has dominion also over the whole. This process is by no means confined to a mythically bound society; as a different order of experience, to be sure, it is the way of the imagination when it is bound, in its own way, by the spell of the creative artist. The judge who has been ridiculed by a powerful satirist comes to stand for—to be—lawyers in general and even the law itself. What starts as local attack ends by calling the whole institution into question. Thus the satirical portraits of Chaucer, who seems to have been thoroughly orthodox in religion, have often been interpreted as evidence of his revolt against the Church; during the Reformation he and Langland were used for purposes doubtless far removed from their intent. Molière proposed in *Tartuffe* to unmask an example of religious hypocrisy. Yet the effect of the play has seemed to many people genuinely subversive, the attack on the hypocrite somehow, insidiously, becoming an attack on religion itself. Two hundred and fifty years after the play was first performed, Brunetière could write that the wound had not closed: ". . . there is no doubt that it was deep; that the hand which made it meant to make it; that therefore it was not only false devotion but also true, which Molière meant to attack. . . ."[35] Brunetière attributes the damage to Molière's evil intentions; in an odd way, if one wants to talk about damage, one is on safer grounds to speak of magic: of synecdoche, of the tainted part becoming through the strange efficacies of art the whole.

The *Tartuffe* dilemma is very ancient; Lucian's dialogue *The Dead Come to Life* turns precisely on it. The question of the dialogue is this: has Lucian's ridicule of individual philosophers (specifically in *Philosophies for Sale*) besmirched Philosophy herself?[36] The problem is treated with the greatest subtlety. Frankness (a transparent alias for Lucian) is hailed up for trial; he is to be accused by Socrates, Plato, Diogenes, and others who are on leave from Hades for a day, and is to be judged by Philosophy. In the course of the trial the following points are established: Philosophy holds that ridicule, far from harming truth,

[35] *Brunetière's Essays in French Literature,* trans. D. Nichol Smith (London, 1898), p. 111.
[36] *Lucian,* trans. Harmon, III, 3-81.

actually enhances it (p. 23); Lucian is found to have ridiculed, not Philosophy, but only impostors and thus to have served truth; and the character of the satirist is established to be that of a "bluff-hater, cheat-hater, liar-hater, vanity-hater," but also that of a "truth-lover, beauty-lover, simplicity-lover," and so on. These latter propensities the satirist has little opportunity to exercise, the world being what it is; but Philosophy consoles him: "the two callings [hating evil and loving good] . . . are but one" (p. 33). Philosophy expresses in a phrase the public rationale of the satirist's activity. Lucian manages his own defense with marvellous skill and impeccable logic; the fact remains, however, that as all readers of Lucian know, Philosophy emerges from his dialogues in very tattered condition indeed.

Swift notoriously found himself in a similar situation with A Tale of a Tub. In the "Apology" which he added to the work in 1710, he reverts at least six times to the contention that the Tale attacks, not religion and learning, but abuses in religion and learning: "Religion they tell us ought not to be ridiculed, and they tell us Truth, yet surely the Corruptions in it may; for we are taught by the tritest Maxim in the World, that Religion being the best of Things, its Corruptions are likely to be the worst." Yet the attack, as Swift's contemporaries saw, could hardly be contained; restricted as the intention may have been, the Tale in effect ramified into an attack on religion itself. I believe that Swift was deeply concerned for the welfare of the Established Church as he saw it; but under the impact of his satire one of the great pillars of society rocked a bit. Swift's strength, as Empson puts it, made his instrument too strong for him. His magic, one might say, was his undoing.

The implications are reasonably clear. The satirist, it is true, claims to be conservative, to be using his art to shore up the foundations of the established order; and insofar as one can place satirists politically, I suspect that a large majority are what would be called conservative. Professor Auerbach has emphasized, for example, that in all Molière's plays there is no criticism whatever of the social, political, or economic bases of life. "Molière's criticism is entirely moralistic; that is to say, it accepts the prevailing structure of society, takes for granted its justification, permanence, and general validity, and castigates the excesses occurring within its limits as ridiculous."[37] Yet who could deny the profoundly anarchic thrust of Alceste's sentiments? The play demands that his passionate utterances be given full weight in the scale which measures his fanatical sincerity against the social hypocrisy of the Orontes, the Célimènes, the Philintes of his world. It demands that he be taken seriously; and the demand enforces the question: what if he *were* taken seriously? Alceste's commitments and criticisms are moral, as Auerbach says, rather than social or political; but in the area of his interest, and given the power of his utterance, the moral subsumes the social. His ideas are radically disruptive. It is hard to conceive the society that could sustain them.

Such ambiguous results seem almost an inevitable consequence of major satire. Let the conscious intent of the artist be what it will, the local attack cannot be contained: the ironic language eats its way in implication through the most powerful-seeming structures.[38] One final example from Swift. The complexly simple projector of *An Argument against Abolishing Christianity*, the "I" of the piece, argues cogently for the retention of nominal Christianity. To restore "real" Christianity, he says, "would indeed be a wild Project; it would be to dig up Foundations; . . . to break the entire Frame and Constitution of Things; to ruin Trade, extinguish Arts and Sciences, with the Professors of them; in short, to turn our Courts, Exchanges, and Shops into Desarts. . . ." One reads this and one can only say, He is right: the fool speaks truth. Between Swift and the projector, of course, there is a considerable ironic remove, just as there is distance between Swift and some of the meanings set in motion by his creature. We may doubt that Swift the Tory politician, Swift the social man, would have sympathized with breaking the "Frame and Constitution of Things." But here Swift is the artist. The pressure of his art works directly against the ostensibly conservative

[37] *Mimesis*, p. 365.
[38] See Bishop Warburton's comment: "The Spaniards have lamented, and I believe truly, that Cervantes's just and inimitable ridicule of *knight-errantry* rooted up, with that folly, a great deal of their *real honour*. And it was apparent, that Butler's fine satire on *fanaticism* contributed not a little . . . to bring *sober piety* into disrepute." *Works*, ed. Richard Hurd (London, 1811), i, 155-56. Cf. Northrop Frye, "The Nature of Satire," pp. 82 ff.

function which it is said to serve. Instead of shoring up foundations, it tears them down. It is revolutionary.

Society has doubtless been wise, in its old pragmatic way, to
suspect the satirist. Whether he is an enchanter wielding the
ambiguous power of magic, or whether he is a "mere" poet, his
relation to society will necessarily be problematic. He is of society in the sense that his art must be grounded in his experience
as social man; but he must also be apart, as he struggles to
achieve aesthetic distance. His practice is often sanative, as he
proclaims; but it may be revolutionary in ways that society cannot possibly approve, and in ways that may not be clear even
to the satirist.

CHAPTER VII

CONCLUSION: THE LIFE OF SATIRE

———————————— ❈ ————————————

Yet primal nature will out. . . . When the harvest has been fully gathered in, it will then be time to say, in regard to the classics both of Greece and of Rome, how far the old lives on in the new, how far what the student in his haste is apt to label "survival" stands for a force still tugging at the heartstrings of even the most sophisticated and lordly heir of the ages.—R. R. MARETT, *Anthropology and the Classics*, "Preface"

———————————— ❈ ————————————

THE REINTRODUCTION OF MAGIC as a constitutive element in the function of satire leads us to a puzzling problem: has the genesis of satire in magical belief any significance for satire today? Is there any relation whatever between the response to the writings of Mary McCarthy or the late English poet Reginald Reynolds, say, and the response which legend attributes to those who heard the verses of Aithirne the Importunate? We shall not be able to answer the question directly, but I propose in this concluding chapter to suggest why I think that the question at least is open.

Belief in the magical power of poetry survived in Ireland into the nineteenth century and probably survives among the folk today. Blind Raftery, who wandered the parishes of Galway and Mayo, was "someway gifted," it was said; people were frightened of him, particularly of his satire and curses (about which strange stories were told), but also, oddly enough, of his praise: it was thought to be unlucky. Lady Gregory gives examples of his satires and quotes an old basketmaker who remembered the poems and the tales of their blighting effect and compared them to stories of an older day: " 'That is why the poets had to be banished before in the time of St. Columcill. Sure no one could stand the satire of them.' "[1]

[1] *Poets and Dreamers* (Dublin, 1903), pp. 1-10.

England has no record of a similar magical tradition, although tales of the lethal powers of verse seized the imagination of Renaissance writers. Thomas Freeman can think of no higher praise for Nashe than to compare him with Archilochus:

> Nash, had Lycambes on earth liuing beene
> The time thou wast, his death had bin al one,
> Had he but mou'd thy tartest Muse to spleene,
> Vnto the forke he had as surely gone:
> For why there liued not that man I thinke,
> Vsde better, or more bitter gall in Inke.[2]

Stories of Irish magical verse were almost as popular as those of the Greek: Sidney, Shakespeare, Jonson, Thomas Randolph, Marston, Otway, Temple—all refer to one or the other. Knowledge of such stories by no means implies belief, of course; rather, the tales of magical efficacy provided metaphors for poetry. When Ben Jonson threatens to write iambics that will make his enemies hang themselves, or when Marston's Lampatho Doria shouts:

> I'll rhyme thee dead.
> Look for the satire. . . .

we understand the language as figurative.[3] On the level of consciousness these are mere images, legitimately hyperbolic because they are "poetic," but not to be taken "seriously," *i.e.*, literally. On a level below consciousness, however, such images function in mysterious ways. What does it mean to say that Jonson and Pope and Byron and Roy Campbell kill their enemies symbolically? What did it mean to John Partridge, the astrologer, to be ridiculed "to death" by Swift and his friends? Satire unquestionably retains its power to hurt: an American poet has described vividly to me the agony he experienced when another writer attempted to demolish him satirically in print. But until we know much more about both the creative process and the actual nature of the response of those who are "in the spell," as we say, of the creative artist, we shall be unable to discuss such matters systematically.

[2] Cited in Thomas Nashe, *Works*, ed. R. B. McKerrow (London, 1904-10), v, 153.
[3] Jonson, *Poetaster*, "To the Reader"; Marston, *What You Will*, ii. i, 121-22.

A major difference between victims of archaic satire and victims today is in their respective attitudes toward magic: they believed in its efficacy, we do not. We do not believe consciously, that is; yet we often behave as though we lived in a world pulsating with magic power. There can be little doubt that below the level of consciousness primitive magic lives on powerfully in us all. "In the human mind," writes Lévy-Bruhl, "whatever may be its intellectual development, subsists an ineradicable foundation of primitive mentality."[4] Freud has demonstrated the similarity between the mechanisms of magic and the mechanisms of various kinds of neurotic behavior; we need not fear that we are becoming obsessional neurotics when we recognize certain of the same mechanisms in our own and our friends' deportment.

Even in much more prosaic areas of human behavior an essentially magical attitude toward many phenomena is considered thoroughly normal. We are quick to perceive evidence of these unconscious forces as they have made their grotesque appearances in the past. We read, for example, of the extraordinary efforts exerted during the French Revolution to destroy emblems of royalty: statues, pictures, inscriptions, memorials of every kind. Even playing cards were replaced throughout the country, kings and queens being the principal victims. The public executioner broke on the scaffold a medal that had been struck off in honor of Lafayette.[5] From the vantage point of 170 years the magical component in such regressive action is unmistakable. But are we not responding to similar primal demands when we treasure the lock of hair of a loved one, or tear up the picture of the girl who has rejected us, or keep as a talisman the pocket torn from Ty Cobb's baseball uniform? or the sleeve from Frank Sinatra's shirt? Objects which once belonged to famous men take on for us the *mana* of those men: George Washington's sword, Voltaire's writing desk, the pen with which General MacArthur signed the peace treaty. I know a museum which once proudly displayed the shoes and stockings worn by a general in World War II. Bits of the true Cross are less vendible today

[4] Cited by E. R. Dodds in the Preface to *The Greeks and the Irrational*.

[5] Ernest F. Henderson, *Symbol and Satire in the French Revolution* (New York 1912), pp. 263-82.

than they were in the Middle Ages, but if Sir Winston Churchill chose to sell the stub of a cigar, he could be fairly sure of commanding an eager market. The unconscious mechanism behind these phenomena is clear: to possess the object is to possess something of the person with whom it was associated, or something of that person's power. This is not to say that autograph collectors are savages—simply that we are all responsive in various ways to magical orders of behavior.[6]

Language affects us similarly. In a discussion of magical language in both primitive and civilized cultures, Malinowski writes of the "very real basis to human belief in the mystic and binding power of words." He speaks of the law: "Here the value of the word, the binding force of a formula, is at the very foundation of order and reliability in human relations. Whether the marriage vows are treated as a sacrament or as a mere legal contract . . . the power of words in establishing a permanent human relation, the sacredness of words and their socially sanctioned inviolability, are absolutely necessary to the existence of social order. If legal phrases, if promises and contracts were not regarded as something more than *flatus vocis*, social order would cease to exist in a complex civilisation as well as in a primitive tribe."[7]

Verbal magic in our culture is ubiquitous, extending far beyond legal and sacral usage; its clearest manifestation is probably in advertising and in propaganda of all kinds.[8] Malinowski draws amusing parallels between advertising formulas of certain cosmetic firms and beauty charms employed by the Trobriand Islanders:

> I smooth out, I improve, I whiten.
> Thy head I smooth out, I improve, I whiten.
> Thy cheeks I smooth out, I improve, I whiten.
> Thy nose I smooth out, I improve, I whiten.
> Thy throat I smooth out, I improve, I whiten. . . .[9]

[6] For the survival of primitive magic in contemporary culture, see Arthur Koestler, "An Essay on Snobbery," *Encounter* (Sept. 1955), pp. 33 ff.; for examples of current "mythological thinking," see W. K. C. Guthrie, *In the Beginning* (Ithaca, N.Y., 1957), pp. 15-16.

[7] *Coral Gardens*, II, 234-35.

[8] See Duncan, "Literature as Magical Art," *Language and Literature in Society*, pp. 20-41.

[9] *Coral Gardens*, II, 237-38.

—so the Islanders. Elizabeth Arden says much the same thing, although somewhat less simply. It is not easy to say which is the "purer" magic.

As we noted at the beginning of the preceding chapter, a magical aura still clings obscurely around the artist. It is manifested in various ways. For example, at certain times the artist will be urged to renounce "art" as such and to become a magician—to revitalize the power of the primitive. ". . . In time of worldwoe," said Thomas Wolfe, "there is no place for the indirect method of satiric writing. . . . We need the blazing indignation, the thunder tones of a Carlisle—or an Isaiah. Satire has its province, but it cannot cope with the problems that vitally and immediately face mankind."[10] Or again, a writer in *Encounter* bitterly criticizes Thomas Mann's entire literary career because Mann, witnessing the collapse of European civilization, chose irony as his most characteristic literary mode. "Is a smile the answer to Buchenwald?" asks this writer. "How surprising it is that the German master, faced with . . . barbarism and inhumanity, should never have used his favourite weapon to express the same savage indignation which it provoked in Swift."[11] These pleas (misconceived as we may think them) arise in response to overwhelming social crises; we call for help upon the manipulators of our symbols: we call upon our artists to abandon art and to make magic.

A passage in D. H. Lawrence's *Plumed Serpent* illustrates finely this dilemma over the function of art. Kate Leslie and her friends are looking at the frescoes in the University in Mexico City: ". . . they were caricatures so crude and so ugly that Kate was merely repelled. They were meant to be shocking, but perhaps the very deliberateness prevents them from being so shocking as they might be. Strident caricatures of the Capitalist and the Church, and of the Rich Woman and of Mammon. . . . To anyone with the spark of human balance, the things are a misdemeanour. . . .

[10] Wolfe's words are quoted by R. W. Madry in the Durham, North Carolina *Sunday Herald-Sun* (Sept. 25, 1938). Cited in M. C. Randolph's unpublished dissertation, "The Neo-Classic Theory of the Formal Verse Satire," p. 398, n. 192.

[11] Gorowny Rees in a review of Erich Heller's *The Ironic German*, *Encounter* (Jan. 1959), p. 82.

" 'Oh no!' said Kate in front of the caricatures. 'They are too ugly. They defeat their own ends.'

" 'But they are meant to be ugly,' said young Garcia. 'They must be ugly, no? Because capitalism is ugly. . . .'

" 'But,' said Kate, 'these caricatures are too intentional. They are like vulgar abuse, not art at all. . . . One must keep a certain balance.'

" 'Not in Mexico!' said the young Mexican. . . . 'In Mexico you can't keep a balance, because things are so bad. . . . You have to hate the capitalist. . . .' "[12]

In this interchange is dramatized an age-old conflict: art as magic and ritual over against the sophisticated view of art as art and not another thing. Society's demands are the determinant; and even in the most sophisticated societies artists will still be called upon to perform their ancient magical role.

One further survival in this catalogue of primitive survivals: it is a tantalizing fact that dozens of the terms we conventionally apply to satire have direct association with the magical power we have been concerned with. Herblock, the cartoonist, speaks of being "disconcerted when I hear someone I've just tried to *annihilate* chuckling on the phone and asking for a drawing." Van Wyck Brooks accuses Joyce of having "*satirized out of existence* so many of the greatest writers. . . ." Louise Bogan, writing of William Plomer's *Borderline Ballads*, says that in his satire Plomer "is *out for blood*"; he "*pinks* his subjects with an *unbuttoned foil*."[13] Consider the terms that we normally use to characterize "harsh" satire—and consider their relation to the Old Irish terms for satire listed in Chapter 1: satire, we say, may be cutting, blistering, biting, killing, stinging, stabbing, scorching, searing, burning, withering, flaying, annihilating; satires are sharp, barbed, poisonous, malignant, deadly, vitriolic, and so on. The list could be indefinitely extended, the metaphors all expressing our latent sense of satire's destructive powers.[14] On the conscious level these *are* metaphors. As Addison writes in *Spec-*

[12] *The Plumed Serpent* (New York, 1933), pp. 48-49.

[13] *Life* (Nov. 19, 1956), p. 156; "Reflections on the Avant-Garde," *New York Times* Book Review (Dec. 30, 1956), p. 10; *New Yorker* (Feb. 4, 1956), p. 102. Italics added.

[14] See M. C. Randolph, "The Medical Concept," *SP*, xxxviii (1941), p. 142.

tator No. 23, the wounds satire gives are imaginary: "a lampoon or a satire do not carry in them robbery or murder"; but yet, he asks, how many would not rather lose their lives than be exposed to the injury they do? We inevitably think of the injury as bodily harm. I believe that no matter how conscious we may be of the metaphoric quality of our terminology, we retain, unconsciously, some sense of the truth to which the metaphors point: the truth of Ashanti and Tlingit experience, for example, as described in Chapter II, or the "truth" of ancient legend. In obscure ways we "know" that satire kills.

Still, despite the evidence of history, despite language and metaphor, despite unacknowledged beliefs, it would be folly to suggest that satire in Western civilized society has any but the most remote affiliations with its ritual origins. When Roy Campbell ends a vituperative poem with an ancient threat: "So will my verse propel you to your doom . . . ," the effect is only ludicrous. Ours is no heroic folk society, no shame culture. Pope's dunces, far from developing blisters, raged and replied in kind. Today, when Auden impales a name on the end of a couplet, or when Mary McCarthy dissects recognizable public figures in her novels, the victims unquestionably are affected: who can doubt that they feel pain? But we need not speak of magic.

And yet still we hesitate, for words move us in mysterious ways. As Eliade says, "the patterns that have come down from the distant past never disappear; they do not lose the possibility of being brought back to life."[15] If we can no longer responsibly refer to magic to account for their strange promptings, alternative explanations are hardly more satisfactory. Consider one more passage from Lawrence, who knew about magic. In *Women in Love* the long spiritual-erotic fencing match between Birkin and Ursula Brangwen is brought to a climax and concluded by a burst of invective. The two are in the country together, enmeshed in their strange struggle of attraction and repulsion. Suddenly Ursula turns on Birkin: " 'You!' she cried. 'You! You truth-lover! You purity-monger! It *stinks*, your truth and your purity. It stinks of the offal you feed on, you scavenger dog, you eater of corpses. You are foul, *foul*. . . . What you are is a foul, deathly thing, obscene, that's what you are, obscene and perverse.

[15] *Patterns in Comparative Religion*, pp. 431-32.

. . . You are so *perverse,* so death-eating.' "[16] Birkin writhes under the vituperation. Yet the outburst functions as though it were an apotropaic spell; it drives out the hesitations, knocks flat the barriers and defenses that have stood in the way of the natural sexual union. It effects catharsis in both attacker and victim. Words of destruction and death issue in the life-fulfilling assurance of the act of fertilization. The ritual union is consummated. From one point of view the scene can stand as an emblem of the promise primitive satire bears. Ursula's outburst cannot, of course, be called satire as we use the term today; but if it is not satire, it is the stuff of which satire is born: a primitive, incantatory invective. And if it is not magic, it yet functions in the reality of this fictional world in ways unfathomable by rational inquiry.

We have dealt with equivocal matters, and I am content, making a virtue of necessity, to leave them so, with the last words going to the poets, some of whom retain a proud and lofty conception of their art, think of themselves still as "reciters of the ritual which is to renew the world."[17] Mr. Eliot's lines from "The Dry Salvages" present powerfully much of what has here been tentatively suggested:

> We had the experience but missed the meaning. . . .
> I have said before
> That the past experience revived in the meaning
> Is not the experience of one life only
> But of many generations—not forgetting
> Something that is probably quite ineffable:
> The backward look behind the assurance
> Of recorded history, the backward half-look
> Over the shoulder, towards the primitive terror.[18]

At the conclusion of his article on Satire in *La Grande Encyclopédie,* M. Brunetière tells briefly the story of the Greek

[16] Chap. XXIII (London, 1921), p. 324.
[17] Howard Nemerov's phrase describing St.-John Perse's conception of his own role as poet. "The Golden Compass Needle," *Sewanee Review* (Winter 1959), p. 98.
[18] From "The Dry Salvages" in *Four Quartets,* copyright 1943, by T. S. Eliot. Reprinted by permission of Harcourt, Brace and Company, Inc.

Archilochus, whose verses caused Lycambes and his daughter to hang themselves. M. Brunetière would have been little attracted to the abyss that falls away behind Eliot's lines, but his final remark comes from similar insight. "Voilà," he says of the Archilochus story and its fatal outcome, "Voilà le fond de toute la satire."

APPENDIX: *THE CURSE*

FROM the earliest records of man we have to the present, among people of every stage of civilization, the curse is one of the most common forms by which man attempts to exercise control over the other. Most simply, a curse is a wish in a magical or religious context; it "is a wish, expressed in words, that evil . . . may befall a certain person."[1] From it come strange and unlikely structures: on its religious side, according to Jane Harrison, it develops into the vow and the prayer; on its secular side into the ordinance and ultimately into the law. The curse is of the essence of law, as we find by examining ancient legal formulas which are built around its sanction. Instead of injunctions saying "do this" or "do not do that," we find "cursed be he who does this," or "cursed be he who does not do that."[2]

A fine example of the curse in ancient Greece is the inscription, taken from two marble pillars, known as the Dirae of Teos:

"Whosoever maketh baneful drugs against the Teans, whether against individuals or the whole people:

"May he perish, both he and his offspring.

"Whosoever hinders corn from being brought into the land of the Teans, either by art or machination, whether by land or sea, and whosoever drives out what has been brought in:

"May he perish, both he and his offspring."

And the final curse, to round off all the other curses into a perfect circle:

"Whosoever of them that hold office doth not make this cursing . . . let him be bound by an overcurse . . . , and whoever

[1] See A. E. Crawley, "Cursing and Blessing," Hastings' *Encyclopaedia of Religion and Ethics,* p. 370 b.
[2] *Prolegomena to the Study of Greek Religion,* pp. 142, 138. While the curse may have been the sanction of the law, laws frequently have had to be passed against the irresponsible use of curses and comparable magic. See Chap. 1, 1 and 3.

either breaks the stelae on which the cursing is written, or cuts out the letters or makes them illegible:

"May he perish, both he and his offspring."[3]

The importance of the curse to the ancient world has been touched upon in Chapter 1 and is so well known as to need little further elaboration. Perhaps a distinction should be made, however, between the public curse, usually an official ceremony serving to promote, through negative means, the welfare of a particular group, and the private curse, originating in personal hatred, envy, or outrage of some kind and directed usually to the more or less painful downfall of the enemy. As an example of the public curse may be cited the ceremonial cursing of the enemies of the state at the opening of important public functions in Athens. In one of his orations Demosthenes demands that "the curse" be recited: "This imprecation, men of Athens, is pronounced, as the law directs, by the marshal on your behalf at every meeting of the Assembly, and again before the Council at all their sessions."[4] The "curses of Buzyges" were ritualistically pronounced by priests of Zeus at the annual festival commemorating the invention of the plow. They were directed at those who failed to provide food and water for persons in distress, who neglected to give proper burial to the dead, etc.[5] The Romans relied heavily on curses as weapons of war, and seem often to have considered them more potent than more conventional weapons; we recall their custom of razing and then cursing conquered cities, most notably, of course, Carthage. Curses might be powerful even in politics. When all other measures to restrain the potential tyrant Crassus had failed, the tribune Ateius hurried to the city gate, cast incense into a blazing brazier (Plutarch's description is most vivid), and invoked curses which were

[3] Compare this final over-curse with a modern instance. The hideous oaths taken recently by the Mau Mau are reported always to have contained this penalty: "If I fail in this may this oath kill me." Philip Mitchell, "Report on Mau Mau," *New Statesman and Nation* (May 28, 1955), p. 740.

[4] *Demosthenes*, "De Falsa Legatione," trans. C. A. Vince and J. H. Vince (London, 1926), pp. 291-93. The exact wording of the curse has not survived, although we have a burlesque form of it in Aristophanes, *Thesmophoriazusae*, ll. 331-51.

[5] Hendrickson, "Archilochus and the Victims of his Iambics," p. 105.

"dreadful and terrifying in themselves, and were reinforced by sundry strange and dreadful gods whom he summoned and called by name. The Romans say that these mysterious and ancient curses have such power that no one involved in them ever escapes, and misfortune falls also upon the one who utters them, wherefore they are not employed at random nor by many."[6] There was muttering in the city, even though it was recognized that Ateius cursed for the city's sake; and Crassus died in Parthia. In the Old Testament Balak called upon Balaam to "curse me this people . . . for he whom thou cursest is cursed." Balaam blessed instead ("How shall I curse whom God hath not cursed?"), but only because of divine intervention. In ancient Ireland druids and saints cursed, for public and private ends, with extraordinary abandon; probably the most dramatic of all cursing contests was that between St. Ruadan and King Diarmit which lasted for a year and eventuated in the total destruction of Tara.[7]

Just as curses have played a more important role in the history of man than blessings, so private curses have always preponderated over public. Aside from literary evidence, which is considerable, the best testimony to the widespread belief of the ancients in the efficacy of the curse is the number of Greek and Roman curse-tablets (*defixiones*) which have been recovered. Many of these small metal tablets dug up from graves or bodies of water where they had been consigned to the underworld contain only the name of the enemy with a nail driven through it. The magical principle operative here we have already considered: the name is no mere sign distinguishing one person from another; by a magical process of identification, the name *is* the person, and he who controls the name controls the man. One tablet bears this simple inscription: "I nail his name, that is himself."[8]

Other inscriptions are extremely elaborate and apparently

[6] "Crassus," *Plutarch's Lives*, trans. Bernadotte Perrin (London, 1916), III, Chap. XVI, 363-65.
[7] "Vita Sancta Ruadani," in Plummer, *Vitae Sanctorum Hiberniae*, II, 247-48.
[8] F. B. Jevons, "Graeco-Italian Magic," in *Anthropology and the Classics*, ed. R. R. Marett (Oxford, 1908), p. 108. For the magical significance of the name in early Irish culture, see Chap. I, 1 and 3 above.

were fabricated with meticulous attention to detail by professional curse-makers. I give one sample in abbreviated form:

"Good and beautiful Proserpina (or Salvia, shouldst thou prefer),[9] mayest thou wrest away the health, body, complexion, strength, and faculties of Plotius and consign him to thy husband, Pluto. . . . Mayest thou consign him to the quartian, tertian, and daily fevers to war and wrestle with him until they snatch away his very soul. Wherefore I hand over this victim to thee, Proserpina (or, shouldst thou prefer, Acherusia). Mayest thou summon for me the three-headed hound Cerberus to tear out the heart of Plotius, and mayest thou pledge thyself to give him three offerings—dates, figs, and a black swine—should he finish his task before the month of March. These offerings, Proserpina, I shall entrust to thee as soon as thou shalt have made good my vow. Proserpina Salvia, I give thee the head of Plotius . . . his brow and eyebrows, eyelids, and pupils, I give thee his ears, nose, nostrils, tongue, lips, and teeth, so he may not speak his pain; his neck, shoulders, arms, and fingers, so that he may not aid himself; his breast, liver, heart, and lungs, so he may not locate his pain; his bowels, belly, navel, and flanks, so he may not sleep the sleep of health. . . . As Plotius has prepared a curse against me, in like manner do I consign him to thee to visit a curse on him ere the end of February. May he most miserably perish and depart this life. . . .[10]

In a curse of this stylized complication, the formal elements are the source of power; the curse must be letter-perfect according to the formula (as in magical spells the world over) or

[9] The *sive . . . sive* (either . . . or) construction is familiar in ancient prayers and curses and is another example of name-magic at work. The curser must exhaust all possibilities as he searches for the essential agency of power, the god's "right" name. In ancient Egypt, for example: "If a divinity was invoked according to the correct forms, especially if one knew how to pronounce its real name, it was compelled to act in conformity to the will of its priest. The sacred words were an incantation that compelled the superior powers to obey the officiating person, no matter what purpose he had in view." Franz Cumont, *The Oriental Religions in Roman Paganism* (Chicago, 1911), p. 93.

[10] Trans. W. Sherwood Fox in his "Cursing as a Fine Art," *Sewanee Review*, xxvii (1919), pp. 467-68. See also J. H. Mozley, "On Cursing in Ancient Times," Appendix to his translation of Ovid, *The Art of Love*, pp. 359-72.

it will fail or perhaps, like some unjust magical satire in Ireland, redound upon the head of the curser.

Of Plotius' fate we know nothing (though we may be sure that he and his enemy believed unreservedly in the malefic power of this form of word-magic); but the Old Testament provides much evidence that the curse, uttered by one of peculiar qualification, might bring immediate and terrible consequences. One of the most dreadful of all curses in the disproportionate violence of its fulfillment, is that of the prophet Elisha:

". . . and as he was going up by the way, there came forth little children out of the city, and mocked him, and said unto him, Go up thou bald head; go up thou bald head.

"And he turned back and looked on them, and cursed them in the name of the LORD. And there came forth two she bears out of the wood, and tare forty and two children of them." (II Kings 2: 23-24)

Usually, however, the curse is conceived of in the Bible as merely a wish which God will fulfill if the wish is just; an unjust curse may be ineffective (Proverbs 26: 2), it may recoil on its utterer (Genesis 12: 3), or it may be turned into a blessing (Numbers 23; Deuteronomy 23: 5). Similarly, it is said in the Talmud that an undeserved curse returns on him who uttered it, but also that the curse of a scholar is unfailing in its effect, whether just or no.[11] When a man is sentenced to death, "a hook must be placed in his mouth in order that he shall not [be able to] curse the king. . . ."[12]

---

[11] Sanhedrin 49a; Berakoth 56a and Makkoth 11a. My references are from the article "Cursing" in the *Jewish Encyclopedia*.

[12] 'Erubin, 19a, trans. Israel W. Slotki in *The Babylonian Talmud*, ed. Epstein. The belief that a condemned man's curse may harm a king, and the custom following on it, is remarkably widespread. Today in Ashanti in West Africa the first thing done to a condemned man is "to drive a small knife through both cheeks and tongue, to prevent the victim 'cursing the King.' " Among the Dahomey the doomed man is gagged with a Y-shaped stick to prevent him "from swearing an oath against the King, since in Dahomey, as elsewhere in West Africa, the power of the oath is greatly feared." R. S. Rattray, *Ashanti*, p. 160 note; Melville J. Herskovits, *Dahomey* (New York, 1938), II, 20-21. Morton W. Bloomfield suggests that the belief may explain the puzzling lines from *Piers Ploughman*:

In Ireland the most powerful of the cursers were the saints, who uttered their maledictions on the slightest provocation. One tale has much in common with the curse of Elisha, although the Irish curse has been ambiguously softened as compared with the stark cruelty of the Old Testament story: "At another time Féchín was in his cell praying, when he heard the noise of the children hurling on the green beside the cell, and they disturbed Féchín at his devotions. Says Féchín: 'I permit you to go and be drowned in the lake, and your souls will be free (to ascend) to heaven.' Then the children went into the lake, and they were drowned and they obtained a reward for their souls. Wherefore from them *Loch Macraide* 'Children's Lake' is (so called) for ever; and God's name and Féchín's were magnified thereby."[13]

The saints' maledictory function had probably been inherited from the druids; and, indeed, except for the doctrinal interpolation, there is little to distinguish between the curse of the one and the curse of the other. Saints had, among other appurtenances, cursing stones, which, upon being turned "widdershins" (left-hand-wise) against an enemy, brought a curse upon him. When St. Maedoc turned his stone three times against an oppressor, death came to the man within a year.[14] St. Patrick relied upon the power of the word alone:

"Some clerics preceded Patrick to the house of Becan, who was so that he had thirty milch herds; yet he denied them meat. . . . Patrick . . . says: 'all so many as the fellow has of cattle and of people, I ordain that by to-morrow there be not a single one of them escaped alive.' The thing came true too, *ut dixit Patricius:*—

> And ʒif the kynge of that kyngedome. come in that tyme,
> There the feloun thole sholde . deth or otherwyse,
> Lawe wolde, he ʒeue hym lyf . if he loked on hym.

The Vision of William concerning Piers the Plowman, ed. W. W. Skeat. B XVIII, ll. 379-81 [Oxford, 1924], I, 546. For information on curses in other cultures, see the chapters on Mantic Literature in each of the three vols. of H. Munro Chadwick and N. Kershaw Chadwick, *The Growth of Literature* (Cambridge, 1932-40), esp. I, 449, 451-52 (Norse); II, 366, 411 (Yugoslav), 581 (Indian); III, 135-37 (Tatar), 266 (Maori).

[13] *Life of St. Féchín of Fore*, trans. Stokes, RC, XII (1891), p. 349. Féchín is said to have died in the year 664 of the Yellow Plague which he and other saints brought down upon the Irish by their pitiless prayers.

[14] Plummer, *Vitae Sanctorum Hiberniae*, I, clxxiii, clvii and note 11.

" 'Becan here and Becan there: be his fastings not many in number; so long as the sun shall travel right-hand-wise, let Becan not make mirth for them [his people].'

"Then the earth swallowed up Becan with his people—with all his wealth, animal and human, simultaneously. . . ."[15]

Clearly it is impossible to distinguish formally between magical satire and the curse. Both have public as well as more obvious private manifestations: Archilochus hurled his maledictions against the public enemy, the Sapaeans; Carpre, the Irish poet, promises to "satirize and shame" the enemy so that through the spell of his art they will not be able to resist warriors. The threat of satire is invoked in treaties, just as from the beginning of historical times the threat of curses has been invoked; witness the close of a treaty between the Hittites and the Egyptians in the thirteenth century B.C.: ". . . should Duppi-Tessub not honor these words of the treaty and the oath, may these gods of the oath destroy Duppi-Tessub together with his person, his wife, his son, his grandson, his house, his land and together with everything that he owns."[16] Archilochus, the archetypal satirist, sometimes calls on the gods to effectuate his will. Patrick, a saint, uses the formula "I ordain" and winds a spell around the name of the victim in a fashion indistinguishable from that of the magician-satirists. Children laugh at Elisha's bald head; he invokes the name of the Lord to slay them. Luaine rejects Aithirne's sexual advances; his satire causes her to die of shame. Satirists and cursers and magicians of all kinds rely upon a magical use of the optative mood, in the formulas "Let him be such-and-such" and "May he be so-and-so." Both satire and curse may be lethal, whether they accord with justice or not; but a tradition exists that the unjust satire and the unjust curse will recoil onto him who utters them. Similarly, there is a tradition that a blessing will neutralize the curse, and praise

[15] "The Colloquy with the Ancients," *Sylva Gadelica*, trans. Standish H. O'Grady (London, 1892), II, 113.
[16] *Ancient Near Eastern Texts Relating to the Old Testament*, ed. James B. Pritchard, 2nd ed. (Princeton, N.J., 1955), p. 205. See pp. 205-06 for a much more elaborate curse.

will wash out satire.[17] Just as it is impossible to disentangle the magical curse from the religious curse, so it is impossible, except in extreme cases, to disentangle magical satire from either. The confusion is inevitable at the cultural stage in which we are interested; for where poet is likely to be prophet and where the crucial matter is power and its manipulation by means of the word, generic distinctions will have little meaning.

One or two *differentiae*, however, may be tentatively pointed out. Magical satire is frequently in verse, the curse in prose, for example. Further, insofar as satire employs ridicule, it may be distinguished from the curse; but while ridicule is associated with satire from the beginning, it is not at this stage central to it. Perhaps the best approach is to look at both curse and satire as relatively undifferentiated responses to the threats and the possibilities of a hostile environment. Behind them both is the will to attack, to do harm, to kill—in some negative way to control one's world.

In *The Marriage of Heaven and Hell*, William Blake asks the prophet Isaiah, "does a firm perswasion that a thing is so, make it so?" Isaiah replies: "All poets believe that it does, & in ages of imagination this firm perswasion removed mountains; but many are not capable of a firm perswasion of anything."[18] The will in ages of imagination was endowed with preternatural power, and not until the firm persuasion disappears do satire and the curse meaningfully diverge and satire begin to take on an independent and remarkably complex life of its own.

[17] "Cursing and Blessing," Hastings' *Encyclopaedia*; E. J. Gwynn, "An Old Irish Tract," *Eriu*, XIII (1942), pp. 57-58.
[18] *The Writings of William Blake*, ed. Geoffrey Keynes (London, 1925), I, 187.

INDEX

Achilles, 130, 132
Addison, Joseph, 268, 281
Adventures of Nera, The, 132
Adventures of the Sons of Eochaid Muigmedón, The, 22
adversarius, 110, 202
Aed, King, 24, 27, 42. *See also* Hugh, King
Aelian, 10
Aeschylus, 89, 91, 94, 109; (as character) 108-09
Aethiopis, 132
Aithirne the Importunate, 27-34, 46, 60, 62-65, 97, 116, 129, 166, 220, 276, 291
Aithirne's Mother, 29
Alceste, 141, 168-84, 209, 213, 219, 220, 274
Alcibiades, in Plutarch, 141-42; in Shakespeare, 154, 161, 163
Aldington, Richard, 233, 237
Aldridge, A. O., 84
Algonquian, 53
Amergen, 31
Amergin White Knee, 19, 34, 61
Anatomy of Melancholy, The, 186, 187
Ancient Laws of Ireland, 25, 31, 40
Annals of the Kingdom of Ireland, by the Four Masters, 34
Apemantus, 150-53, 157-60, 164-67
Apo ceremony, 78, 83
Apollonius of Tyana, 6
apologia, 113-15, 124, 127, 225, 229, 230, 231, 262, 265, 266, 269, 273
Apuleius, 186-88, 191
Arabian satire, 15-18, 19, 103, 259
Arbuthnot, John, 217
Archilochus, 3-15, 19, 23, 29, 30, 35, 47, 59, 77, 86, 100, 105-08, 115, 116, 121, 124-26, 129, 133, 220, 242, 259, 261, 267, 277, 284, 291
Aretino, 17, 259, 267
Aristophanes, 92-93, 98, 101, 105, 108, 112, 127, 261, 267; *Acharnians,* 5; *The Frogs,* 94, 108-09; *The Knights,* 92, 100, 261; *Lysistrata,* 94; *Thesmophoriazusae,* 93, 286; *Wasps,* 108
Aristotle, 4, 6, 84, 93, 100, 105
Ashanti, 76-83, 140, 221, 282, 289

Athenis, 13
Atreus, house of, 8
Auden, W. H., 12, 27, 225, 239, 282
Auerbach, Erich, 192-94, 273-74
Augustus, 121, 260
Aurelius, Marcus, 216
Austen, Jane, 187, 269
Azande, 56

Bacchylides, 90
Bailey, Cyril, 119, 120
BaKxatla, 52, 57
Barber, C. L., 139
Bardic Association, see Proceedings of the Great Bardic Institution, The
Barrymore, John, 85
Bayle, Pierre, 80, 267-69
Beals, Ralph L., 70
Bell, David, 34
Bell, H. Idris, 34
Bell, John, 197
Benedict, Ruth, 50-51, 53-54, 67-68
Beowulf, 132, 135
Bergson, Henri, 214
Bernini, 87
Bible, 16, 17, 174, 243, 287, 289-91
Birket-Smith, Kaj, 71, 73
Blake, William, 166, 292
BLAST, 224
blight, 33-34, 61-62, 166, 276
blisters, 25-29, 32, 115, 281-82
Bloomfield, Morton W., 289
Bogan, Louise, 281
Boileau, 181, 233, 265, 269
Bolingbroke, 206
Book of Conquests of Ireland, The, 34
Book of Leinster, 65
Borgerhoff, E. B. O., 168, 174
Bosman, William, 78
Bosworth, Joseph, 135
Brauer, H., 87
Brave New World, 186, 192
Bray, René, 168-69
Bres Mac Eladain, 38, 45, 62
Bricriu Poison-tongue, 131-32, 135, 136, 141
Broccardo, Antonio, 259
Brooks, Van Wyck, 281
Brown, T. E., 209

Harvey, Gabriel, 267
Hatch, W. J., 58
Hauvette, Amédée, 133, 140
Heinsius, Daniel, 116-17
Hemingway, Ernest, 223
Henderson, Ernest F., 278
Henderson, George, 132
Hendrickson, G. L., 8, 9, 11, 14, 93,
    101, 102, 104, 105, 112, 114, 121,
    123, 124, 128, 286
Herblock, 281
Herero, 57
Herskovits, Melville J., 81, 289
Highet, Gilbert, 116, 125
hijá, 15-17, 103
Hild, J. A., 119
Hipponax, 12-13, 35, 59, 100, 105,
    106, 121, 133, 268
Hirusan, 44-47
Hittites, 291
Hoare, Dorothy M., 132
Holyday, Barten, 117
Homer, 4, 7, 89, 130-31, 135, 140
Hooke, S. H., 61
Hopkins, G. M., 222
Horace, 7, 8, 11, 27, 39, 99, 100-29,
    159, 174, 181, 221, 230, 260, 261,
    262, 265, 266, 267
Hos, 80
Hrafn, 75
Huart, Clément, 17
Hugh, King, 42-46, 95. *See also* Aed,
    King
Huizinga, Johan, 10, 16, 62-63, 64, 71
Hull, Eleanor, 65
Huvelin, Paul, 122-23
Hyde, Douglas, 19
Hyman, Stanley E., 61

"iambics," 3-14, 47, 59, 100, 105-07,
    126, 277
Ibis, see Ovid
Icelandic saga, 75
image magic, 87-88
*Instructions of King Cormac MacAirt,
    The*, 40-41
Intoxication of the Ulstermen, The, 33
invective, 3-14, 17, 59, 70, 92, 93, 100,
    106, 113, 116, 121, 126, 134, 140,
    167, 182, 220, 251, 260, 263-64,
    282, 283
Irish satire, 18-48, 61-65, 66, 259, 276

Jaeger, Werner, 11, 108
James I, King, 266

James, Henry, 199
Jandal, 18
Jarír, 18
Jarwal ibn Aus, 17, 30
Jevons, F. B., 287
John, Augustus, 234
Johnson, Samuel, 35, 49, 156, 198,
    233, 264, 268
Jonson, Ben, 3, 12-13, 35, 36, 127,
    261-63, 277; *Every Man Out of his
    Humour*, 137, 263, 271; *Poetaster*,
    3, 47, 127, 263, 277
Joyce, James, 225, 226-27, 236, 281
Juvenal, 31, 40, 99, 100-29, 162-63,
    182, 207, 261, 265, 266, 270

Kahler, Erich, 83
Kaplan, Abraham, 92
Kaye, Sir, 132
Keating, Geoffrey, 24
Keith, A. Berriedale, 5
Kelsen, Hans, 56
Kenner, Hugh, 225, 234, 236
Kenney, James F., 23
Kirk, Russell, 237, 240
Knapp, C., 104
Knight, G. Wilson, 146, 211
Koestler, Arthur, 279
Koyemci, 58
Kraus, Karl, 256
Kris, Ernst, 87-88, 92, 98, 252, 257-58
Kroeber, A. L., 49
Kuraver, 57

Laidcenn, 33, 61, 166, 249
lampoon, 4, 17, 33, 70, 78, 80, 83,
    108, 229
Langer, Suzanne K., 55, 91
Langland, William, 272. *See also* Piers
    Ploughman
La Rochefoucauld, 68
Lasserre, François, 7, 11, 12
Lattimore, Richard, 11
law, the, 24-25, 40, 105, 120-25, 260-
    65, 272, 279, 285
"Law, The" (game), 74
Lawrence, D. H., 225, 280, 282-83
Lear, King, 33, 145, 160, 166, 167,
    179
Leavis, F. R., 211
*Lebor Gabála Erenn: The Book of the
    Taking of Ireland*, 60
Lejay, Paul, 105-06, 112, 125
Leo, Friedrich, 106
Leonidas, 133